FANTAMIR

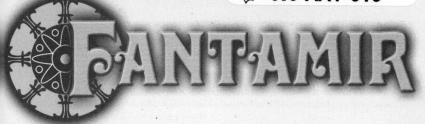

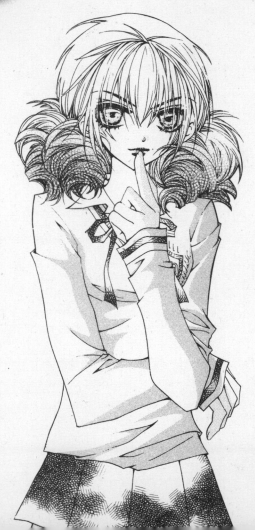

Fantamir Volume 3

Created by Eun-Jin Seo

Translation - Lauren Na
English Adaptation - Barb Lien-Cooper
Retouch and Lettering - Star Print Brokers
Production Artist - Mike Estacio
Graphic Designer - Louis Csontos

Editor - Hyun Joo Kim
Digital Imaging Manager - Chris Buford
Pre-Production Supervisor - Lucas Rivera
Production Manager - Elisabeth Brizzi
Managing Editor - Vy Nguyen
Creative Director - Anne Marie Horne
Editor-in-Chief - Rob Tokar
Publisher - Mike Kiley
President and C.O.O. - John Parker
C.E.O. and Chief Creative Officer - Stu Levy

A TOKYOPOP® Manga

TOKYOPOP and are trademarks or registered trademarks of TOKYOPOP Inc.

TOKYOPOP Inc.
5900 Wilshire Blvd. Suite 2000
Los Angeles, CA 90036

E-mail: info@TOKYOPOP.com
Come visit us online at www.TOKYOPOP.com

ISBN: 978-1-4278-0292-7

First TOKYOPOP printing: May 2008

10 9 8 7 6 5 4 3 2 1

Printed in the USA

FANTAMIR

EUN-JIN SEO
VOL. 3

HAMBURG // LONDON // LOS ANGELES // TOKYO

MIR

BORN TO INHERIT HER MOTHER'S POSITION AS THE GREAT SORCERESS, SHE GREW UP IN A TEMPLE FAR AWAY FROM SOCIETY. DUE TO AN INCIDENT THAT CAUSED HER TO LOSE HER SUPERNATURAL POWERS, MIR DECIDED TO RUN AWAY FROM HOME. HOWEVER, SHE NOW ATTENDS THE SHINDANSOO ACADEMY (HER MOTHER'S ALMA MATER) THAT SEEMS TO HARBOR HER FAMILY'S SECRET.

BA-RI/HAE-RANG

BA-RI IS THE HEAD WONHWA AT THE SHINDANSOO ACADEMY, WHICH MAKES HER THE PRIM AND PROPER QUEEN OF THE SCHOOL. BUT BA-RI REALLY IS HAE-RANG, AN UNRULY GUY WITH A TENDENCY TO POP UP IN FRONT OF MIR AT THE MOST INOPPORTUNE TIMES. HIS TWIN SISTER, THE REAL BA-RI, WAS KILLED WHEN SHE WAS YOUNG AND HAE-RANG HAS TO POSE AS HIS SISTER TO BE THE CANDIDATE TO BECOME THE NEXT GREAT SORCERESS.

BE-HYUNG-RANG

AS THE HANDSOME AND SMART STUDENT PRESIDENT OF THE SHINDANSOO ACADEMY, HE SHOULD BE THE MOST POPULAR GUY AT SCHOOL. BUT HE'S ACTUALLY REGARDED AS A CREEPY NERD WHO, FOR SOME ODD REASON, IS ALLOWED TO HANG AROUND BA-RI. BE-HYUNG-RANG ALONE KNOWS OF BA-RI'S SECRET AND FAMILY HISTORY.

PREVIOUSLY IN...

MIR IS AN AVERAGE 17-YEAR-OLD GIRL WHOSE GOAL IN LIFE IS TO MAKE 100 BEST FRIENDS...**NOW**. SHE DIDN'T USED TO BE SUCH A NORMAL GIRL. IN FACT, SHE USED TO BE THE GREAT SORCERESS CANDIDATE WHO WAS BORN WITH SUPERNATURAL ABILITIES AND SHOULDERED THE FATE OF HER ENTIRE FAMILY. BECAUSE THE GREAT SORCERESS IS A POSITION OF ENORMOUS POWER AND AUTHORITY, MIR'S FAMILY HAD EDGED OUT OTHER CLANS THAT WERE VYING FOR THE POWER. MIR'S MOTHER, JOON-JUNG, HAD TO GO AS FAR AS FIGHT HER BEST FRIEND, NAM-MO, TO THE DEATH WHEN THEY WERE YOUNG.

BUT MIR'S LIFE CHANGED DRAMATICALLY WHEN SHE LOST ALL HER POWERS IN AN EVENT SHE CAN NO LONGER REMEMBER. SHE WAS THEN FORCED TO LIVE ALONE IN ISOLATION, CUT OFF FROM OUTSIDE CONTACTS IN FEAR OF ENEMIES FINDING OUT HER CLAN'S VULNERABLE POSITION. AFTER YEARS OF ALIENATION MIR DECIDED TO RUN AWAY FROM HOME AND PLUNGED INTO GENERAL SOCIETY HOPING TO EXPERIENCE NEW THINGS AND SHED HER LONELY PAST.

MIR'S NOW ENROLLED IN THE SHINDANSOO ACADEMY WHERE, SINCE HER FIRST DAY, SHE NOTICED THE SCHOOL IS FAR FROM NORMAL. THE SCHOOL HAS TWO RULING GROUPS, THE WONHWA AND THE HWARANG, THAT GOVERN THE ENTIRE SCHOOL BODY, AND TO CHALLENGE THEIR RULE, ONE HAS TO CHALLENGE THEM TO A DUEL. UNFORTUNATELY FOR MIR, SHE SOMEHOW FINDS HERSELF DUELING THE HEAD WONHWA BA-RI ONLY A FEW DAYS INTO HER NEW LIFE. FORTUNATELY, MIR WINS AND SHE AND BA-RI ARE NOW BEST OF FRIENDS.

ALTHOUGH MIR'S ON HER WAY TO ACHIEVE HER GREAT GOAL OF MAKING 100 BEST FRIENDS, SHE RUNS SMACK INTO THE VERY THING SHE'S BEEN TRYING TO RUN AWAY FROM—HER FAMILY. AS IT TURNS OUT, THE SHINDANSOO ACADEMY IS JOON-JUNG'S ALMA MATER WHERE SHE AND NAM-MO WERE WONHWAS OF THEIR TIME, DURING WHICH THE DUEL TO THE DEATH TOOK PLACE. NAM-MO, WHO WAS GRAVELY WOUNDED BUT SPARED HER LIFE, NOW RUNS THE ACADEMY AND PLANS TO TAKE REVENGE ON JOON-JUNG BY SEATING HER DAUGHTER BA-RI AS THE NEXT GREAT SORCERESS.

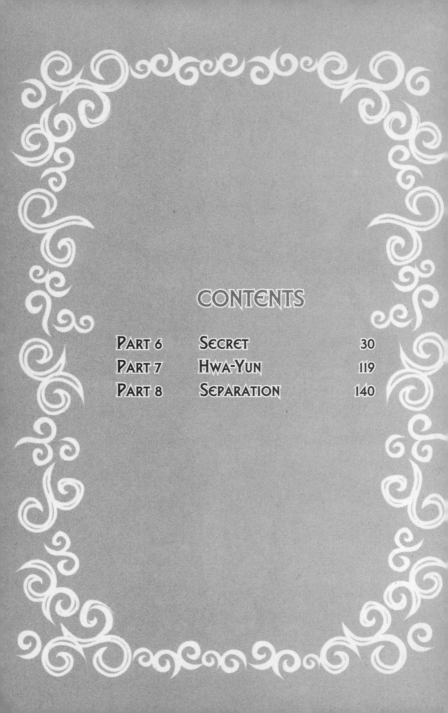

CONTENTS

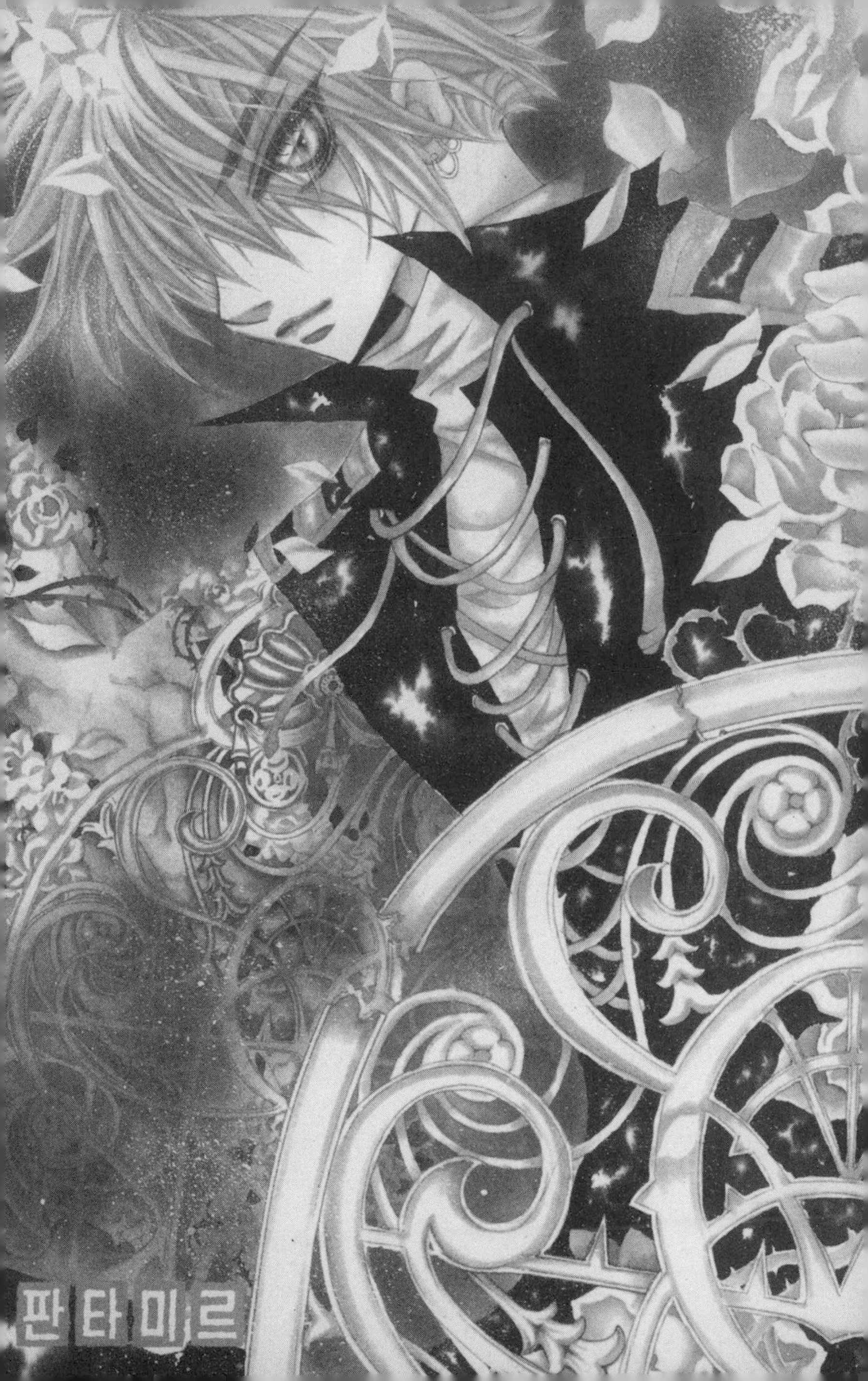
판타미르

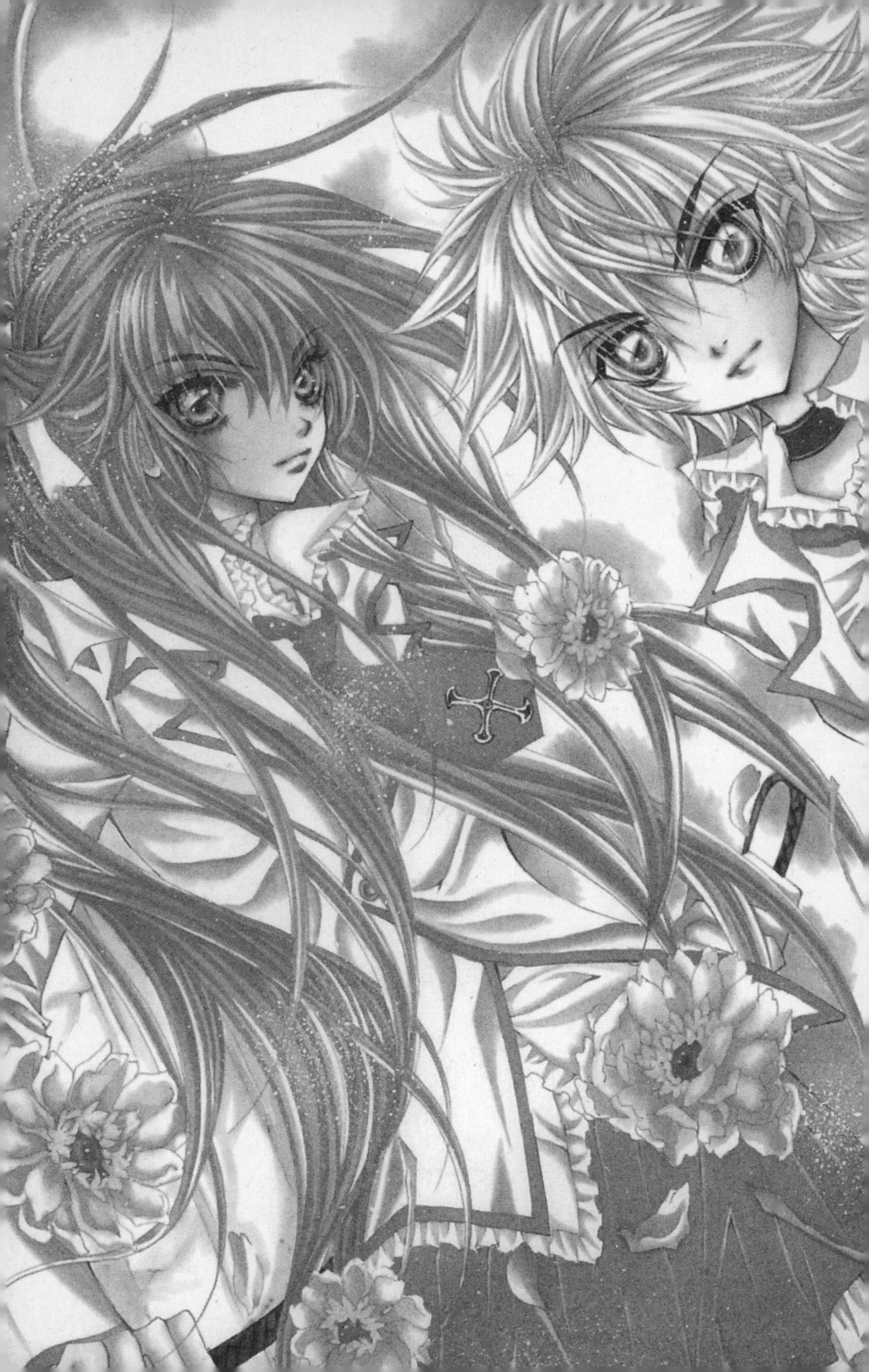

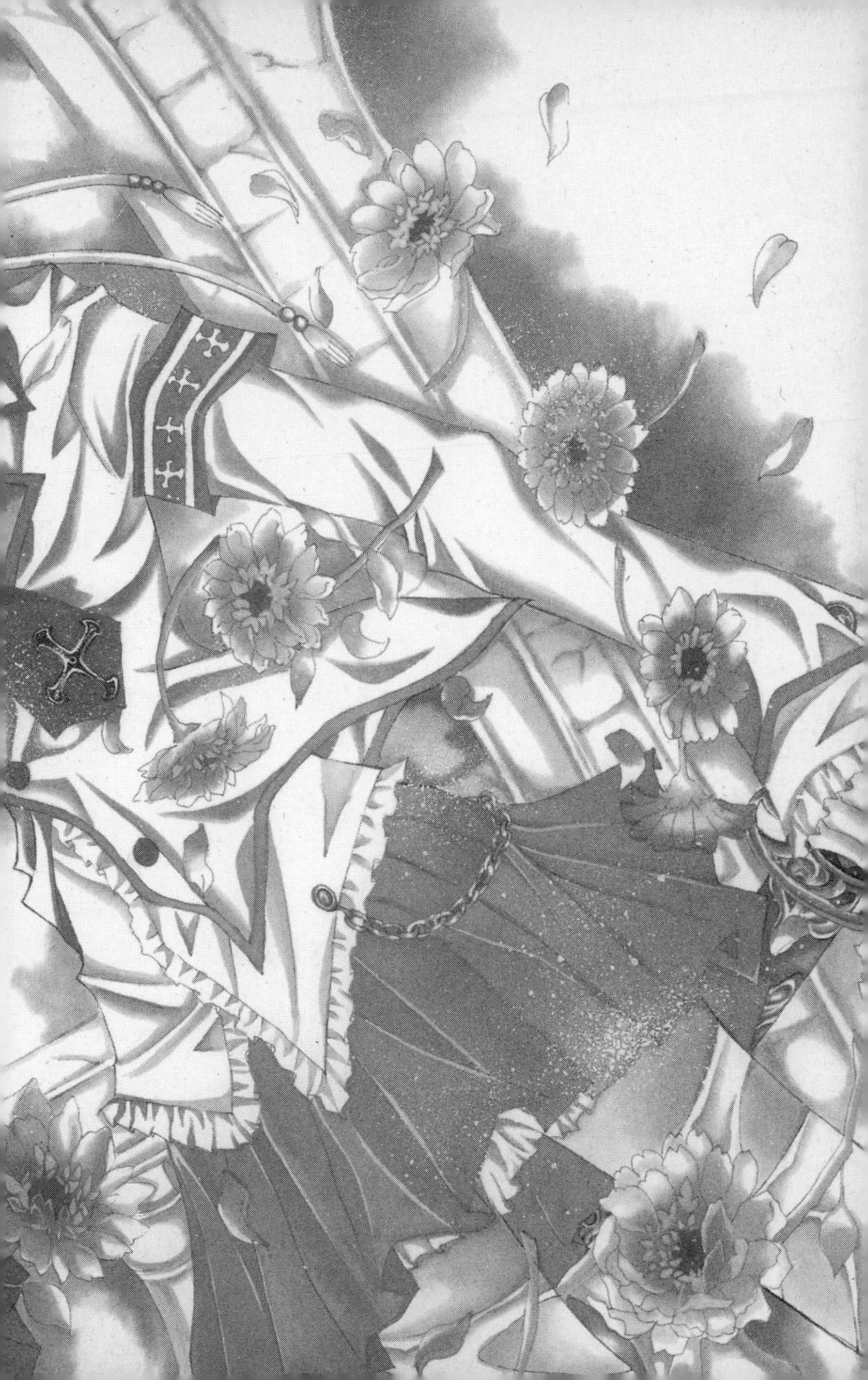

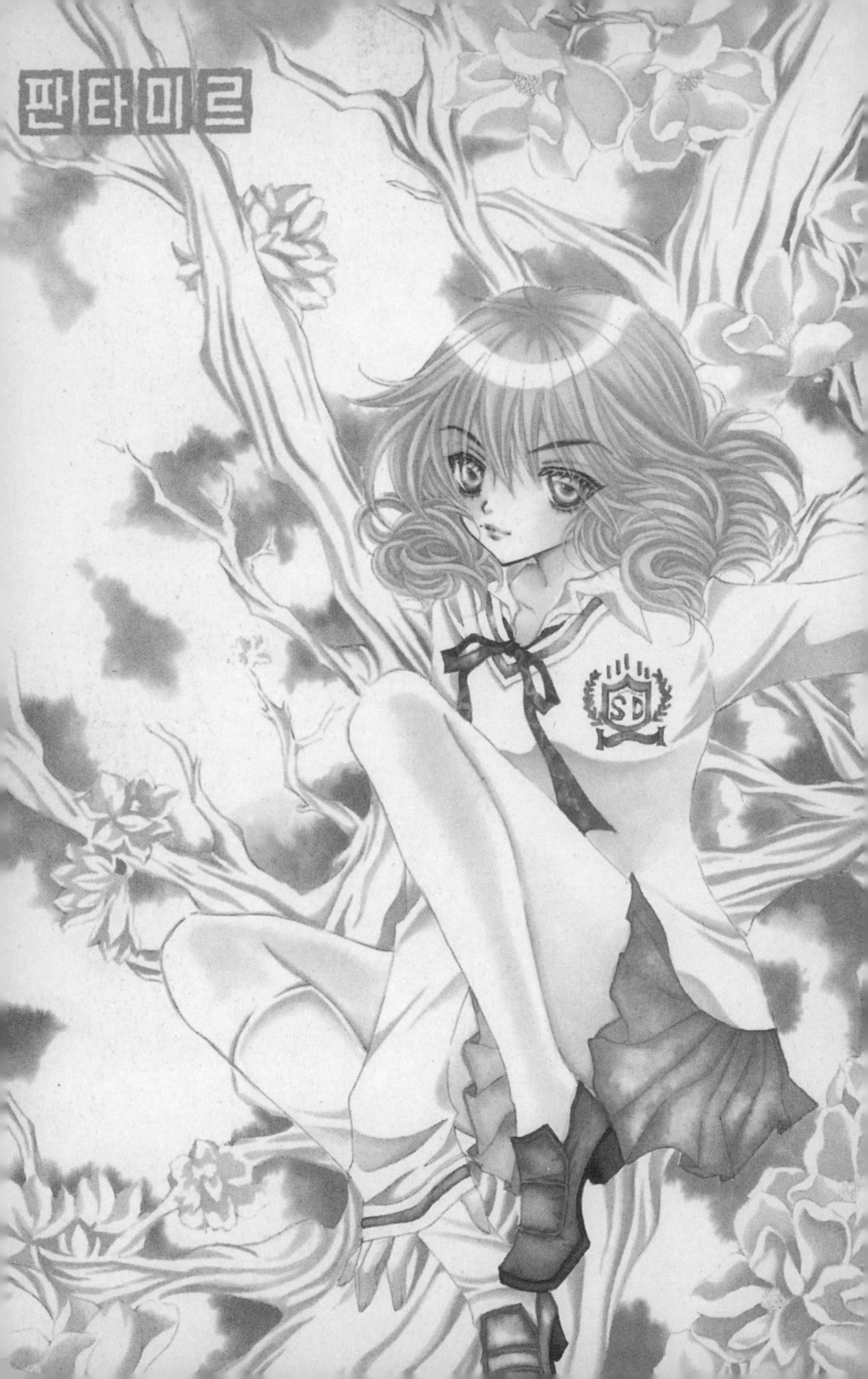
판타미르

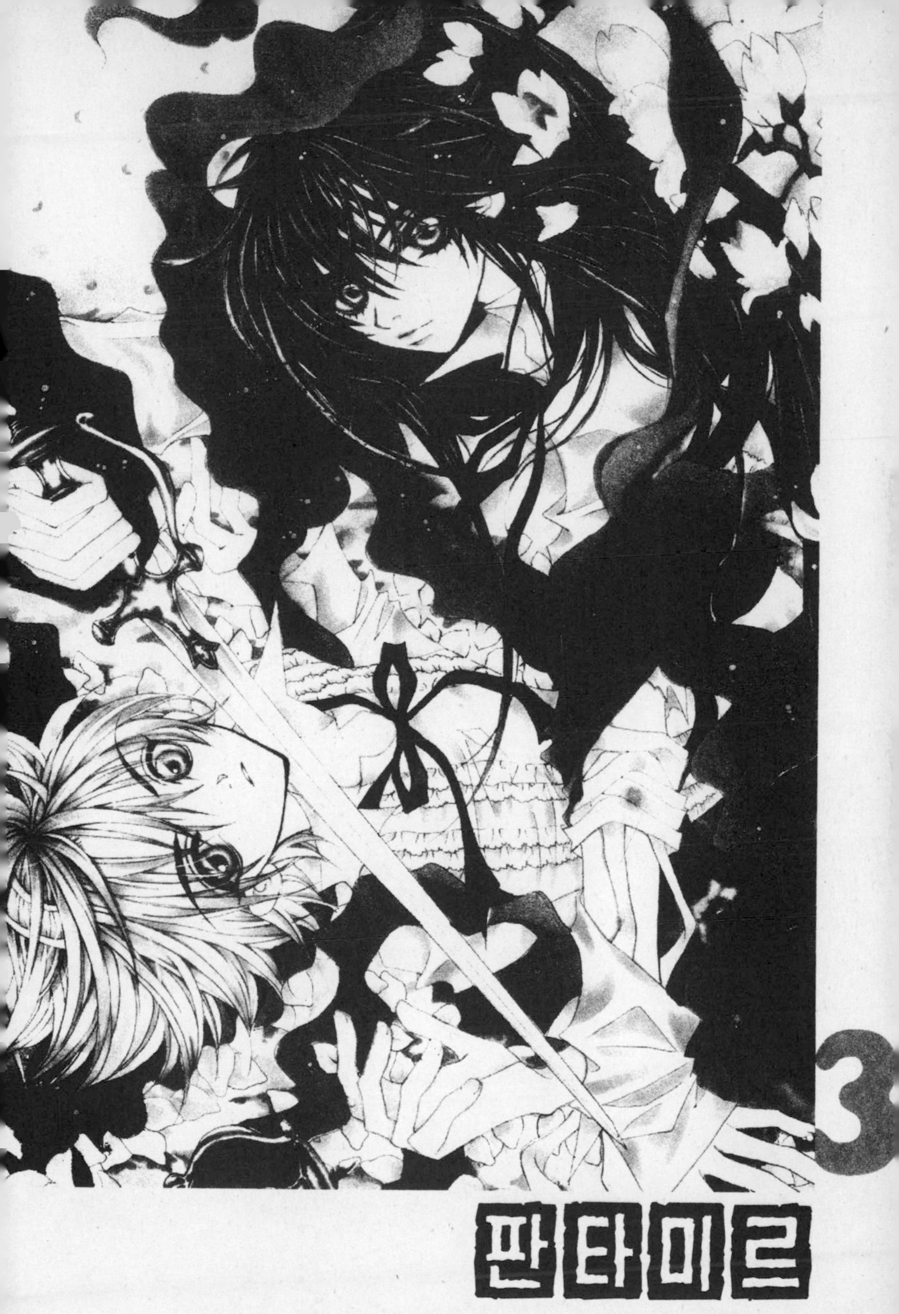

3

판타미르

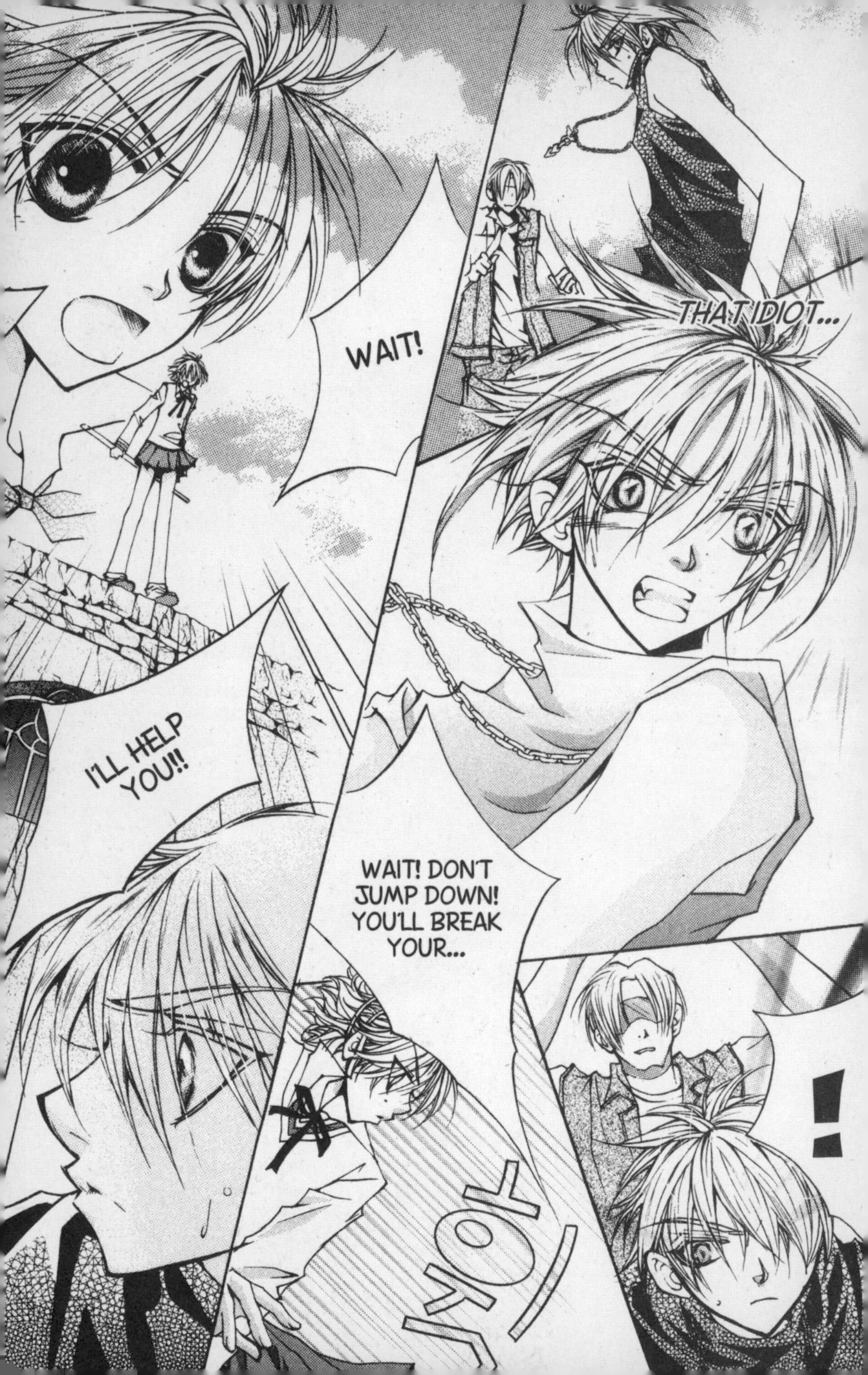
WAIT!
THAT IDIOT...
I'LL HELP YOU!!
WAIT! DON'T JUMP DOWN! YOU'LL BREAK YOUR...
YOI
!

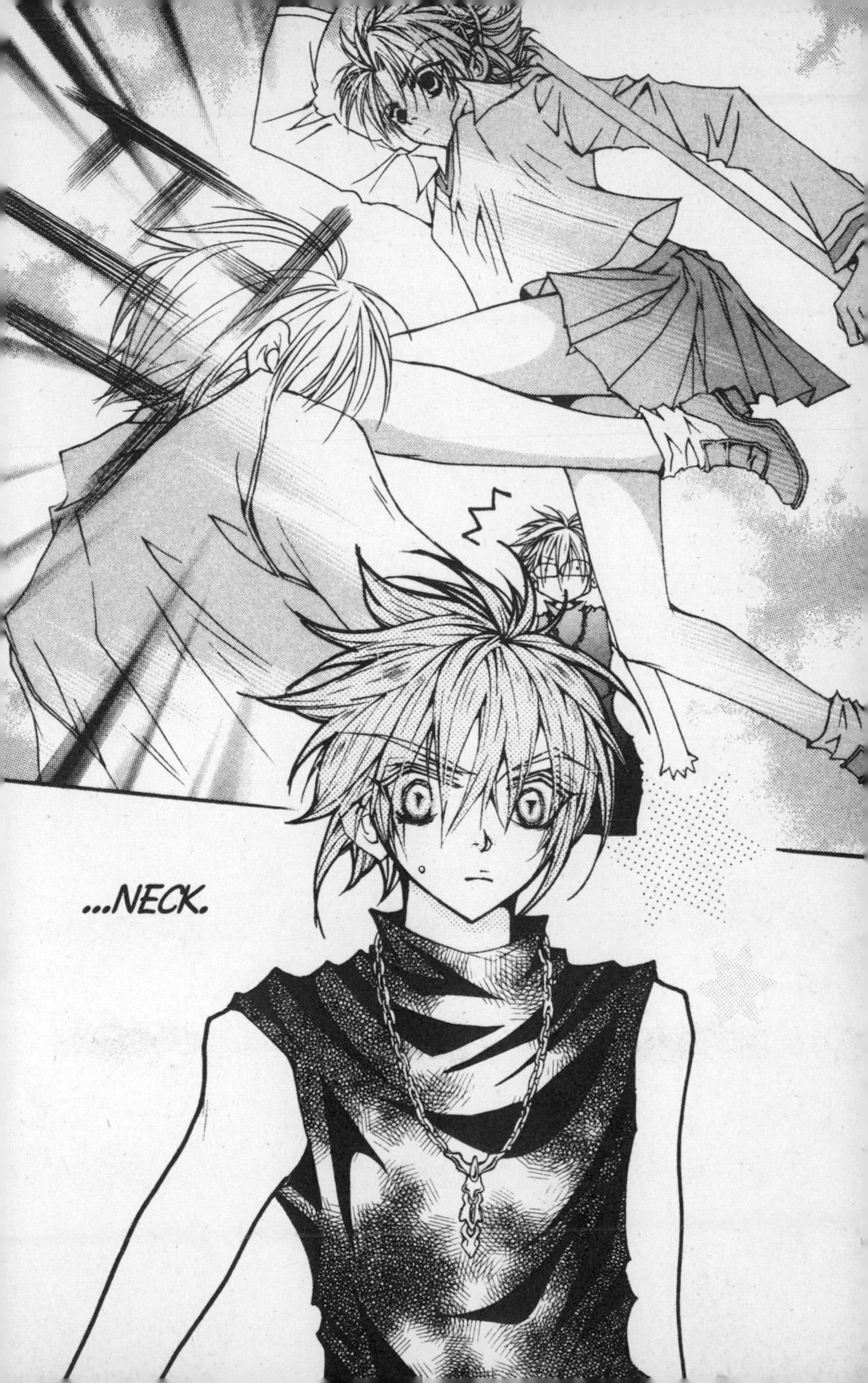
...NECK.

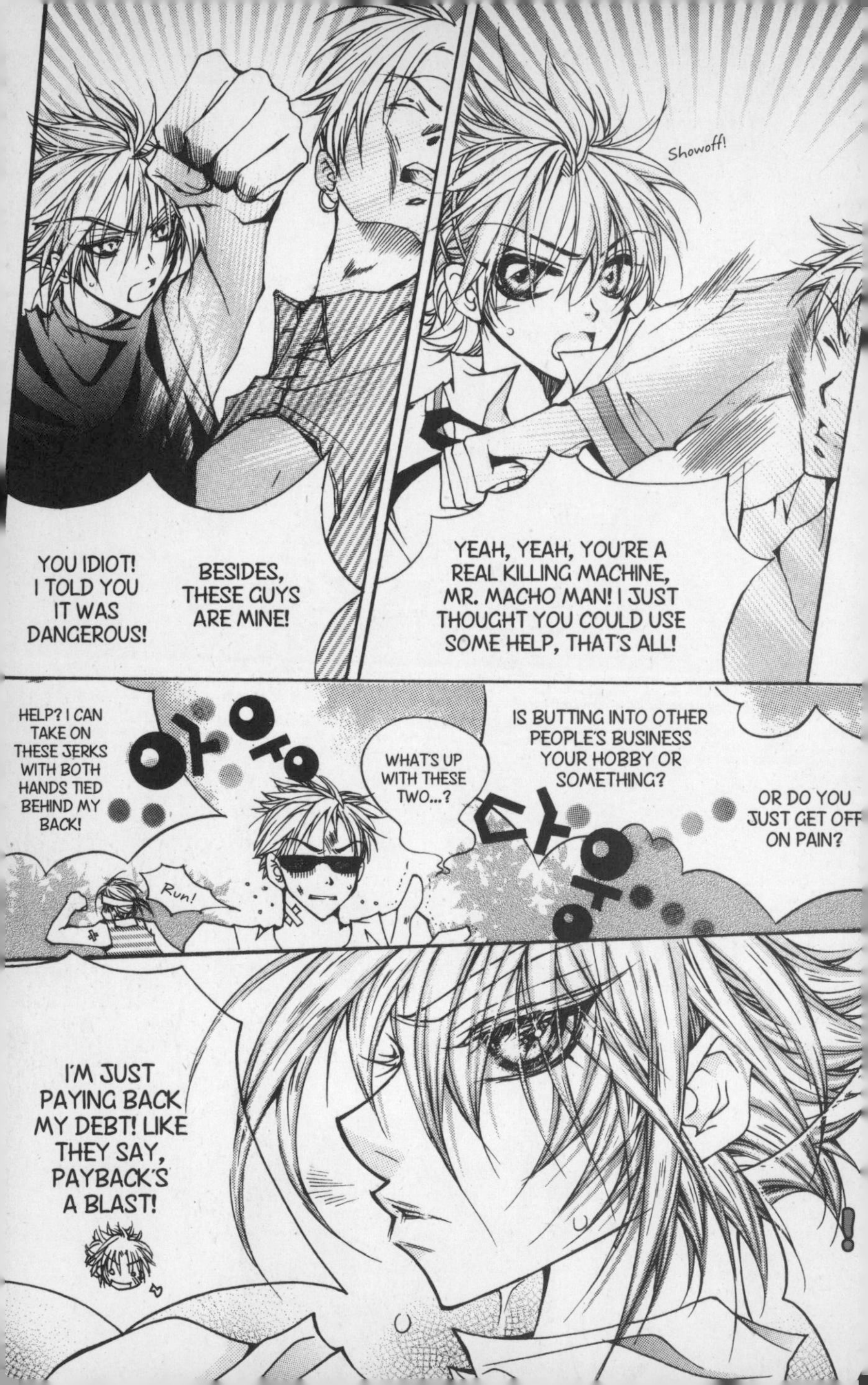
YOU IDIOT! I TOLD YOU IT WAS DANGEROUS!
BESIDES, THESE GUYS ARE MINE!
Showoff!
YEAH, YEAH, YOU'RE A REAL KILLING MACHINE, MR. MACHO MAN! I JUST THOUGHT YOU COULD USE SOME HELP, THAT'S ALL!
HELP? I CAN TAKE ON THESE JERKS WITH BOTH HANDS TIED BEHIND MY BACK!
Run!
WHAT'S UP WITH THESE TWO...?
IS BUTTING INTO OTHER PEOPLE'S BUSINESS YOUR HOBBY OR SOMETHING?
OR DO YOU JUST GET OFF ON PAIN?
I'M JUST PAYING BACK MY DEBT! LIKE THEY SAY, PAYBACK'S A BLAST!

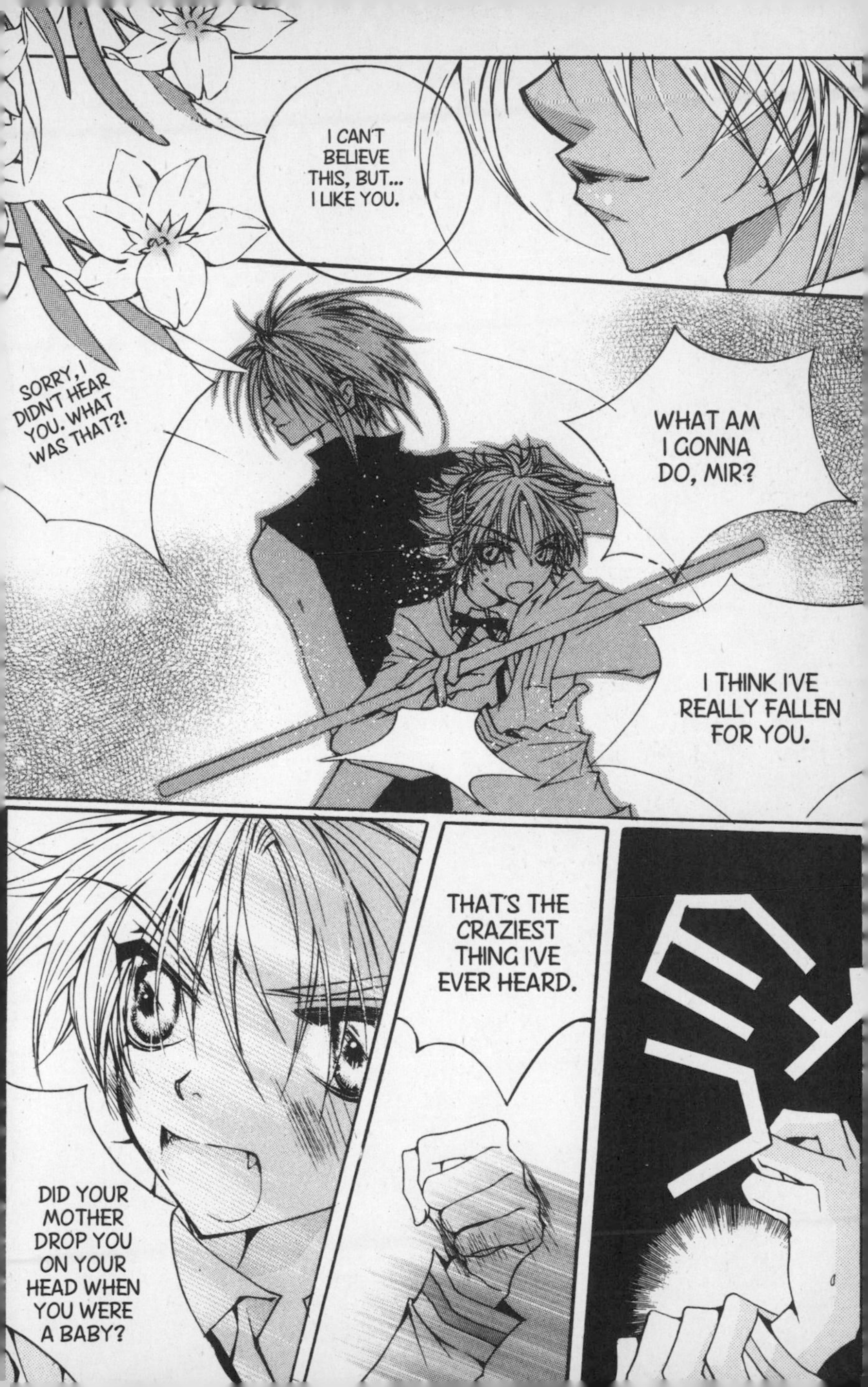
I CAN'T BELIEVE THIS, BUT... I LIKE YOU.
SORRY, I DIDN'T HEAR YOU. WHAT WAS THAT?!
WHAT AM I GONNA DO, MIR?
I THINK I'VE REALLY FALLEN FOR YOU.
DID YOUR MOTHER DROP YOU ON YOUR HEAD WHEN YOU WERE A BABY?
THAT'S THE CRAZIEST THING I'VE EVER HEARD.

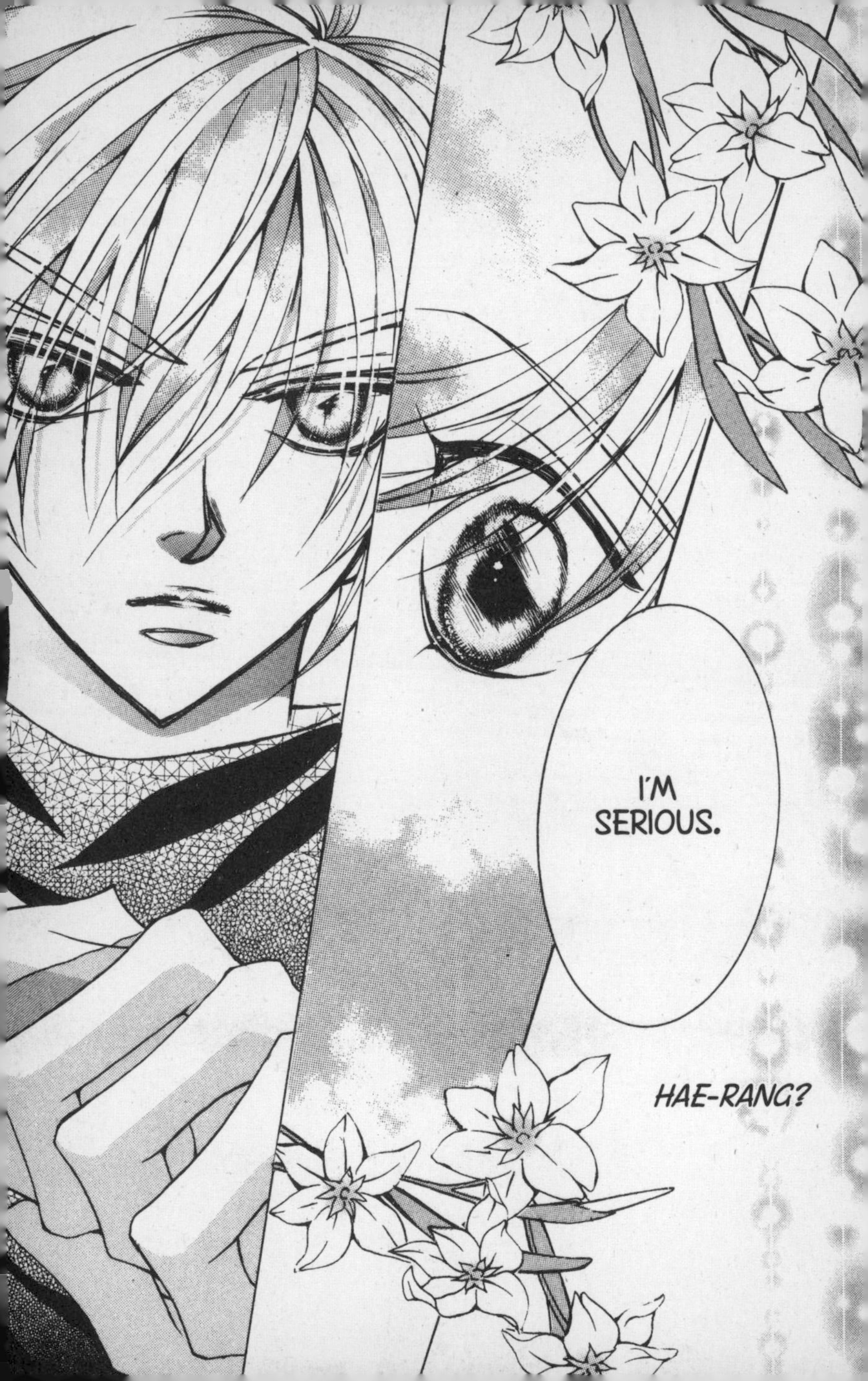
I'M SERIOUS.
HAE-RANG?

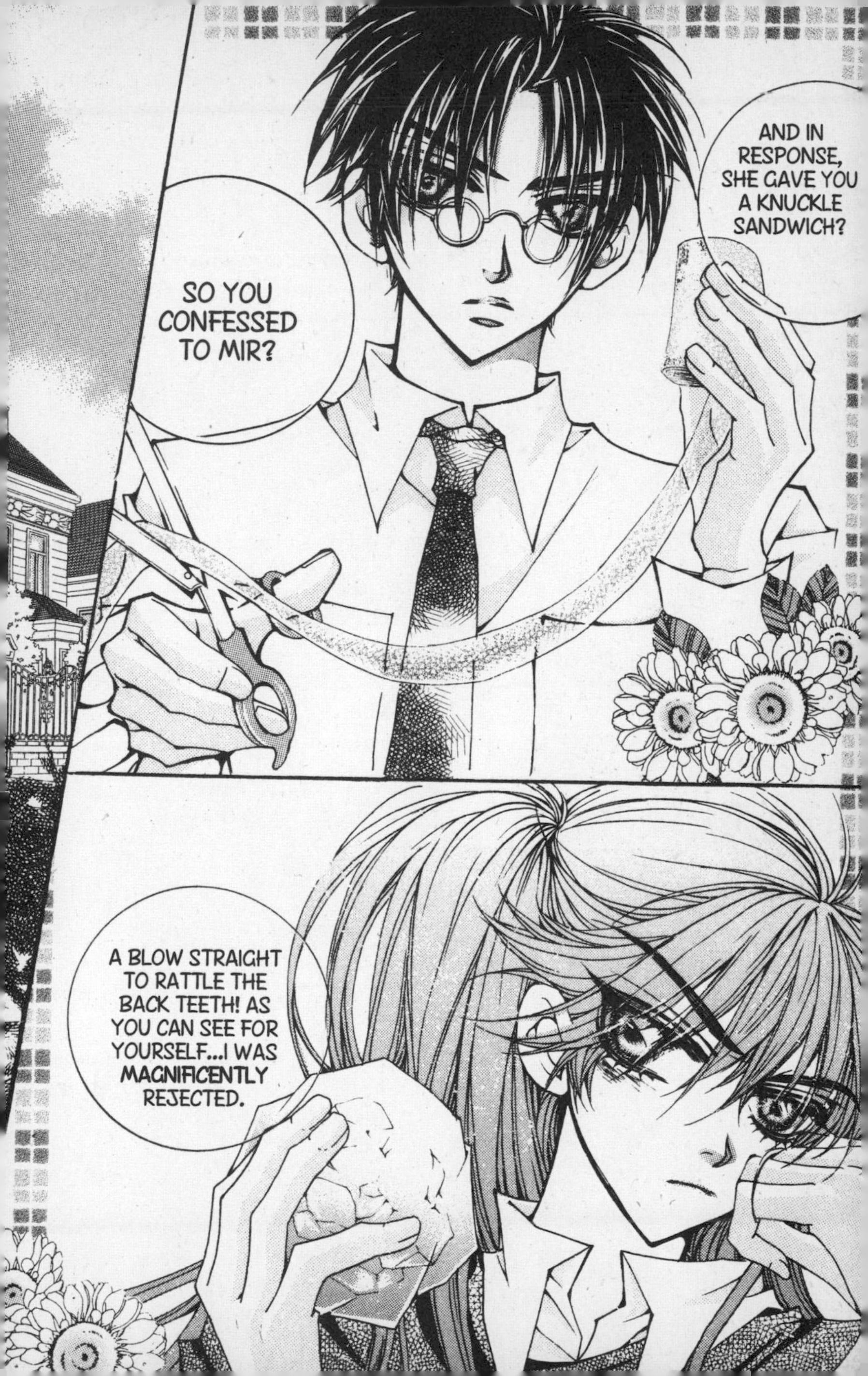
SO YOU CONFESSED TO MIR?
AND IN RESPONSE, SHE GAVE YOU A KNUCKLE SANDWICH?
A BLOW STRAIGHT TO RATTLE THE BACK TEETH! AS YOU CAN SEE FOR YOURSELF...I WAS MAGNIFICENTLY REJECTED.

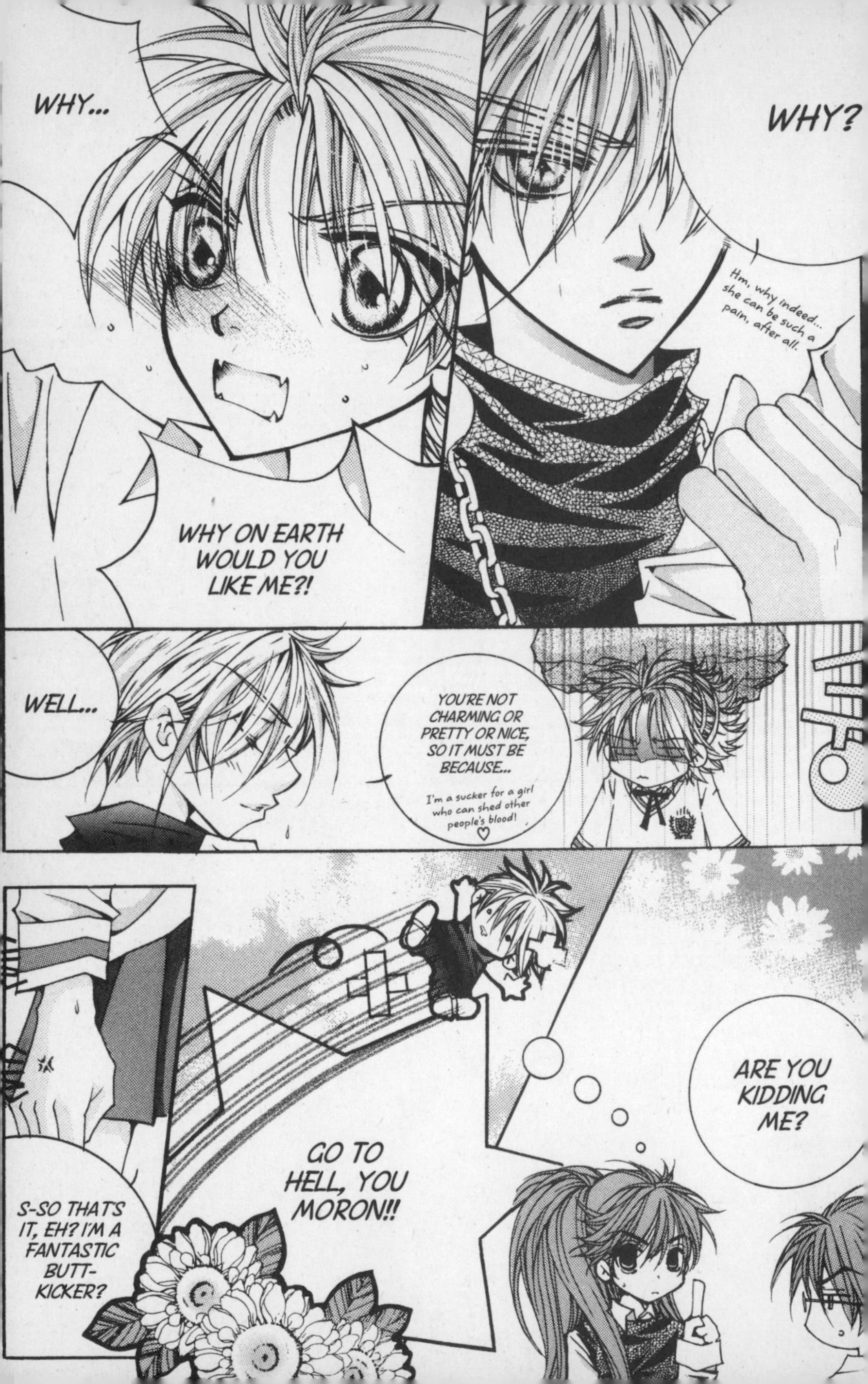
WHY...
WHY ON EARTH WOULD YOU LIKE ME?!
WHY?
Hm, why indeed... she can be such a pain, after all.
WELL...
YOU'RE NOT CHARMING OR PRETTY OR NICE, SO IT MUST BE BECAUSE...
I'm a sucker for a girl who can shed other people's blood! ♡
S-SO THAT'S IT, EH? I'M A FANTASTIC BUTT-KICKER?
GO TO HELL, YOU MORON!!
ARE YOU KIDDING ME?

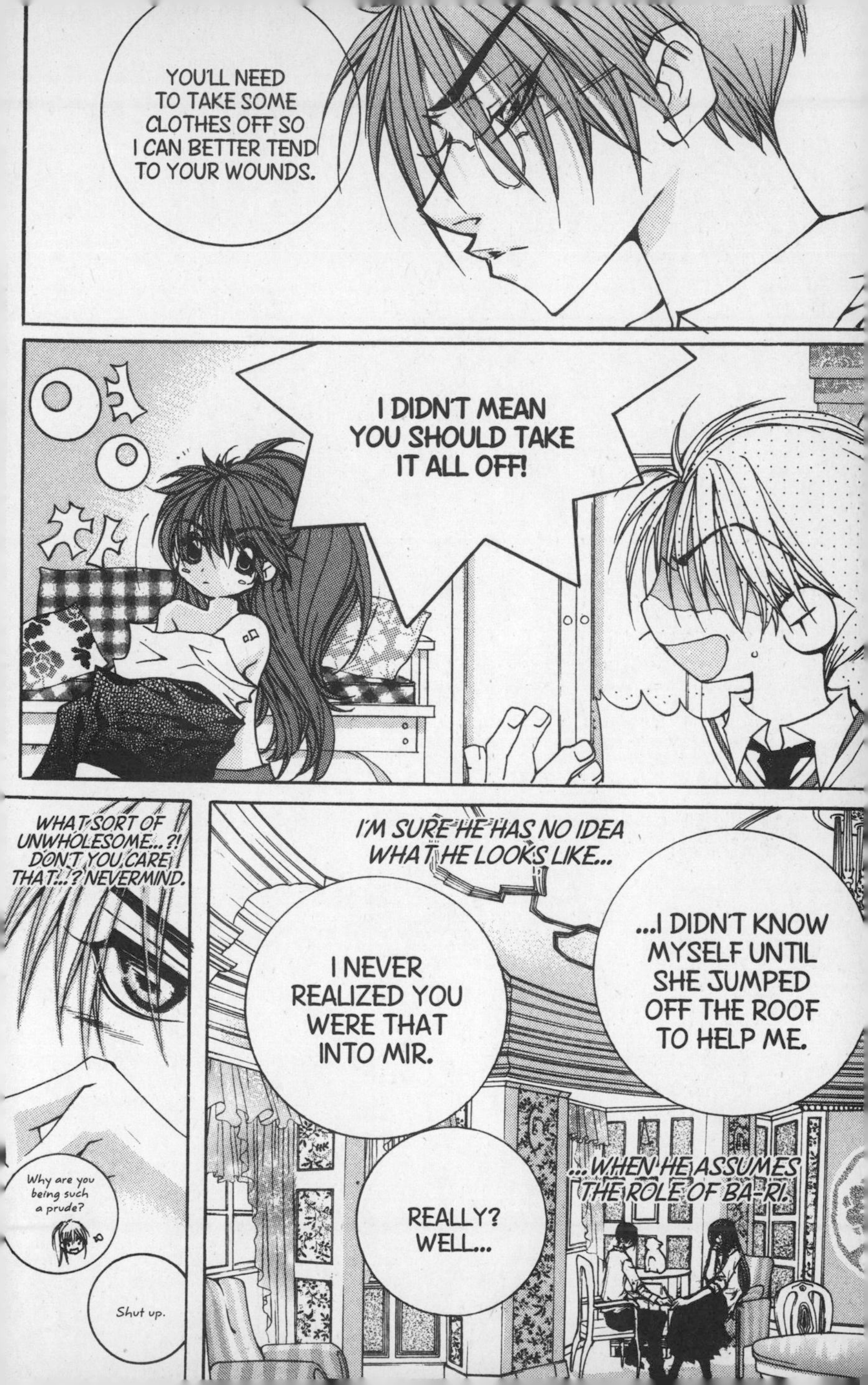
YOU'LL NEED TO TAKE SOME CLOTHES OFF SO I CAN BETTER TEND TO YOUR WOUNDS.
I DIDN'T MEAN YOU SHOULD TAKE IT ALL OFF!
WHAT SORT OF UNWHOLESOME...?! DON'T YOU CARE THAT...? NEVERMIND.
Why are you being such a prude?
Shut up.
I'M SURE HE HAS NO IDEA WHAT HE LOOKS LIKE...
I NEVER REALIZED YOU WERE THAT INTO MIR.
...I DIDN'T KNOW MYSELF UNTIL SHE JUMPED OFF THE ROOF TO HELP ME.
REALLY? WELL...
...WHEN HE ASSUMES THE ROLE OF BA-RI.

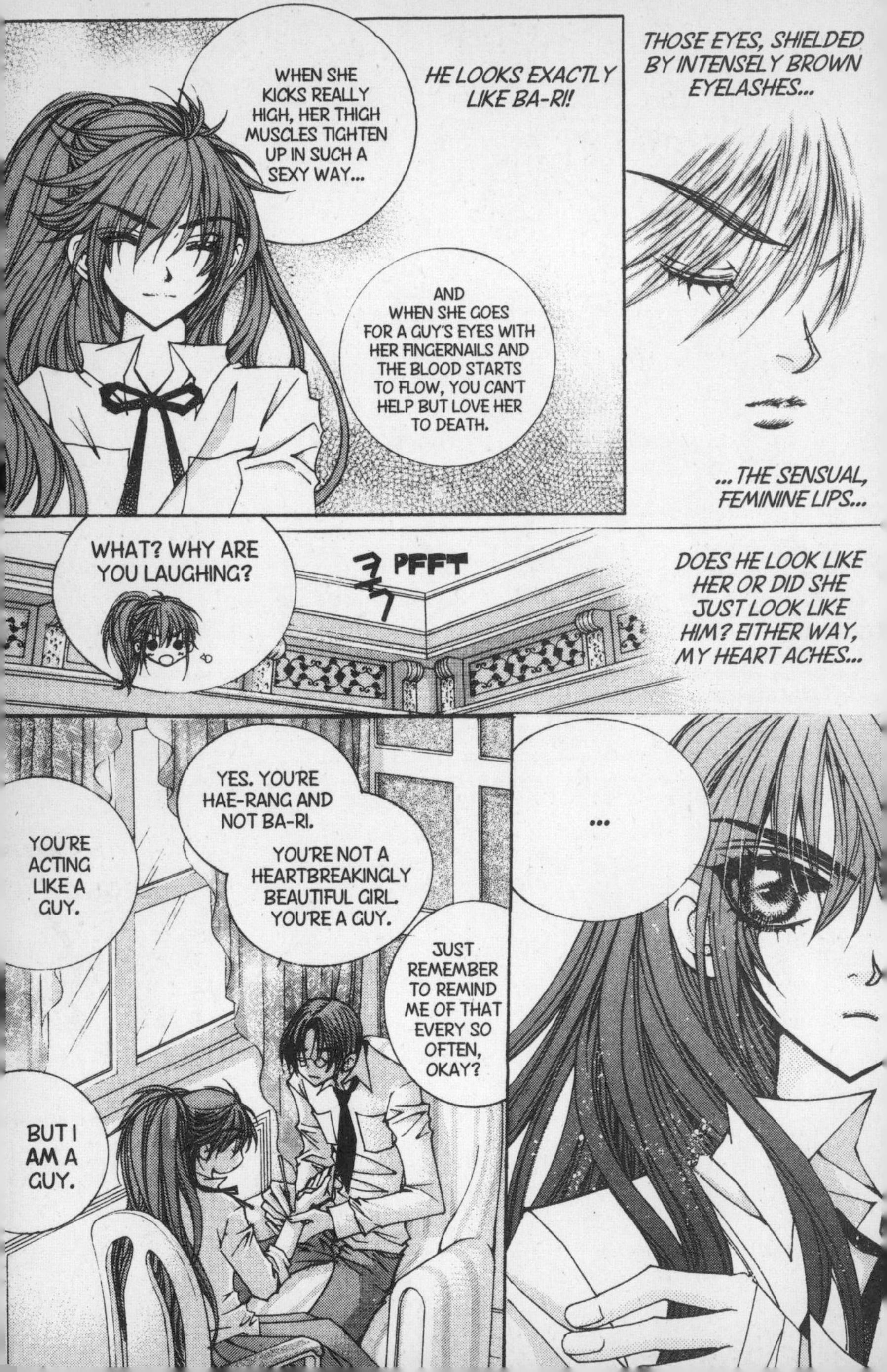
WHEN SHE KICKS REALLY HIGH, HER THIGH MUSCLES TIGHTEN UP IN SUCH A SEXY WAY...
HE LOOKS EXACTLY LIKE BA-RI!
AND WHEN SHE GOES FOR A GUY'S EYES WITH HER FINGERNAILS AND THE BLOOD STARTS TO FLOW, YOU CAN'T HELP BUT LOVE HER TO DEATH.
THOSE EYES, SHIELDED BY INTENSELY BROWN EYELASHES...
...THE SENSUAL, FEMININE LIPS...
WHAT? WHY ARE YOU LAUGHING?
PFFT
DOES HE LOOK LIKE HER OR DID SHE JUST LOOK LIKE HIM? EITHER WAY, MY HEART ACHES...
YOU'RE ACTING LIKE A GUY.
YES. YOU'RE HAE-RANG AND NOT BA-RI.
YOU'RE NOT A HEARTBREAKINGLY BEAUTIFUL GIRL. YOU'RE A GUY.
JUST REMEMBER TO REMIND ME OF THAT EVERY SO OFTEN, OKAY?
BUT I AM A GUY.
...

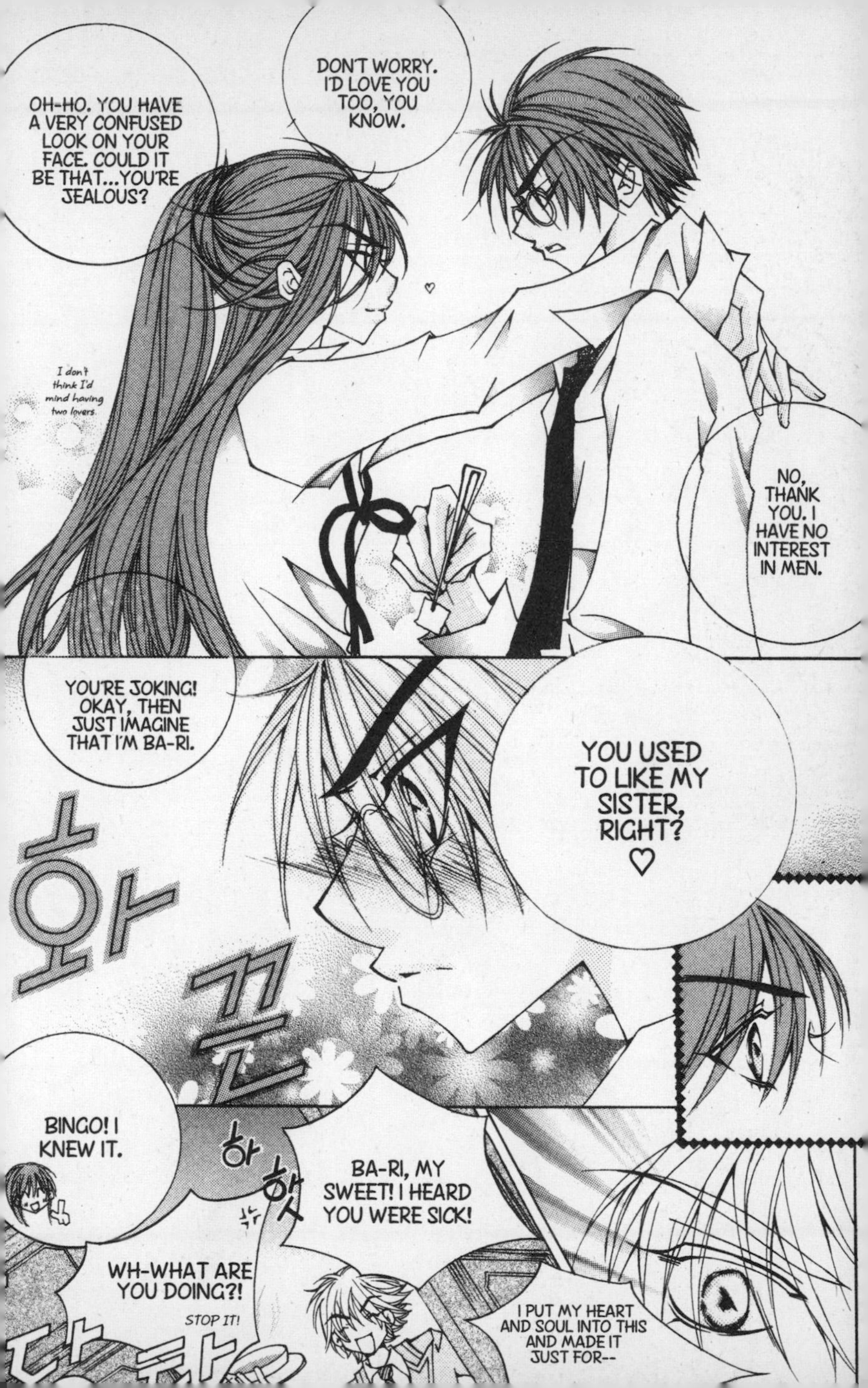
OH-HO. YOU HAVE A VERY CONFUSED LOOK ON YOUR FACE. COULD IT BE THAT...YOU'RE JEALOUS?
DON'T WORRY. I'D LOVE YOU TOO, YOU KNOW.
I don't think I'd mind having two lovers.
NO, THANK YOU. I HAVE NO INTEREST IN MEN.
YOU'RE JOKING! OKAY, THEN JUST IMAGINE THAT I'M BA-RI.
YOU USED TO LIKE MY SISTER, RIGHT? ♡
BINGO! I KNEW IT.
하
핫
BA-RI, MY SWEET! I HEARD YOU WERE SICK!
WH-WHAT ARE YOU DOING?!
STOP IT!
I PUT MY HEART AND SOUL INTO THIS AND MADE IT JUST FOR--

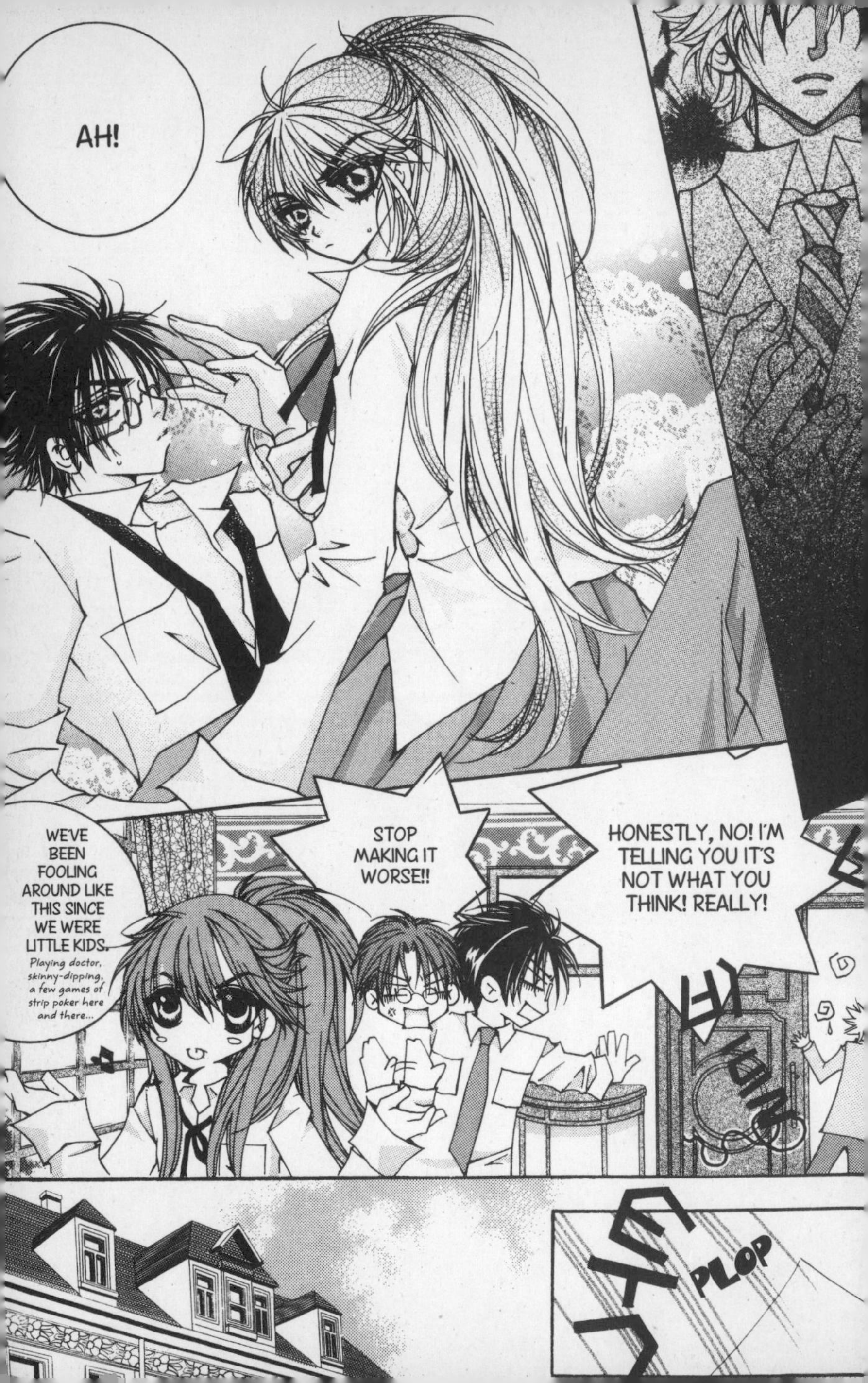
AH!
WE'VE BEEN FOOLING AROUND LIKE THIS SINCE WE WERE LITTLE KIDS.
Playing doctor, skinny-dipping, a few games of strip poker here and there...
STOP MAKING IT WORSE!!
HONESTLY, NO! I'M TELLING YOU IT'S NOT WHAT YOU THINK! REALLY!
PLOP

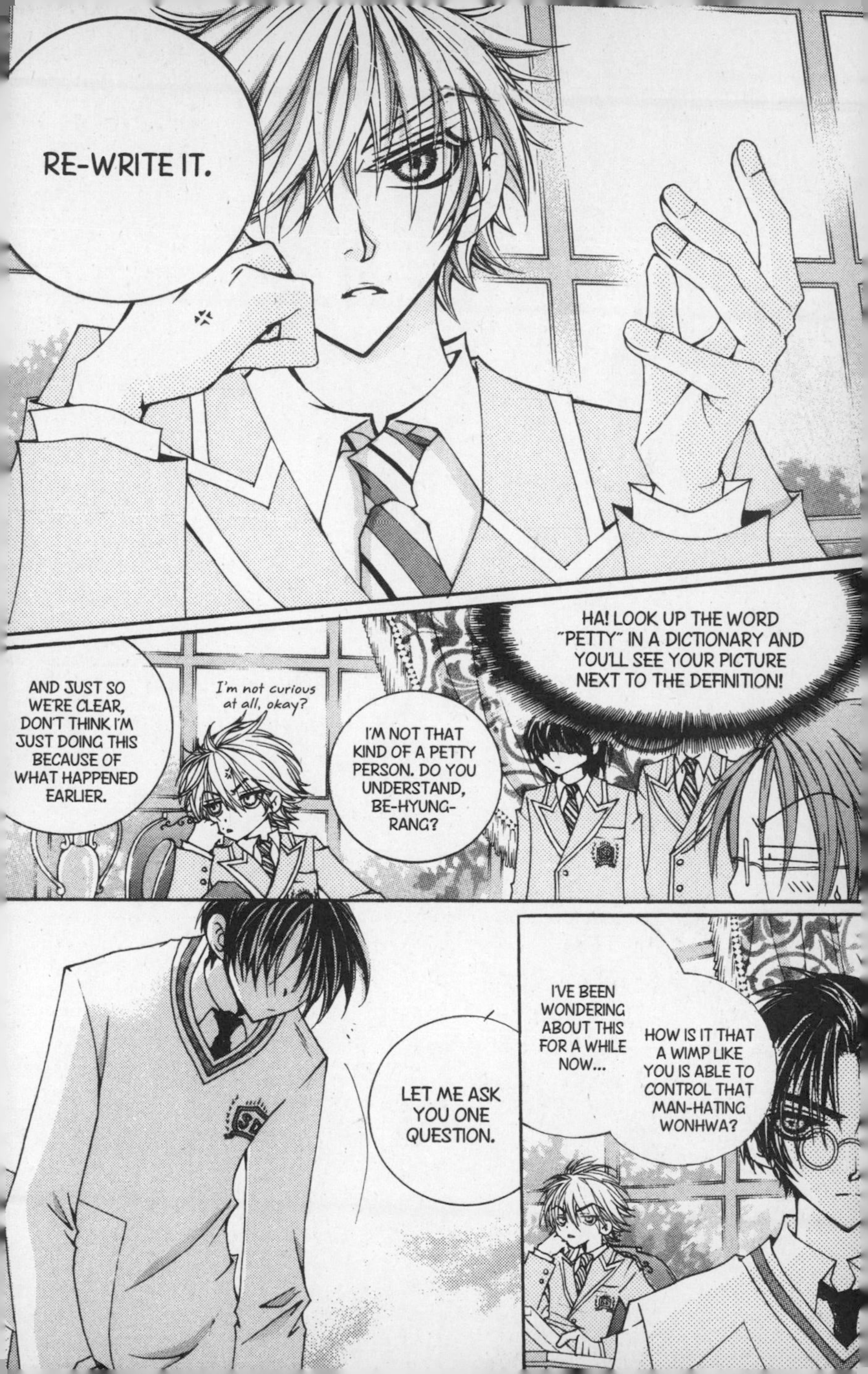
RE-WRITE IT.
AND JUST SO WE'RE CLEAR, DON'T THINK I'M JUST DOING THIS BECAUSE OF WHAT HAPPENED EARLIER.
I'm not curious at all, okay?
I'M NOT THAT KIND OF A PETTY PERSON. DO YOU UNDERSTAND, BE-HYUNG-RANG?
HA! LOOK UP THE WORD "PETTY" IN A DICTIONARY AND YOU'LL SEE YOUR PICTURE NEXT TO THE DEFINITION!
LET ME ASK YOU ONE QUESTION.
I'VE BEEN WONDERING ABOUT THIS FOR A WHILE NOW...
HOW IS IT THAT A WIMP LIKE YOU IS ABLE TO CONTROL THAT MAN-HATING WONHWA?

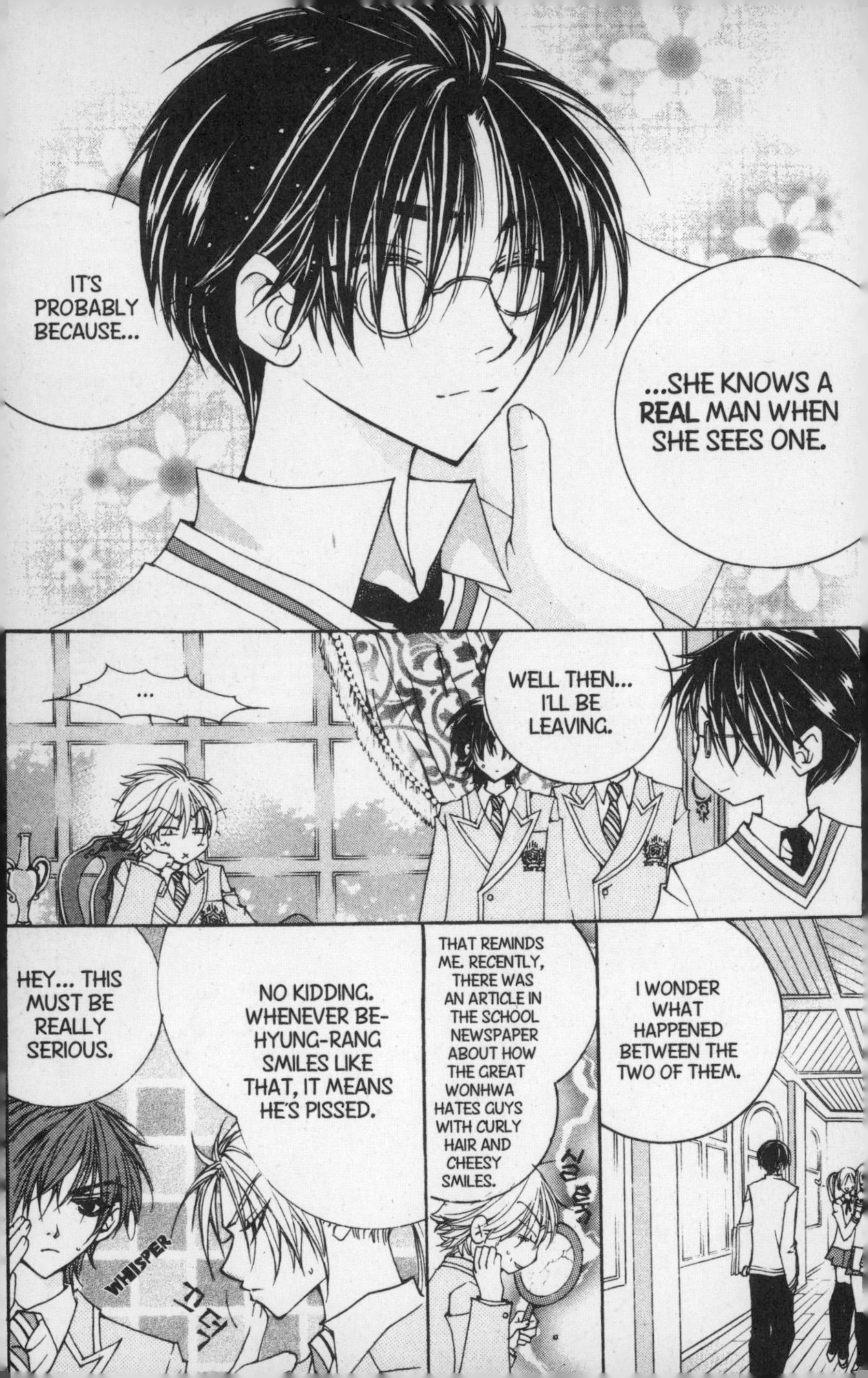
IT'S PROBABLY BECAUSE...
...SHE KNOWS A REAL MAN WHEN SHE SEES ONE.
...
WELL THEN... I'LL BE LEAVING.
HEY... THIS MUST BE REALLY SERIOUS.
NO KIDDING. WHENEVER BE-HYUNG-RANG SMILES LIKE THAT, IT MEANS HE'S PISSED.
WHISPER
THAT REMINDS ME. RECENTLY, THERE WAS AN ARTICLE IN THE SCHOOL NEWSPAPER ABOUT HOW THE GREAT WONHWA HATES GUYS WITH CURLY HAIR AND CHEESY SMILES.
I WONDER WHAT HAPPENED BETWEEN THE TWO OF THEM.

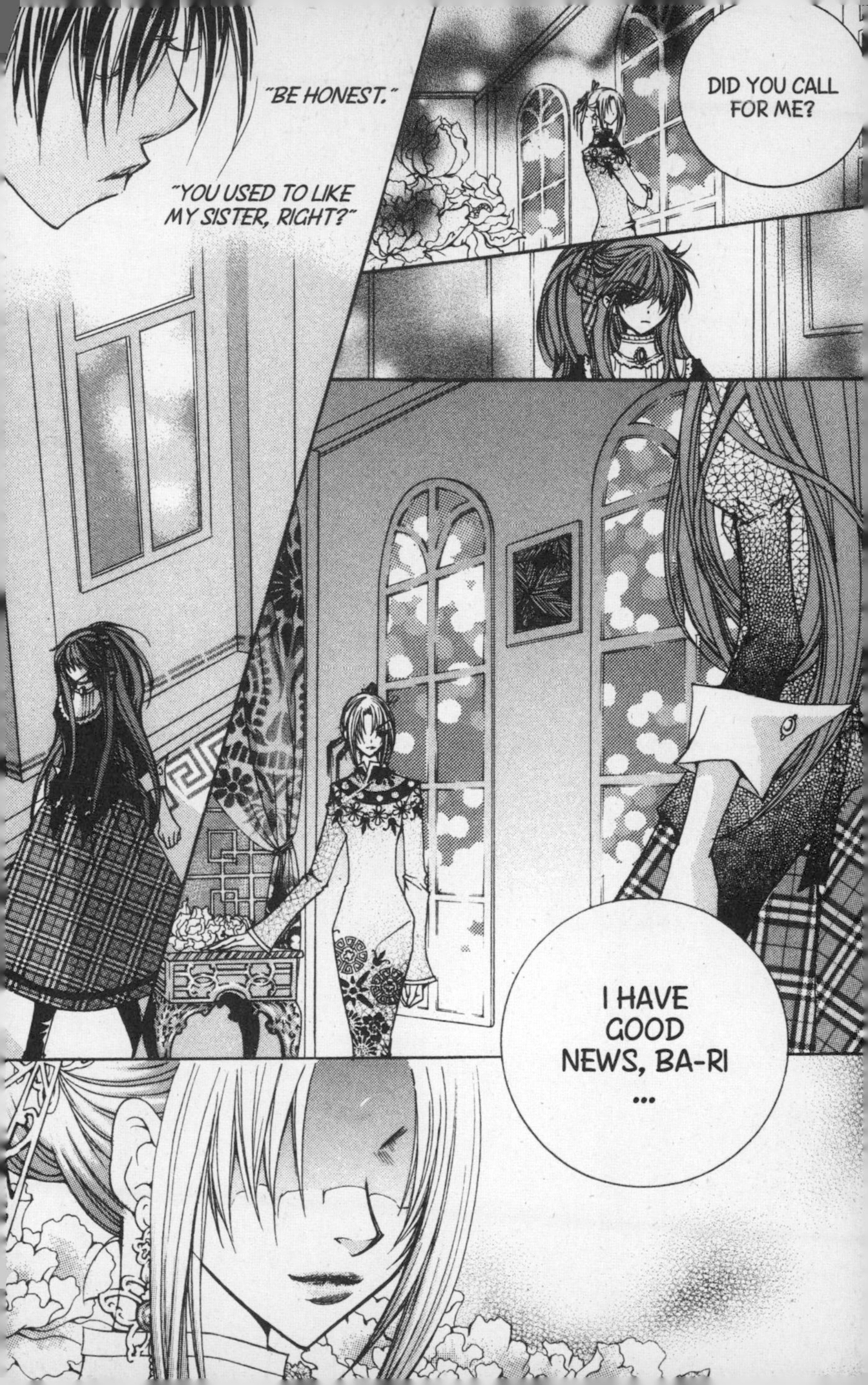
"BE HONEST."
"YOU USED TO LIKE MY SISTER, RIGHT?"
DID YOU CALL FOR ME?
I HAVE GOOD NEWS, BA-RI ...

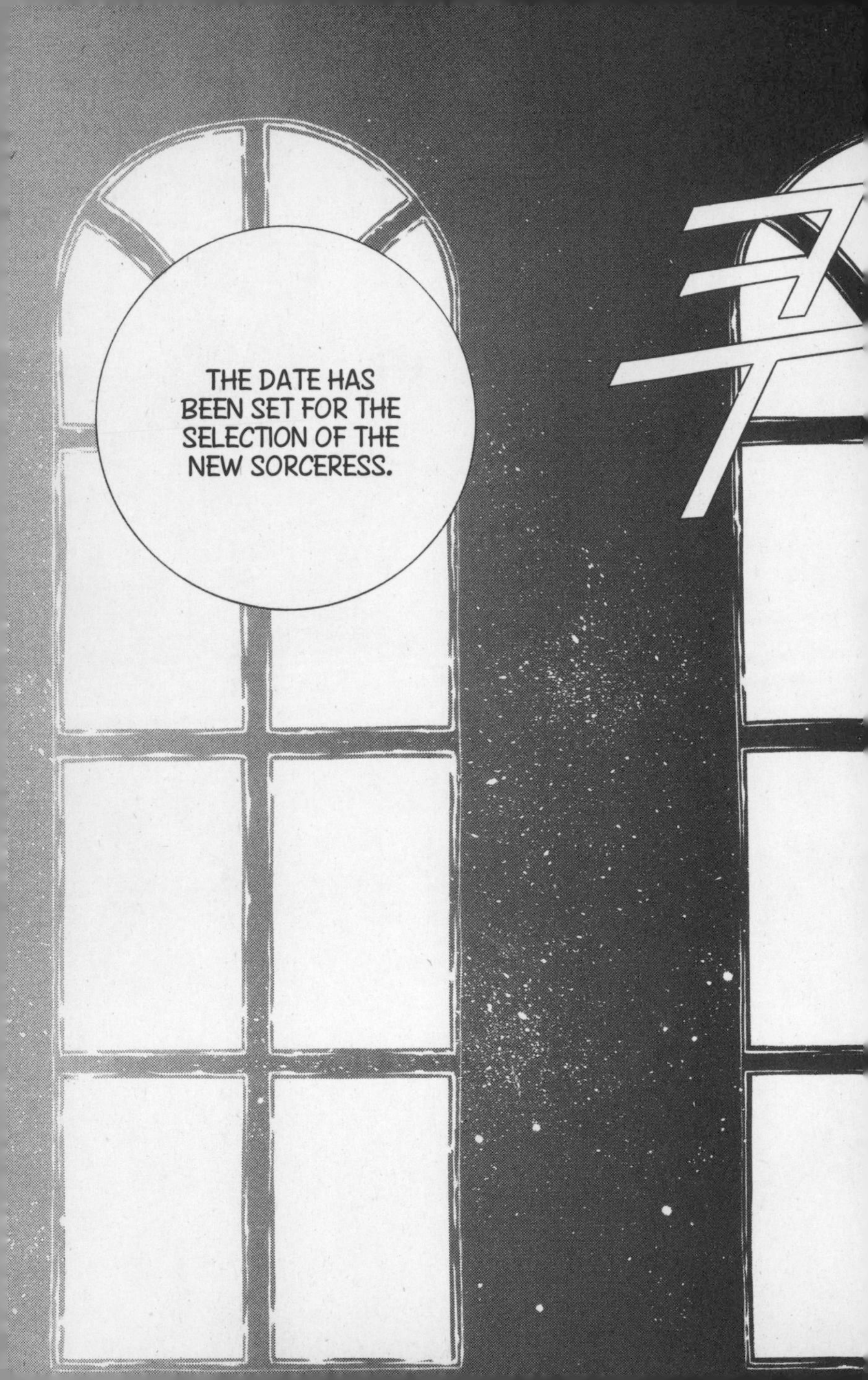
THE DATE HAS BEEN SET FOR THE SELECTION OF THE NEW SORCERESS.

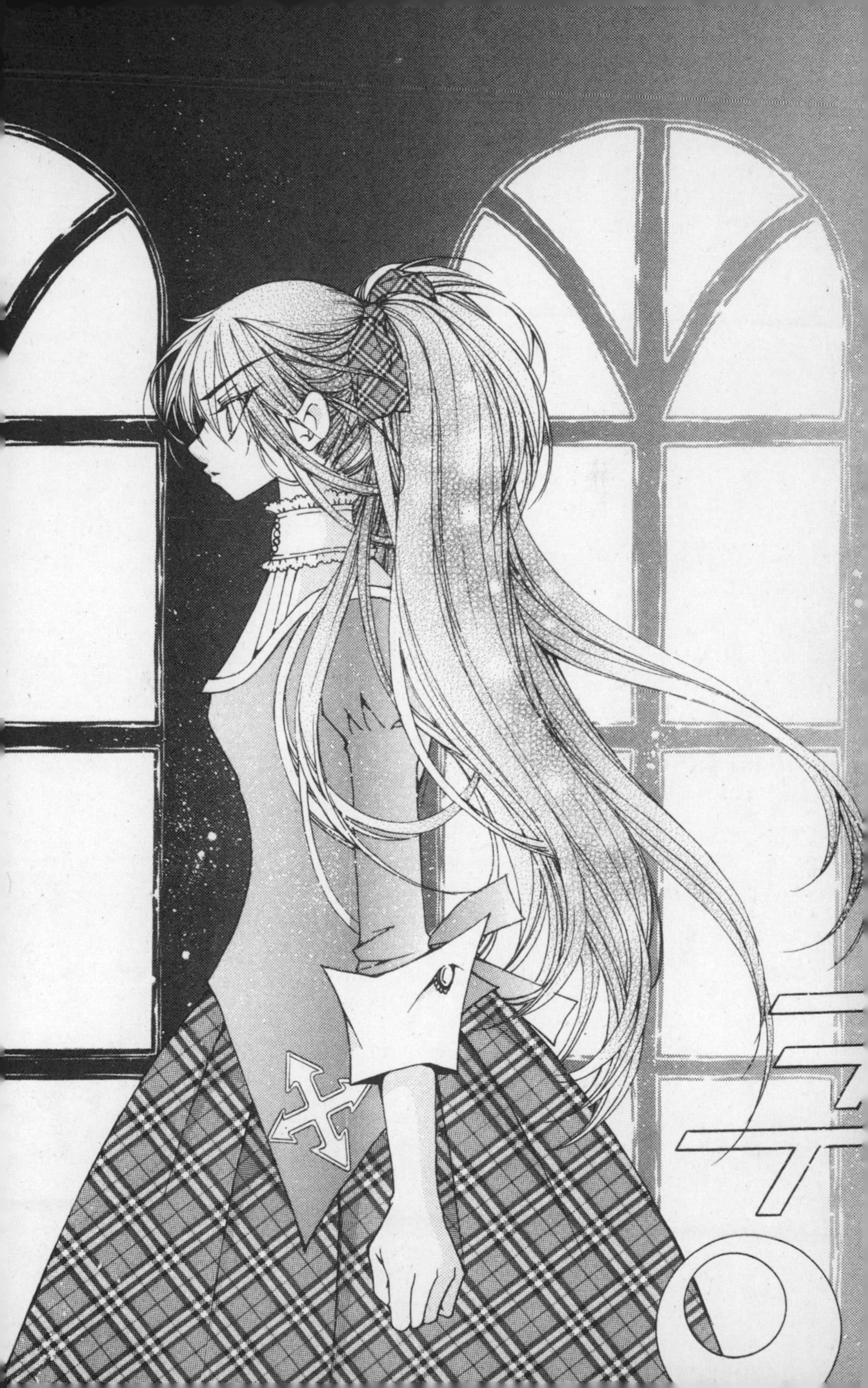

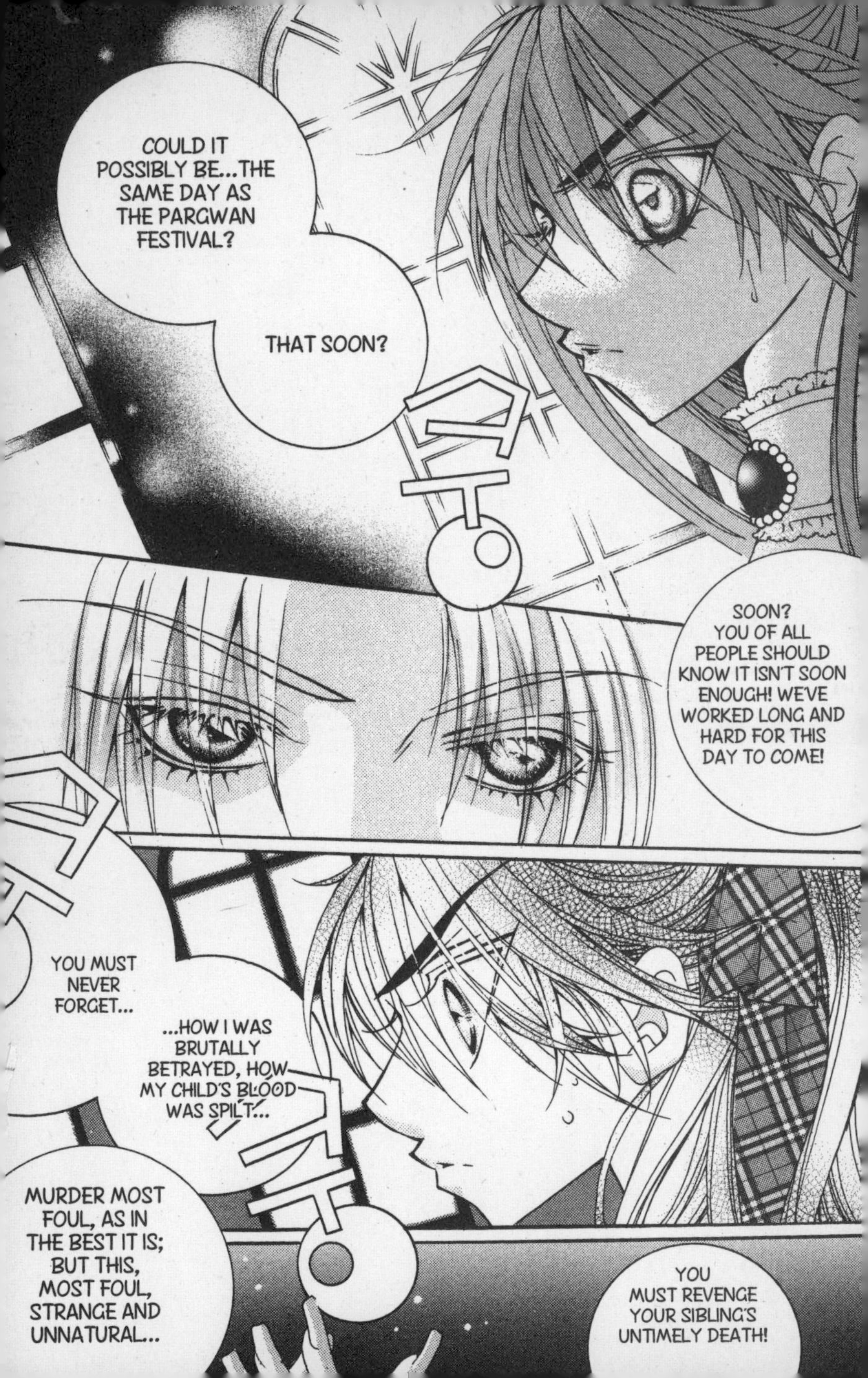
COULD IT POSSIBLY BE...THE SAME DAY AS THE PARGWAN FESTIVAL?
THAT SOON?
SOON? YOU OF ALL PEOPLE SHOULD KNOW IT ISN'T SOON ENOUGH! WE'VE WORKED LONG AND HARD FOR THIS DAY TO COME!
YOU MUST NEVER FORGET...
...HOW I WAS BRUTALLY BETRAYED, HOW MY CHILD'S BLOOD WAS SPILT...
MURDER MOST FOUL, AS IN THE BEST IT IS; BUT THIS, MOST FOUL, STRANGE AND UNNATURAL...
YOU MUST REVENGE YOUR SIBLING'S UNTIMELY DEATH!

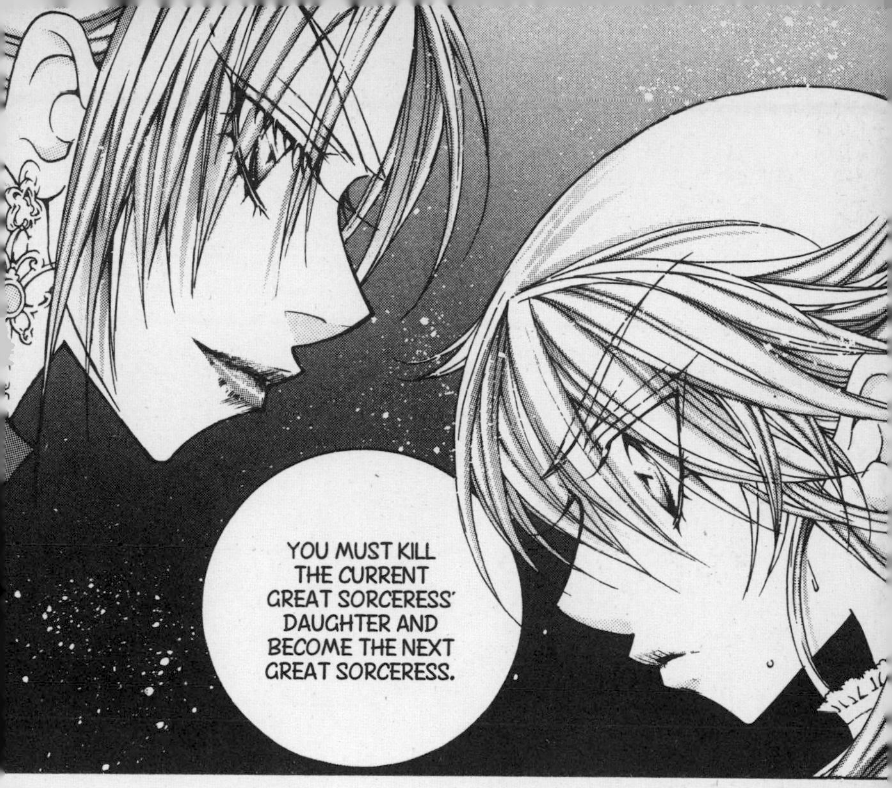
YOU MUST KILL THE CURRENT GREAT SORCERESS' DAUGHTER AND BECOME THE NEXT GREAT SORCERESS.

KILL MIR...?

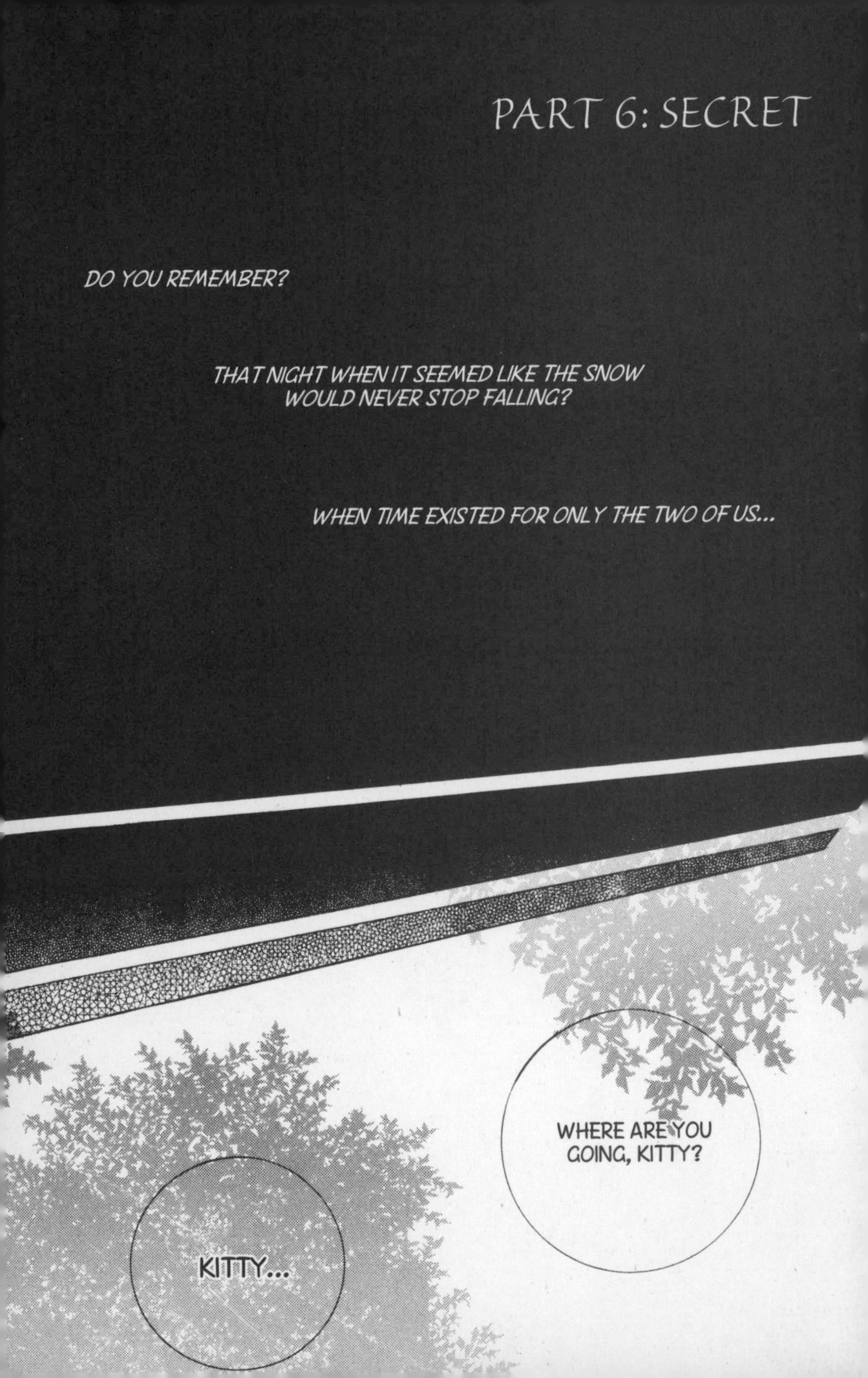
PART 6: SECRET
DO YOU REMEMBER?
THAT NIGHT WHEN IT SEEMED LIKE THE SNOW WOULD NEVER STOP FALLING?
WHEN TIME EXISTED FOR ONLY THE TWO OF US...
KITTY...
WHERE ARE YOU GOING, KITTY?

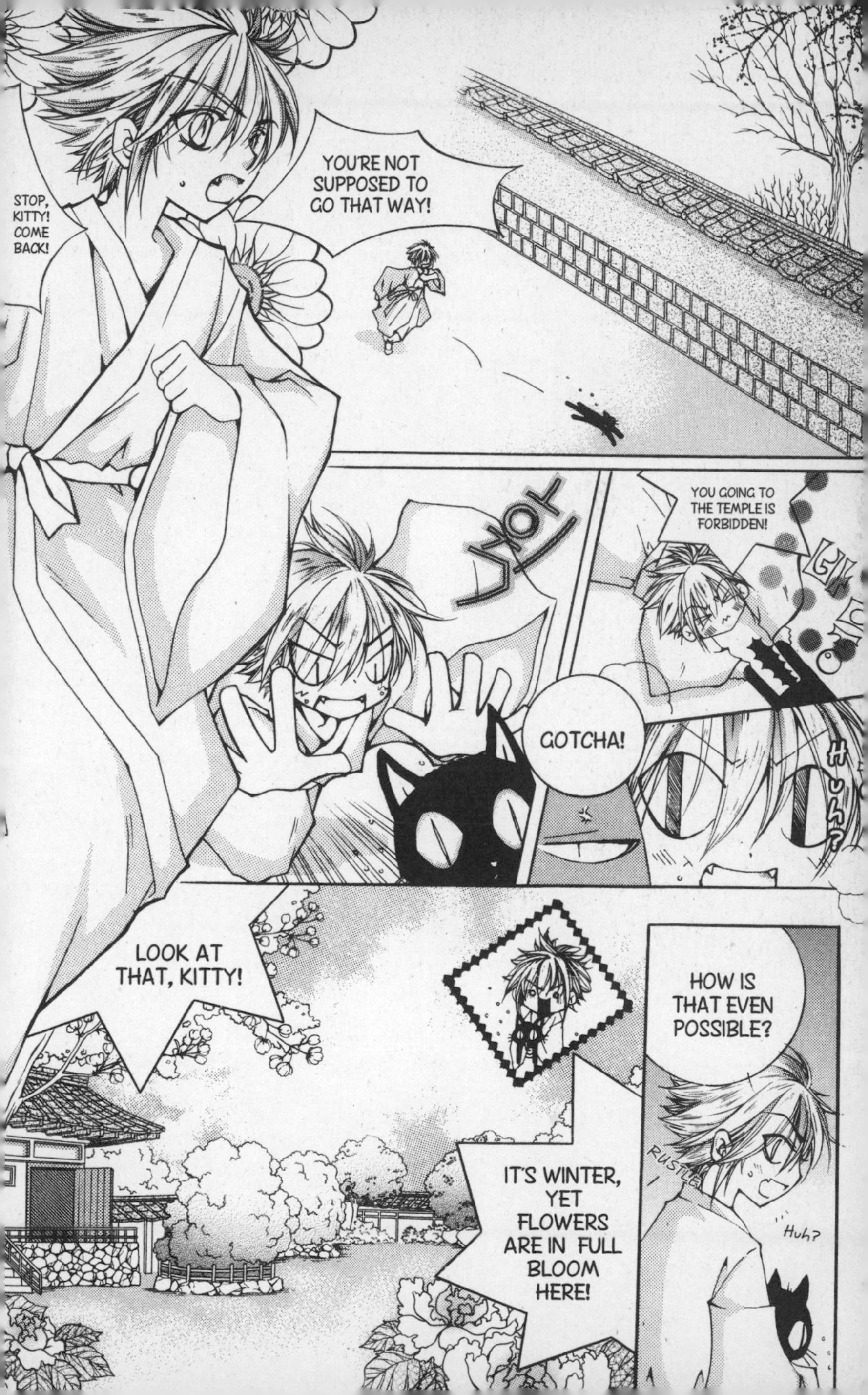
STOP, KITTY! COME BACK!
YOU'RE NOT SUPPOSED TO GO THAT WAY!
GOTCHA!
YOU GOING TO THE TEMPLE IS FORBIDDEN!
Huh?
LOOK AT THAT, KITTY!
IT'S WINTER, YET FLOWERS ARE IN FULL BLOOM HERE!
HOW IS THAT EVEN POSSIBLE?
RUSTLE
Huh?

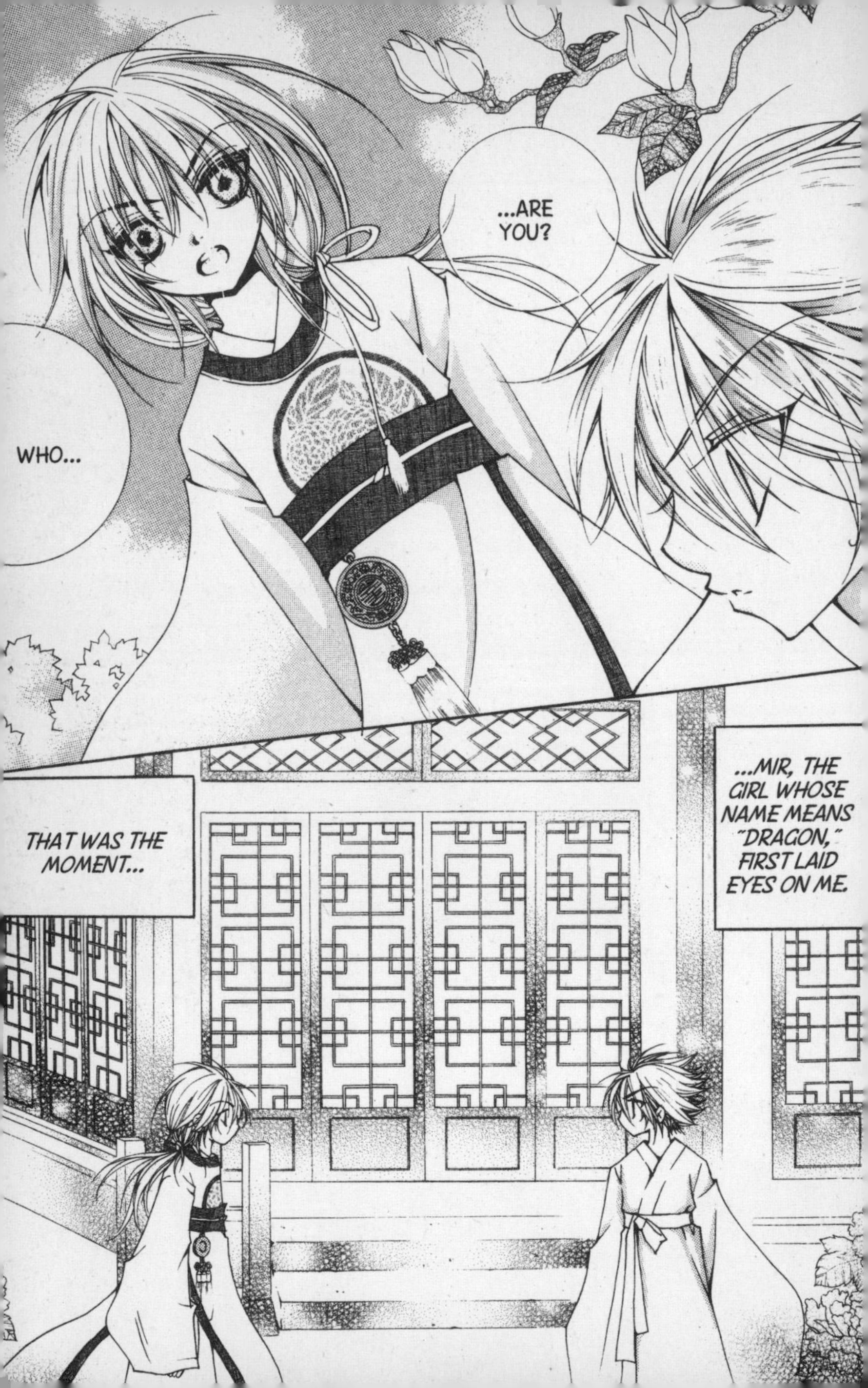
WHO...
...ARE YOU?
THAT WAS THE MOMENT...
...MIR, THE GIRL WHOSE NAME MEANS "DRAGON," FIRST LAID EYES ON ME.

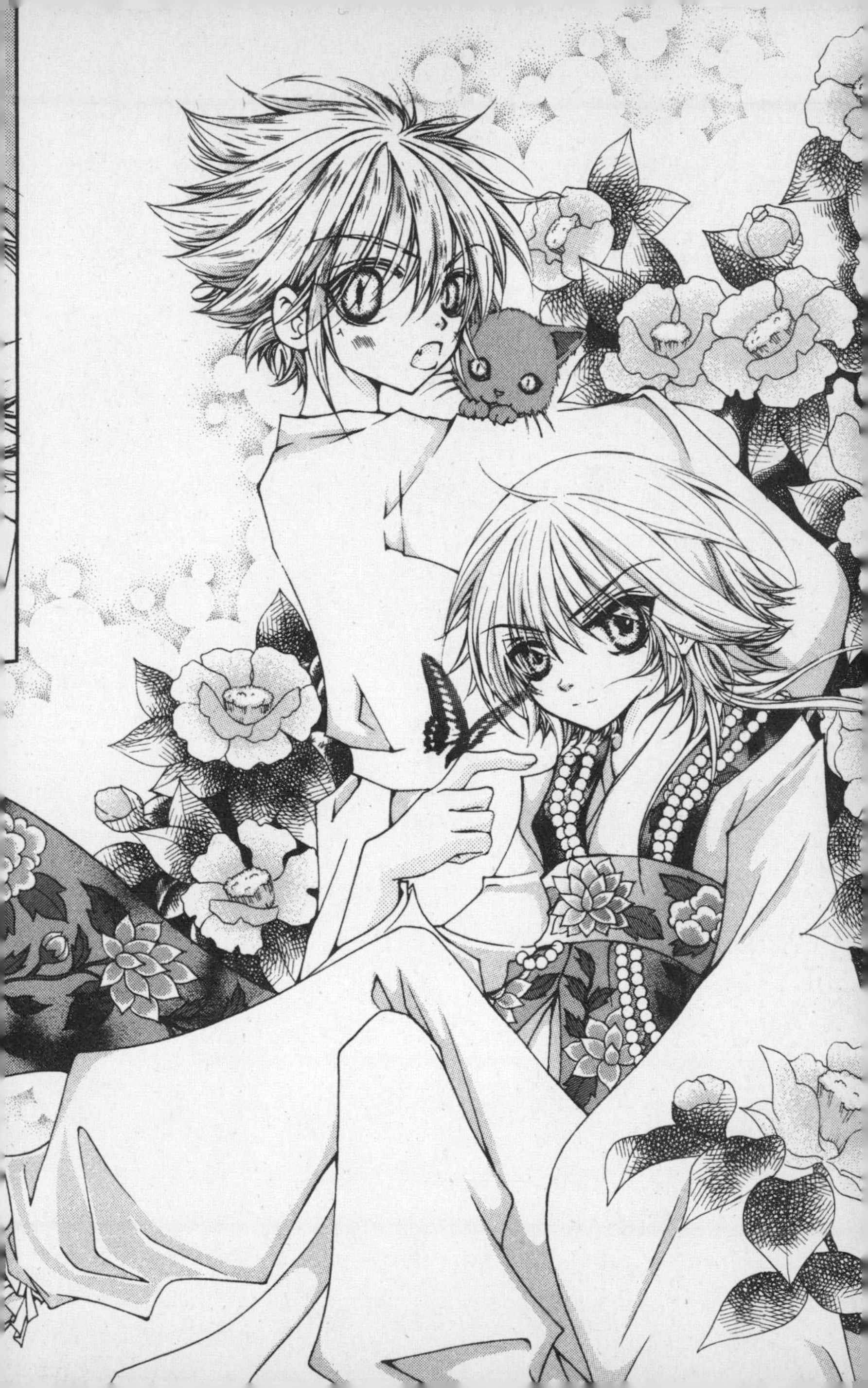

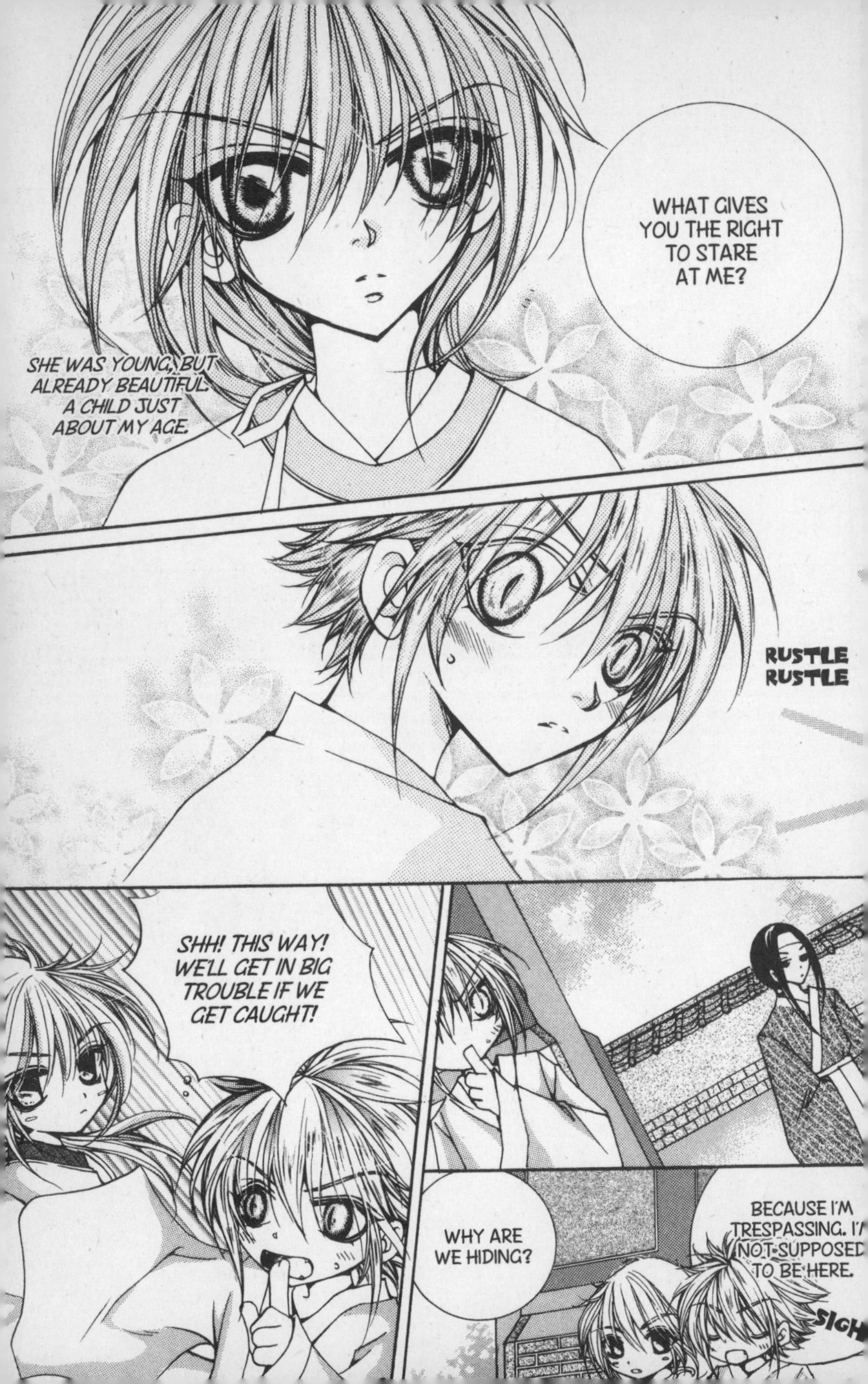
SHE WAS YOUNG, BUT ALREADY BEAUTIFUL. A CHILD JUST ABOUT MY AGE.
WHAT GIVES YOU THE RIGHT TO STARE AT ME?
RUSTLE RUSTLE
SHH! THIS WAY! WE'LL GET IN BIG TROUBLE IF WE GET CAUGHT!
WHY ARE WE HIDING?
BECAUSE I'M TRESPASSING. I' NOT SUPPOSED TO BE HERE.
SIGH

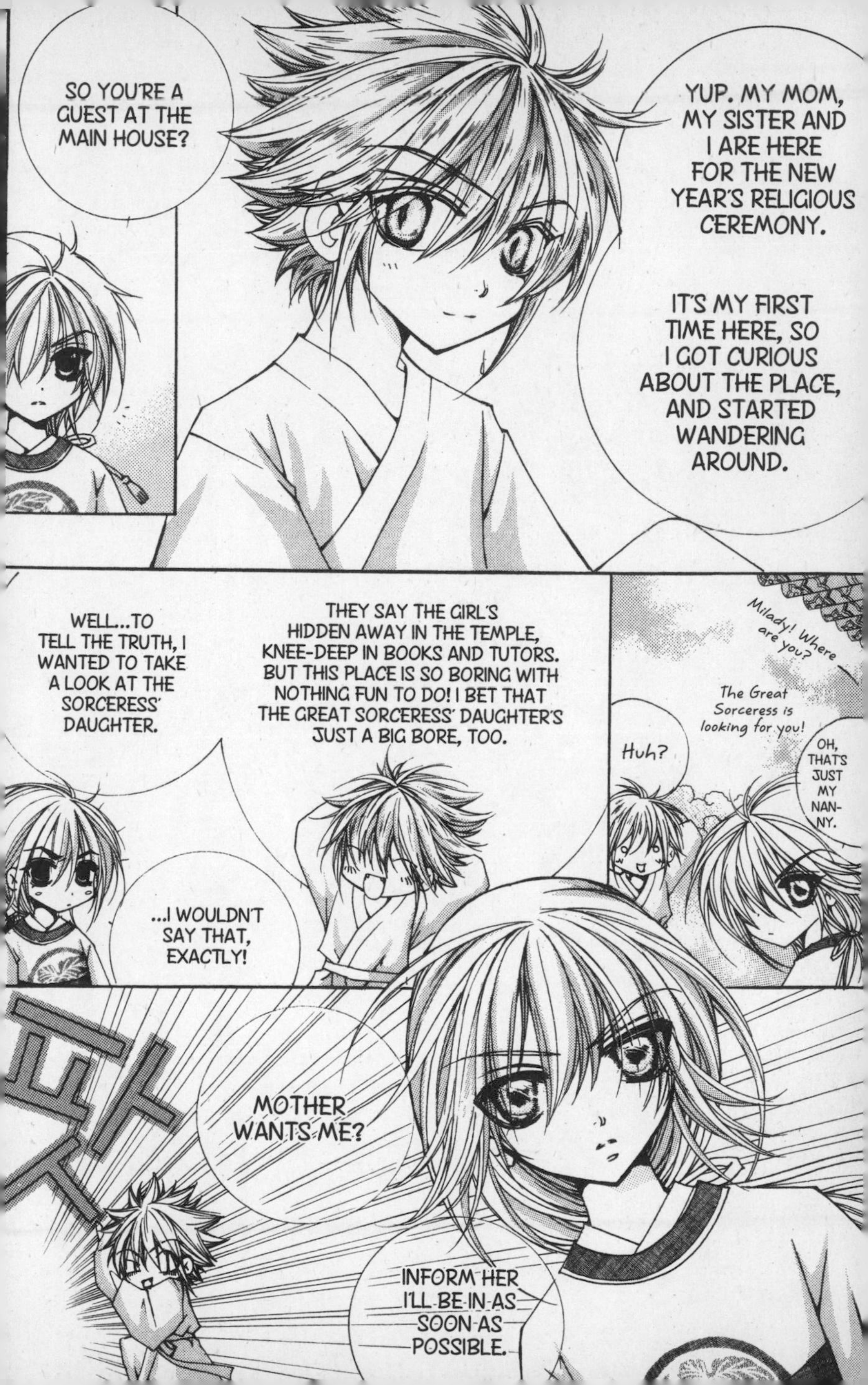
SO YOU'RE A GUEST AT THE MAIN HOUSE?
YUP. MY MOM, MY SISTER AND I ARE HERE FOR THE NEW YEAR'S RELIGIOUS CEREMONY.
IT'S MY FIRST TIME HERE, SO I GOT CURIOUS ABOUT THE PLACE, AND STARTED WANDERING AROUND.
WELL...TO TELL THE TRUTH, I WANTED TO TAKE A LOOK AT THE SORCERESS' DAUGHTER.
THEY SAY THE GIRL'S HIDDEN AWAY IN THE TEMPLE, KNEE-DEEP IN BOOKS AND TUTORS. BUT THIS PLACE IS SO BORING WITH NOTHING FUN TO DO! I BET THAT THE GREAT SORCERESS' DAUGHTER'S JUST A BIG BORE, TOO.
...I WOULDN'T SAY THAT, EXACTLY!
Milady! Where are you?
The Great Sorceress is looking for you!
Huh?
OH, THAT'S JUST MY NANNY.
MOTHER WANTS ME?
INFORM HER I'LL BE IN AS SOON AS POSSIBLE.

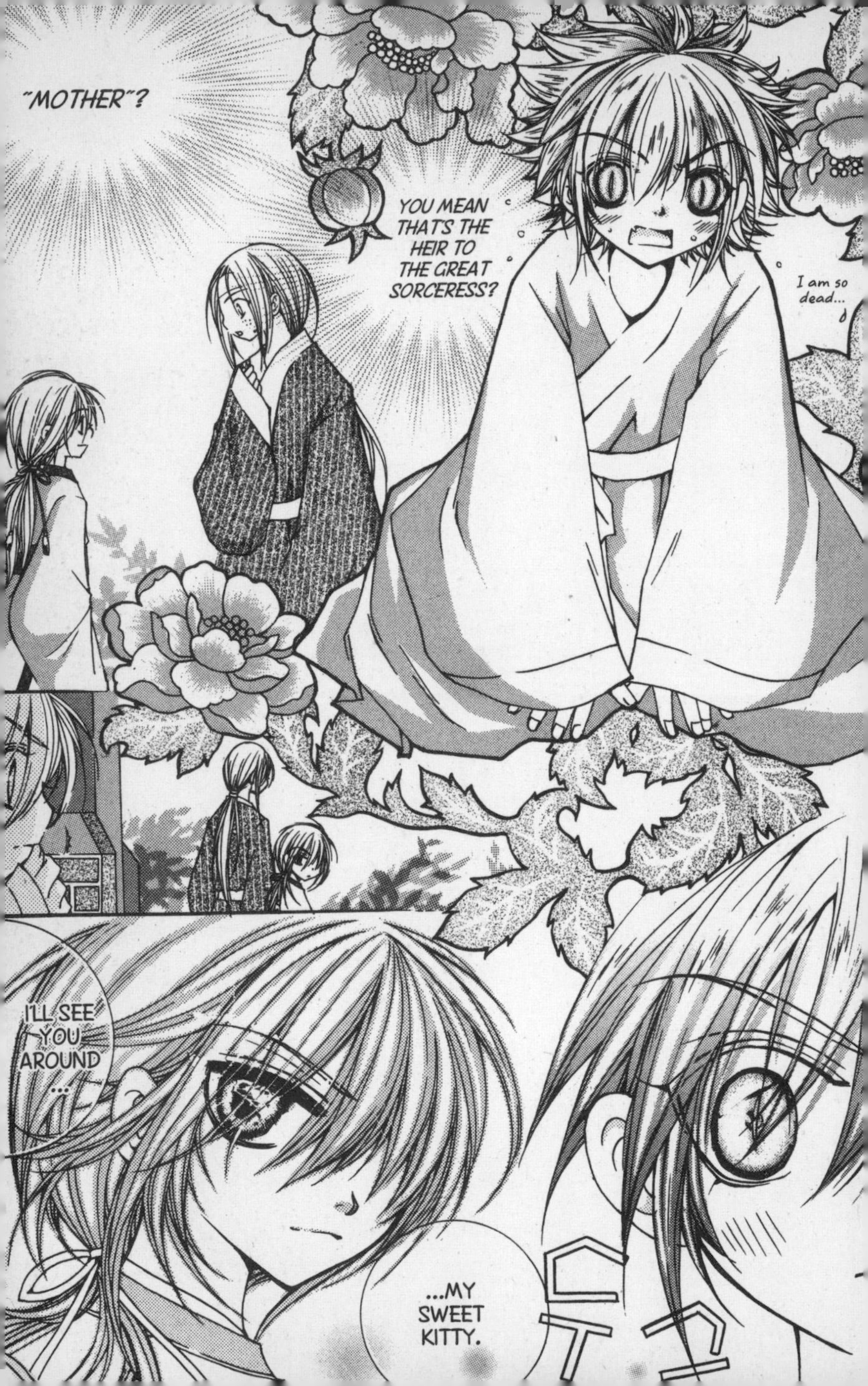
"MOTHER"?
YOU MEAN THAT'S THE HEIR TO THE GREAT SORCERESS?
I am so dead...
I'LL SEE YOU AROUND...
...MY SWEET KITTY.

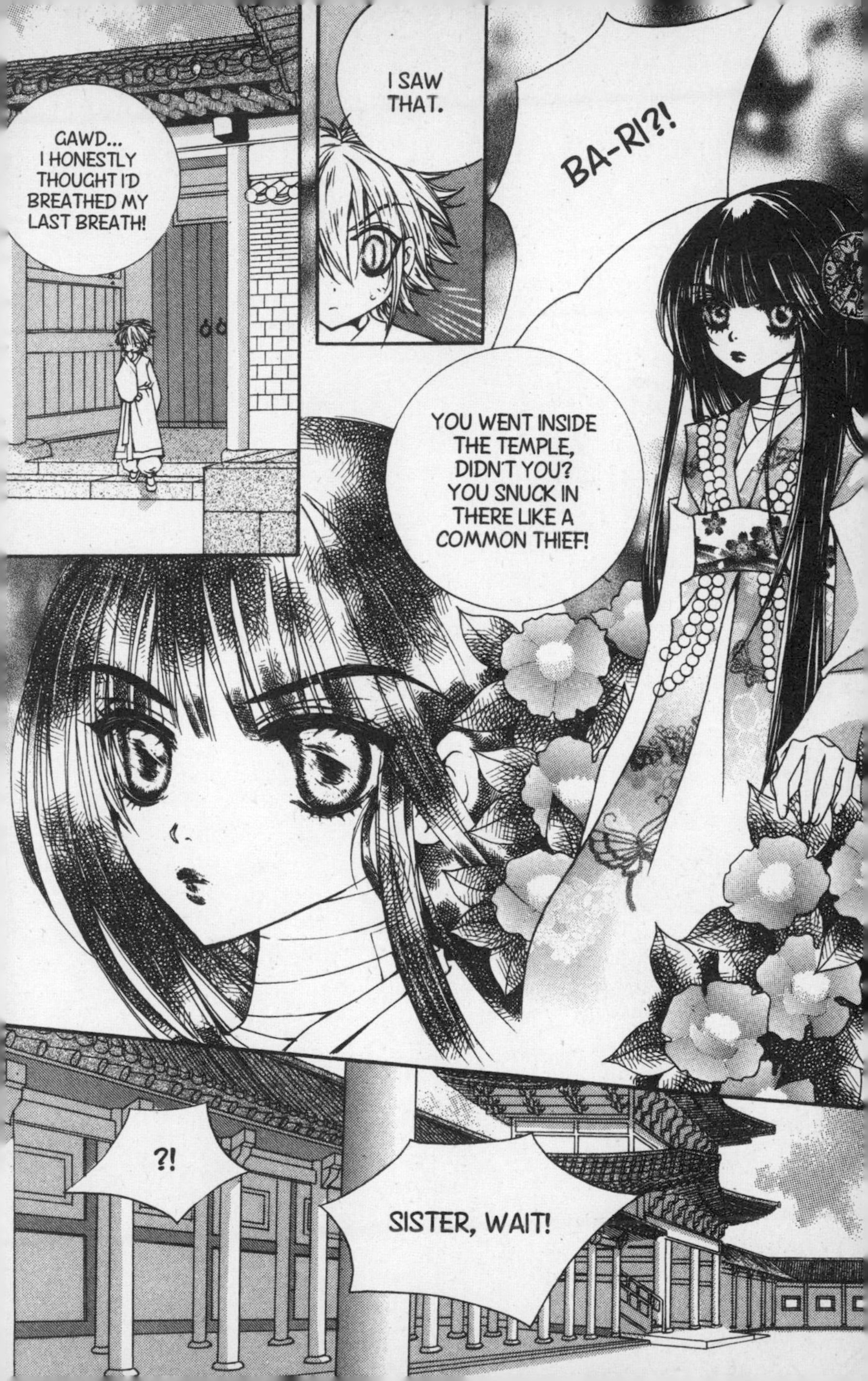
GAWD... I HONESTLY THOUGHT I'D BREATHED MY LAST BREATH!
I SAW THAT.
BA-RI?!
YOU WENT INSIDE THE TEMPLE, DIDN'T YOU? YOU SNUCK IN THERE LIKE A COMMON THIEF!
?!
SISTER, WAIT!

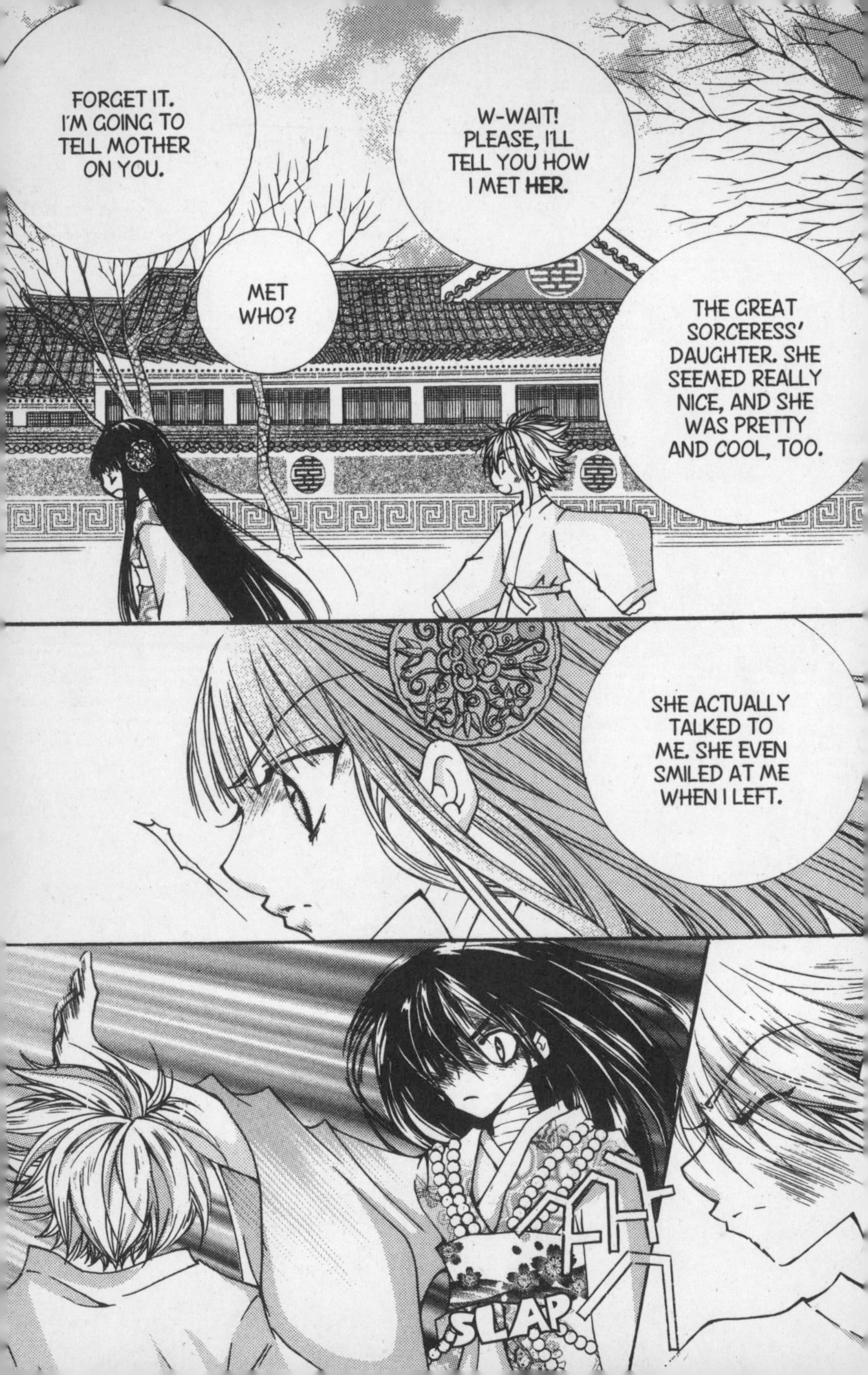

FORGET IT. I'M GOING TO TELL MOTHER ON YOU.
W-WAIT! PLEASE, I'LL TELL YOU HOW I MET HER.
MET WHO?
THE GREAT SORCERESS' DAUGHTER. SHE SEEMED REALLY NICE, AND SHE WAS PRETTY AND COOL, TOO.
SHE ACTUALLY TALKED TO ME. SHE EVEN SMILED AT ME WHEN I LEFT.
SLAP

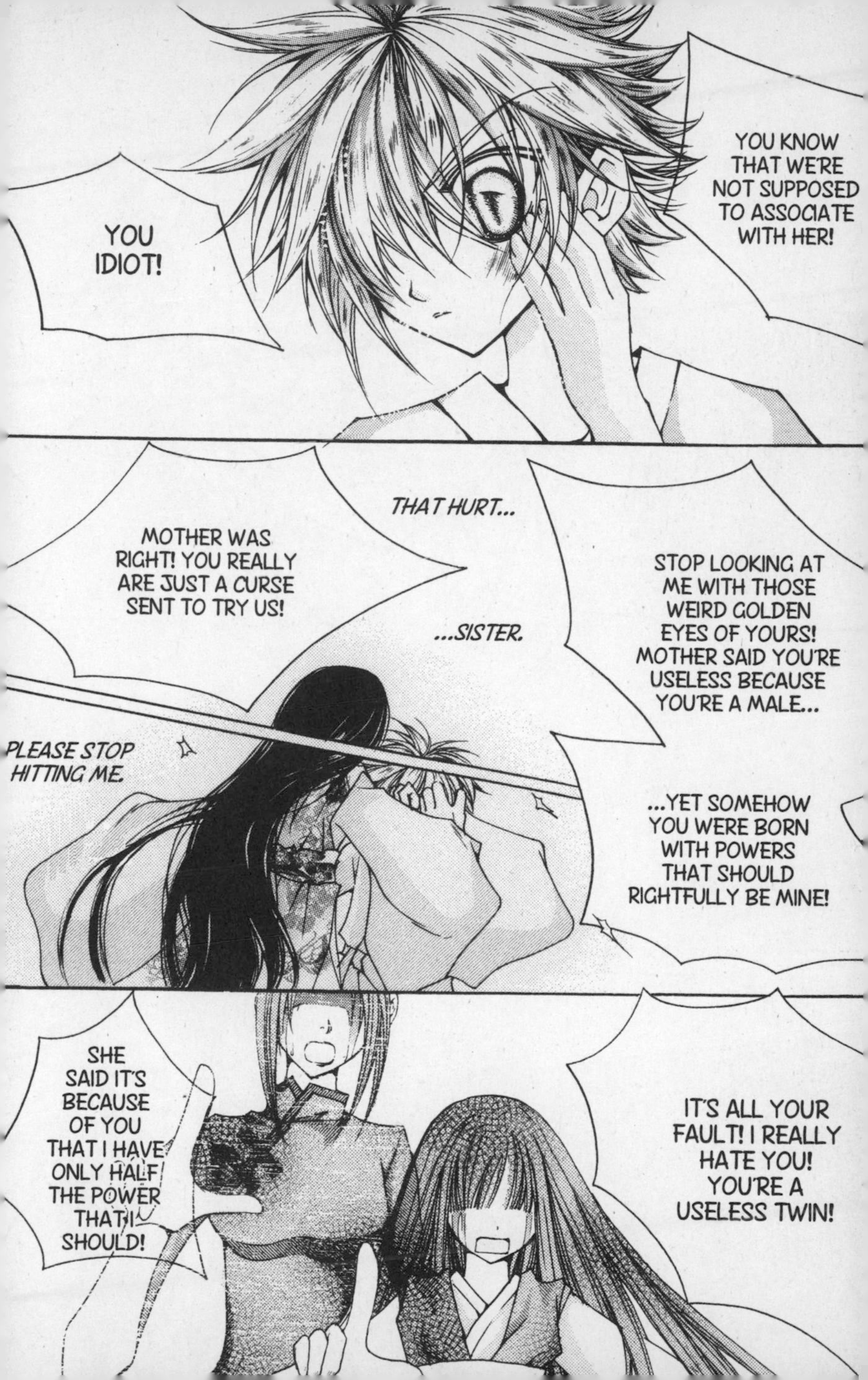
YOU IDIOT!
YOU KNOW THAT WE'RE NOT SUPPOSED TO ASSOCIATE WITH HER!
MOTHER WAS RIGHT! YOU REALLY ARE JUST A CURSE SENT TO TRY US!
THAT HURT...
...SISTER.
PLEASE STOP HITTING ME.
STOP LOOKING AT ME WITH THOSE WEIRD GOLDEN EYES OF YOURS! MOTHER SAID YOU'RE USELESS BECAUSE YOU'RE A MALE...
...YET SOMEHOW YOU WERE BORN WITH POWERS THAT SHOULD RIGHTFULLY BE MINE!
SHE SAID IT'S BECAUSE OF YOU THAT I HAVE ONLY HALF THE POWER THAT I SHOULD!
IT'S ALL YOUR FAULT! I REALLY HATE YOU! YOU'RE A USELESS TWIN!

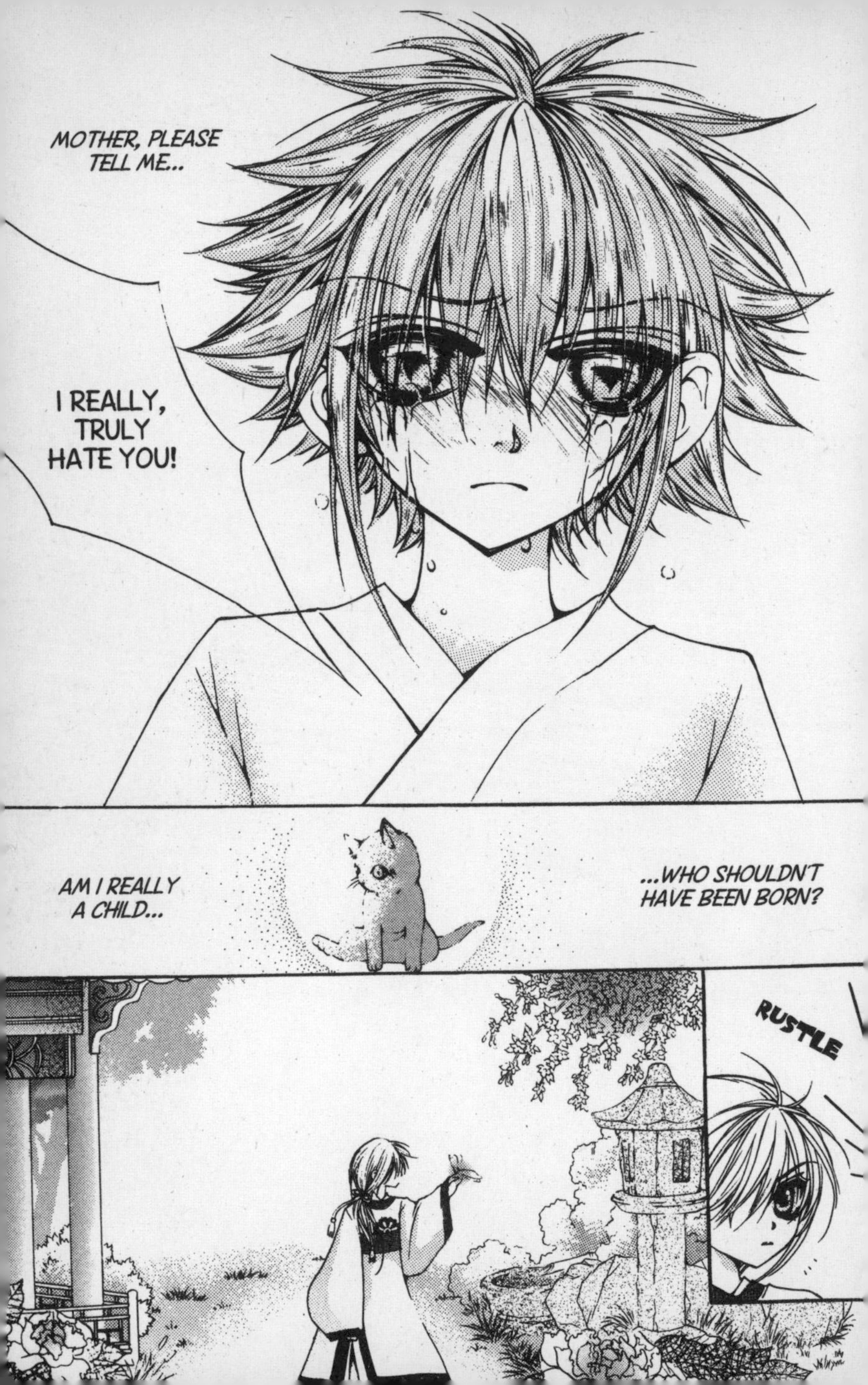
MOTHER, PLEASE TELL ME...
I REALLY, TRULY HATE YOU!
AM I REALLY A CHILD...
...WHO SHOULDN'T HAVE BEEN BORN?
RUSTLE

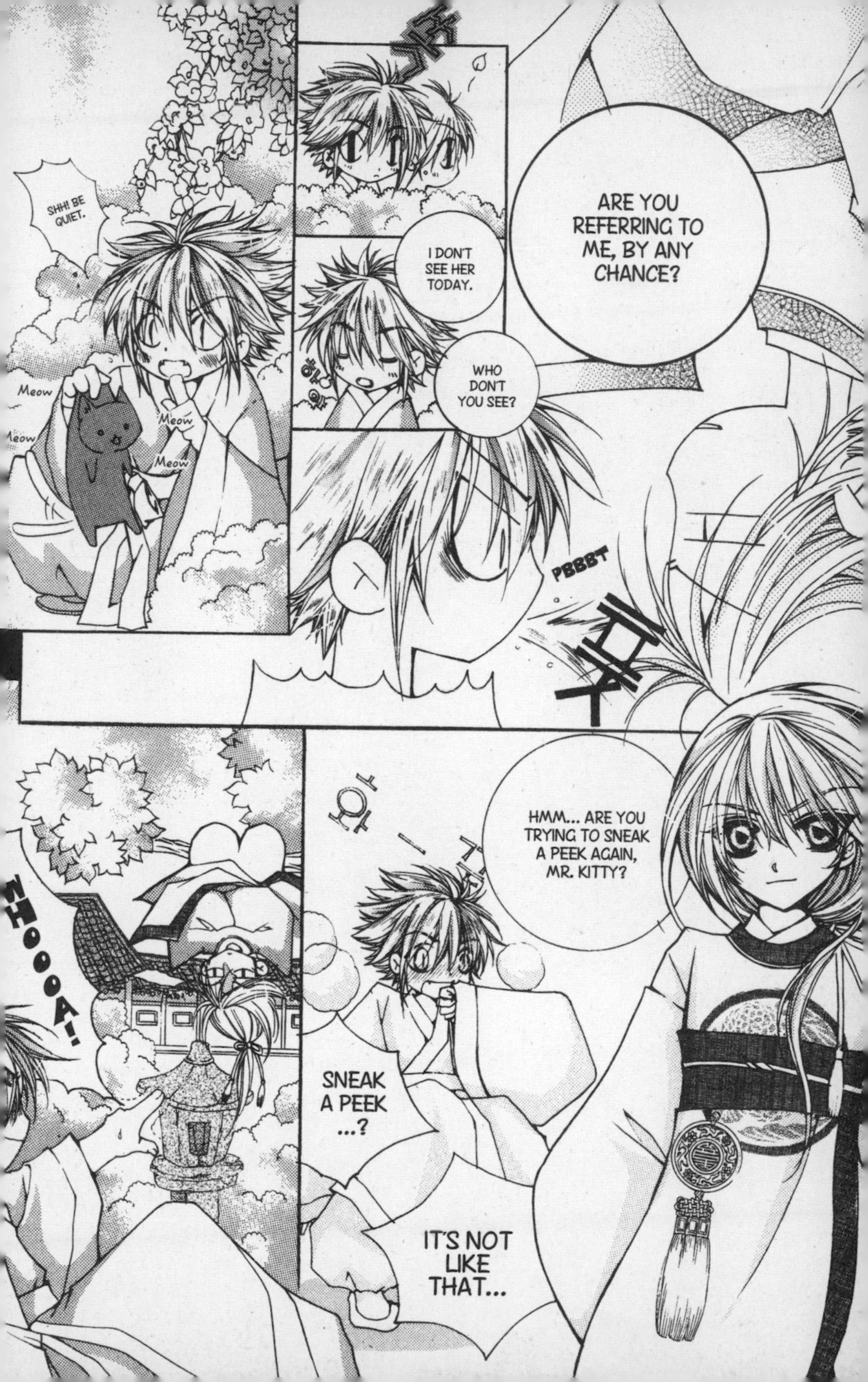

SHH! BE QUIET.
Meow
Meow
Meow
Meow
I DON'T SEE HER TODAY.
WHO DON'T YOU SEE?
ARE YOU REFERRING TO ME, BY ANY CHANCE?
PBBBT
WHOOOA!
HMM... ARE YOU TRYING TO SNEAK A PEEK AGAIN, MR. KITTY?
SNEAK A PEEK ...?
IT'S NOT LIKE THAT...

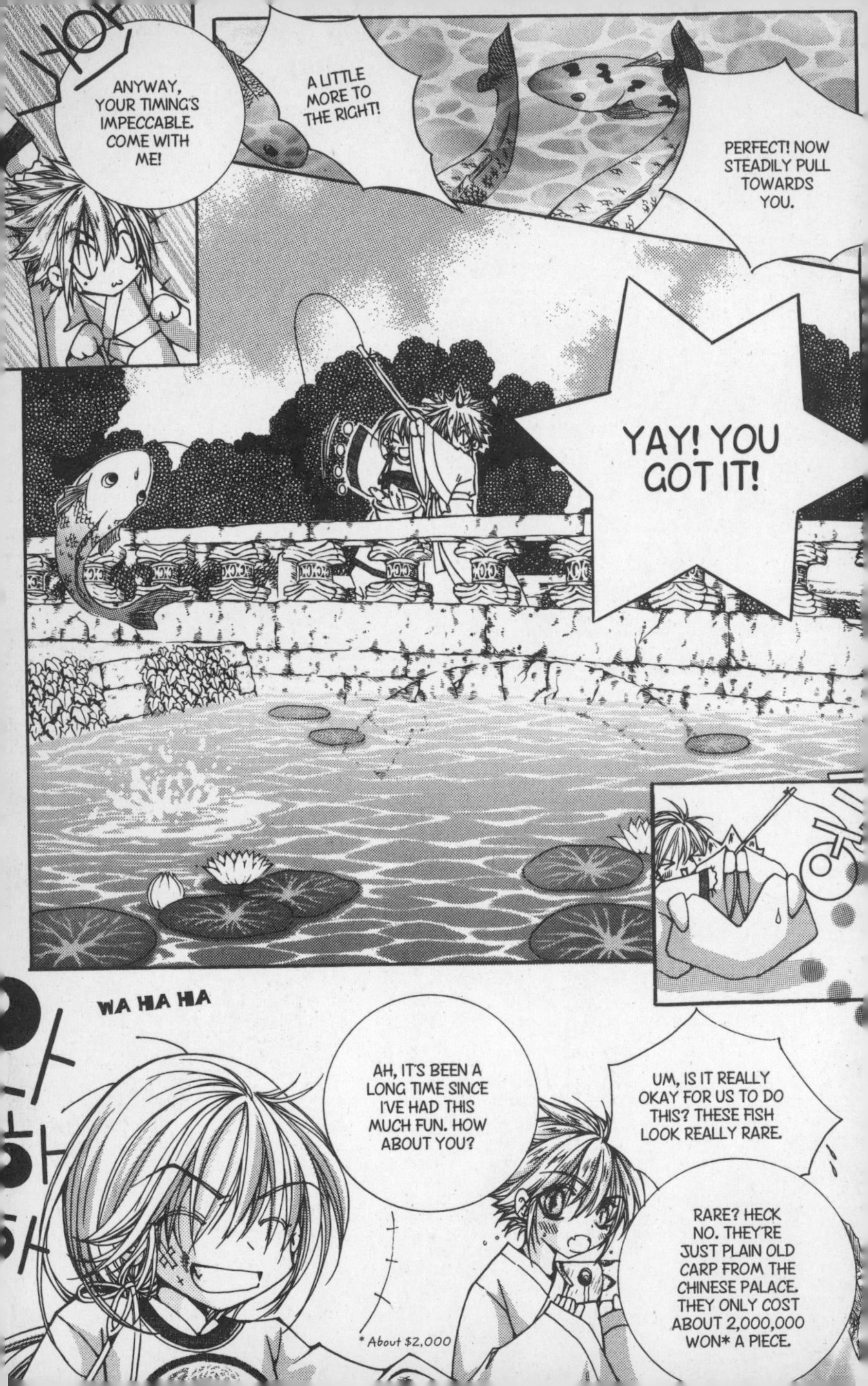
ANYWAY, YOUR TIMING'S IMPECCABLE. COME WITH ME!
A LITTLE MORE TO THE RIGHT!
PERFECT! NOW STEADILY PULL TOWARDS YOU.
YAY! YOU GOT IT!
WA HA HA
AH, IT'S BEEN A LONG TIME SINCE I'VE HAD THIS MUCH FUN. HOW ABOUT YOU?
UM, IS IT REALLY OKAY FOR US TO DO THIS? THESE FISH LOOK REALLY RARE.
RARE? HECK NO. THEY'RE JUST PLAIN OLD CARP FROM THE CHINESE PALACE. THEY ONLY COST ABOUT 2,000,000 WON* A PIECE.
* About $2,000

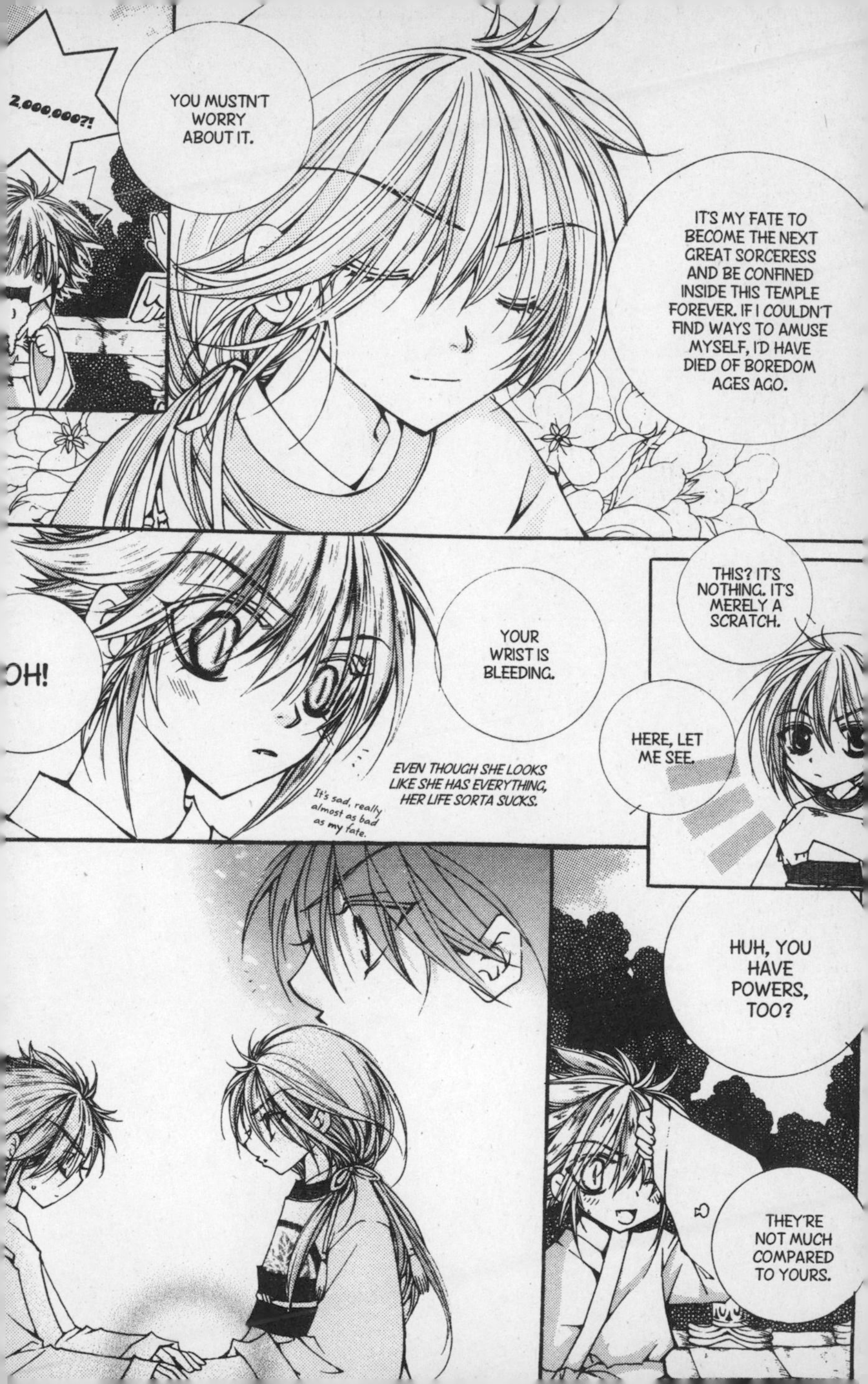
2,000,000?!
YOU MUSTN'T WORRY ABOUT IT.
IT'S MY FATE TO BECOME THE NEXT GREAT SORCERESS AND BE CONFINED INSIDE THIS TEMPLE FOREVER. IF I COULDN'T FIND WAYS TO AMUSE MYSELF, I'D HAVE DIED OF BOREDOM AGES AGO.
OH!
YOUR WRIST IS BLEEDING.
EVEN THOUGH SHE LOOKS LIKE SHE HAS EVERYTHING, HER LIFE SORTA SUCKS.
It's sad, really almost as bad as my fate.
THIS? IT'S NOTHING. IT'S MERELY A SCRATCH.
HERE, LET ME SEE.
HUH, YOU HAVE POWERS, TOO?
THEY'RE NOT MUCH COMPARED TO YOURS.

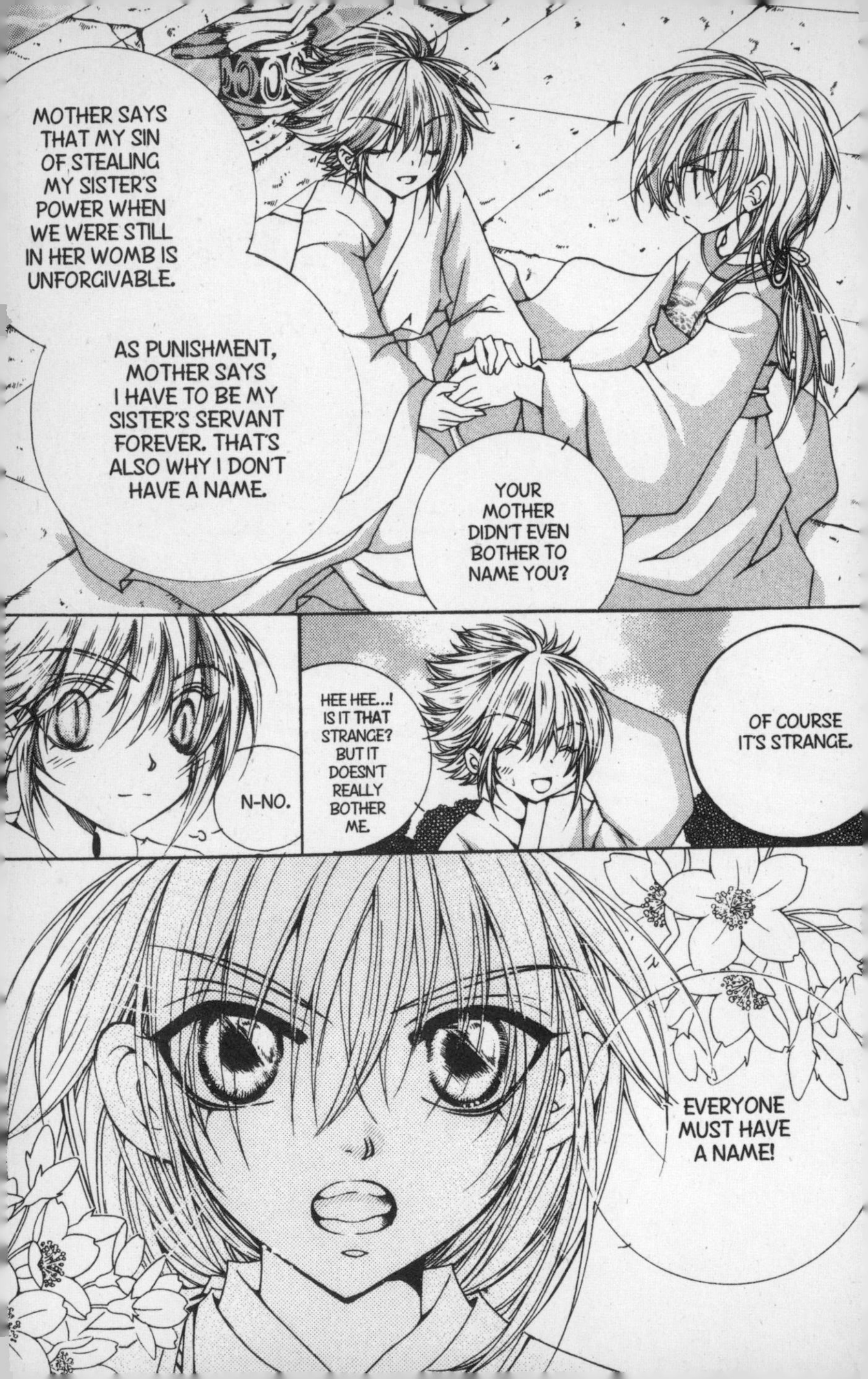
MOTHER SAYS THAT MY SIN OF STEALING MY SISTER'S POWER WHEN WE WERE STILL IN HER WOMB IS UNFORGIVABLE.
AS PUNISHMENT, MOTHER SAYS I HAVE TO BE MY SISTER'S SERVANT FOREVER. THAT'S ALSO WHY I DON'T HAVE A NAME.
YOUR MOTHER DIDN'T EVEN BOTHER TO NAME YOU?
N-NO.
HEE HEE...! IS IT THAT STRANGE? BUT IT DOESN'T REALLY BOTHER ME.
OF COURSE IT'S STRANGE.
EVERYONE MUST HAVE A NAME!

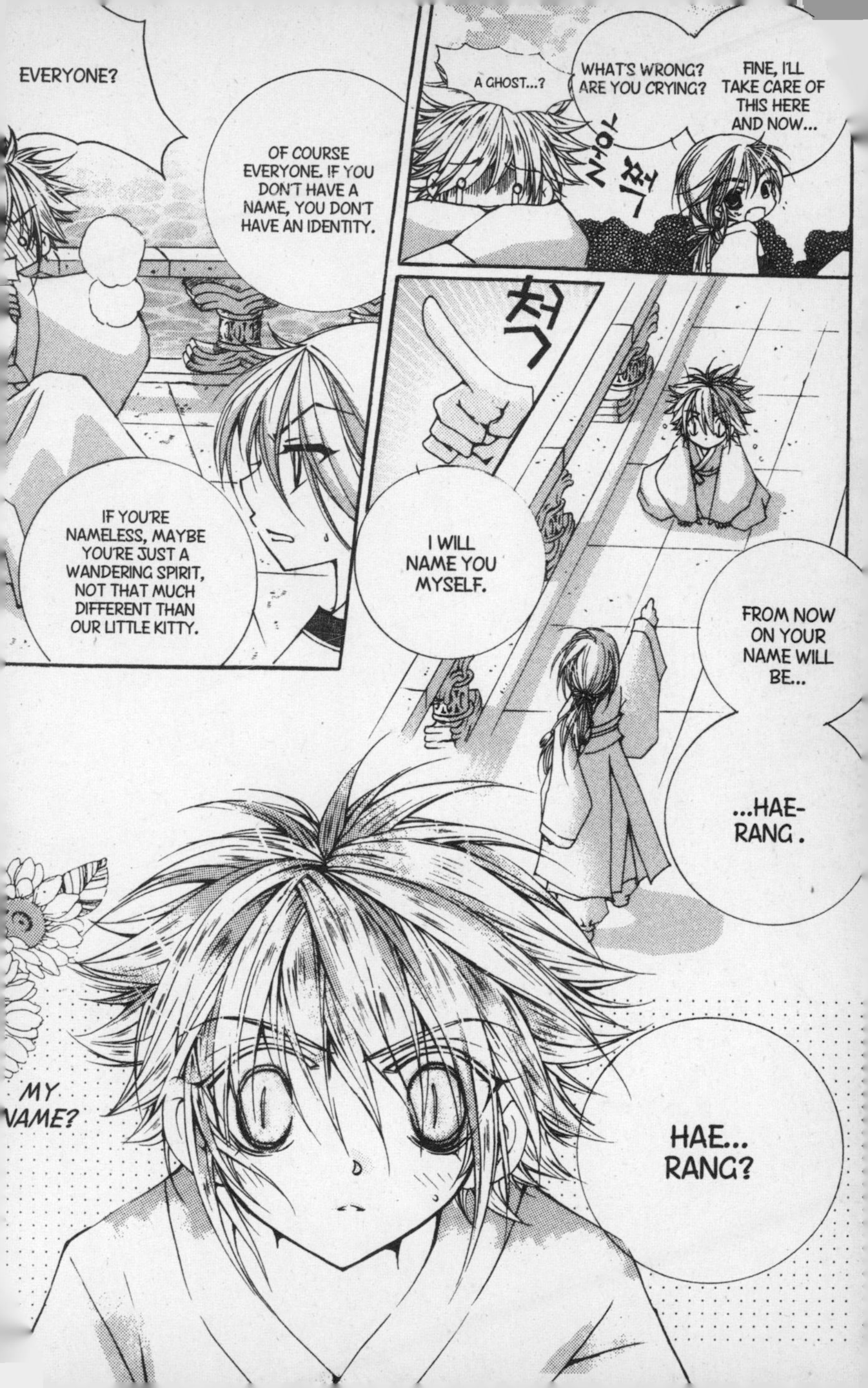
EVERYONE?
OF COURSE EVERYONE. IF YOU DON'T HAVE A NAME, YOU DON'T HAVE AN IDENTITY.
IF YOU'RE NAMELESS, MAYBE YOU'RE JUST A WANDERING SPIRIT, NOT THAT MUCH DIFFERENT THAN OUR LITTLE KITTY.
A GHOST...?
WHAT'S WRONG? ARE YOU CRYING?
FINE, I'LL TAKE CARE OF THIS HERE AND NOW...
척
I WILL NAME YOU MYSELF.
FROM NOW ON YOUR NAME WILL BE...
...HAE-RANG.
MY NAME?
HAE... RANG?

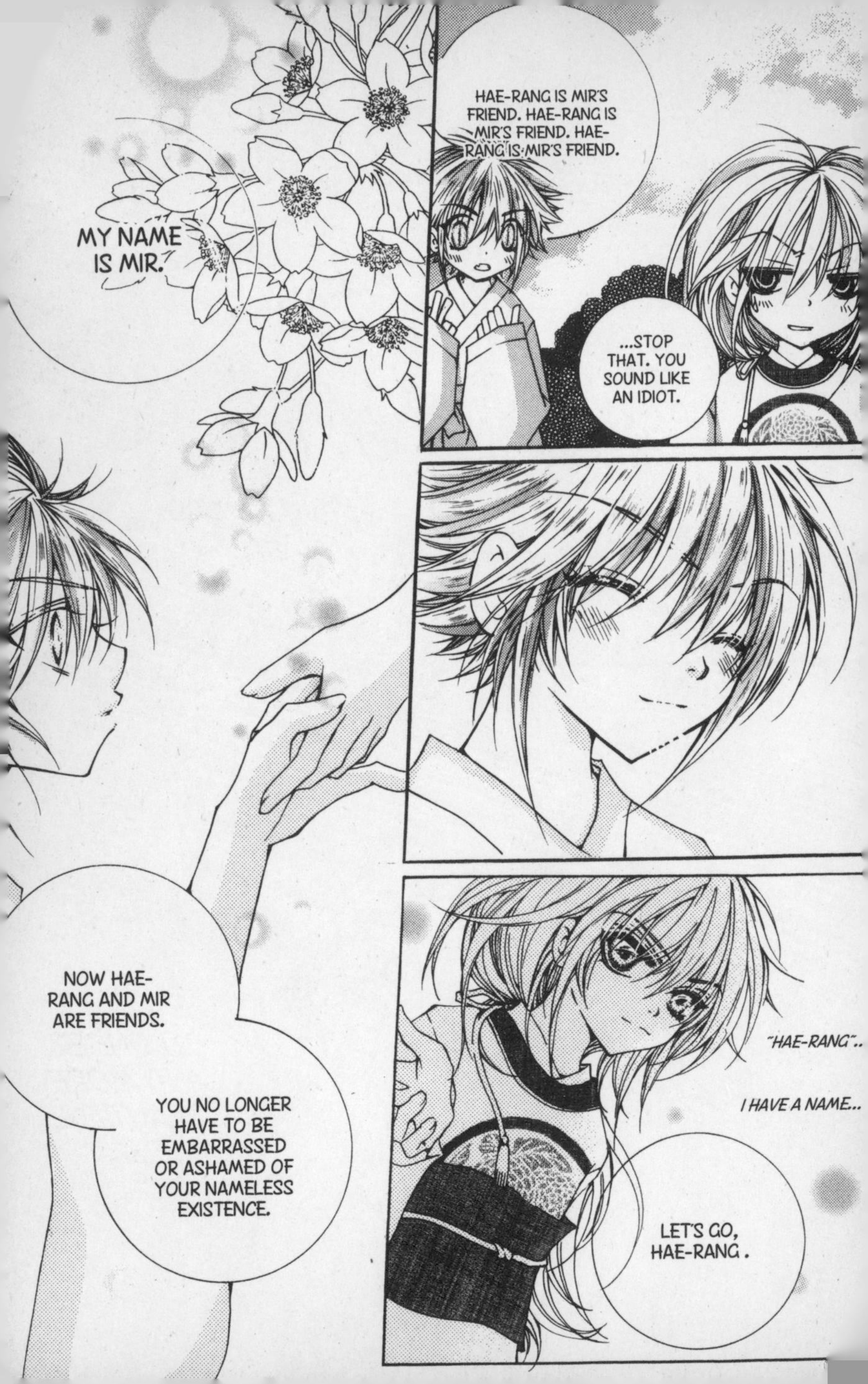
MY NAME IS MIR.
NOW HAE-RANG AND MIR ARE FRIENDS.
YOU NO LONGER HAVE TO BE EMBARRASSED OR ASHAMED OF YOUR NAMELESS EXISTENCE.
HAE-RANG IS MIR'S FRIEND. HAE-RANG IS MIR'S FRIEND. HAE-RANG IS MIR'S FRIEND.
...STOP THAT. YOU SOUND LIKE AN IDIOT.
"HAE-RANG"..
I HAVE A NAME..
LET'S GO, HAE-RANG.

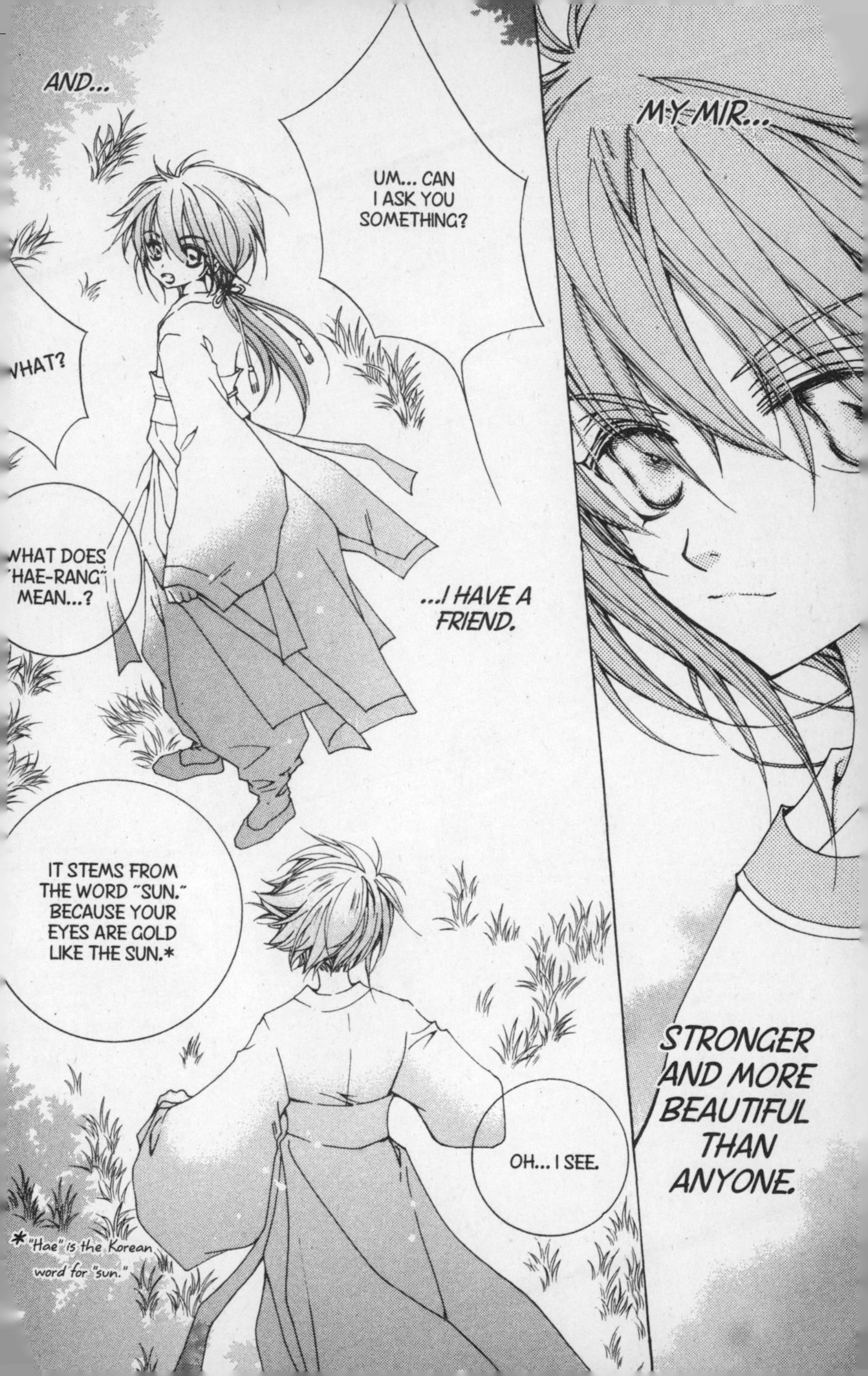
AND...
UM... CAN I ASK YOU SOMETHING?
WHAT?
WHAT DOES "HAE-RANG" MEAN...?
...I HAVE A FRIEND.
IT STEMS FROM THE WORD "SUN." BECAUSE YOUR EYES ARE GOLD LIKE THE SUN.*
OH... I SEE.
M-Y MIR...
STRONGER AND MORE BEAUTIFUL THAN ANYONE.

* "Hae" is the Korean word for "sun."

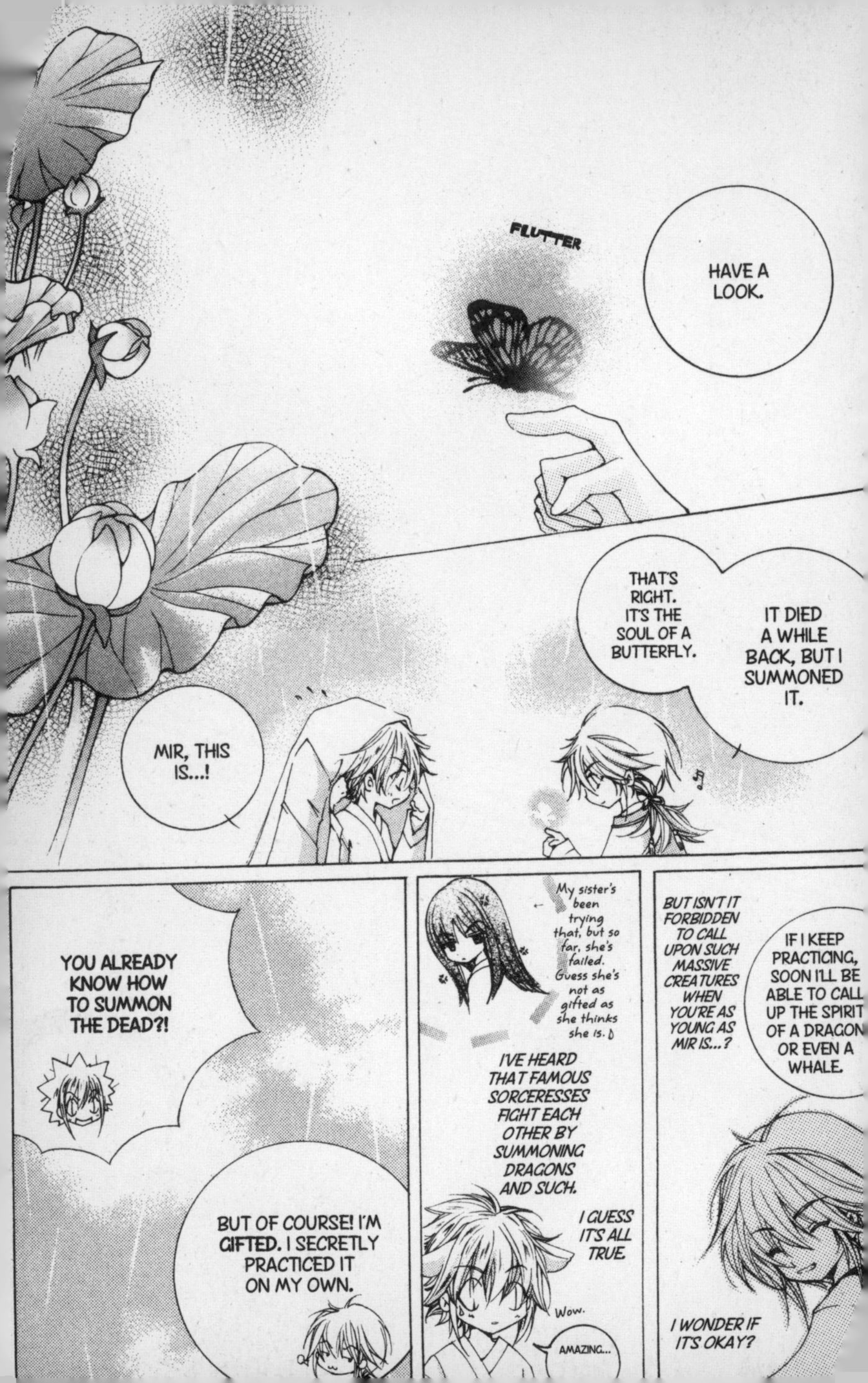
FLUTTER
HAVE A LOOK.
MIR, THIS IS...!
THAT'S RIGHT. IT'S THE SOUL OF A BUTTERFLY.
IT DIED A WHILE BACK, BUT I SUMMONED IT.
YOU ALREADY KNOW HOW TO SUMMON THE DEAD?!
BUT OF COURSE! I'M GIFTED. I SECRETLY PRACTICED IT ON MY OWN.
My sister's been trying that, but so far, she's failed. Guess she's not as gifted as she thinks she is.
I'VE HEARD THAT FAMOUS SORCERESSES FIGHT EACH OTHER BY SUMMONING DRAGONS AND SUCH.
I GUESS IT'S ALL TRUE.
Wow.
AMAZING...
BUT ISN'T IT FORBIDDEN TO CALL UPON SUCH MASSIVE CREATURES WHEN YOU'RE AS YOUNG AS MIR IS...?
IF I KEEP PRACTICING, SOON I'LL BE ABLE TO CALL UP THE SPIRIT OF A DRAGON OR EVEN A WHALE.
I WONDER IF IT'S OKAY?

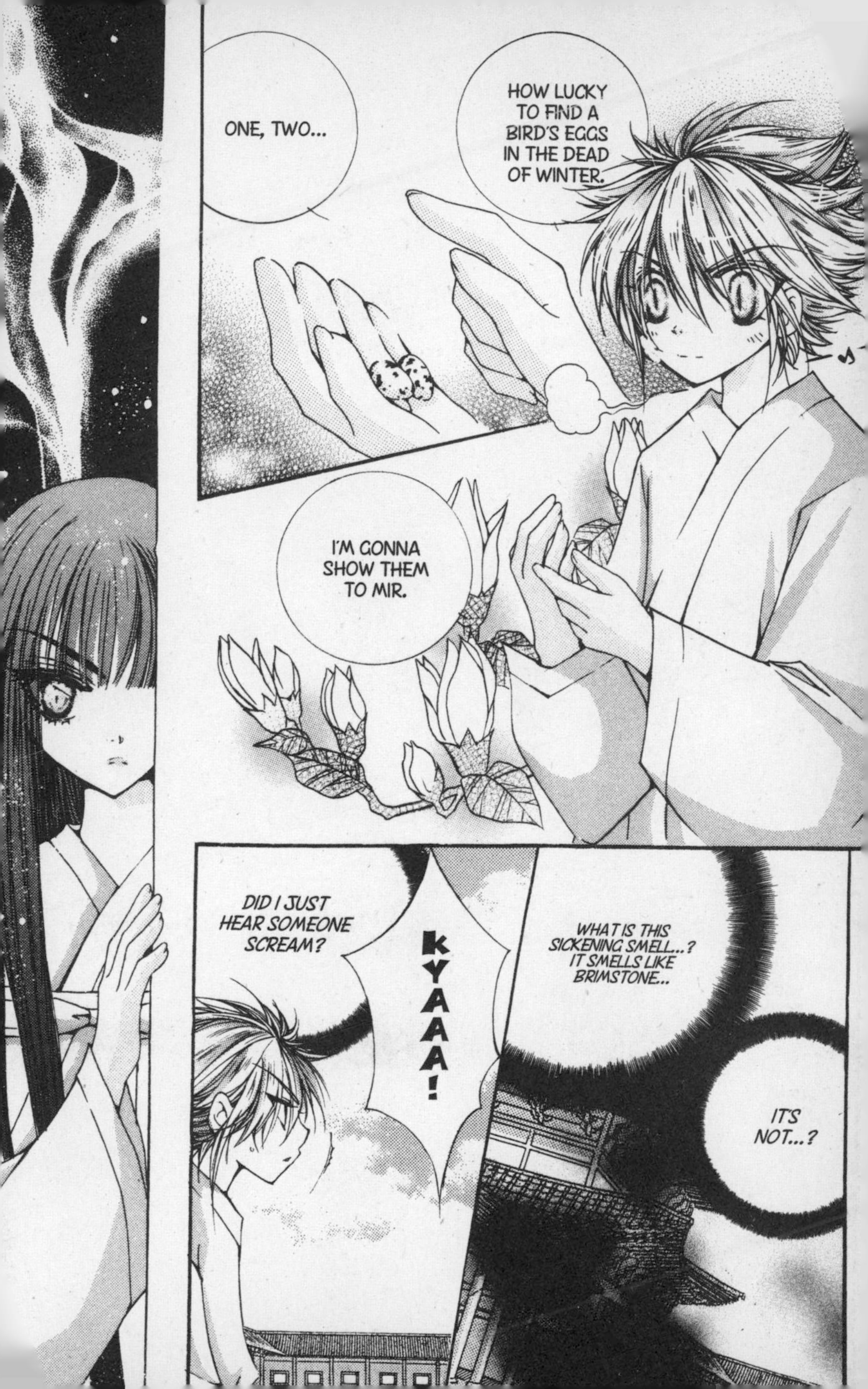
ONE, TWO...
HOW LUCKY TO FIND A BIRD'S EGGS IN THE DEAD OF WINTER.
I'M GONNA SHOW THEM TO MIR.
DID I JUST HEAR SOMEONE SCREAM?
KYAAA!
WHAT IS THIS SICKENING SMELL...? IT SMELLS LIKE BRIMSTONE...
ITS NOT...?

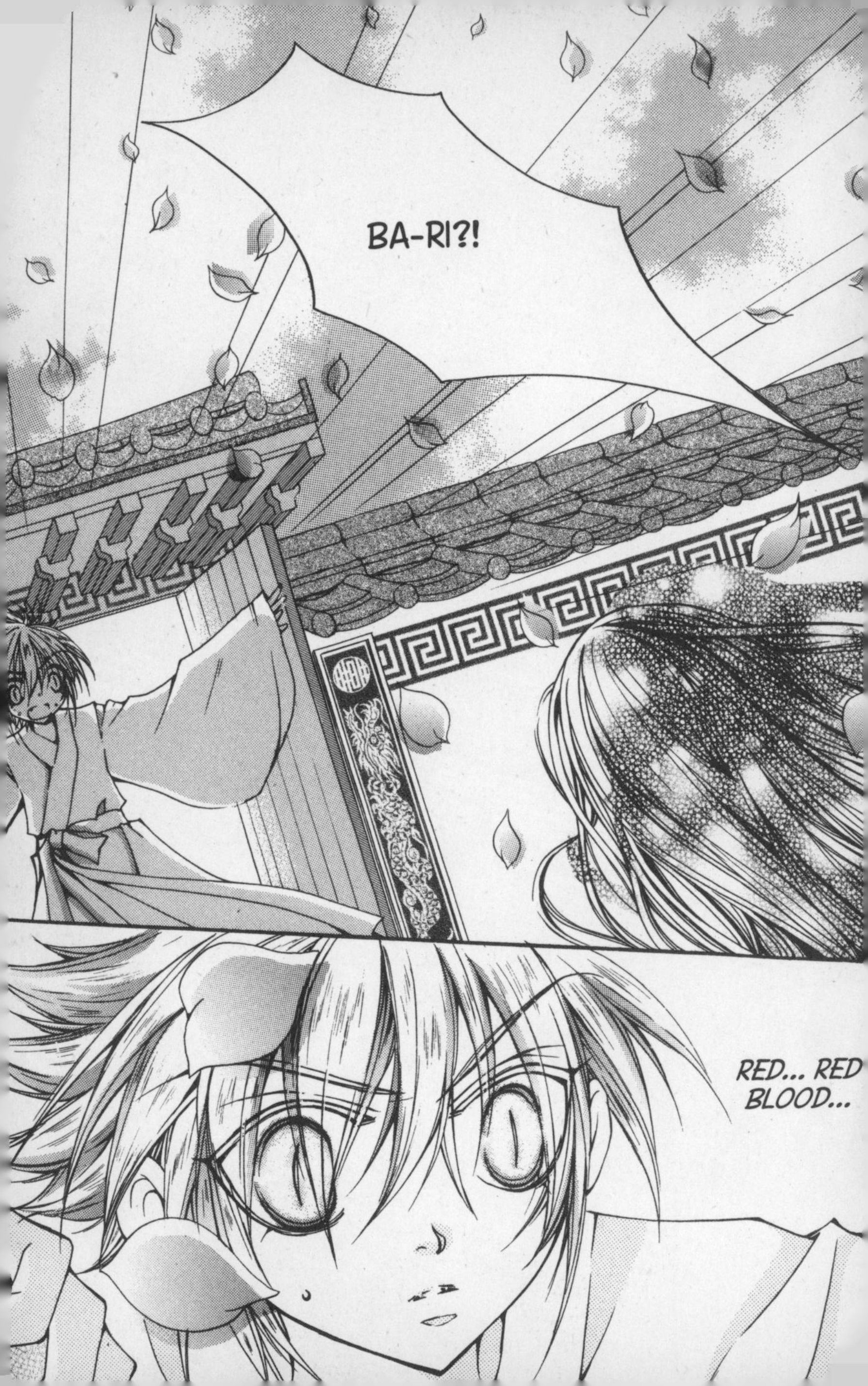
BA-RI?!
RED... RED BLOOD...

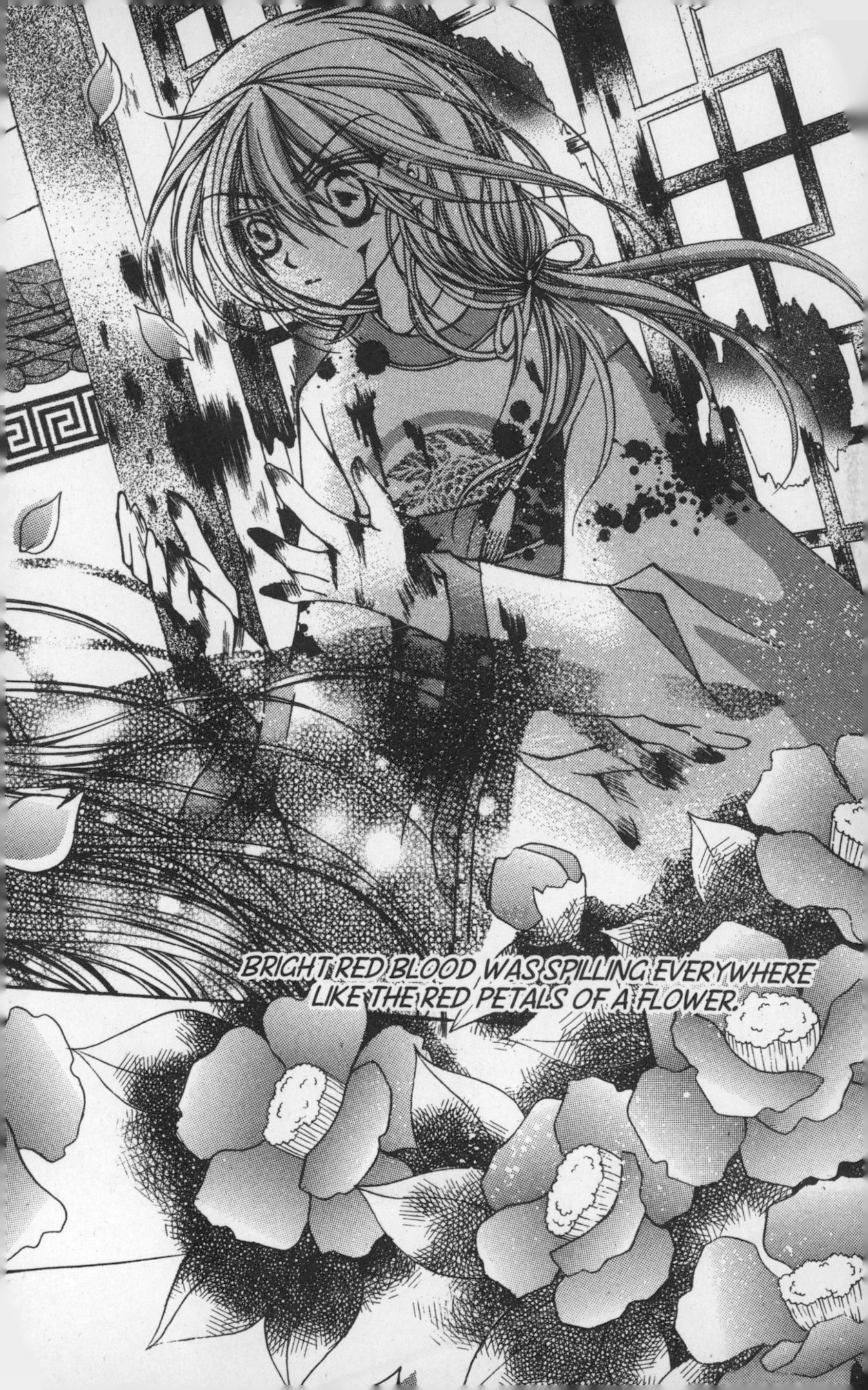
BRIGHT RED BLOOD WAS SPILLING EVERYWHERE
LIKE THE RED PETALS OF A FLOWER.

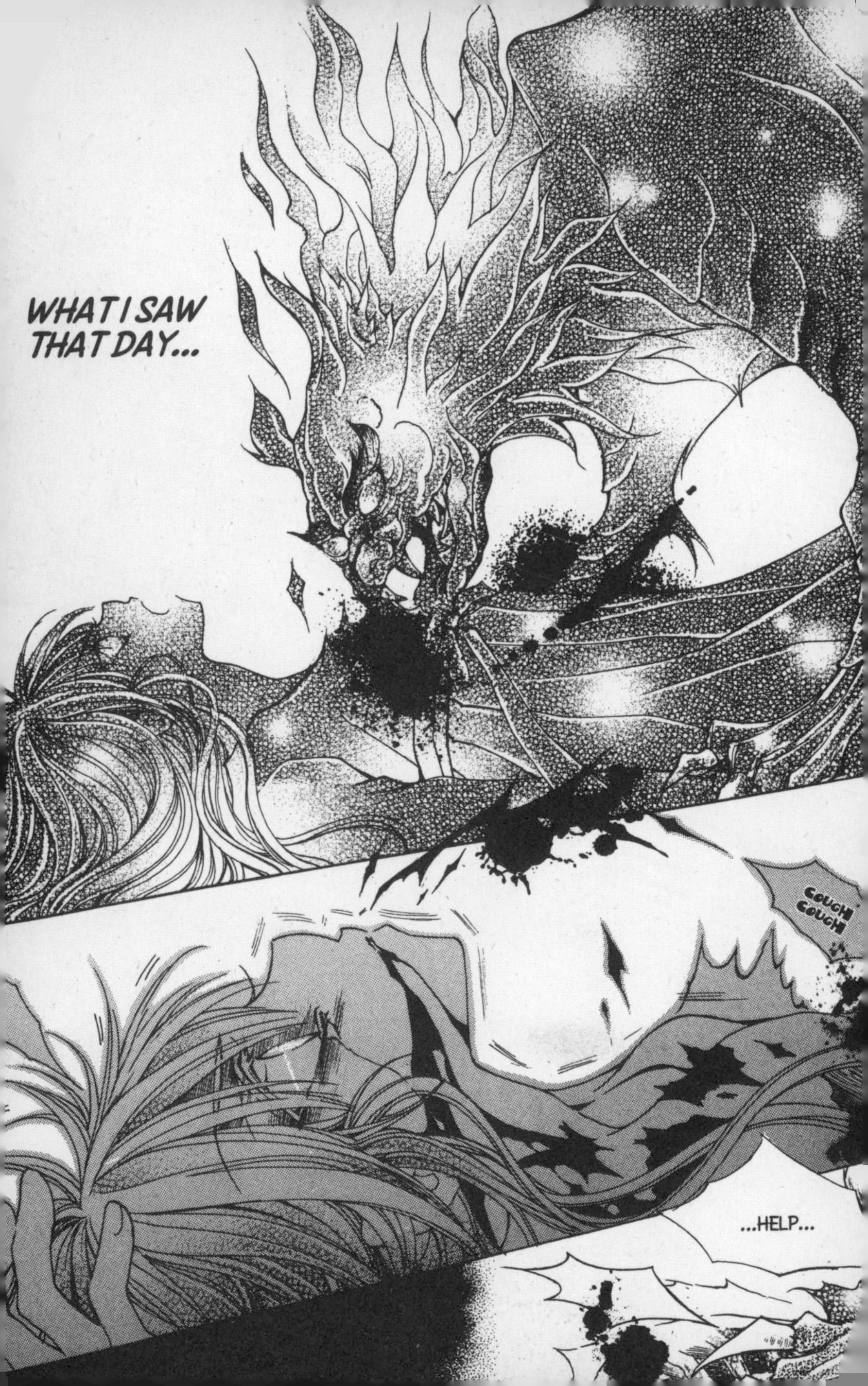
WHAT I SAW THAT DAY...
COUGH COUGH
...HELP...

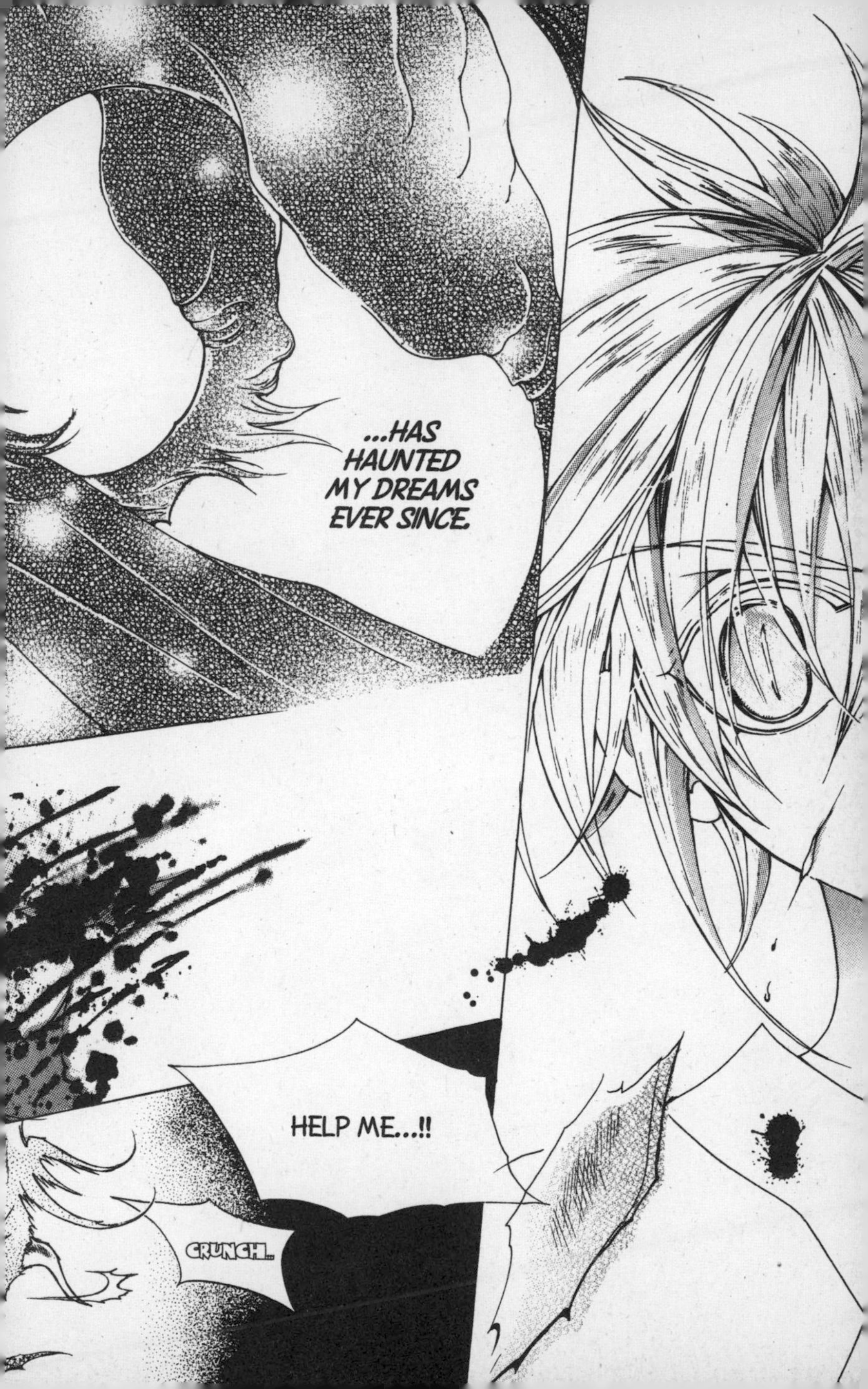
...HAS HAUNTED MY DREAMS EVER SINCE.
HELP ME...!!
CRUNCH...

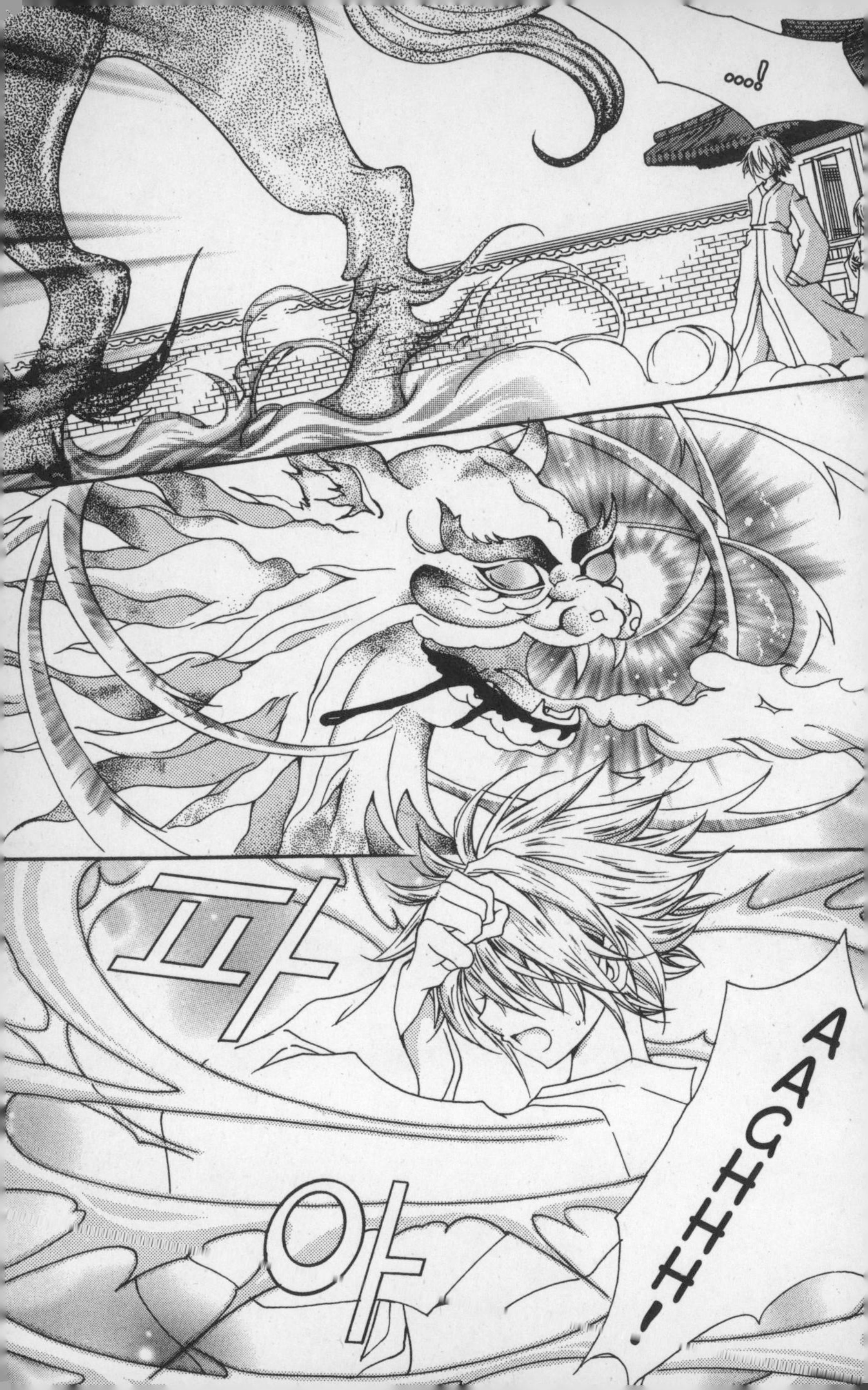
ooo!
파
야
AAGHHH!

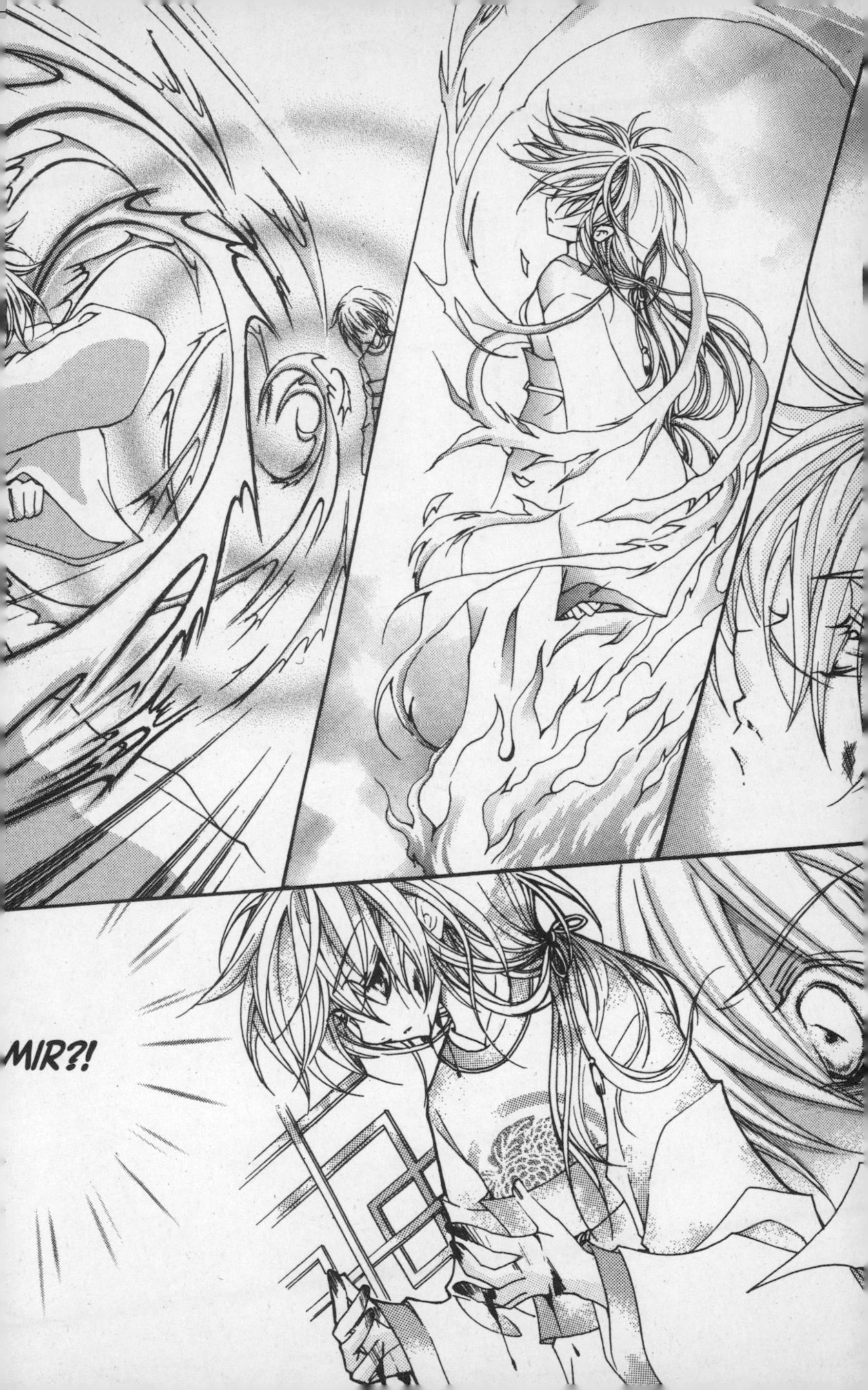
MIR?!

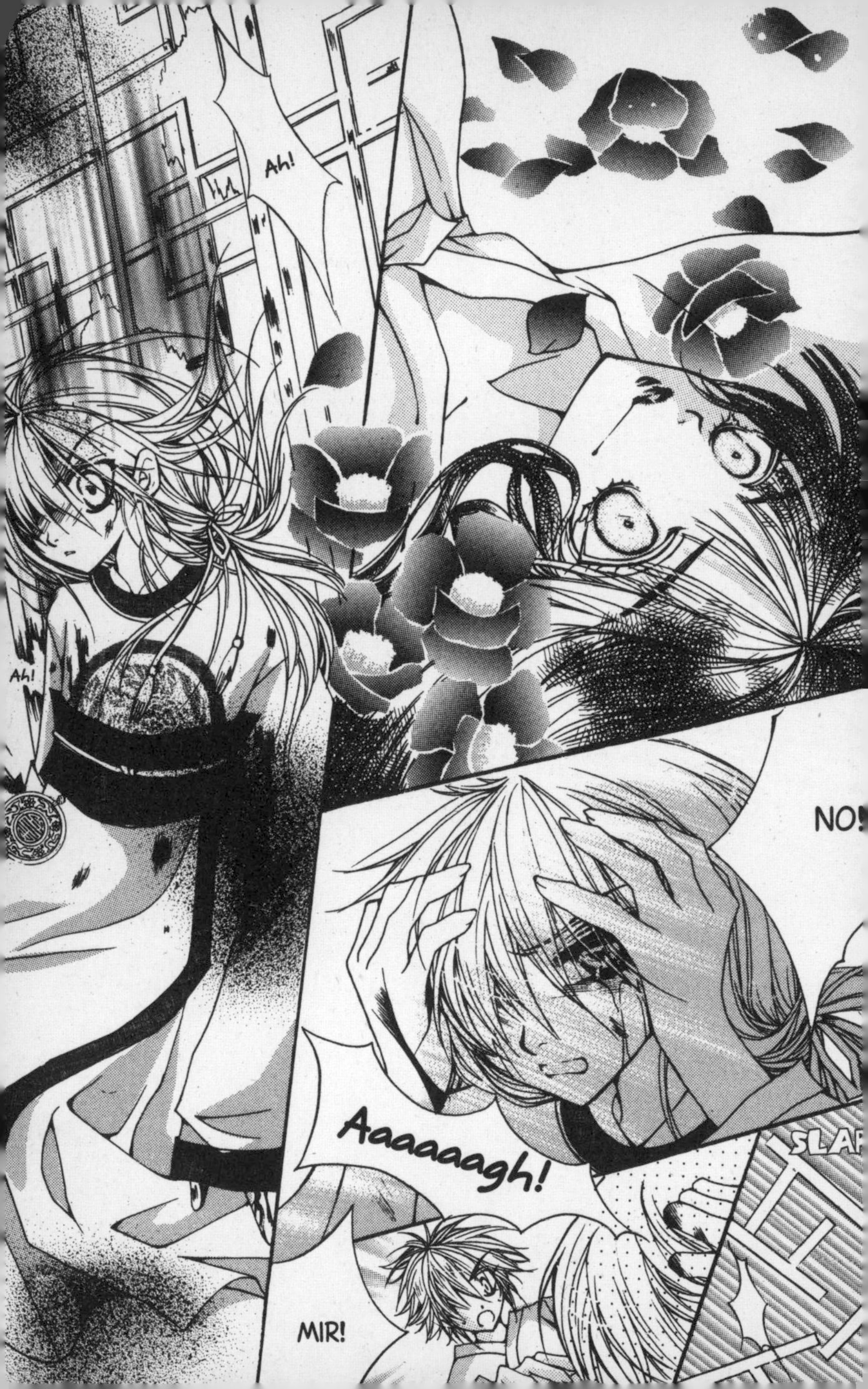

Ah!
Ah!
NO!
Aaaaaaagh!
SLAP
MIR!

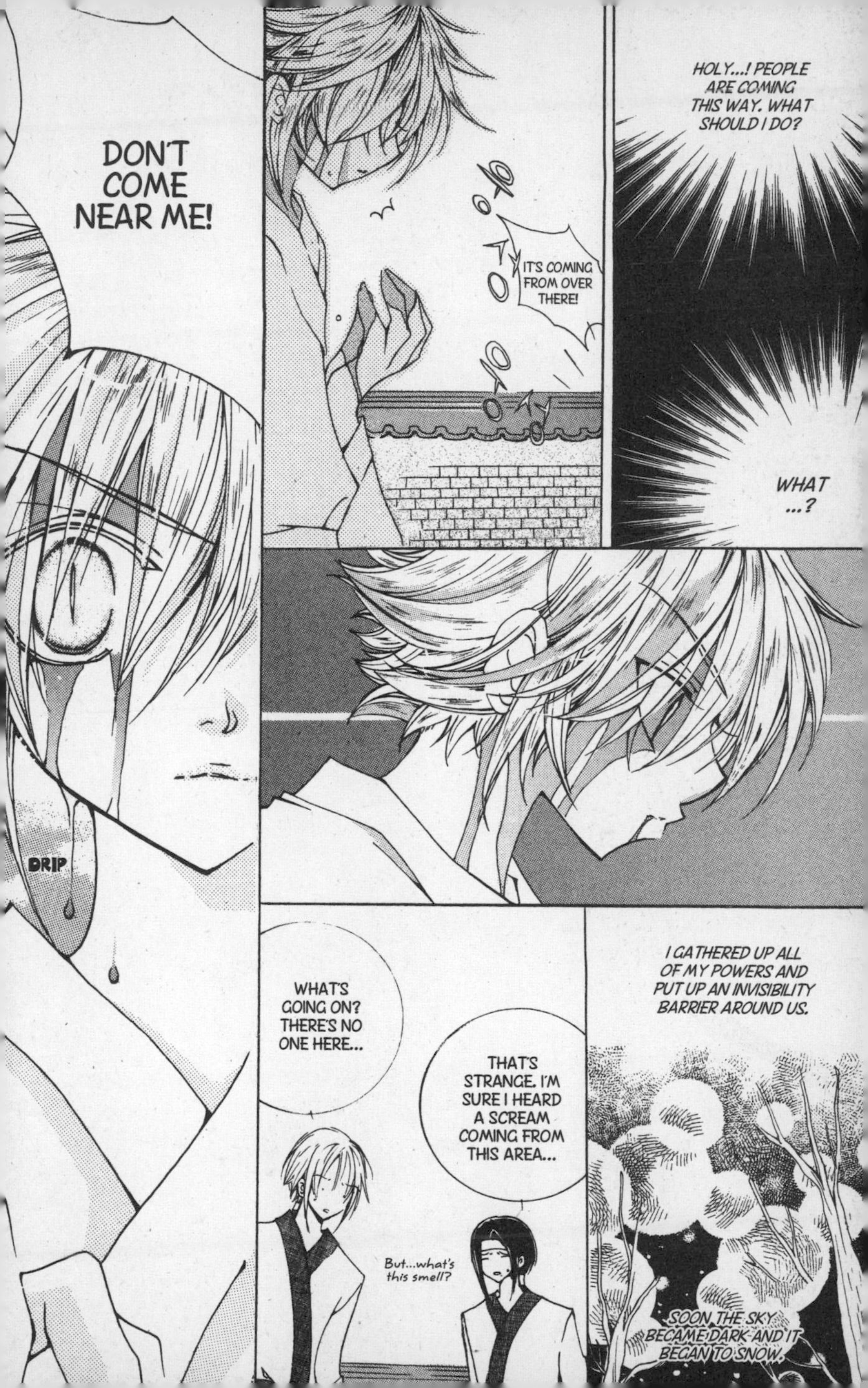
DON'T COME NEAR ME!
DRIP
IT'S COMING FROM OVER THERE!
HOLY...! PEOPLE ARE COMING THIS WAY. WHAT SHOULD I DO?
WHAT ...?
WHAT'S GOING ON? THERE'S NO ONE HERE...
THAT'S STRANGE. I'M SURE I HEARD A SCREAM COMING FROM THIS AREA...
But...what's this smell?
I GATHERED UP ALL OF MY POWERS AND PUT UP AN INVISIBILITY BARRIER AROUND US.
SOON THE SKY BECAME DARK AND IT BEGAN TO SNOW.

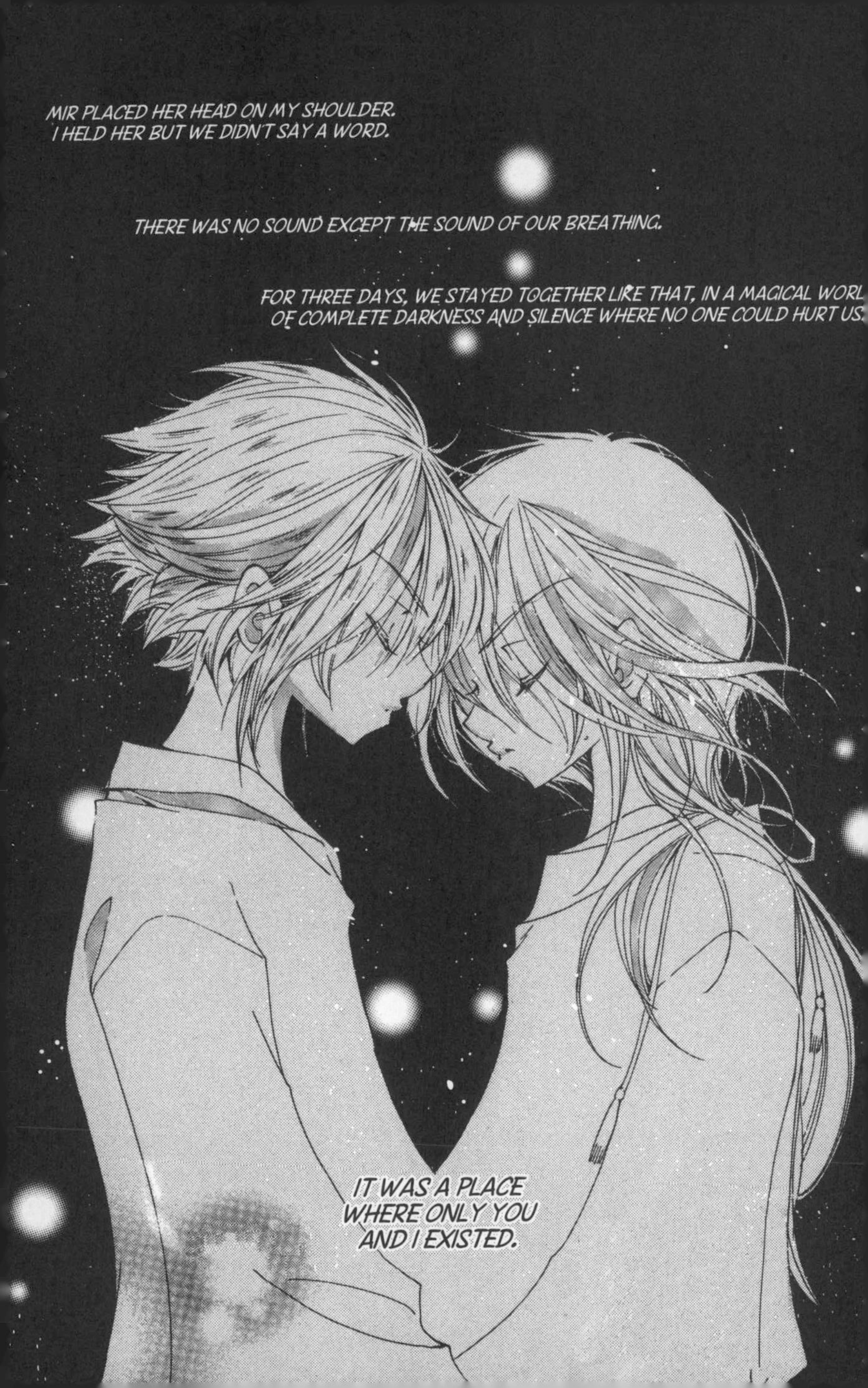
MIR PLACED HER HEAD ON MY SHOULDER. I HELD HER BUT WE DIDN'T SAY A WORD.
THERE WAS NO SOUND EXCEPT THE SOUND OF OUR BREATHING.
FOR THREE DAYS, WE STAYED TOGETHER LIKE THAT, IN A MAGICAL WORL OF COMPLETE DARKNESS AND SILENCE WHERE NO ONE COULD HURT US.
IT WAS A PLACE WHERE ONLY YOU AND I EXISTED.

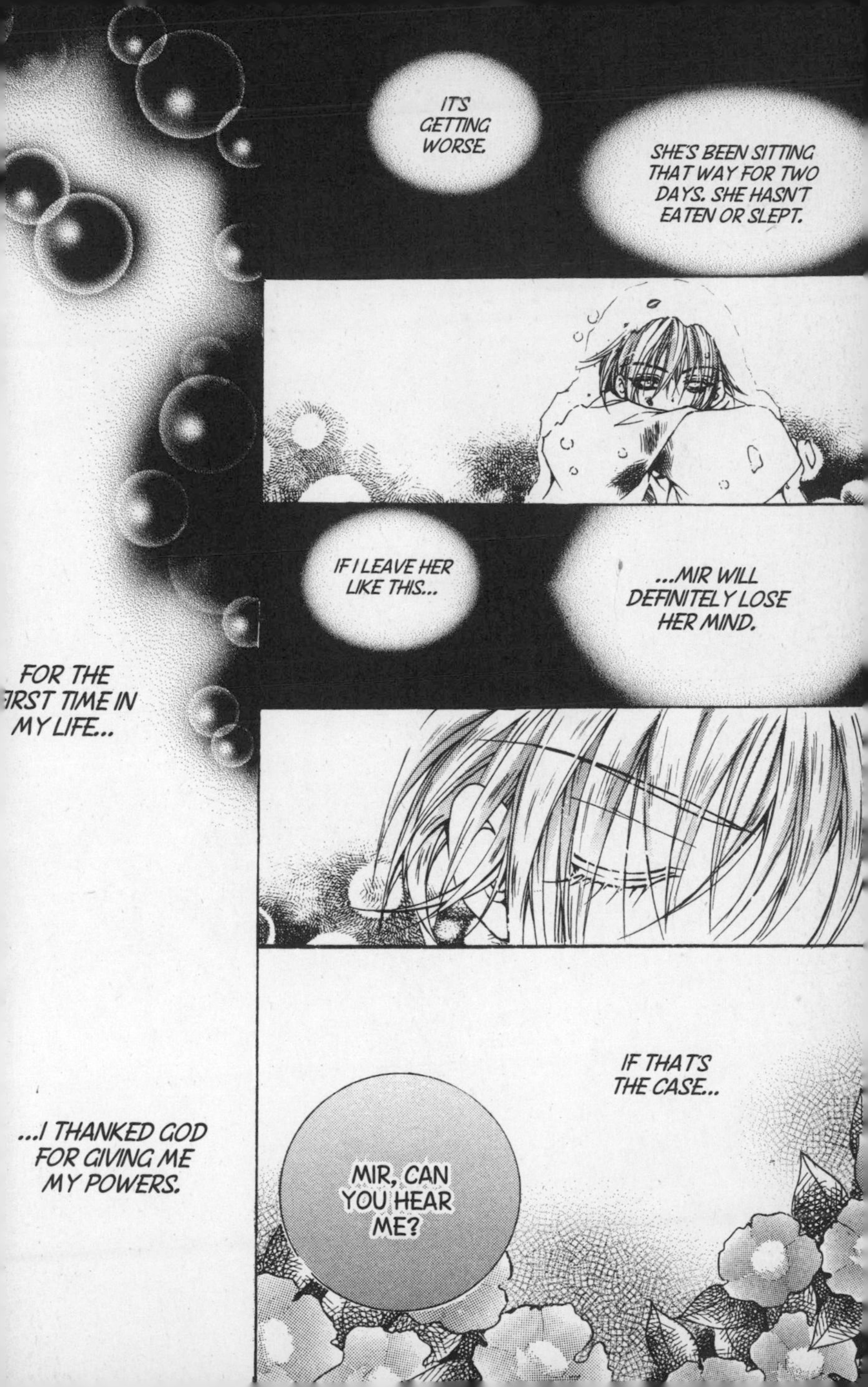

FOR THE FIRST TIME IN MY LIFE...
...I THANKED GOD FOR GIVING ME MY POWERS.
IT'S GETTING WORSE.
SHE'S BEEN SITTING THAT WAY FOR TWO DAYS. SHE HASN'T EATEN OR SLEPT.
IF I LEAVE HER LIKE THIS...
...MIR WILL DEFINITELY LOSE HER MIND.
IF THAT'S THE CASE...
MIR, CAN YOU HEAR ME?

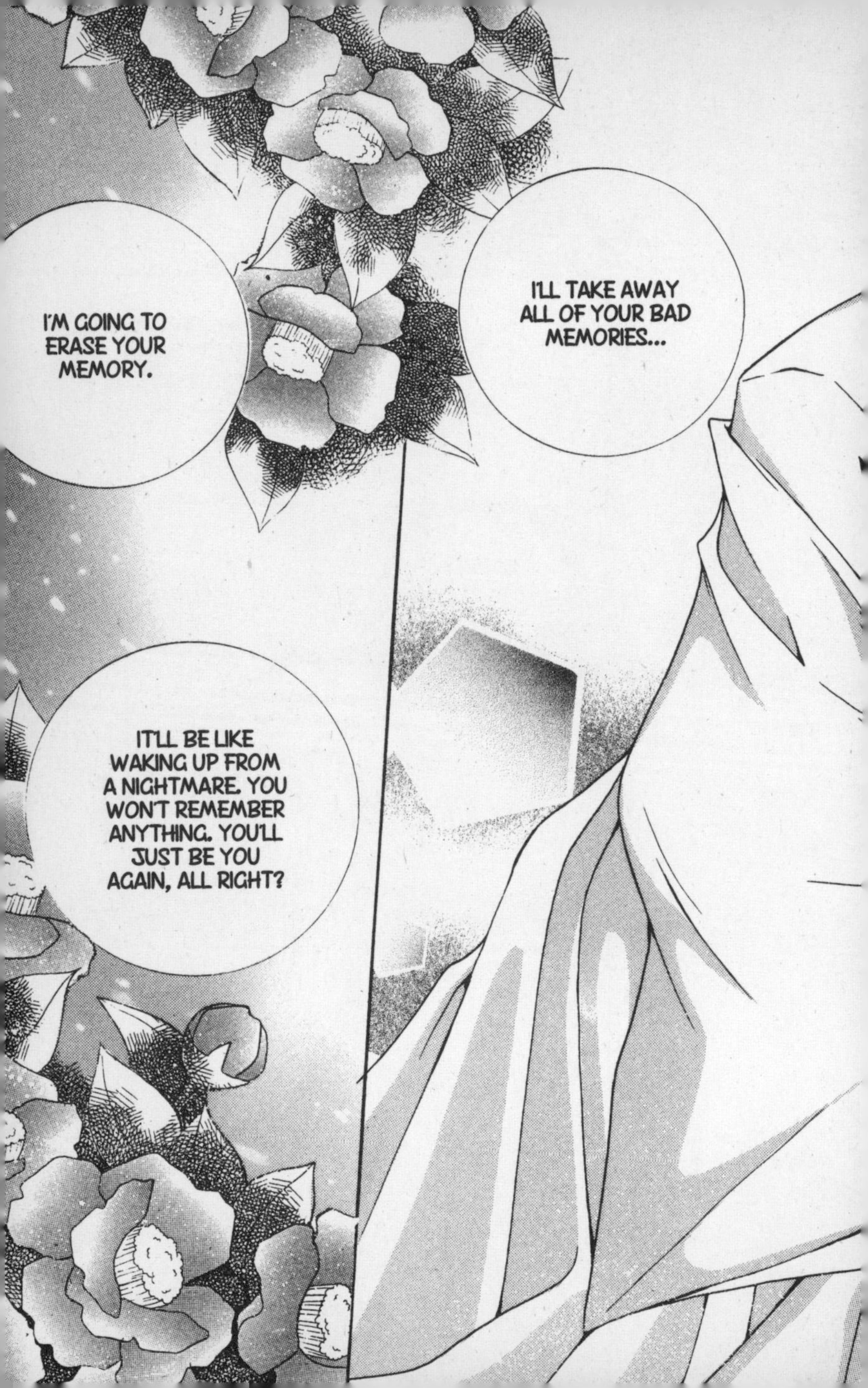
I'M GOING TO ERASE YOUR MEMORY.
IT'LL BE LIKE WAKING UP FROM A NIGHTMARE. YOU WON'T REMEMBER ANYTHING. YOU'LL JUST BE YOU AGAIN, ALL RIGHT?
I'LL TAKE AWAY ALL OF YOUR BAD MEMORIES...

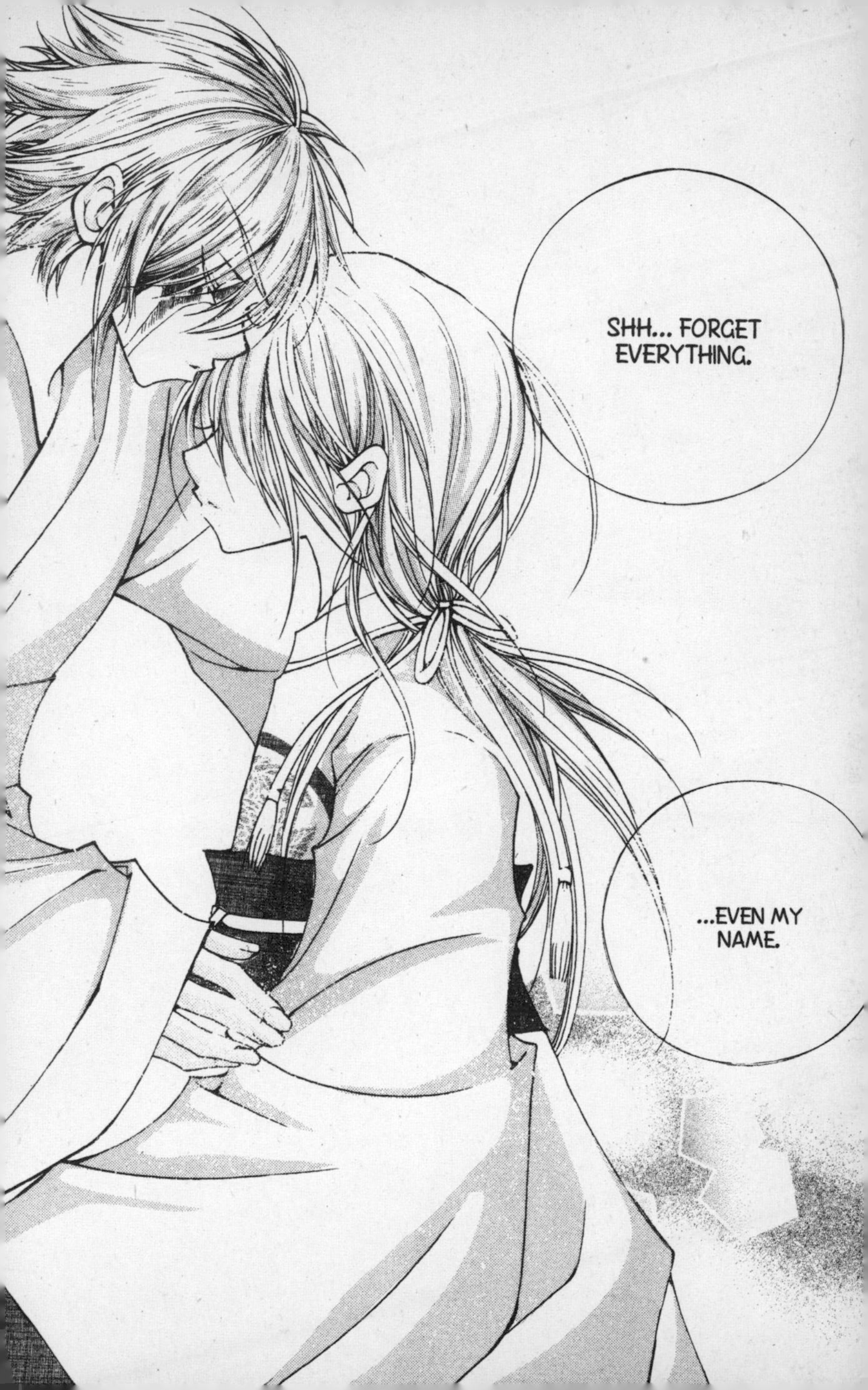
SHH... FORGET EVERYTHING.
...EVEN MY NAME.

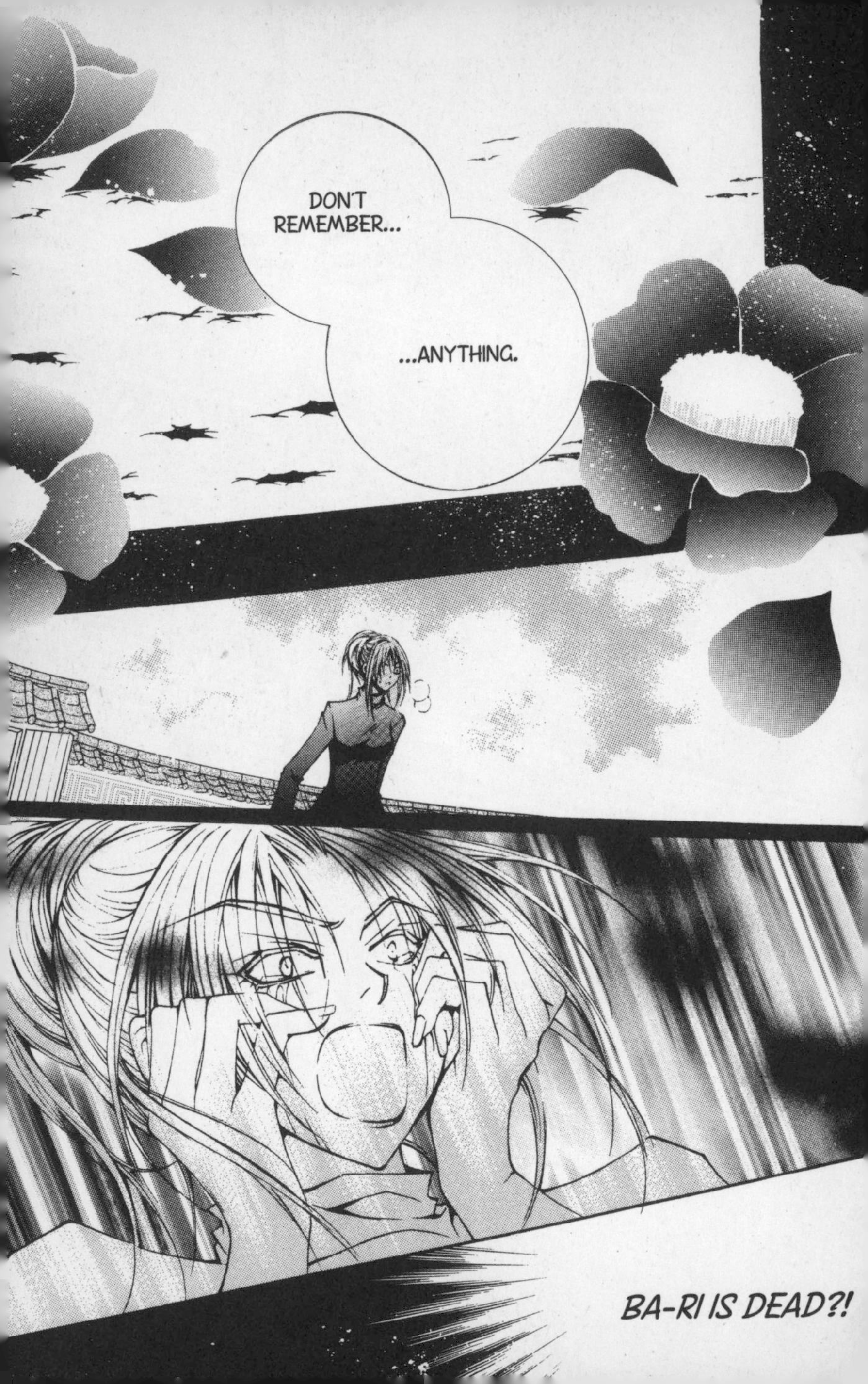
DON'T REMEMBER...
...ANYTHING.
BA-RI IS DEAD?!

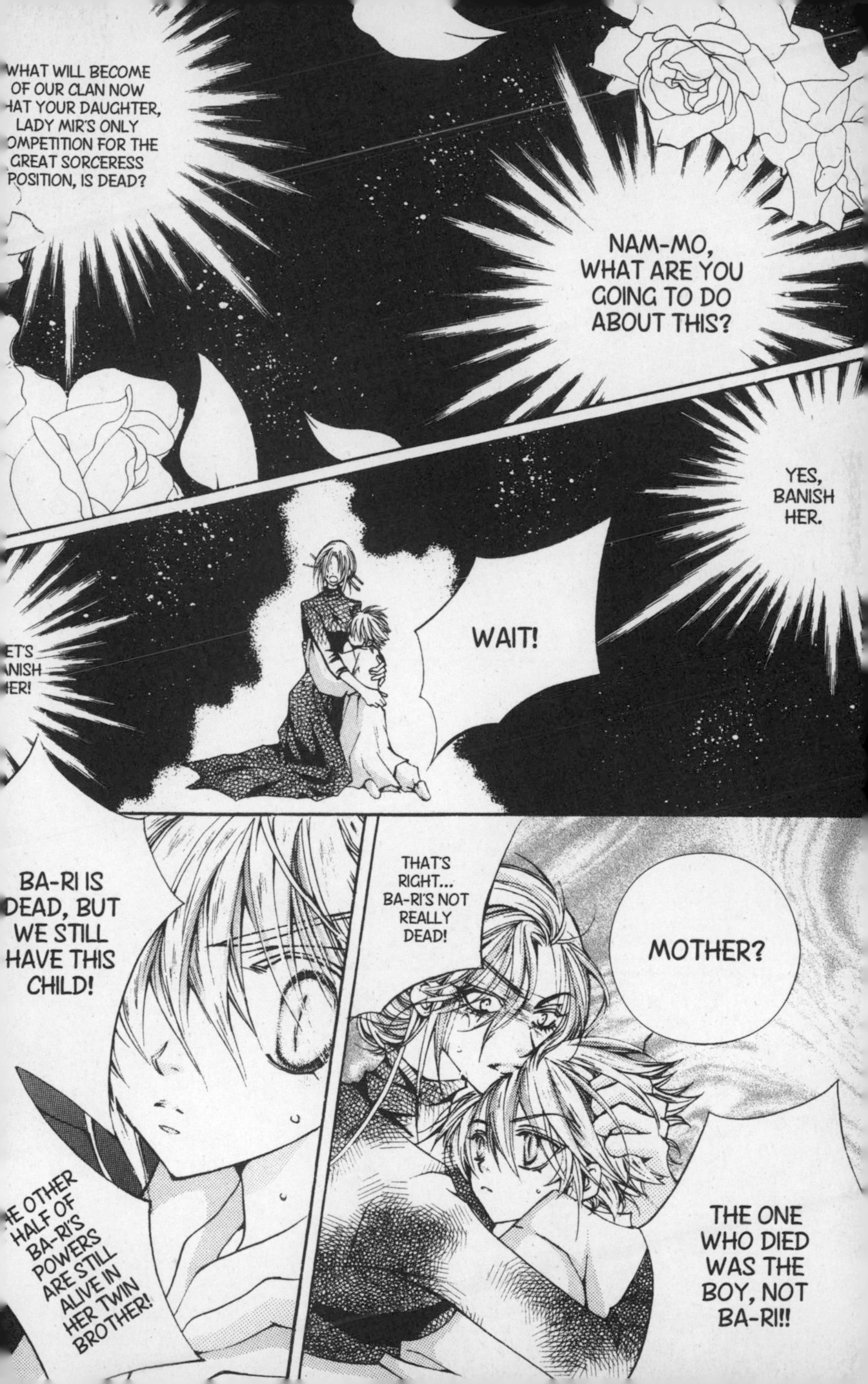
WHAT WILL BECOME OF OUR CLAN NOW HAT YOUR DAUGHTER, LADY MIR'S ONLY OMPETITION FOR THE GREAT SORCERESS POSITION, IS DEAD?
NAM-MO, WHAT ARE YOU GOING TO DO ABOUT THIS?
YES, BANISH HER.
ET'S ANISH ER!
WAIT!
BA-RI IS DEAD, BUT WE STILL HAVE THIS CHILD!
HE OTHER HALF OF BA-RI'S POWERS ARE STILL ALIVE IN HER TWIN BROTHER!
THAT'S RIGHT... BA-RI'S NOT REALLY DEAD!
MOTHER?
THE ONE WHO DIED WAS THE BOY, NOT BA-RI!!

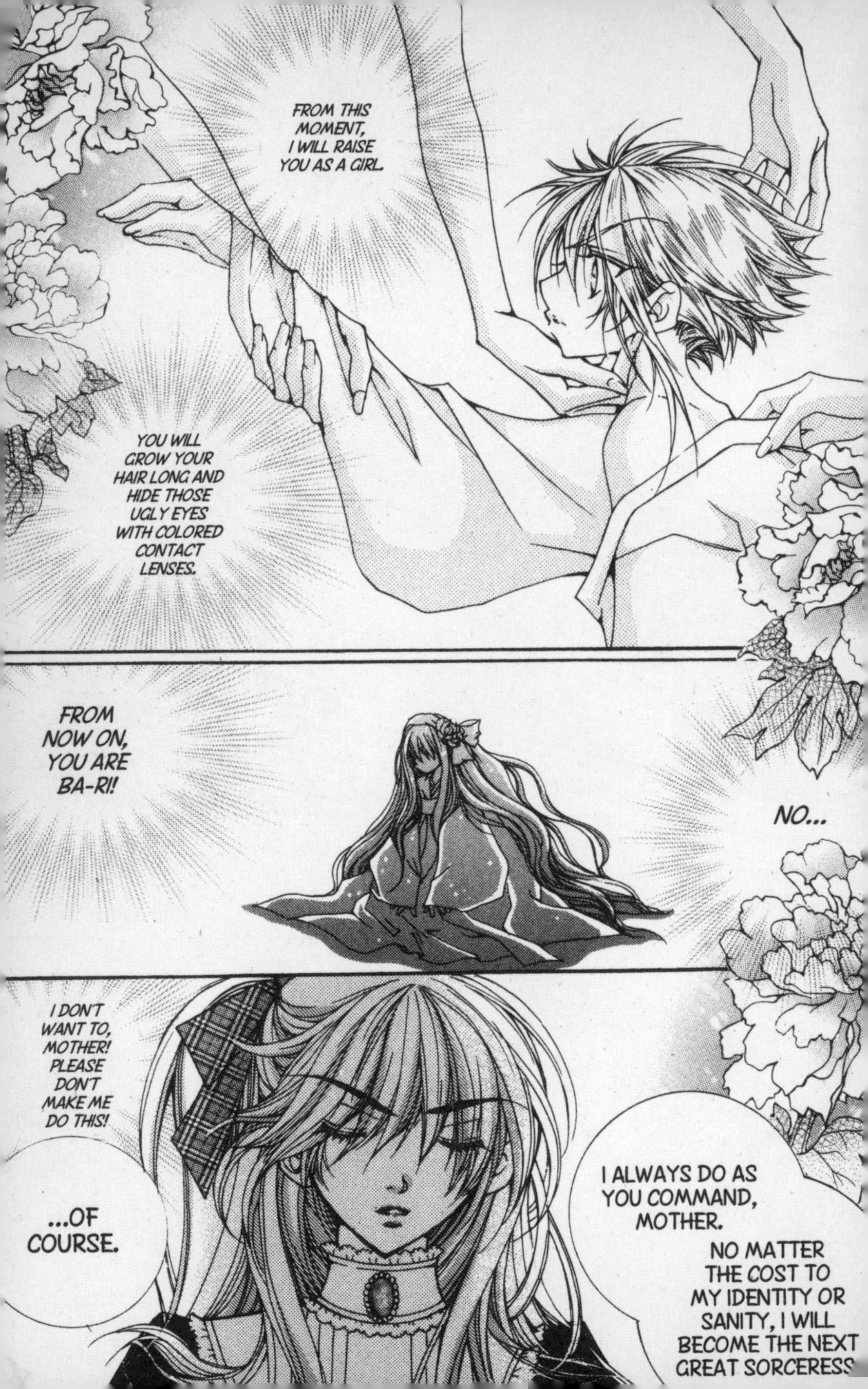
FROM THIS MOMENT, I WILL RAISE YOU AS A GIRL.
YOU WILL GROW YOUR HAIR LONG AND HIDE THOSE UGLY EYES WITH COLORED CONTACT LENSES.
FROM NOW ON, YOU ARE BA-RI!
NO...
I DON'T WANT TO, MOTHER! PLEASE DON'T MAKE ME DO THIS!
...OF COURSE.
I ALWAYS DO AS YOU COMMAND, MOTHER.
NO MATTER THE COST TO MY IDENTITY OR SANITY, I WILL BECOME THE NEXT GREAT SORCERESS

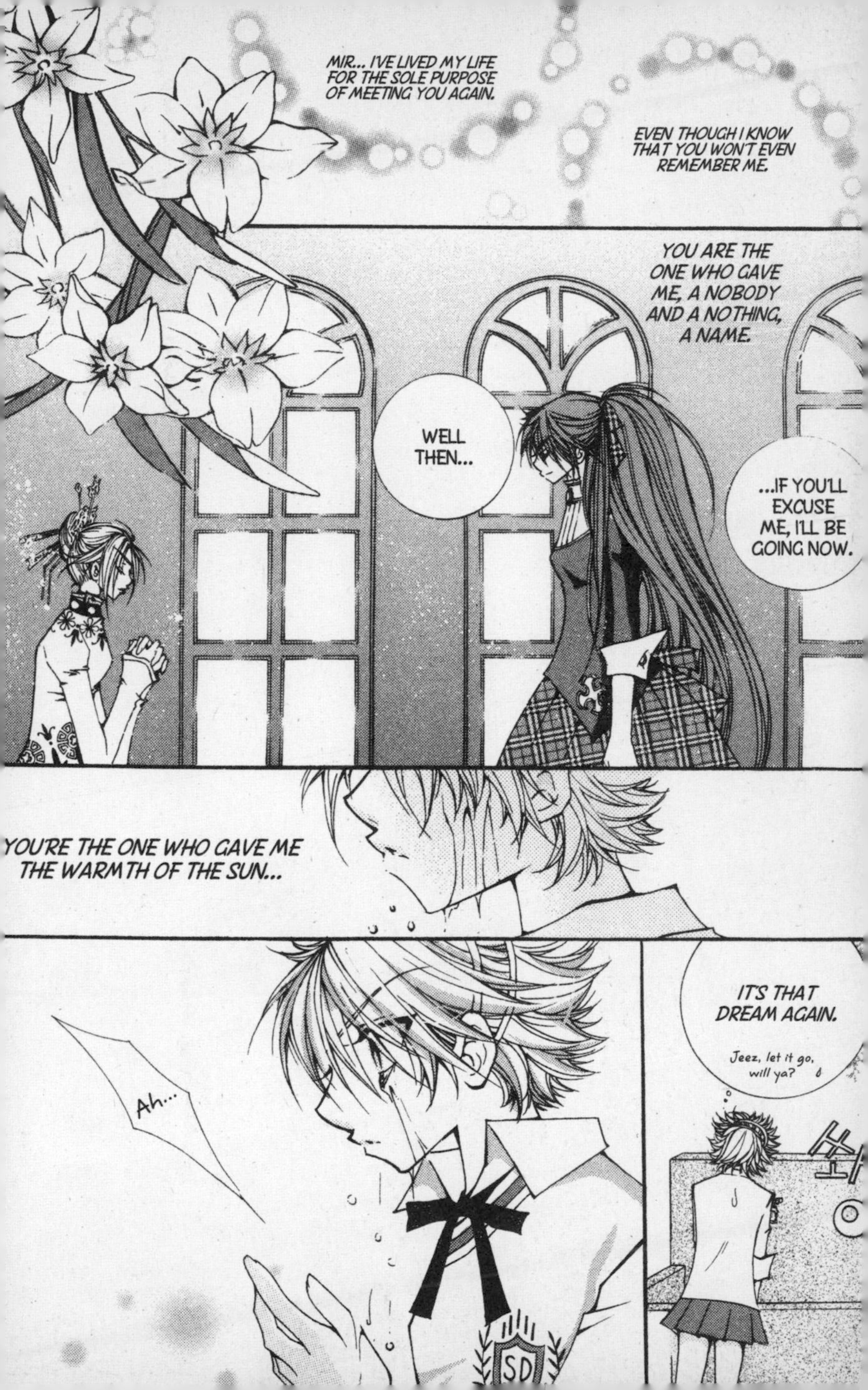
MIR... I'VE LIVED MY LIFE FOR THE SOLE PURPOSE OF MEETING YOU AGAIN.
EVEN THOUGH I KNOW THAT YOU WON'T EVEN REMEMBER ME.
YOU ARE THE ONE WHO GAVE ME, A NOBODY AND A NOTHING, A NAME.
WELL THEN...
...IF YOU'LL EXCUSE ME, I'LL BE GOING NOW.
YOU'RE THE ONE WHO GAVE ME THE WARMTH OF THE SUN...
Ah...
IT'S THAT DREAM AGAIN.
Jeez, let it go, will ya?

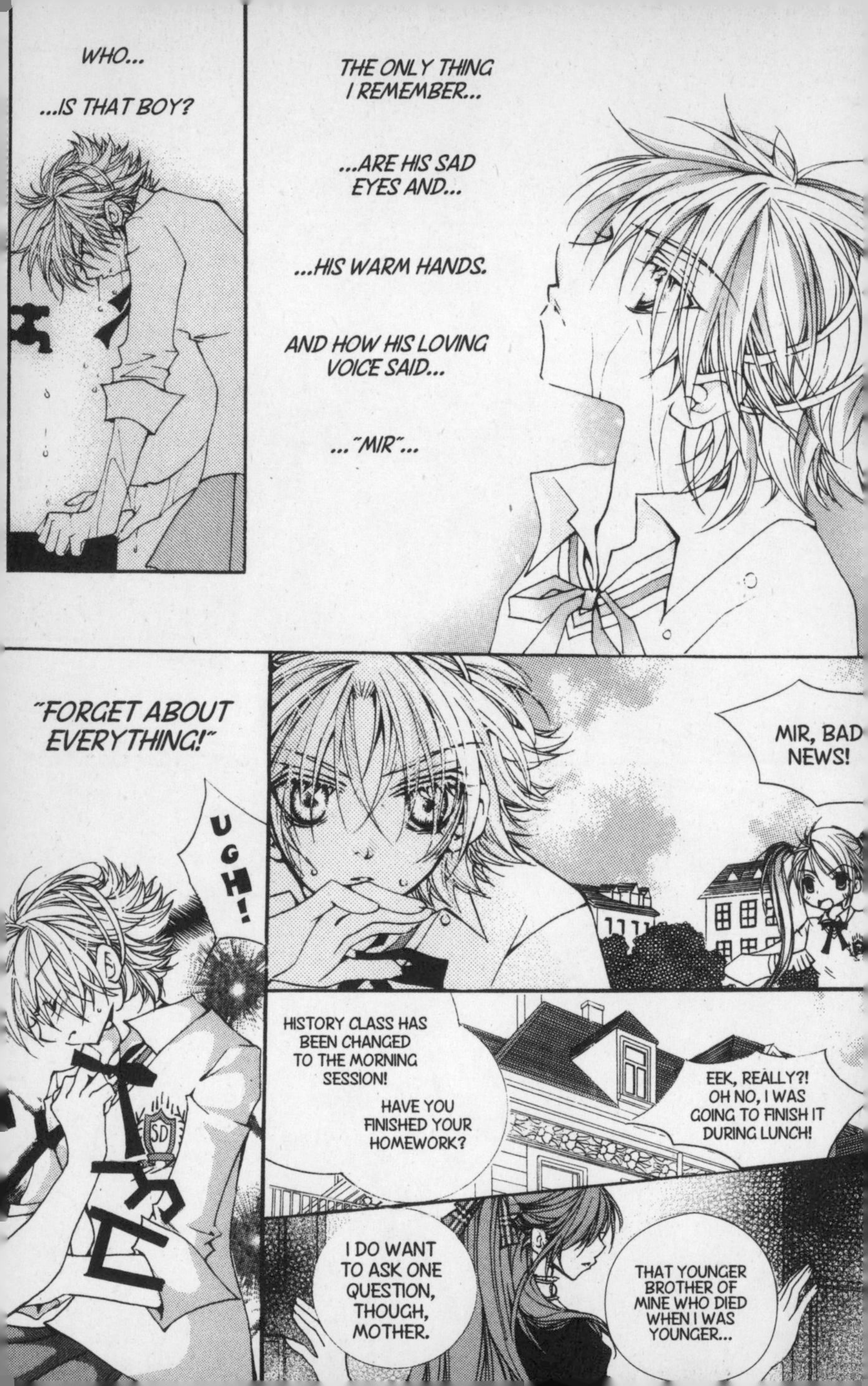

WHO...
...IS THAT BOY?
THE ONLY THING I REMEMBER...
...ARE HIS SAD EYES AND...
...HIS WARM HANDS.
AND HOW HIS LOVING VOICE SAID...
..."MIR"...
"FORGET ABOUT EVERYTHING!"
UGH!
MIR, BAD NEWS!
HISTORY CLASS HAS BEEN CHANGED TO THE MORNING SESSION!
HAVE YOU FINISHED YOUR HOMEWORK?
EEK, REALLY?! OH NO, I WAS GOING TO FINISH IT DURING LUNCH!
I DO WANT TO ASK ONE QUESTION, THOUGH, MOTHER.
THAT YOUNGER BROTHER OF MINE WHO DIED WHEN I WAS YOUNGER...

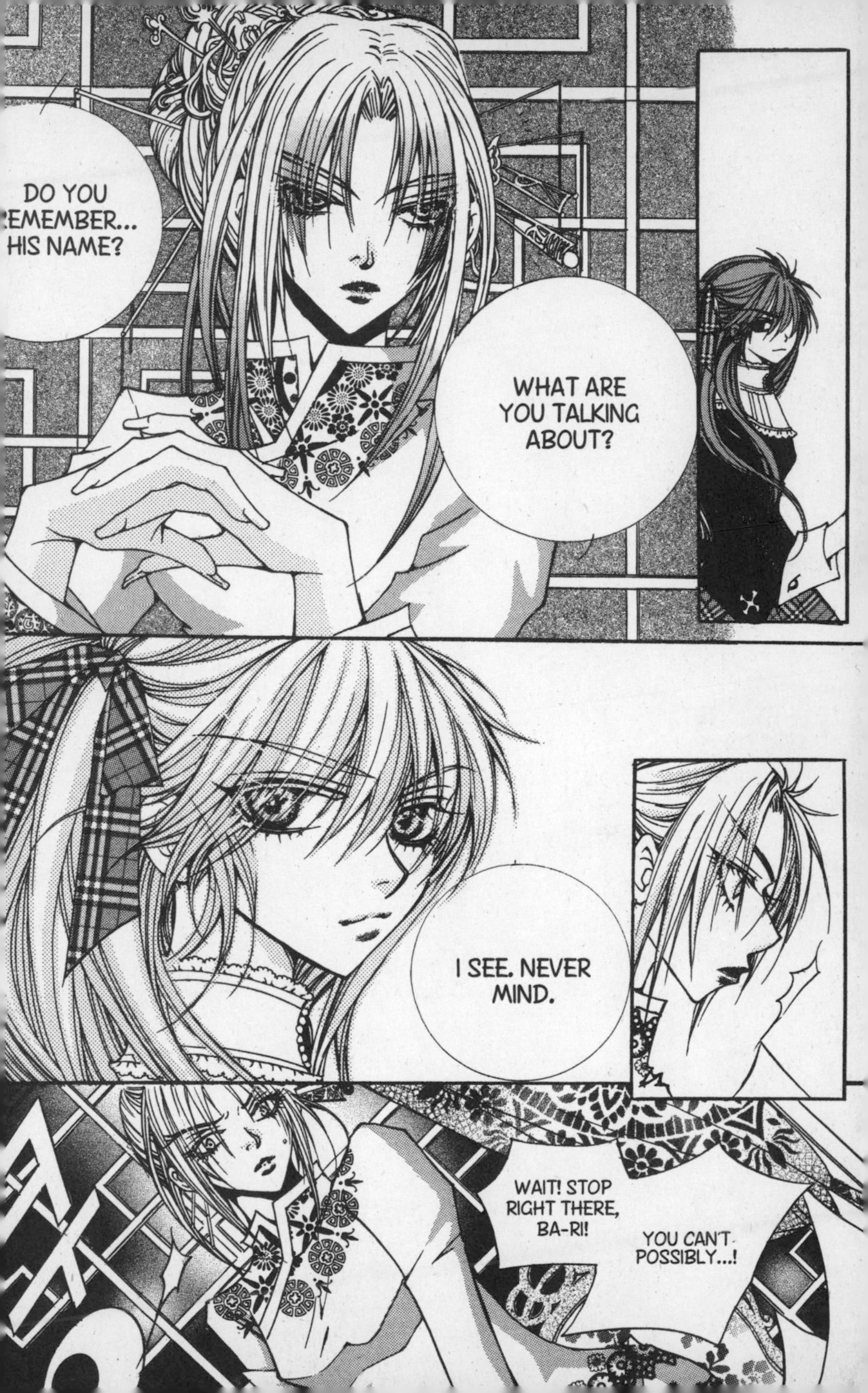
DO YOU REMEMBER... HIS NAME?
WHAT ARE YOU TALKING ABOUT?
I SEE. NEVER MIND.
WAIT! STOP RIGHT THERE, BA-RI!
YOU CAN'T POSSIBLY...!

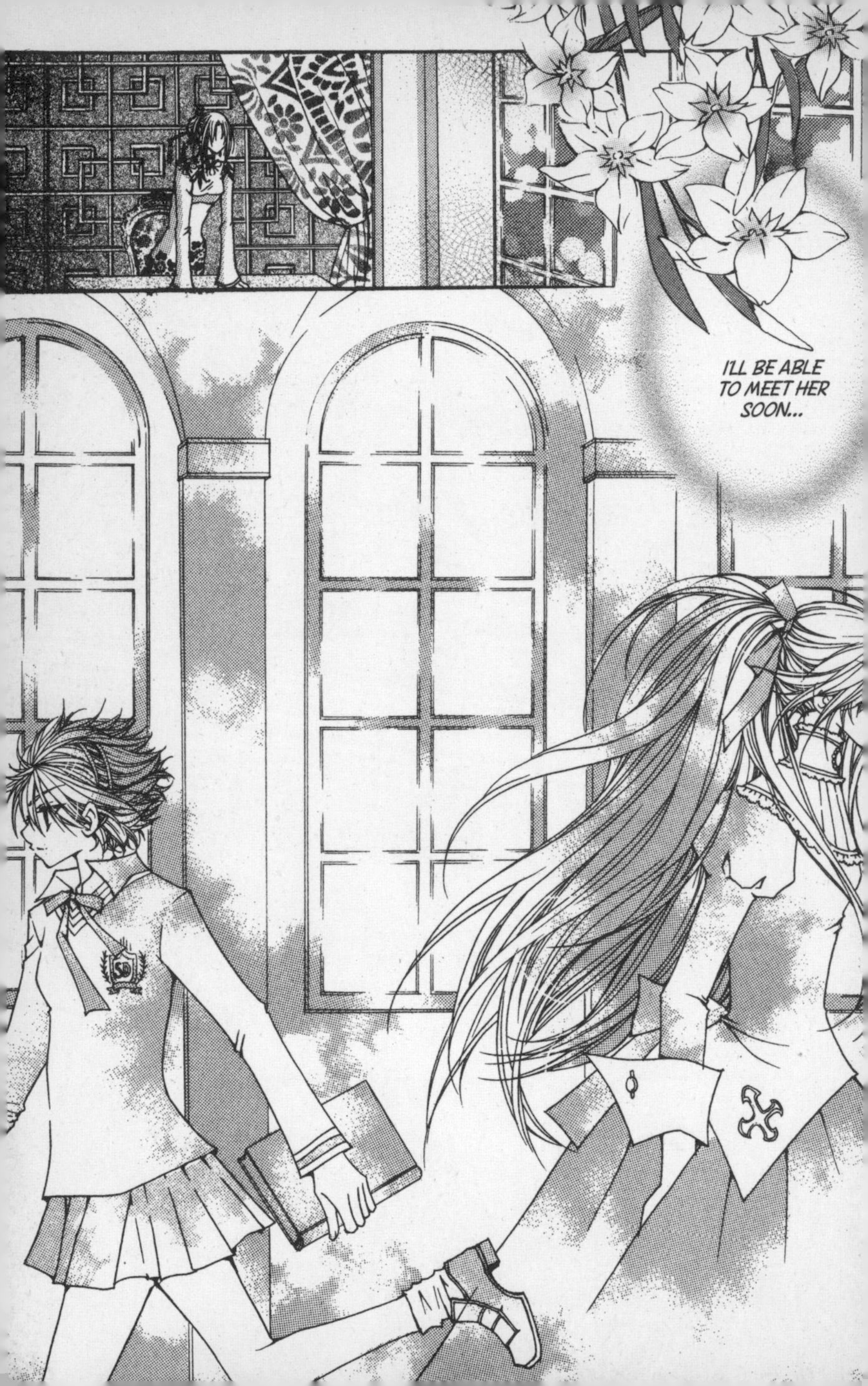
I'LL BE ABLE TO MEET HER SOON...

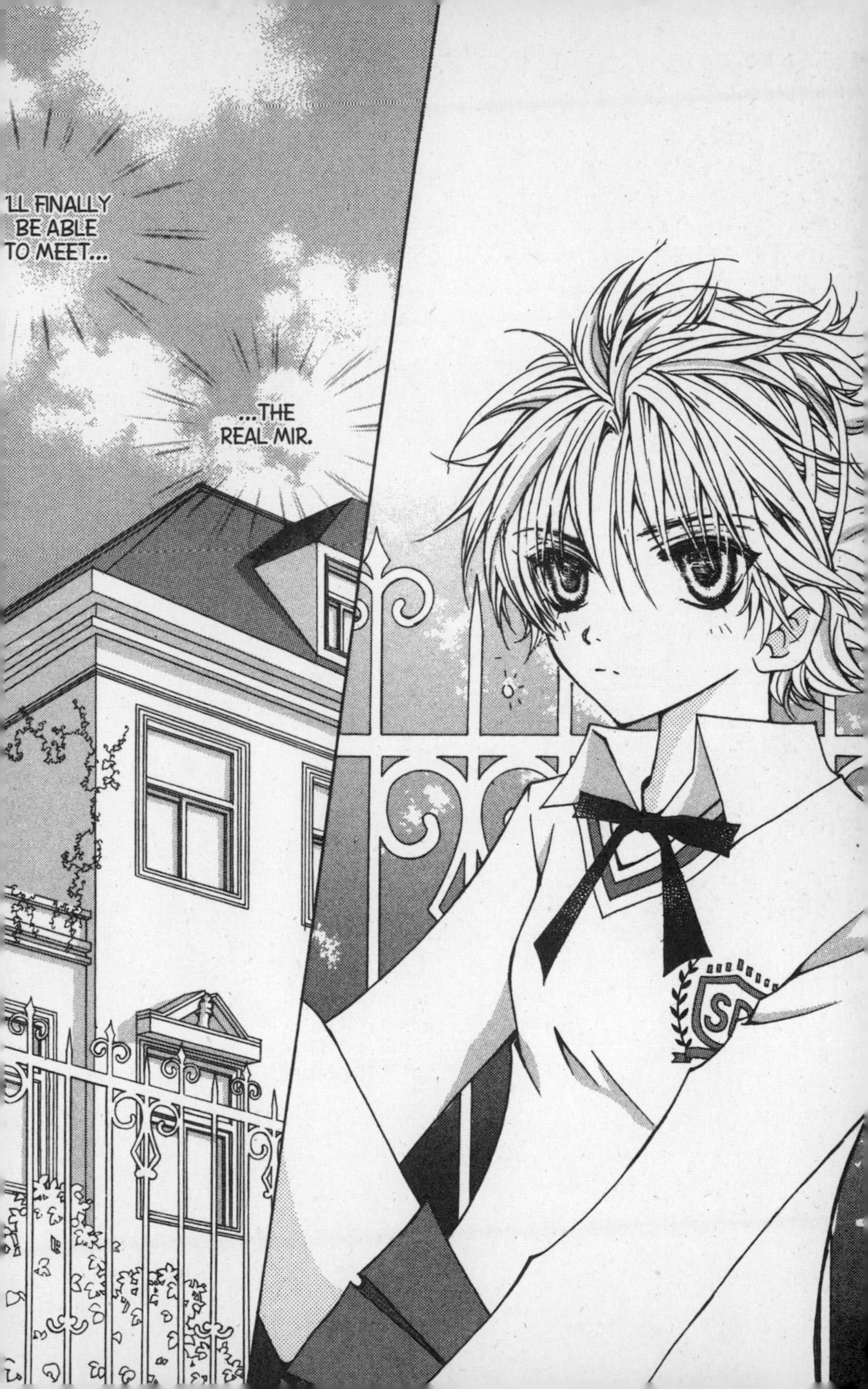
'LL FINALLY BE ABLE TO MEET...
...THE REAL MIR.

FANTAMIR

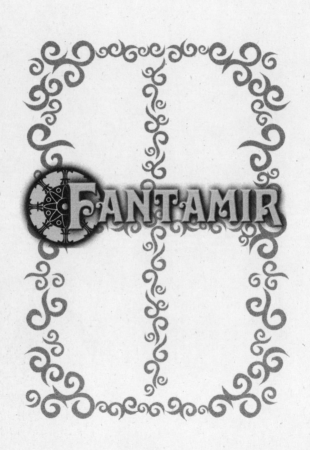

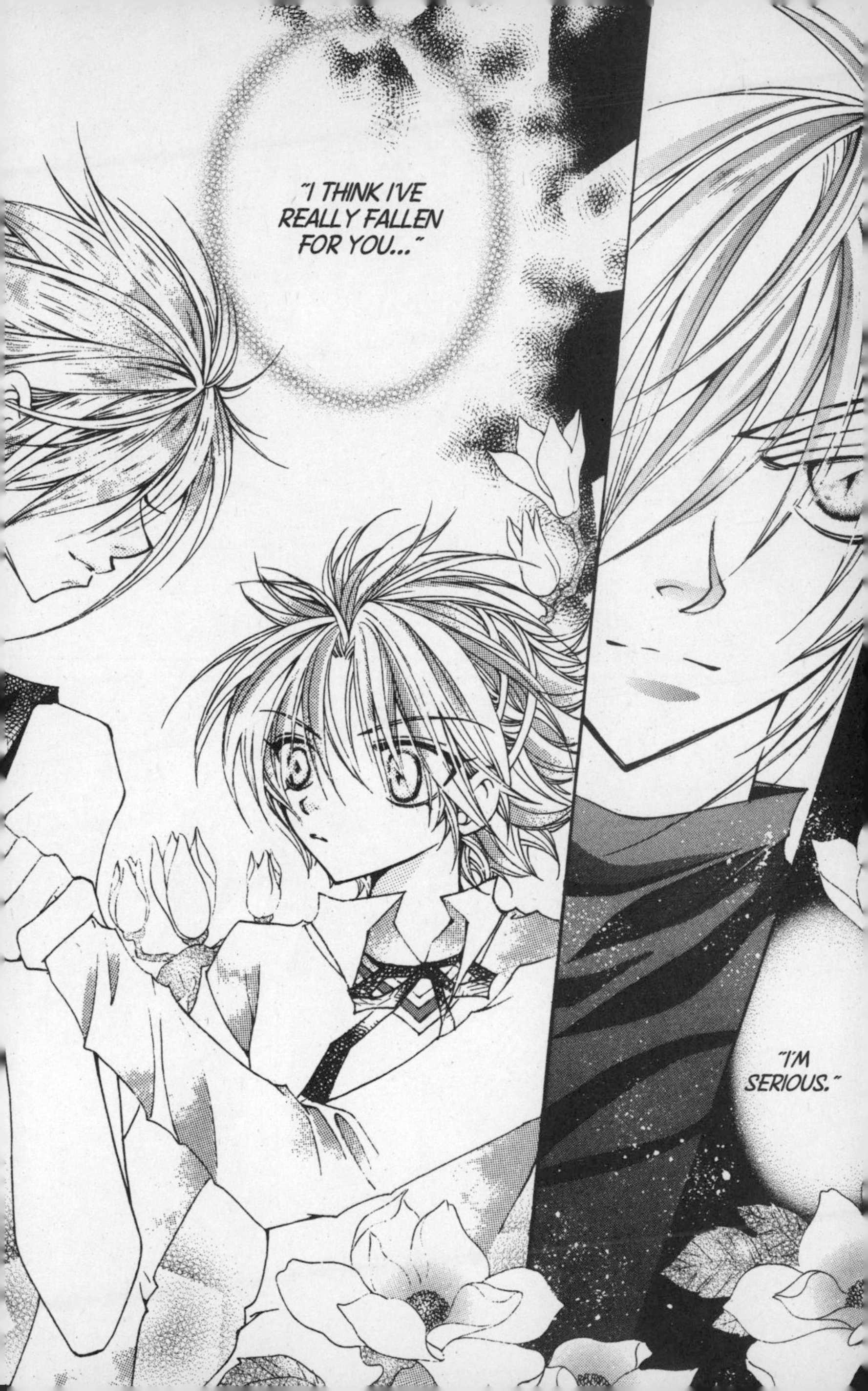
"I THINK I'VE REALLY FALLEN FOR YOU..."
"I'M SERIOUS."

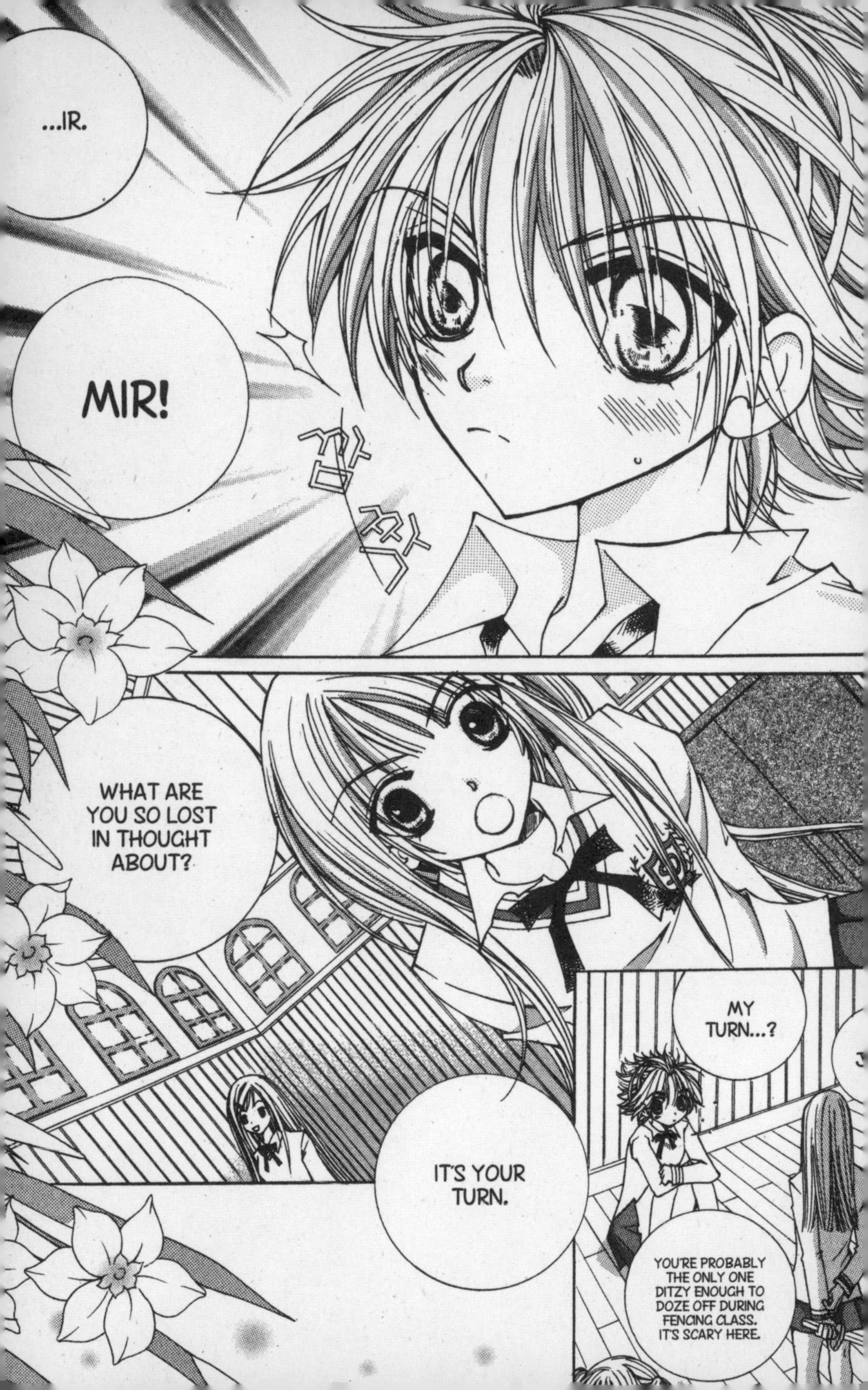
...IR.
MIR!
WHAT ARE YOU SO LOST IN THOUGHT ABOUT?
IT'S YOUR TURN.
MY TURN...?
YOU'RE PROBABLY THE ONLY ONE DITZY ENOUGH TO DOZE OFF DURING FENCING CLASS. IT'S SCARY HERE.

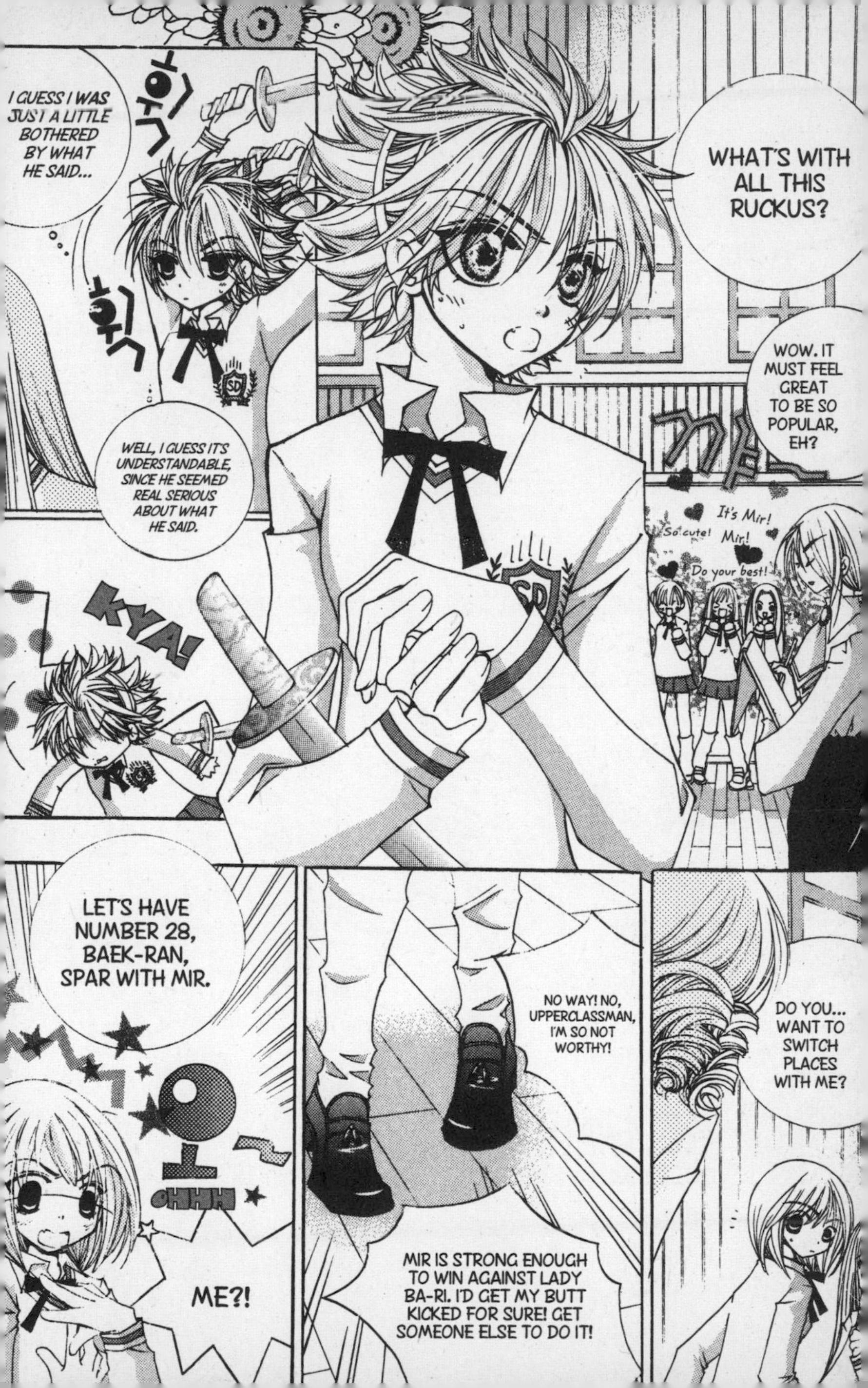
I GUESS I WAS JUST A LITTLE BOTHERED BY WHAT HE SAID...
WELL, I GUESS ITS UNDERSTANDABLE, SINCE HE SEEMED REAL SERIOUS ABOUT WHAT HE SAID.
WHAT'S WITH ALL THIS RUCKUS?
WOW. IT MUST FEEL GREAT TO BE SO POPULAR, EH?
It's Mir!
So cute!
Mir!
Do your best!
KYA!
LET'S HAVE NUMBER 28, BAEK-RAN, SPAR WITH MIR.
OHHH
ME?!
NO WAY! NO, UPPERCLASSMAN, I'M SO NOT WORTHY!
MIR IS STRONG ENOUGH TO WIN AGAINST LADY BA-RI. I'D GET MY BUTT KICKED FOR SURE! GET SOMEONE ELSE TO DO IT!
DO YOU... WANT TO SWITCH PLACES WITH ME?

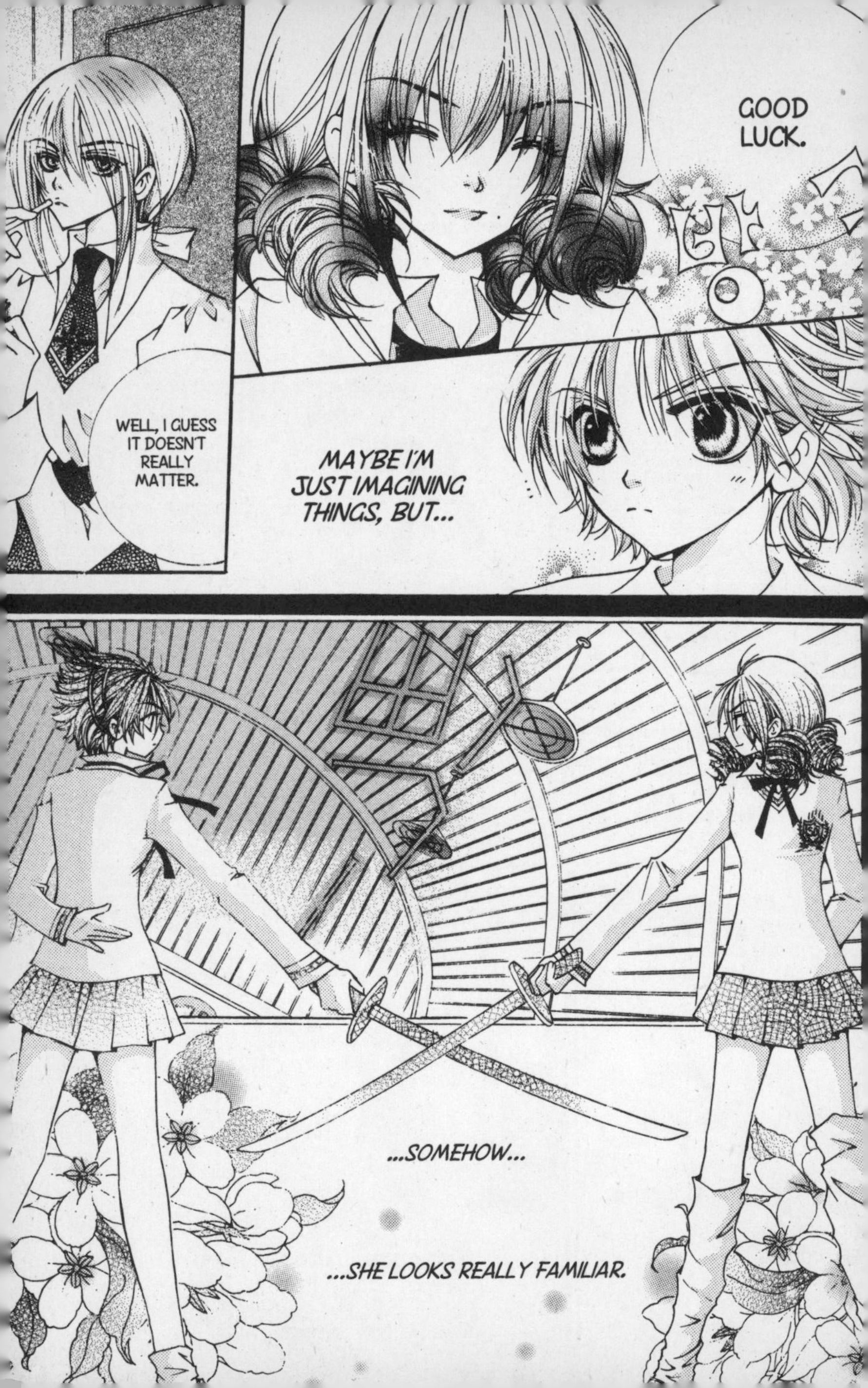
WELL, I GUESS IT DOESN'T REALLY MATTER.
GOOD LUCK.
MAYBE I'M JUST IMAGINING THINGS, BUT...
...SOMEHOW...
...SHE LOOKS REALLY FAMILIAR.

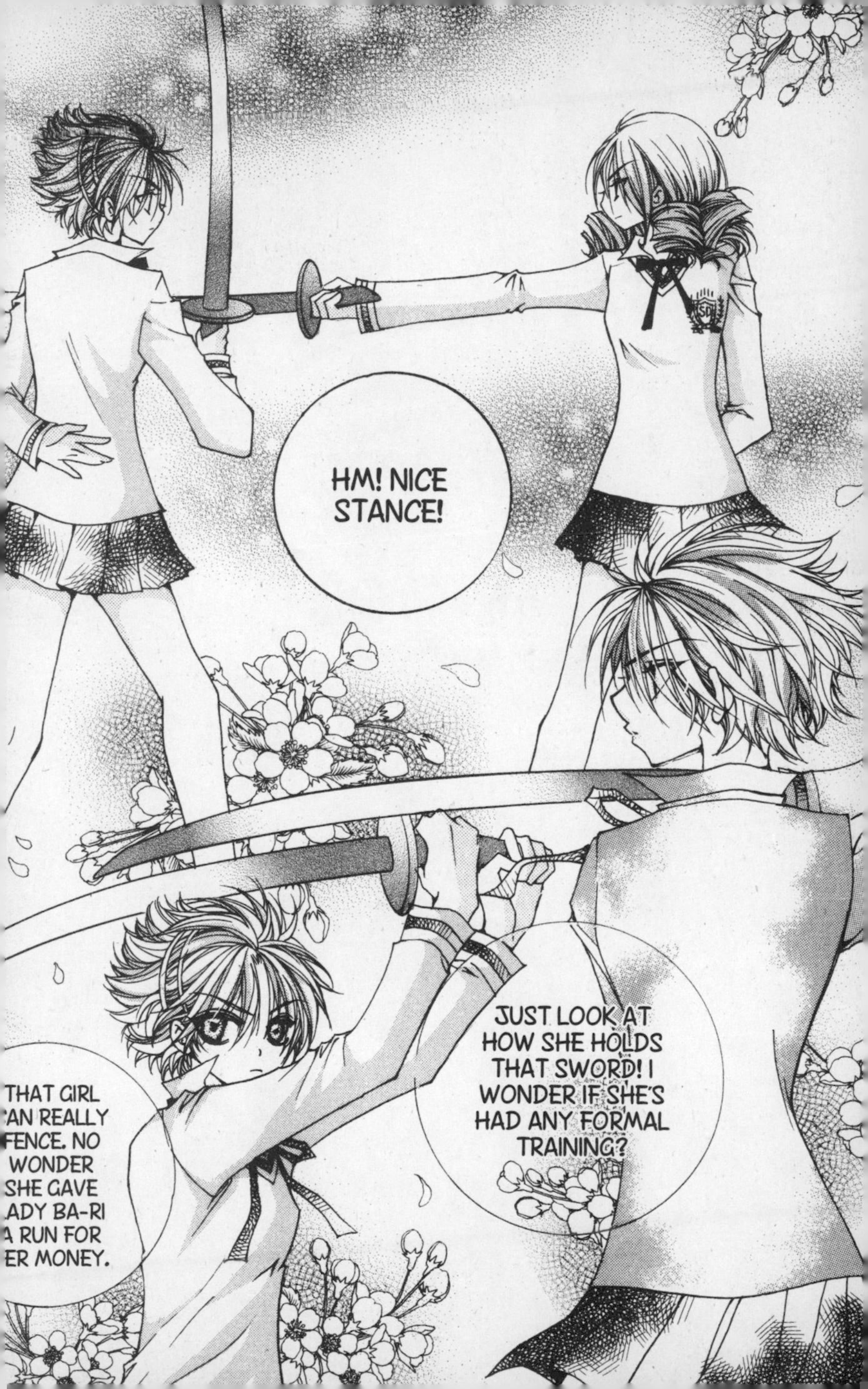
HM! NICE STANCE!
THAT GIRL CAN REALLY FENCE. NO WONDER SHE GAVE LADY BA-RI A RUN FOR HER MONEY.
JUST LOOK AT HOW SHE HOLDS THAT SWORD! I WONDER IF SHE'S HAD ANY FORMAL TRAINING?

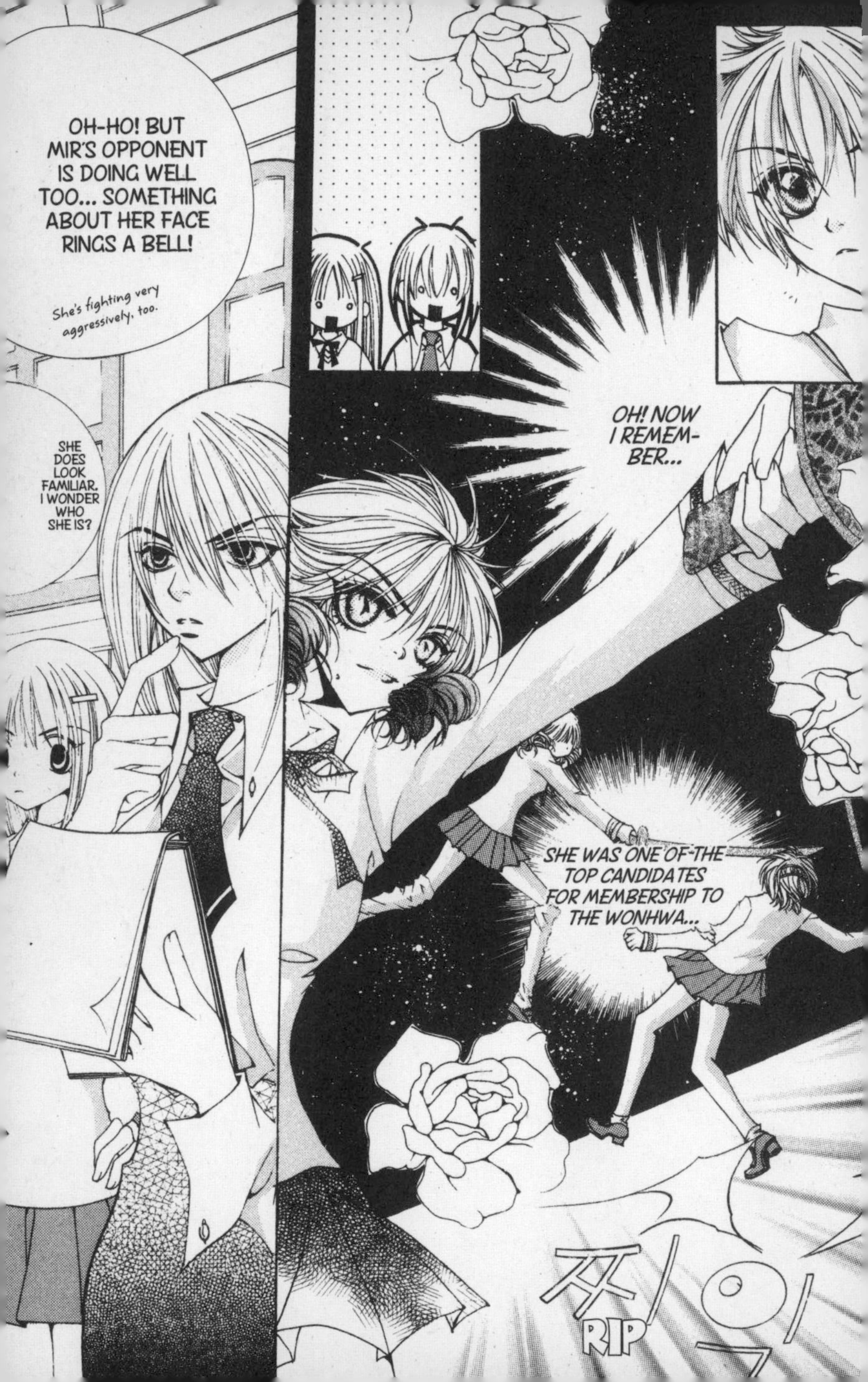
OH-HO! BUT MIR'S OPPONENT IS DOING WELL TOO... SOMETHING ABOUT HER FACE RINGS A BELL!
She's fighting very aggressively, too.
SHE DOES LOOK FAMILIAR. I WONDER WHO SHE IS?
OH! NOW I REMEM-BER...
SHE WAS ONE OF THE TOP CANDIDATES FOR MEMBERSHIP TO THE WONHWA...
RIP

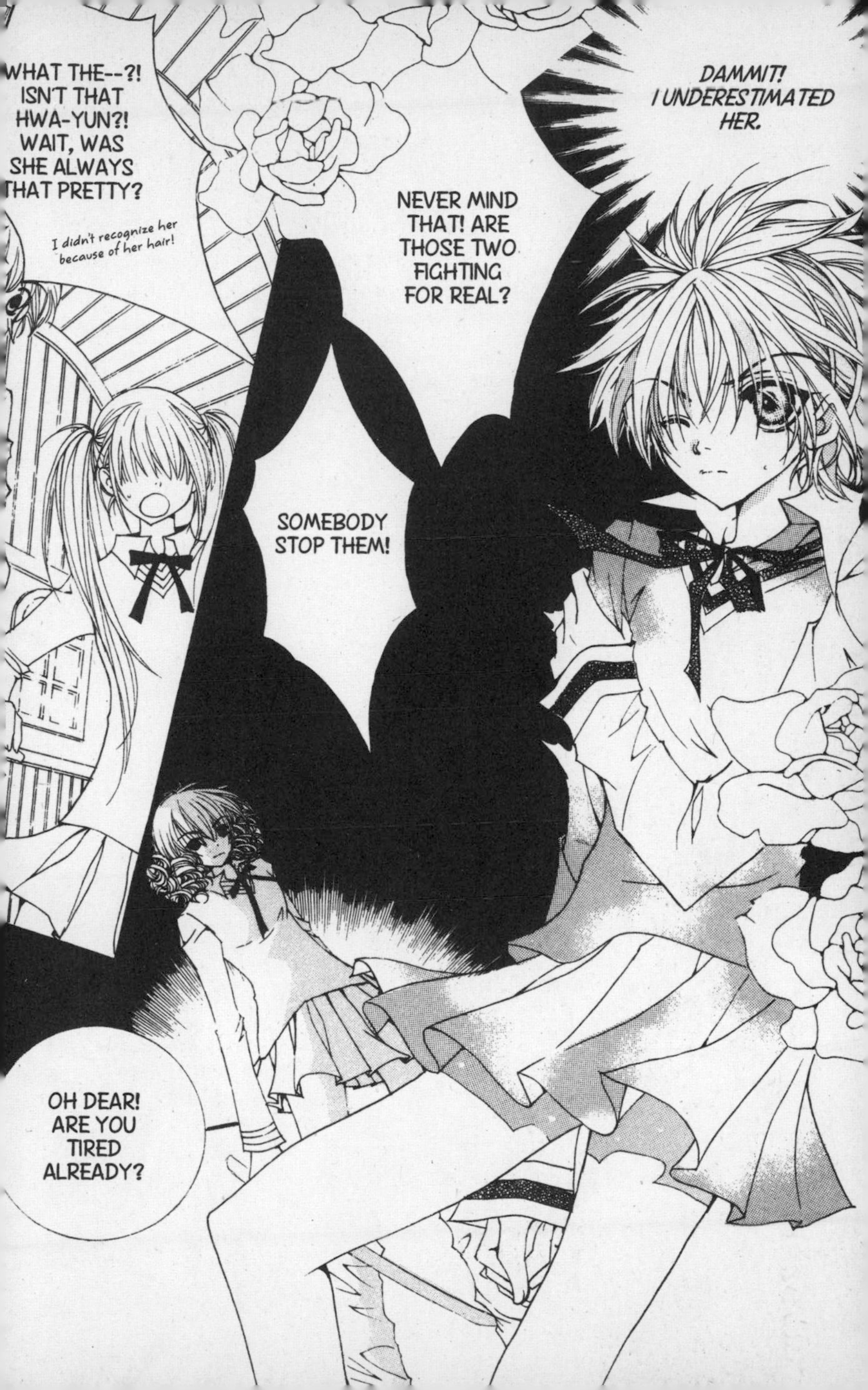

WHAT THE--?! ISN'T THAT HWA-YUN?! WAIT, WAS SHE ALWAYS THAT PRETTY?
I didn't recognize her because of her hair!
DAMMIT! I UNDERESTIMATED HER.
NEVER MIND THAT! ARE THOSE TWO FIGHTING FOR REAL?
SOMEBODY STOP THEM!
OH DEAR! ARE YOU TIRED ALREADY?

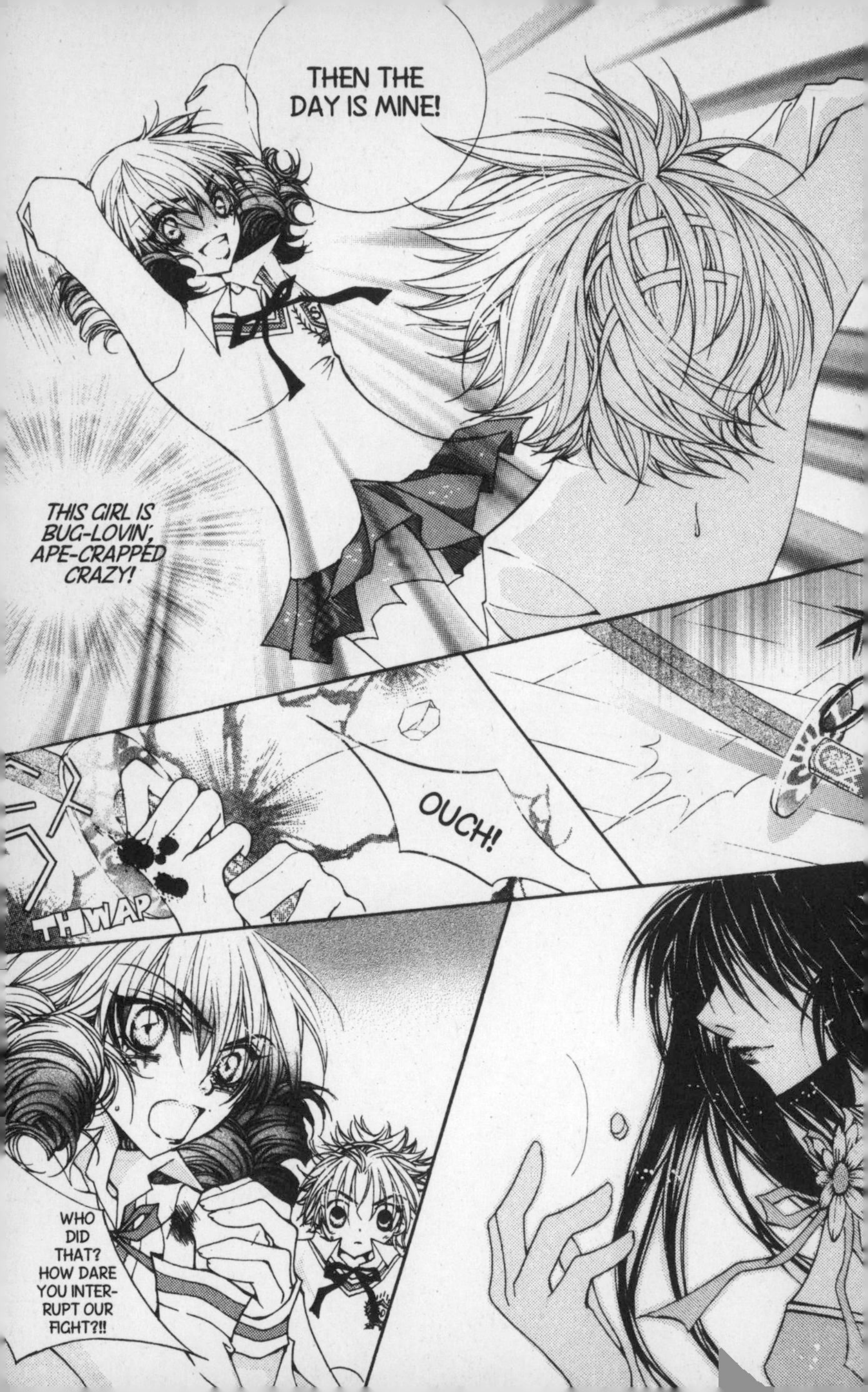
THEN THE DAY IS MINE!
THIS GIRL IS BUG-LOVIN', APE-CRAPPED CRAZY!
THWAP
OUCH!
WHO DID THAT? HOW DARE YOU INTER-RUPT OUR FIGHT?!!

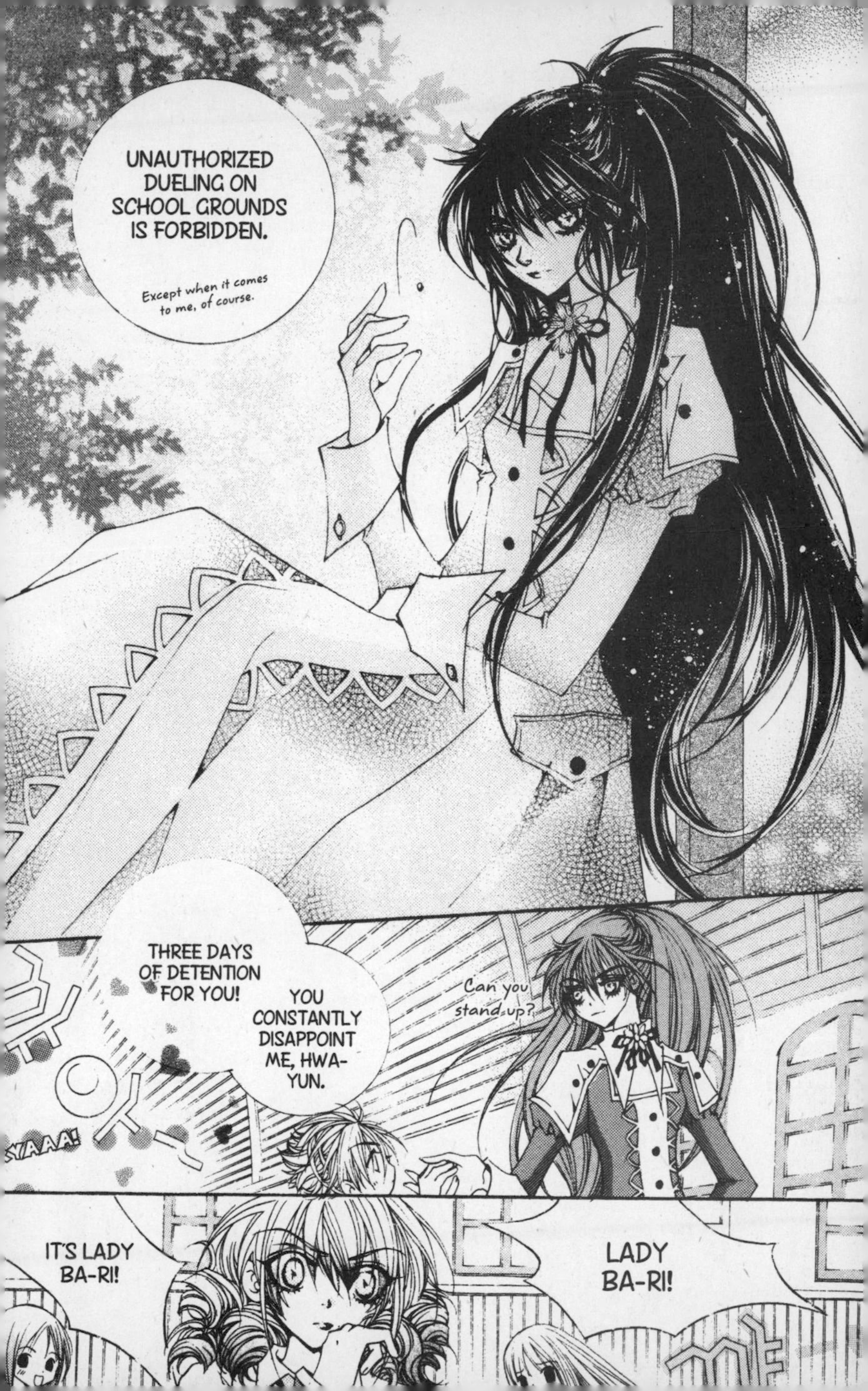
UNAUTHORIZED DUELING ON SCHOOL GROUNDS IS FORBIDDEN.
Except when it comes to me, of course.
THREE DAYS OF DETENTION FOR YOU!
YOU CONSTANTLY DISAPPOINT ME, HWA-YUN.
Can you stand up?
YAAA!
IT'S LADY BA-RI!
LADY BA-RI!

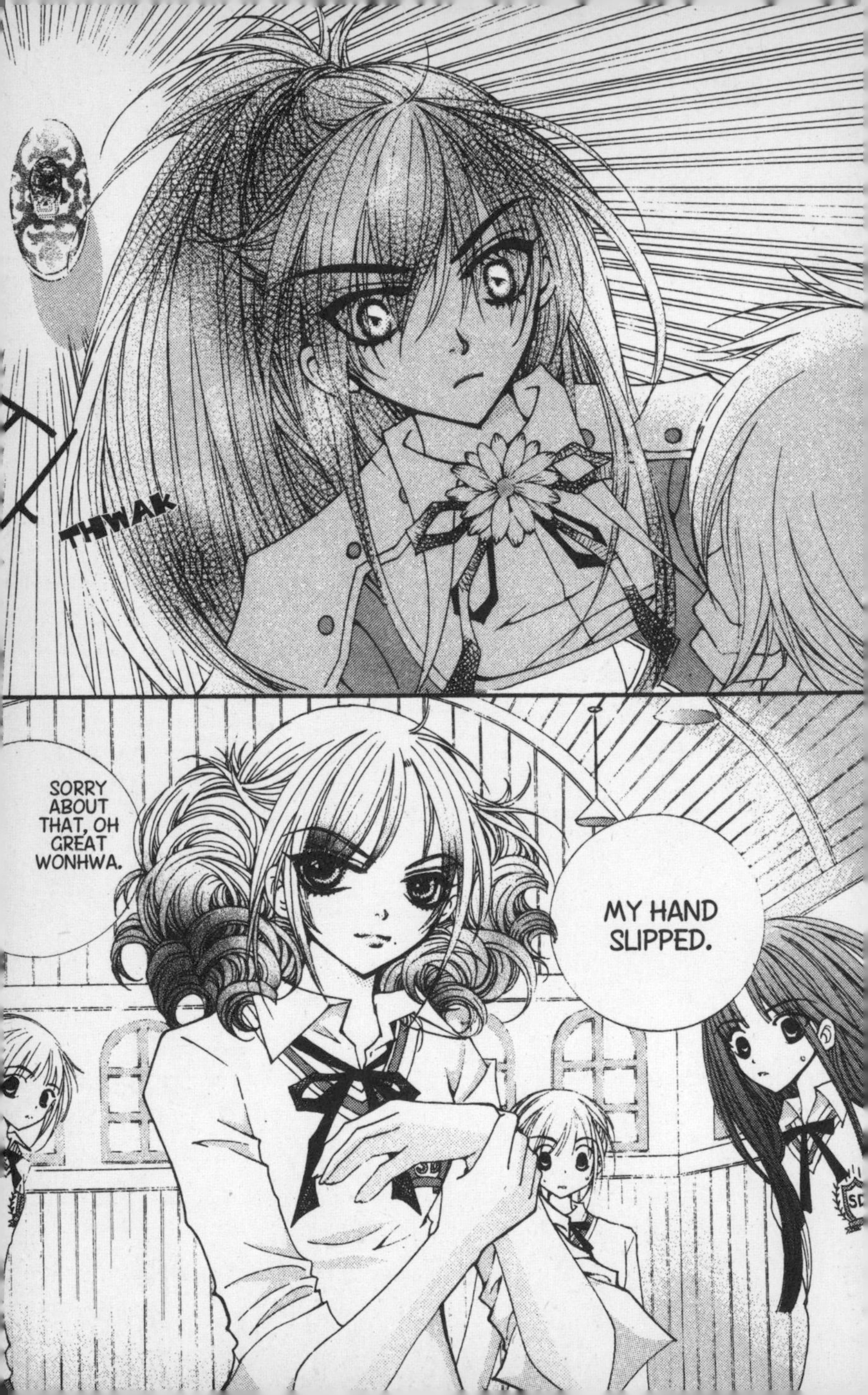
THWAK
MY HAND SLIPPED.
SORRY ABOUT THAT, OH GREAT WONHWA.

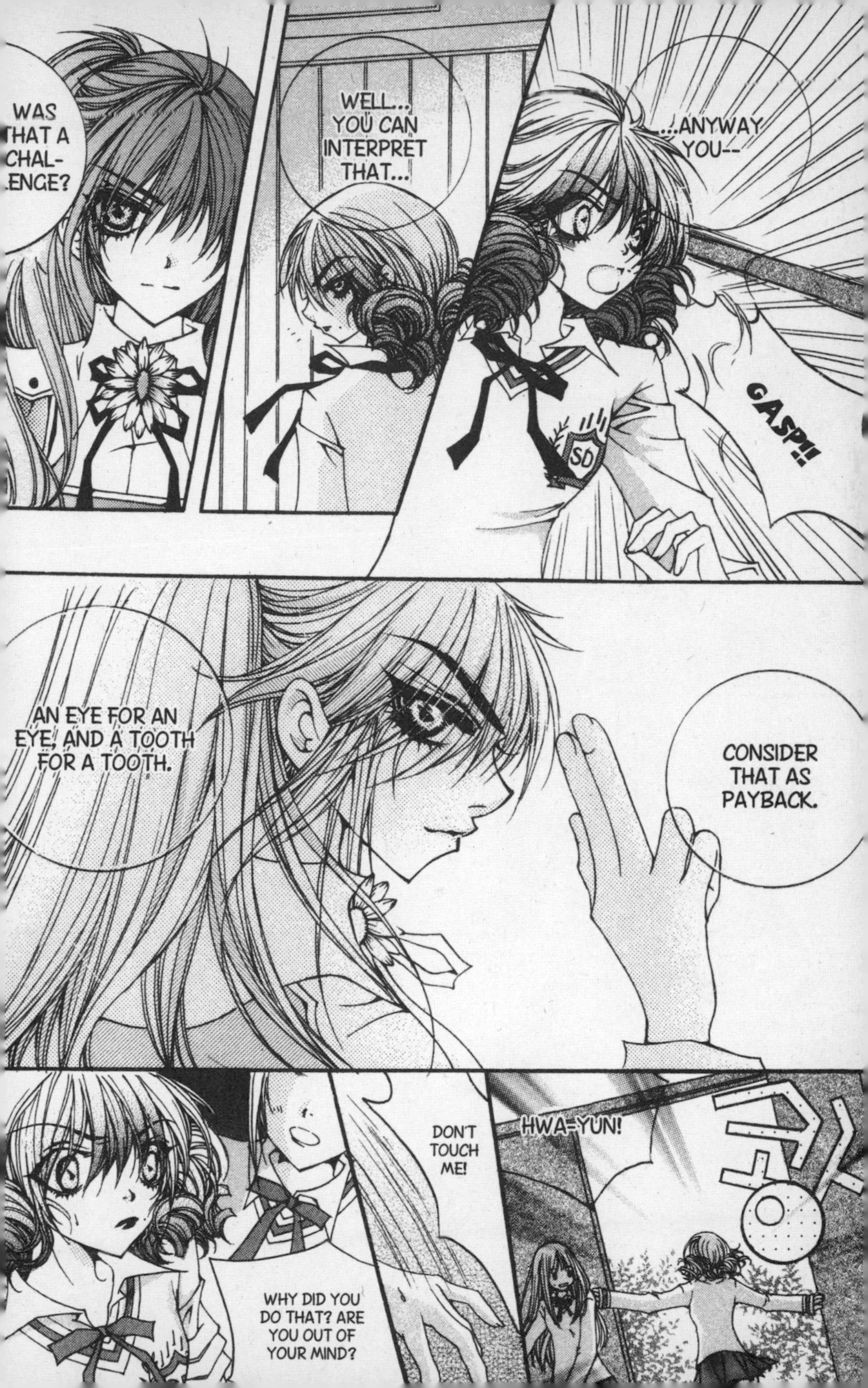
WAS THAT A CHAL-LENGE?
WELL... YOU CAN INTERPRET THAT...
...ANYWAY YOU--
GASP!!
AN EYE FOR AN EYE, AND A TOOTH FOR A TOOTH.
CONSIDER THAT AS PAYBACK.
DON'T TOUCH ME!
WHY DID YOU DO THAT? ARE YOU OUT OF YOUR MIND?
HWA-YUN!

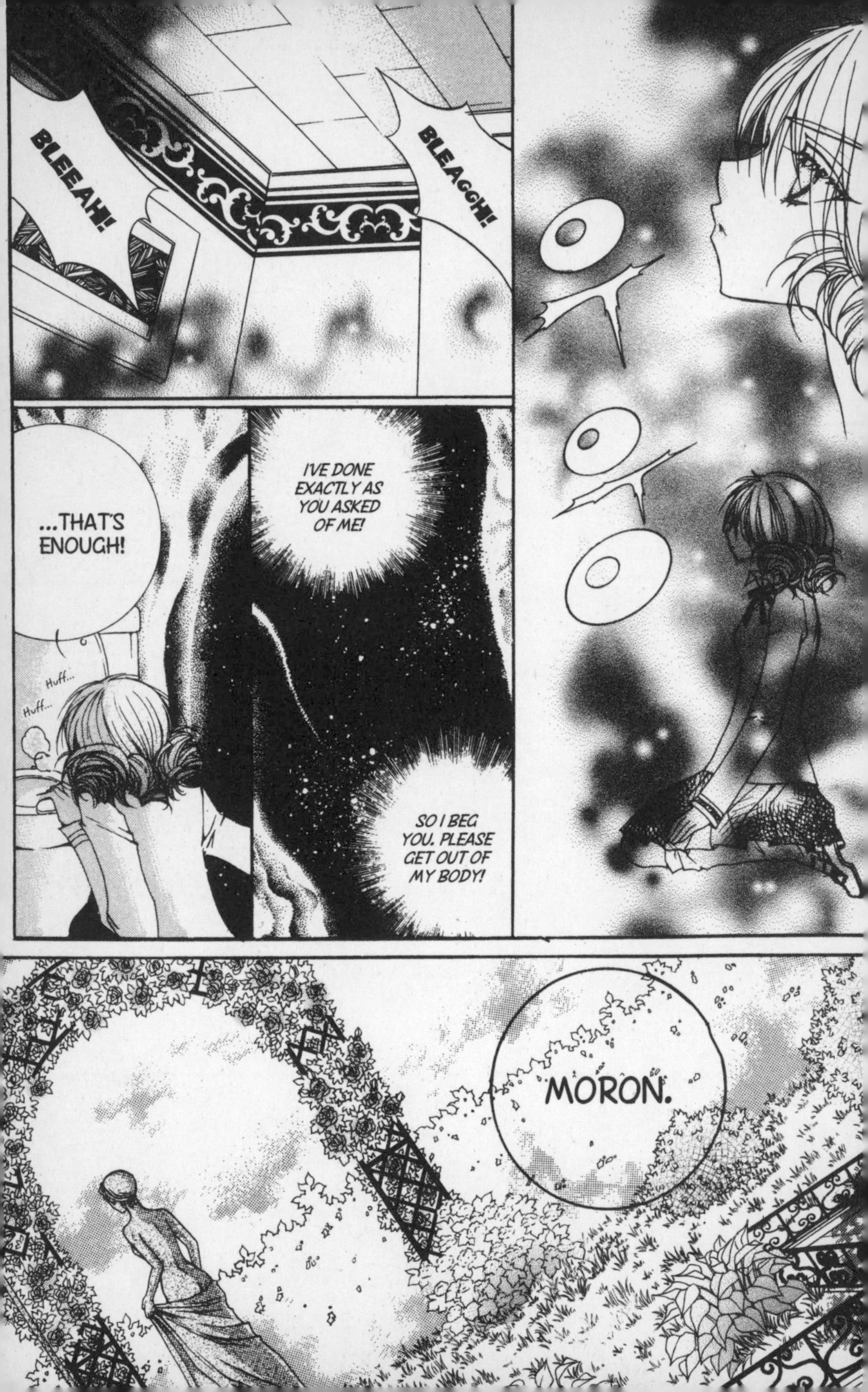
BLEEAH!
BLEAGGH!
...THAT'S ENOUGH!
Huff...
Huff...
I'VE DONE EXACTLY AS YOU ASKED OF ME!
SO I BEG YOU. PLEASE GET OUT OF MY BODY!
MORON.

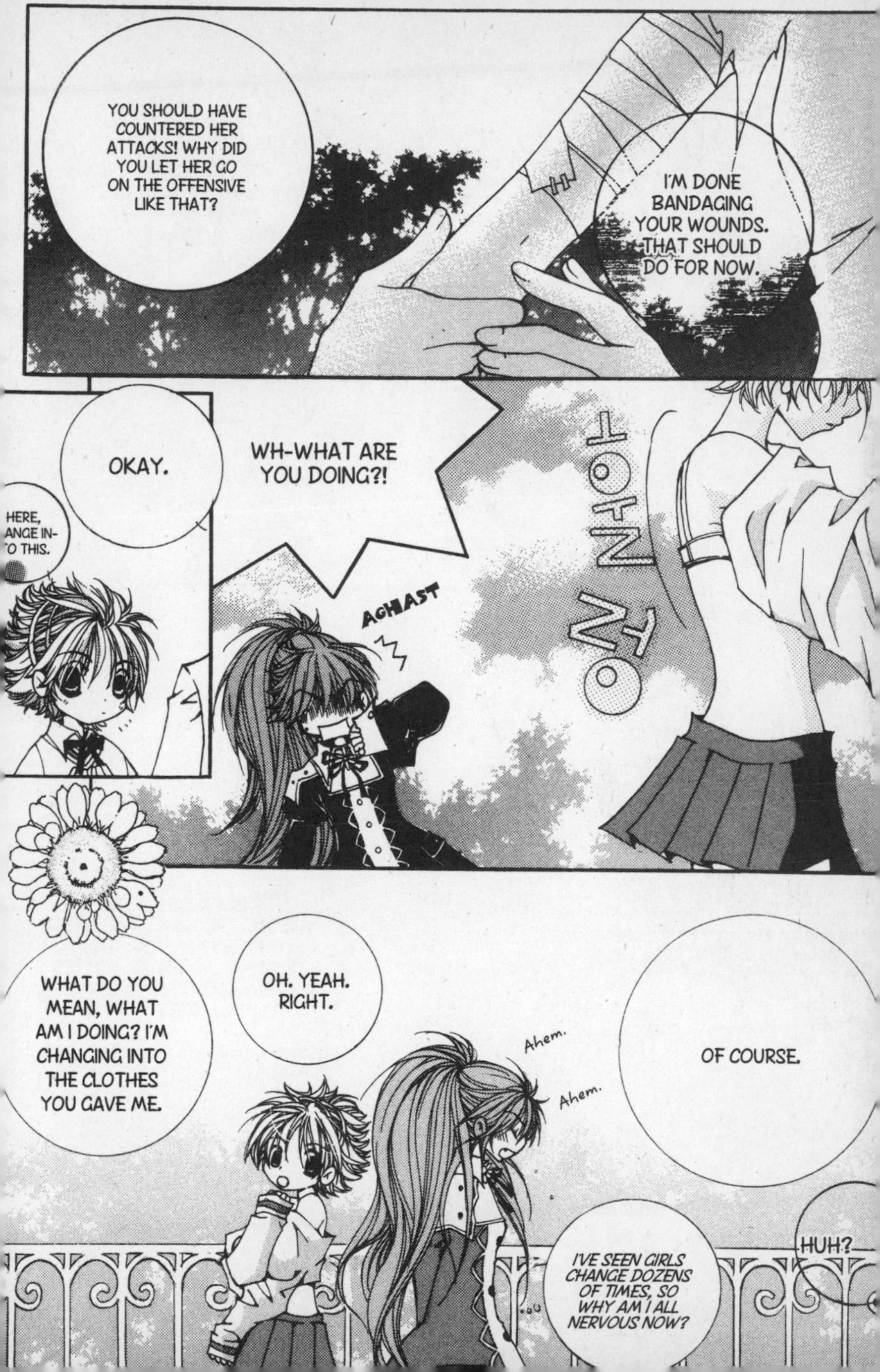
YOU SHOULD HAVE COUNTERED HER ATTACKS! WHY DID YOU LET HER GO ON THE OFFENSIVE LIKE THAT?
I'M DONE BANDAGING YOUR WOUNDS. THAT SHOULD DO FOR NOW.
OKAY.
HERE, ANGE IN- O THIS.
WH-WHAT ARE YOU DOING?!
AGHAST
TO NOTO
WHAT DO YOU MEAN, WHAT AM I DOING? I'M CHANGING INTO THE CLOTHES YOU GAVE ME.
OH. YEAH. RIGHT.
Ahem.
Ahem.
OF COURSE.
I'VE SEEN GIRLS CHANGE DOZENS OF TIMES, SO WHY AM I ALL NERVOUS NOW?
HUH?

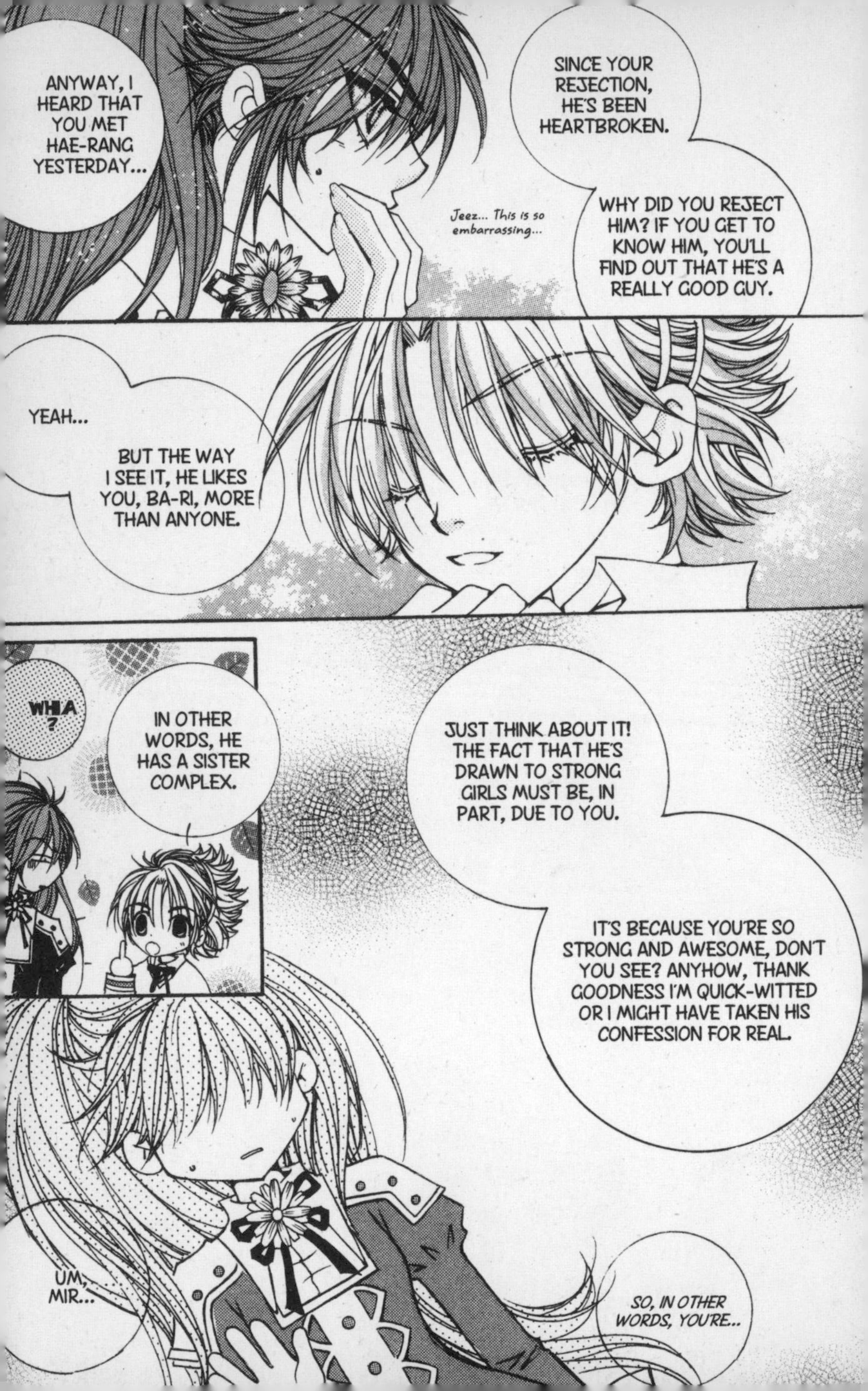
ANYWAY, I HEARD THAT YOU MET HAE-RANG YESTERDAY...
SINCE YOUR REJECTION, HE'S BEEN HEARTBROKEN.
Jeez... This is so embarrassing...
WHY DID YOU REJECT HIM? IF YOU GET TO KNOW HIM, YOU'LL FIND OUT THAT HE'S A REALLY GOOD GUY.
YEAH...
BUT THE WAY I SEE IT, HE LIKES YOU, BA-RI, MORE THAN ANYONE.
WHA?
IN OTHER WORDS, HE HAS A SISTER COMPLEX.
JUST THINK ABOUT IT! THE FACT THAT HE'S DRAWN TO STRONG GIRLS MUST BE, IN PART, DUE TO YOU.
IT'S BECAUSE YOU'RE SO STRONG AND AWESOME, DON'T YOU SEE? ANYHOW, THANK GOODNESS I'M QUICK-WITTED OR I MIGHT HAVE TAKEN HIS CONFESSION FOR REAL.
UM, MIR...
SO, IN OTHER WORDS, YOU'RE...

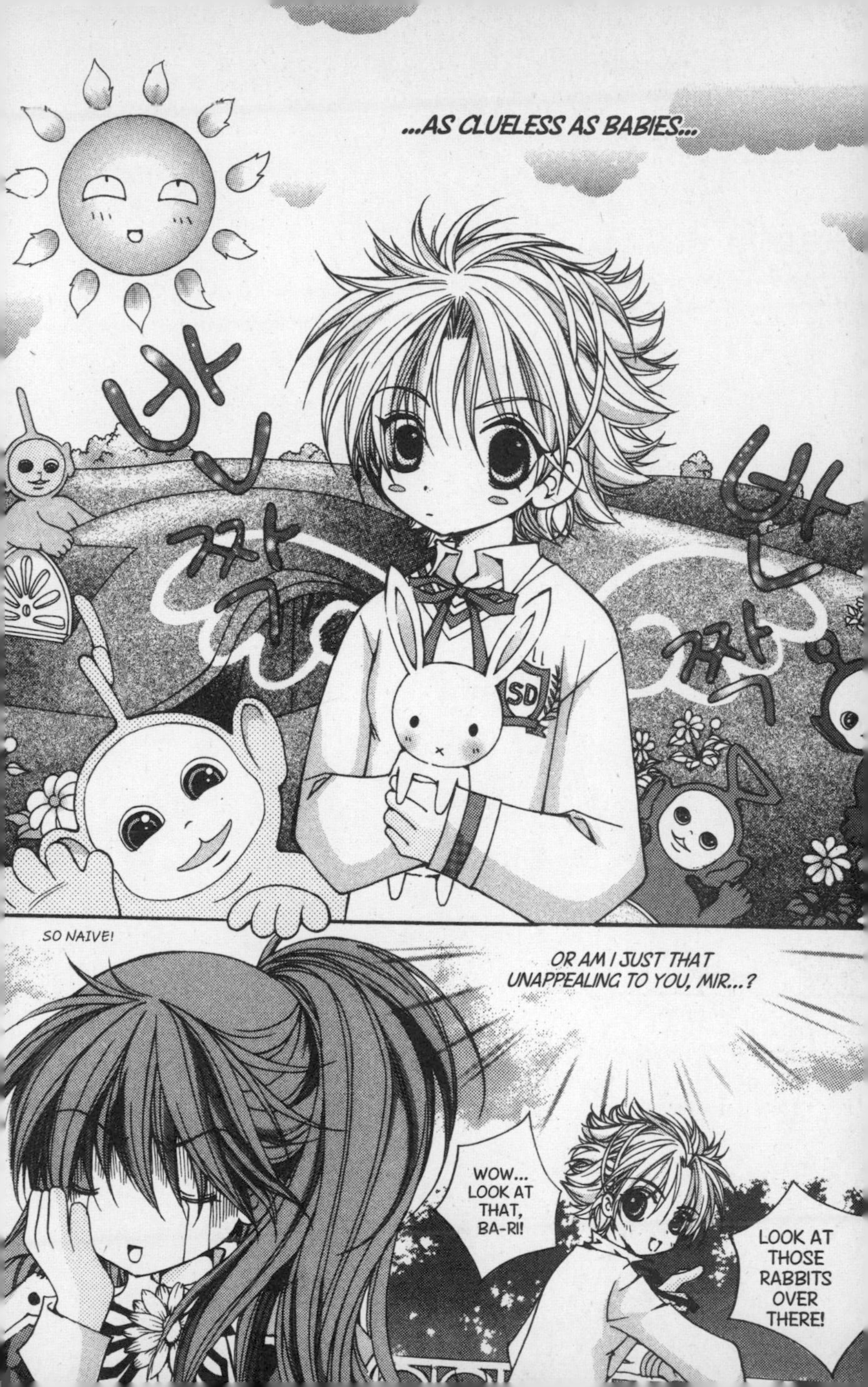
...AS CLUELESS AS BABIES...
반짝
반짝
SO NAIVE!
OR AM I JUST THAT UNAPPEALING TO YOU, MIR...?
WOW... LOOK AT THAT, BA-RI!
LOOK AT THOSE RABBITS OVER THERE!

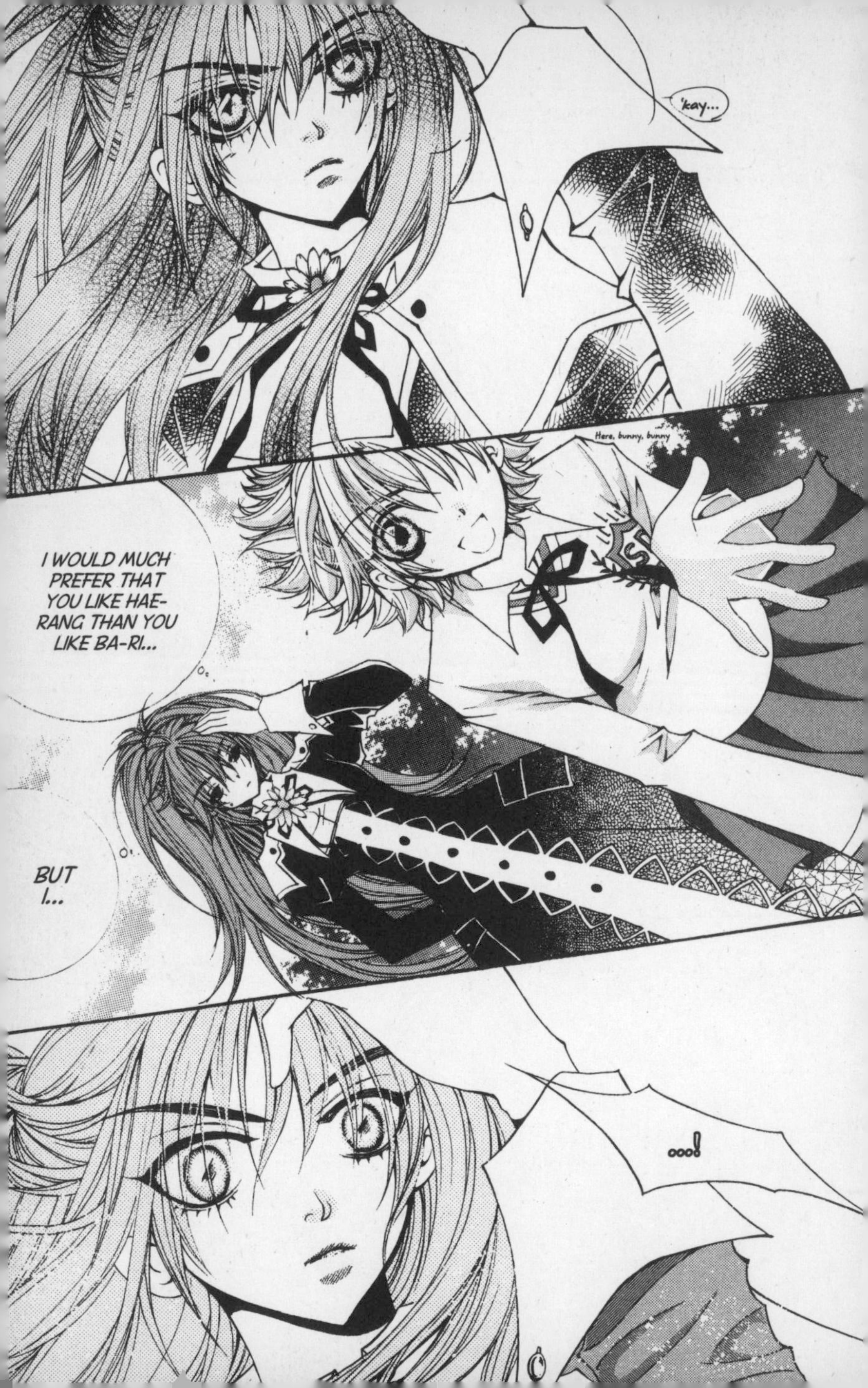
'kay...
Here, bunny, bunny
I WOULD MUCH PREFER THAT YOU LIKE HAE-RANG THAN YOU LIKE BA-RI...
BUT I...
ooo!

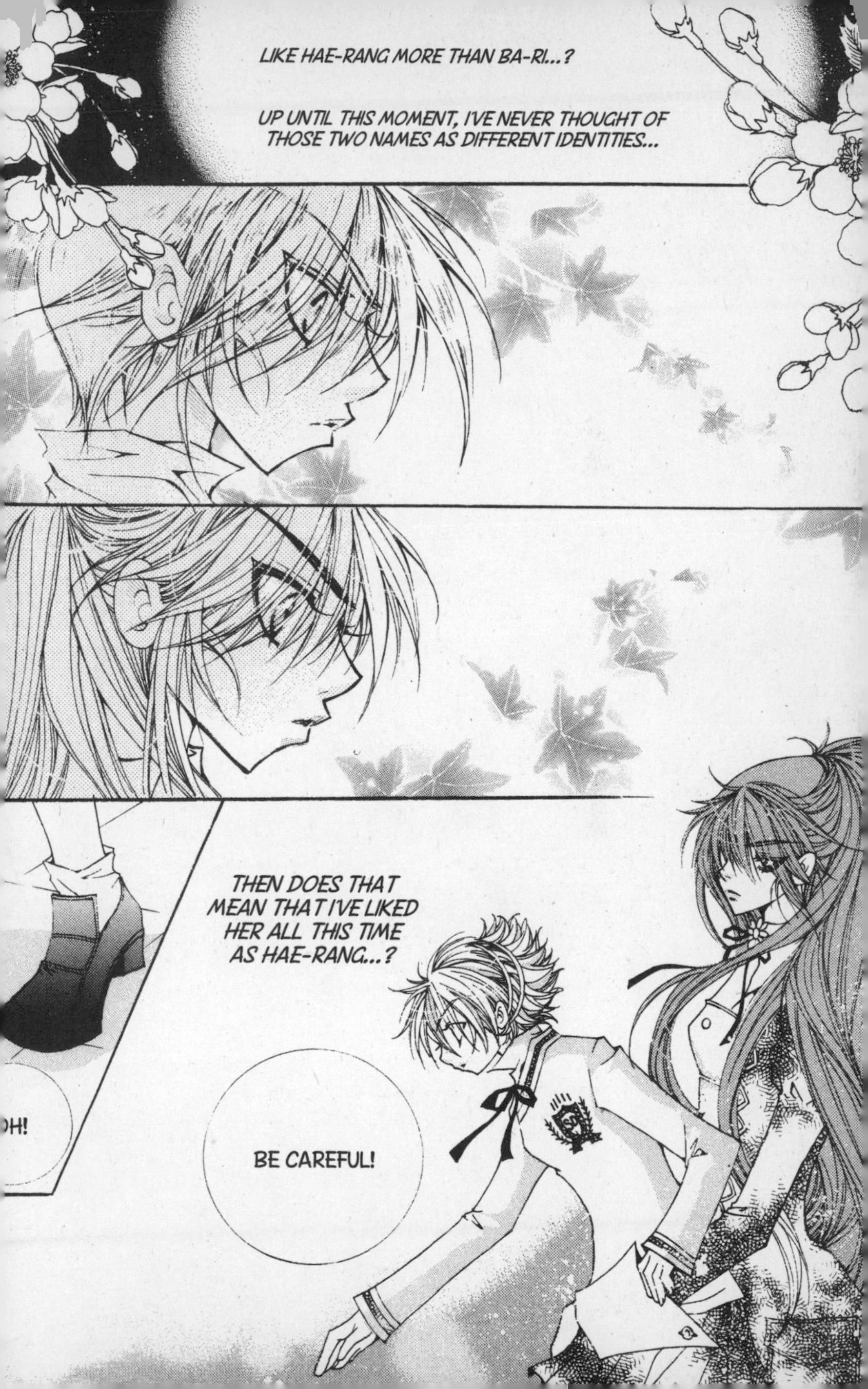
LIKE HAE-RANG MORE THAN BA-RI...?
UP UNTIL THIS MOMENT, I'VE NEVER THOUGHT OF THOSE TWO NAMES AS DIFFERENT IDENTITIES...
THEN DOES THAT MEAN THAT I'VE LIKED HER ALL THIS TIME AS HAE-RANG...?
BE CAREFUL!

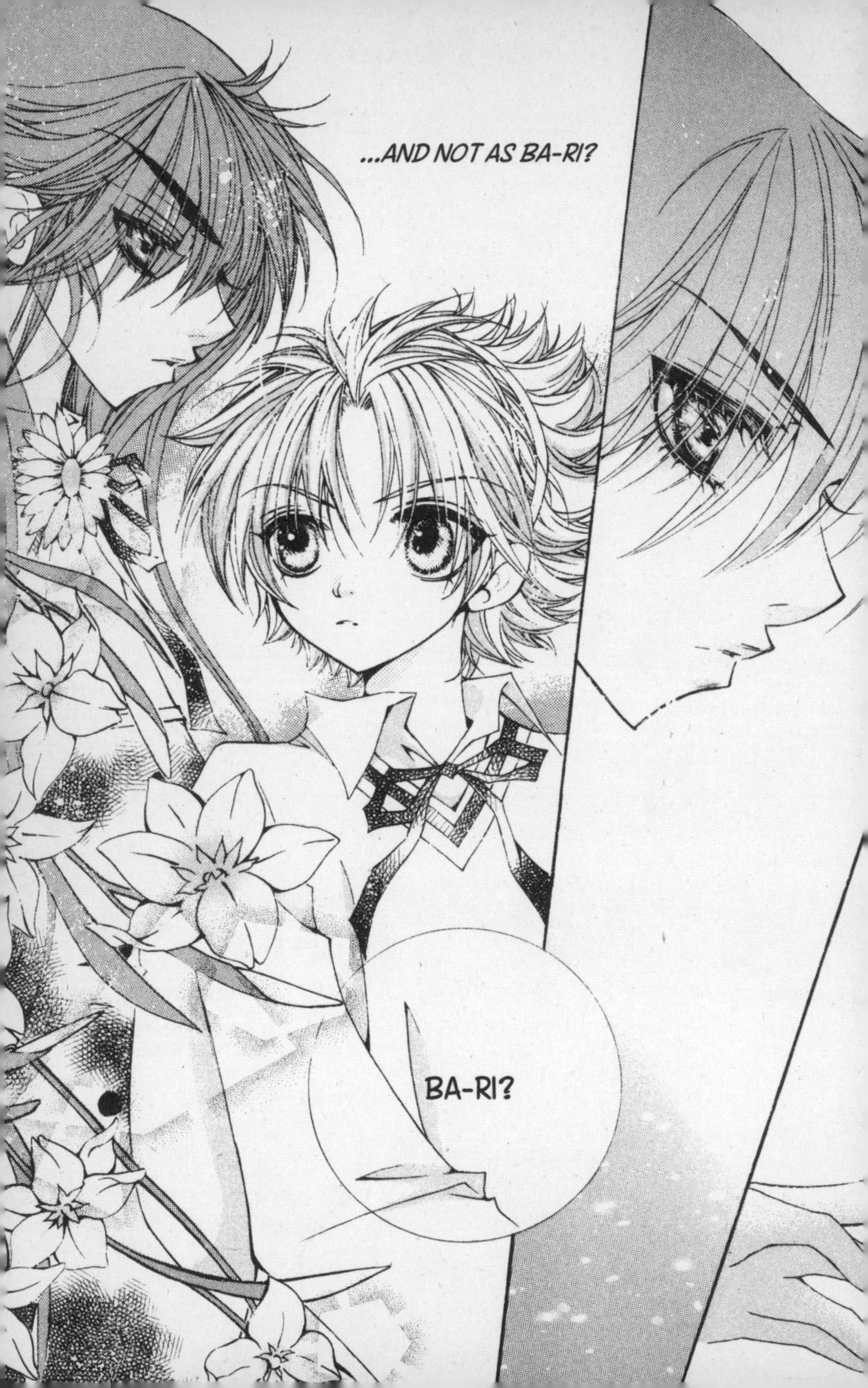
...AND NOT AS BA-RI?
BA-RI?

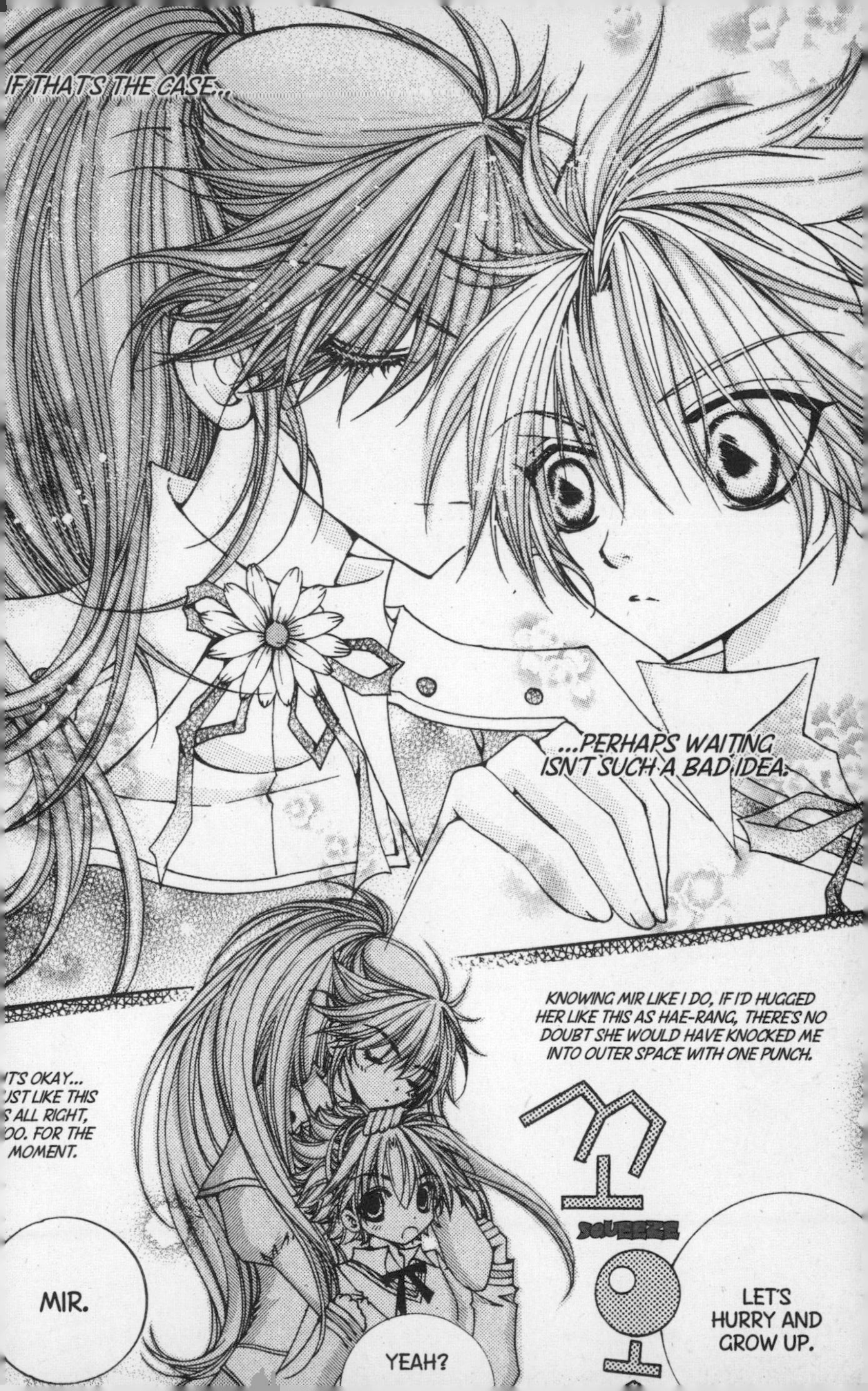
IF THAT'S THE CASE...
...PERHAPS WAITING ISN'T SUCH A BAD IDEA.
KNOWING MIR LIKE I DO, IF I'D HUGGED HER LIKE THIS AS HAE-RANG, THERE'S NO DOUBT SHE WOULD HAVE KNOCKED ME INTO OUTER SPACE WITH ONE PUNCH.
ITS OKAY... UST LIKE THIS S ALL RIGHT, OO. FOR THE MOMENT.
SQUEEZE
MIR.
YEAH?
LET'S HURRY AND GROW UP.

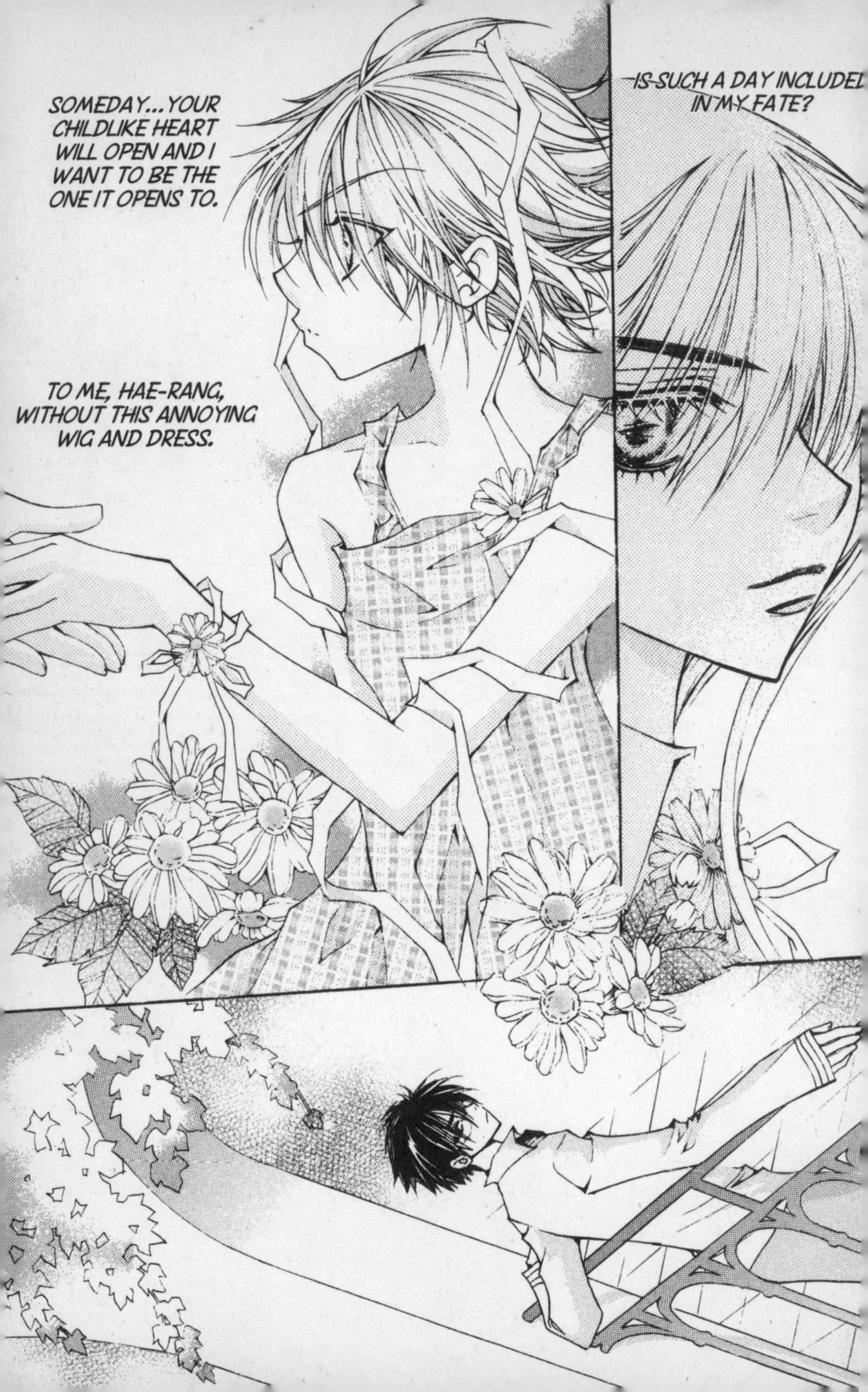
SOMEDAY...YOUR CHILDLIKE HEART WILL OPEN AND I WANT TO BE THE ONE IT OPENS TO.
TO ME, HAE-RANG, WITHOUT THIS ANNOYING WIG AND DRESS.
IS SUCH A DAY INCLUDED IN MY FATE?

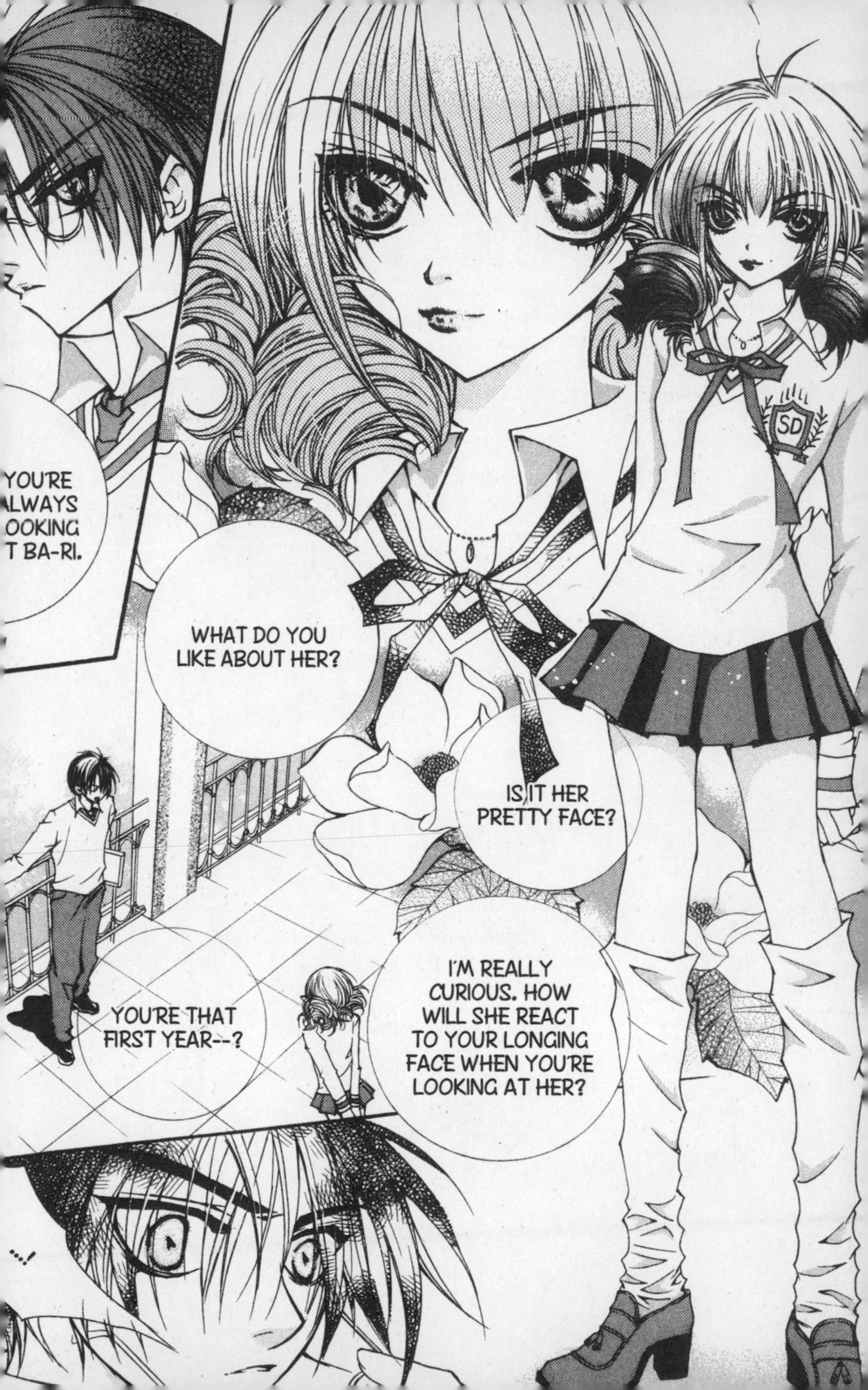
YOU'RE LWAYS OOKING T BA-RI.
YOU'RE THAT FIRST YEAR--?
...!
WHAT DO YOU LIKE ABOUT HER?
IS IT HER PRETTY FACE?
I'M REALLY CURIOUS. HOW WILL SHE REACT TO YOUR LONGING FACE WHEN YOU'RE LOOKING AT HER?

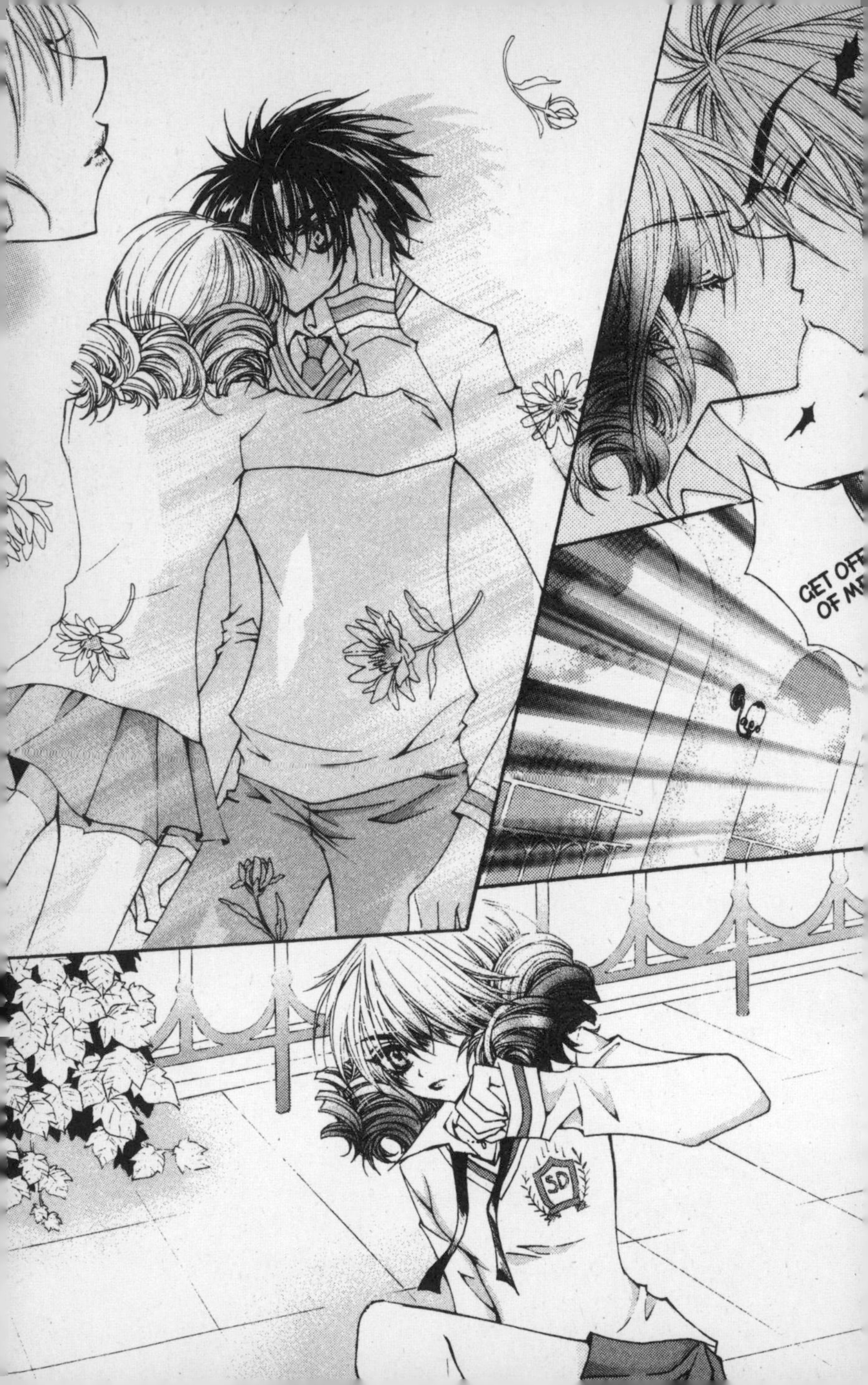
GET OFF OF ME

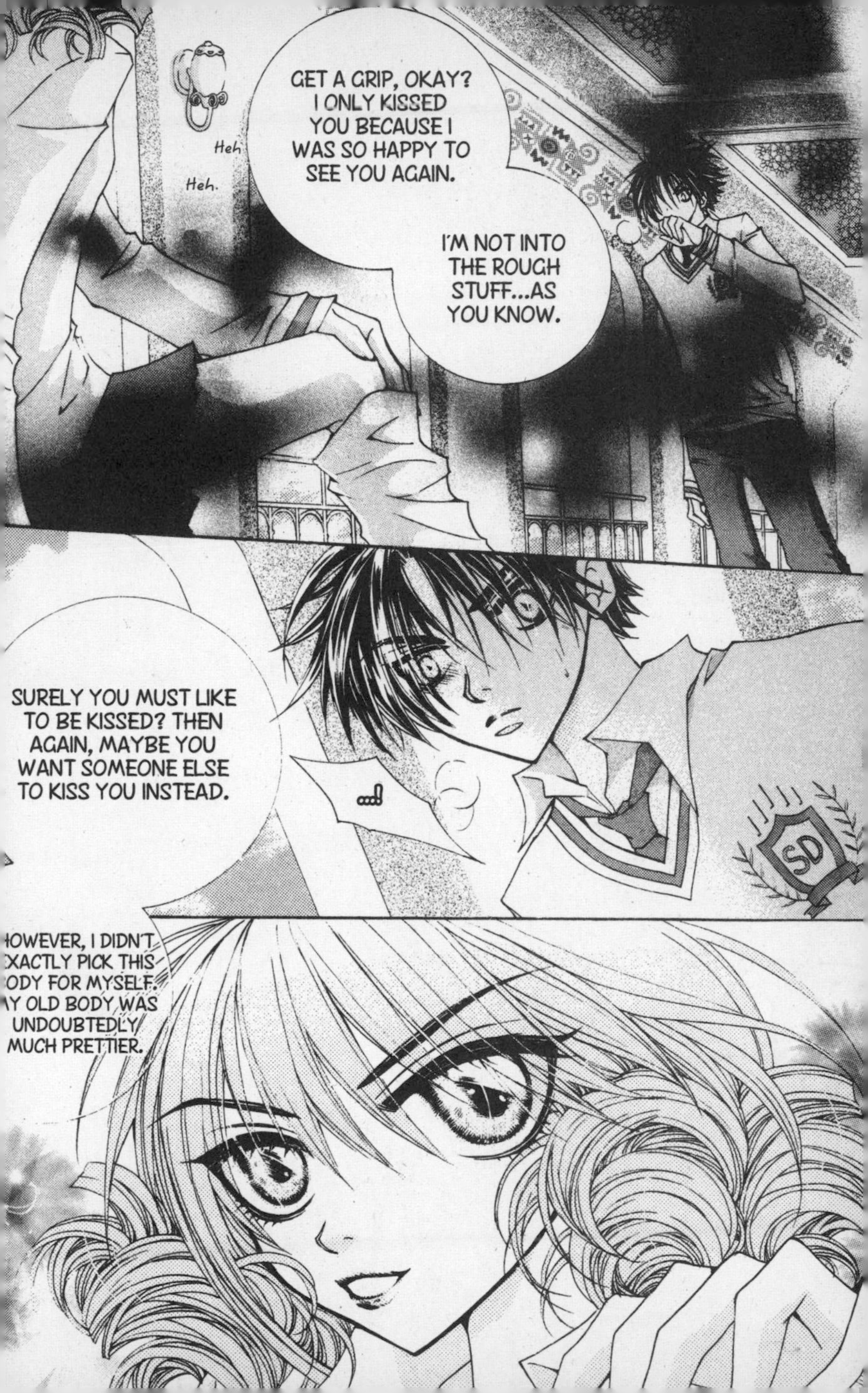
Heh
Heh.
GET A GRIP, OKAY? I ONLY KISSED YOU BECAUSE I WAS SO HAPPY TO SEE YOU AGAIN.
I'M NOT INTO THE ROUGH STUFF...AS YOU KNOW.
SURELY YOU MUST LIKE TO BE KISSED? THEN AGAIN, MAYBE YOU WANT SOMEONE ELSE TO KISS YOU INSTEAD.
SD
OWEVER, I DIDN'T XACTLY PICK THIS ODY FOR MYSELF. Y OLD BODY WAS UNDOUBTEDLY MUCH PRETTIER.

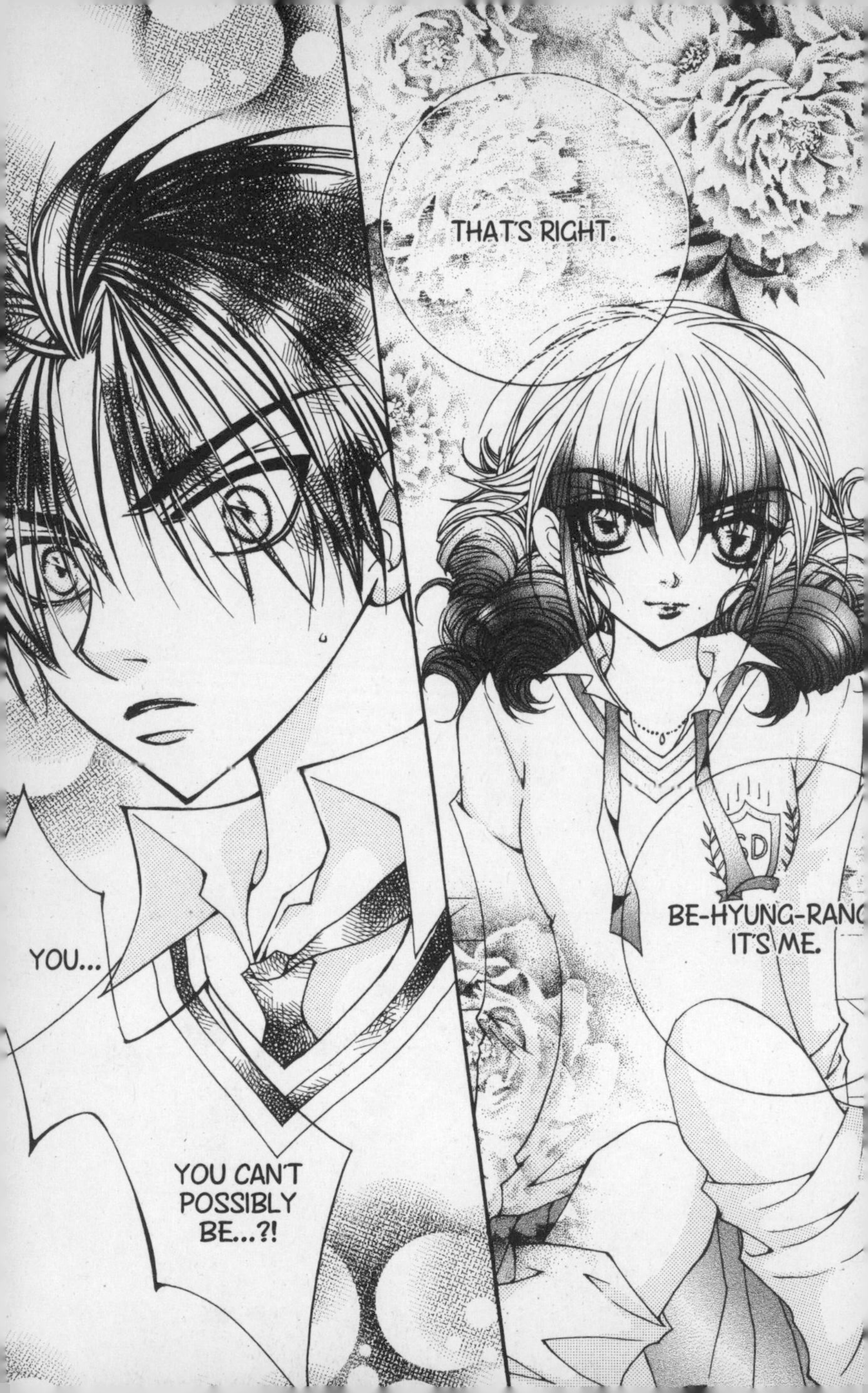
YOU...
YOU CAN'T POSSIBLY BE...?!
THAT'S RIGHT.
BE-HYUNG-RANG IT'S ME.

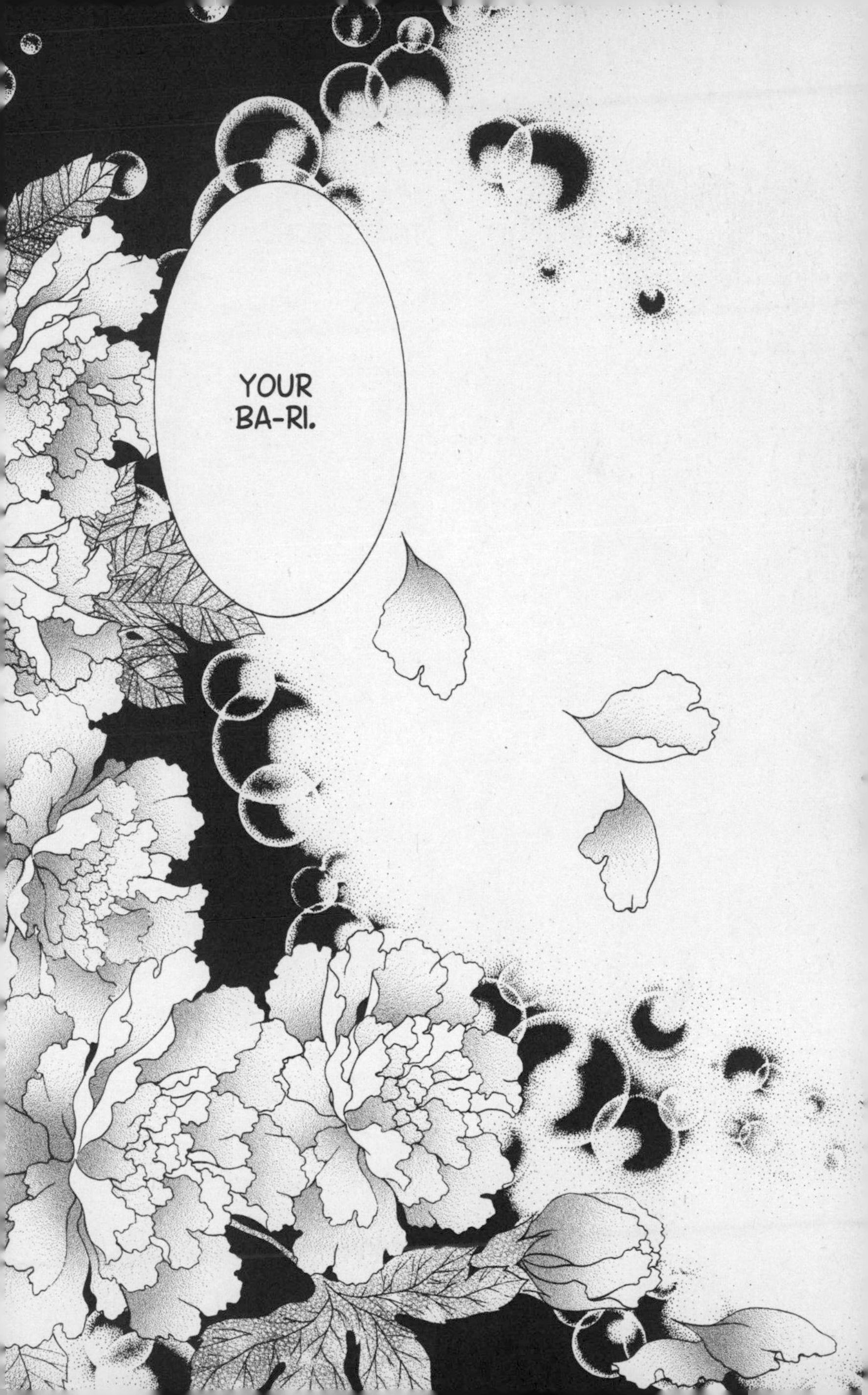
YOUR BA-RI.

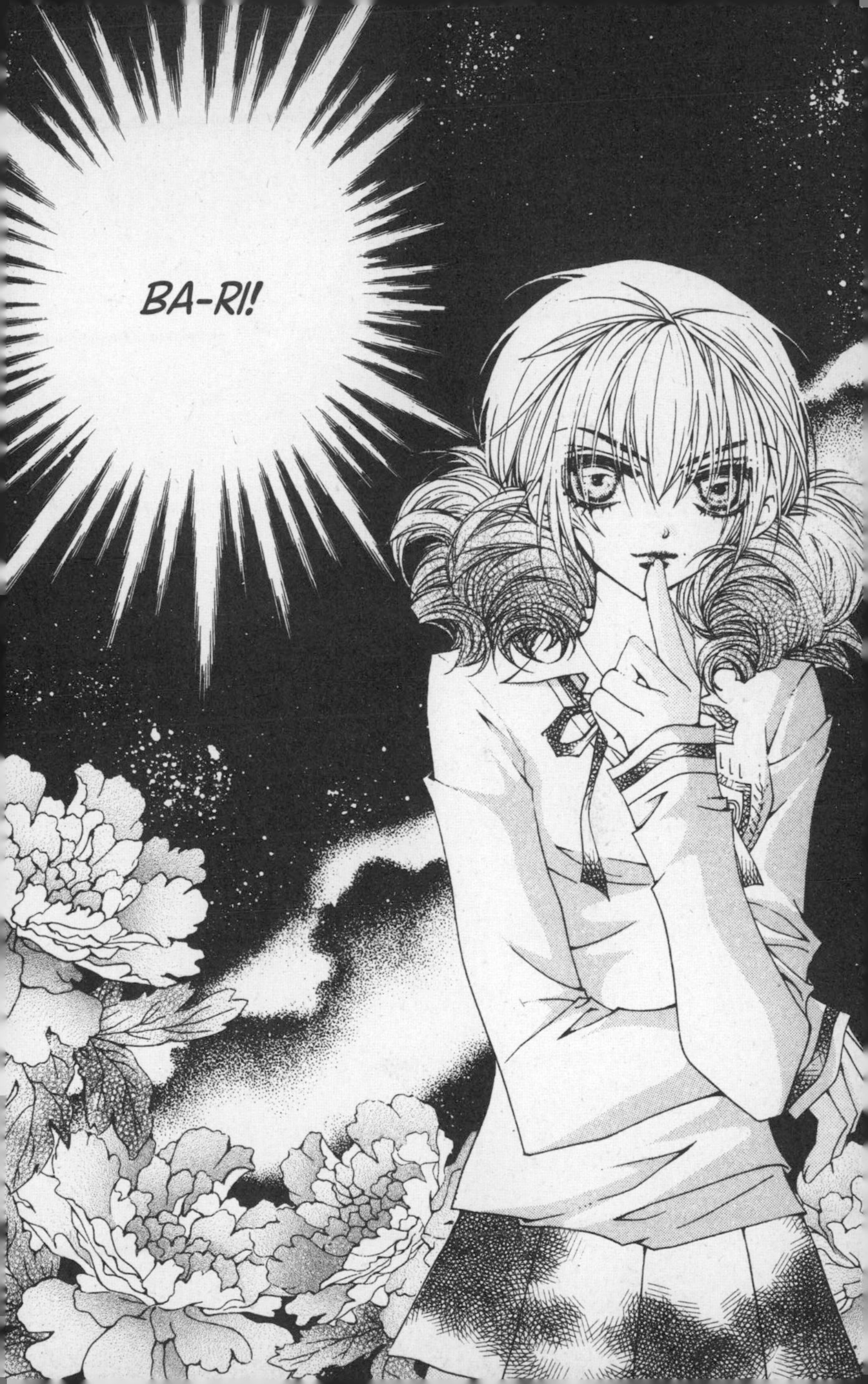
BA-RI!

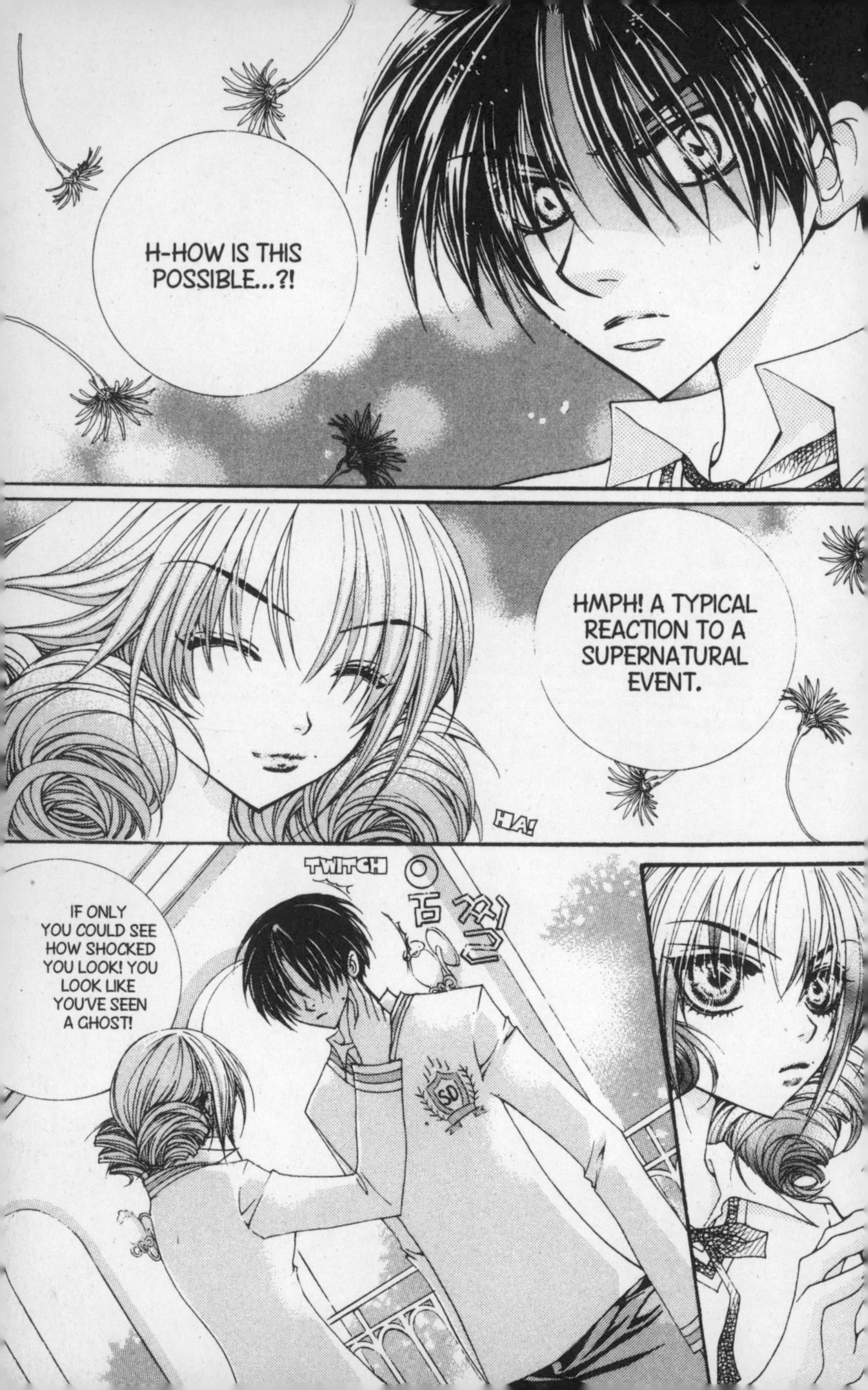
H-HOW IS THIS POSSIBLE...?!
HMPH! A TYPICAL REACTION TO A SUPERNATURAL EVENT.
HA!
TWITCH
IF ONLY YOU COULD SEE HOW SHOCKED YOU LOOK! YOU LOOK LIKE YOU'VE SEEN A GHOST!

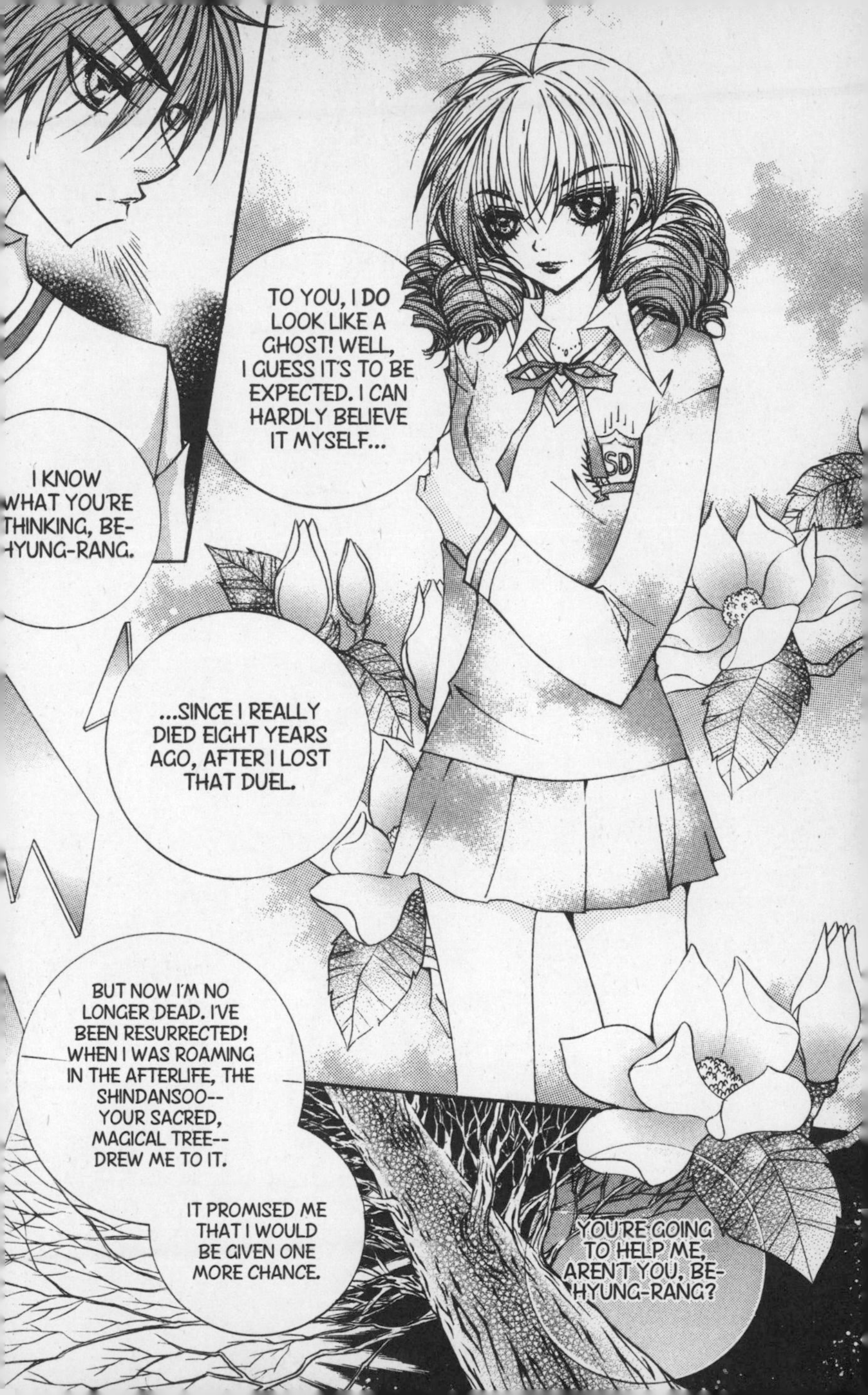
TO YOU, I DO LOOK LIKE A GHOST! WELL, I GUESS IT'S TO BE EXPECTED. I CAN HARDLY BELIEVE IT MYSELF...
I KNOW WHAT YOU'RE THINKING, BE-HYUNG-RANG.
...SINCE I REALLY DIED EIGHT YEARS AGO, AFTER I LOST THAT DUEL.
BUT NOW I'M NO LONGER DEAD. I'VE BEEN RESURRECTED! WHEN I WAS ROAMING IN THE AFTERLIFE, THE SHINDANSOO-- YOUR SACRED, MAGICAL TREE-- DREW ME TO IT.
IT PROMISED ME THAT I WOULD BE GIVEN ONE MORE CHANCE.
YOU'RE GOING TO HELP ME, AREN'T YOU, BE-HYUNG-RANG?

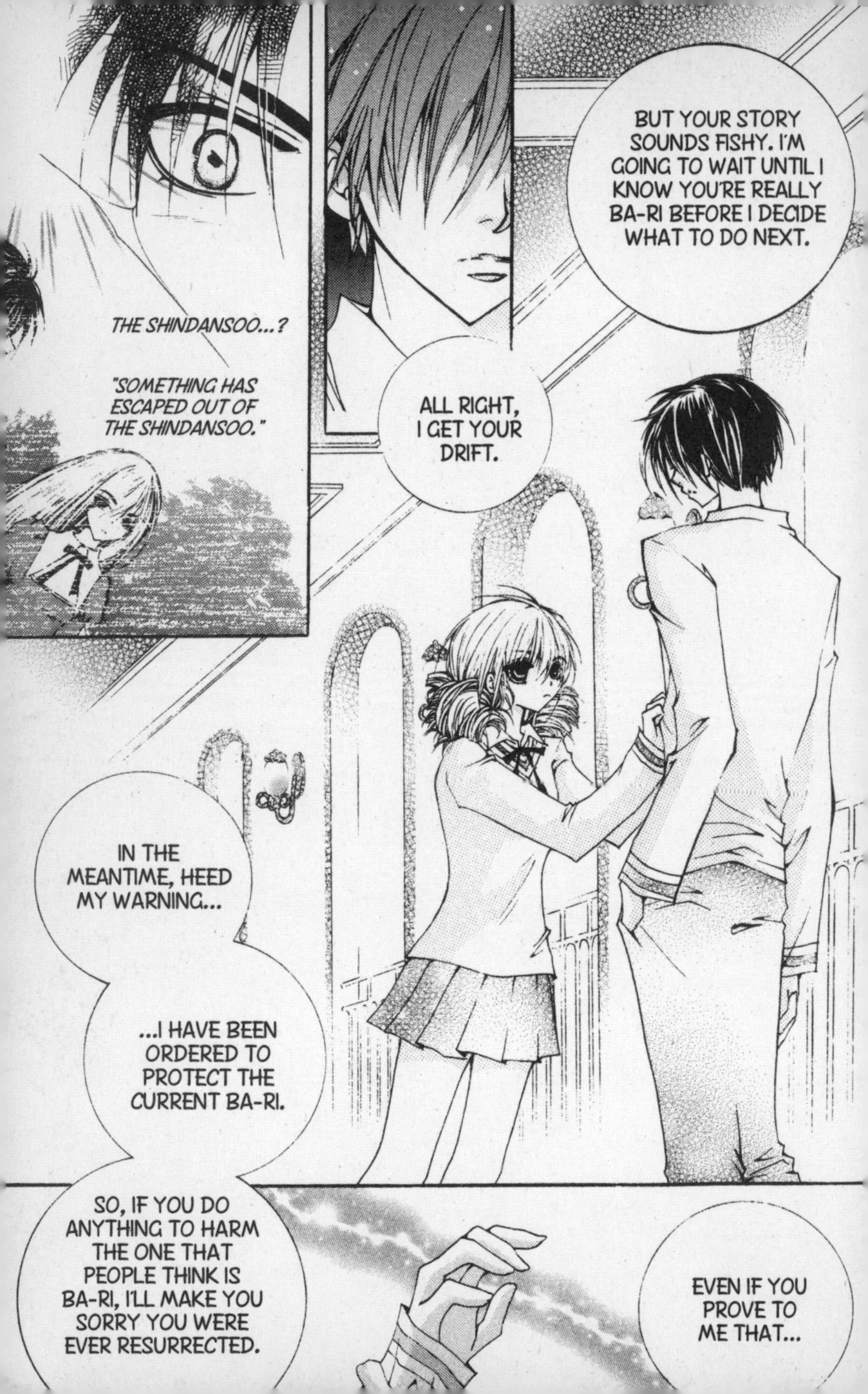
THE SHINDANSOO...?
"SOMETHING HAS ESCAPED OUT OF THE SHINDANSOO."
ALL RIGHT, I GET YOUR DRIFT.
BUT YOUR STORY SOUNDS FISHY. I'M GOING TO WAIT UNTIL I KNOW YOU'RE REALLY BA-RI BEFORE I DECIDE WHAT TO DO NEXT.
IN THE MEANTIME, HEED MY WARNING...
...I HAVE BEEN ORDERED TO PROTECT THE CURRENT BA-RI.
SO, IF YOU DO ANYTHING TO HARM THE ONE THAT PEOPLE THINK IS BA-RI, I'LL MAKE YOU SORRY YOU WERE EVER RESURRECTED.
EVEN IF YOU PROVE TO ME THAT...

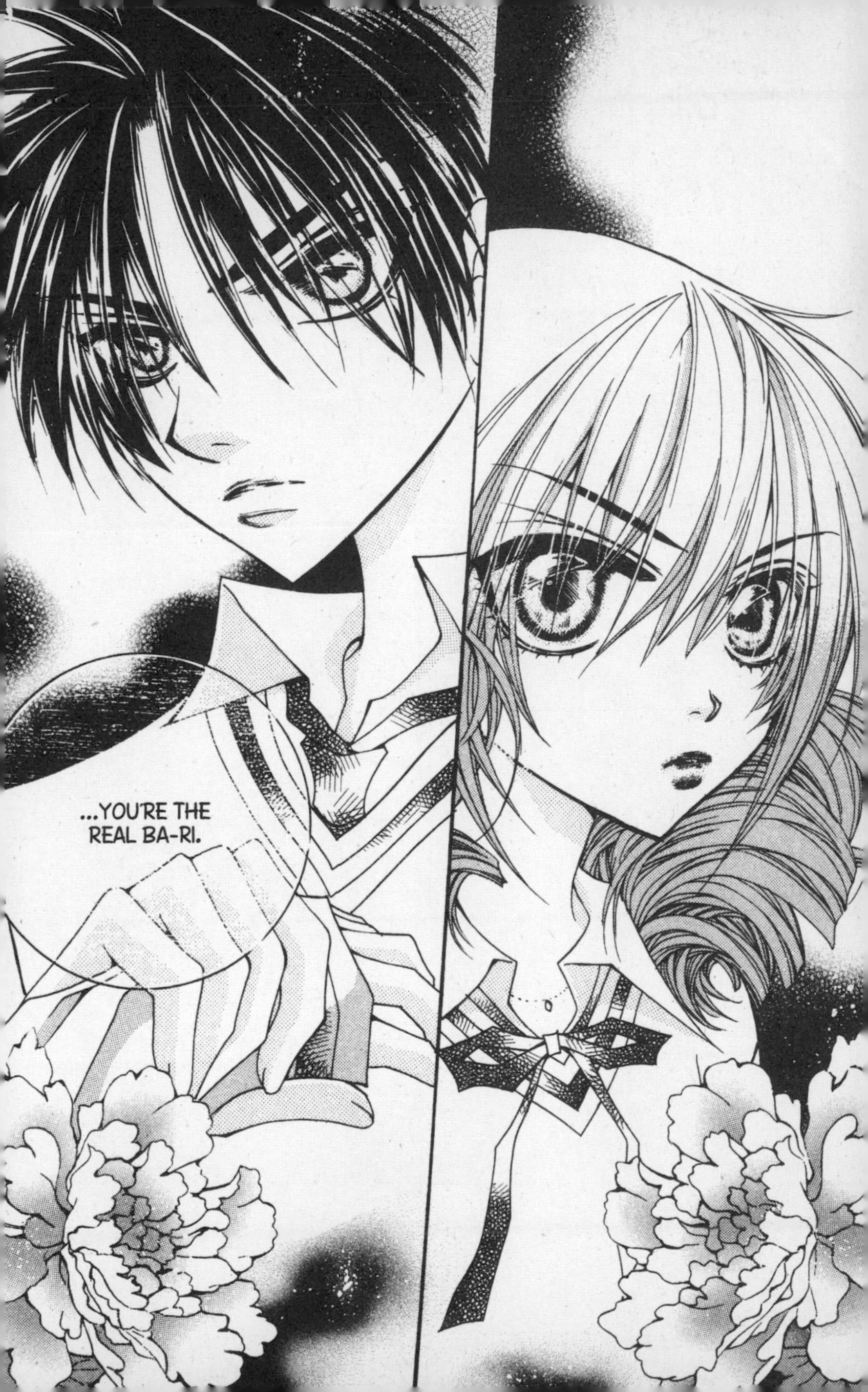
...YOU'RE THE REAL BA-RI.

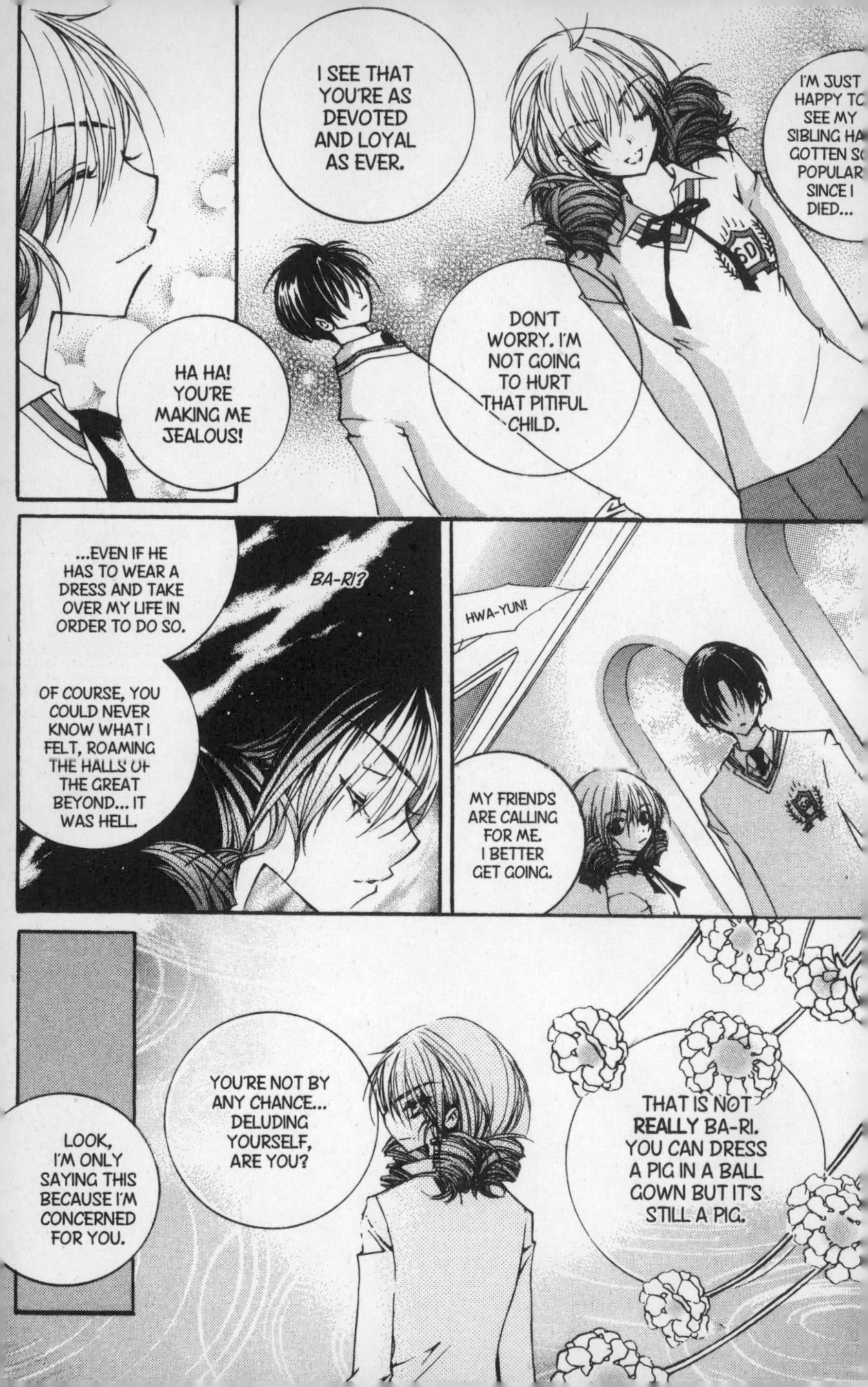

I SEE THAT YOU'RE AS DEVOTED AND LOYAL AS EVER.
I'M JUST HAPPY TO SEE MY SIBLING HA GOTTEN SO POPULAR SINCE I DIED...
HA HA! YOU'RE MAKING ME JEALOUS!
DON'T WORRY. I'M NOT GOING TO HURT THAT PITIFUL CHILD.
...EVEN IF HE HAS TO WEAR A DRESS AND TAKE OVER MY LIFE IN ORDER TO DO SO.
BA-RI?
OF COURSE, YOU COULD NEVER KNOW WHAT I FELT, ROAMING THE HALLS OF THE GREAT BEYOND... IT WAS HELL.
HWA-YUN!
MY FRIENDS ARE CALLING FOR ME. I BETTER GET GOING.
LOOK, I'M ONLY SAYING THIS BECAUSE I'M CONCERNED FOR YOU.
YOU'RE NOT BY ANY CHANCE... DELUDING YOURSELF, ARE YOU?
THAT IS NOT REALLY BA-RI. YOU CAN DRESS A PIG IN A BALL GOWN BUT IT'S STILL A PIG.

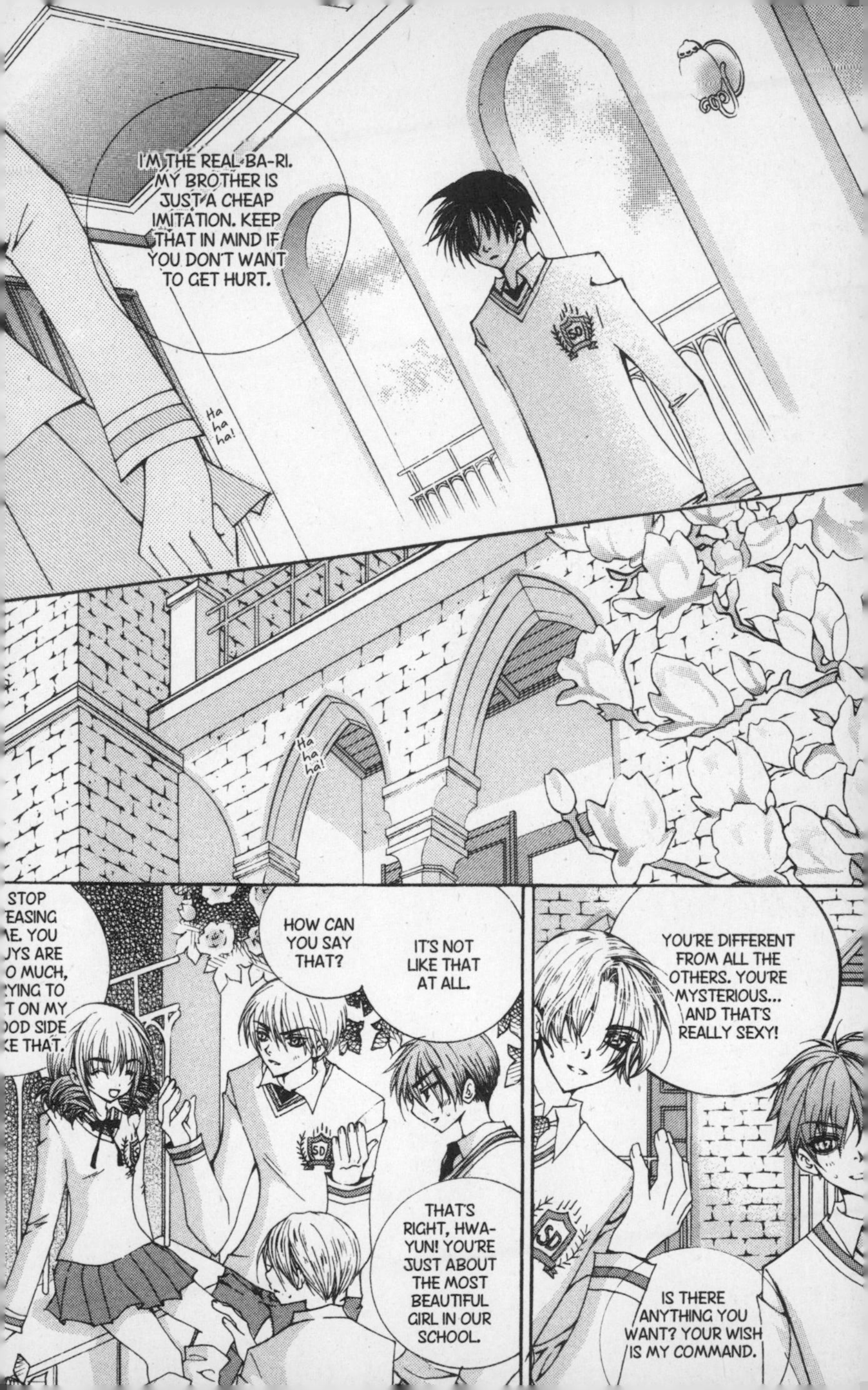
I'M THE REAL BA-RI. MY BROTHER IS JUST A CHEAP IMITATION. KEEP THAT IN MIND IF YOU DON'T WANT TO GET HURT.
Ha ha ha!
Ha ha ha!
STOP TEASING ME. YOU GUYS ARE SO MUCH, TRYING TO GET ON MY GOOD SIDE LIKE THAT.
HOW CAN YOU SAY THAT?
IT'S NOT LIKE THAT AT ALL.
THAT'S RIGHT, HWA-YUN! YOU'RE JUST ABOUT THE MOST BEAUTIFUL GIRL IN OUR SCHOOL.
YOU'RE DIFFERENT FROM ALL THE OTHERS. YOU'RE MYSTERIOUS... AND THAT'S REALLY SEXY!
IS THERE ANYTHING YOU WANT? YOUR WISH IS MY COMMAND.

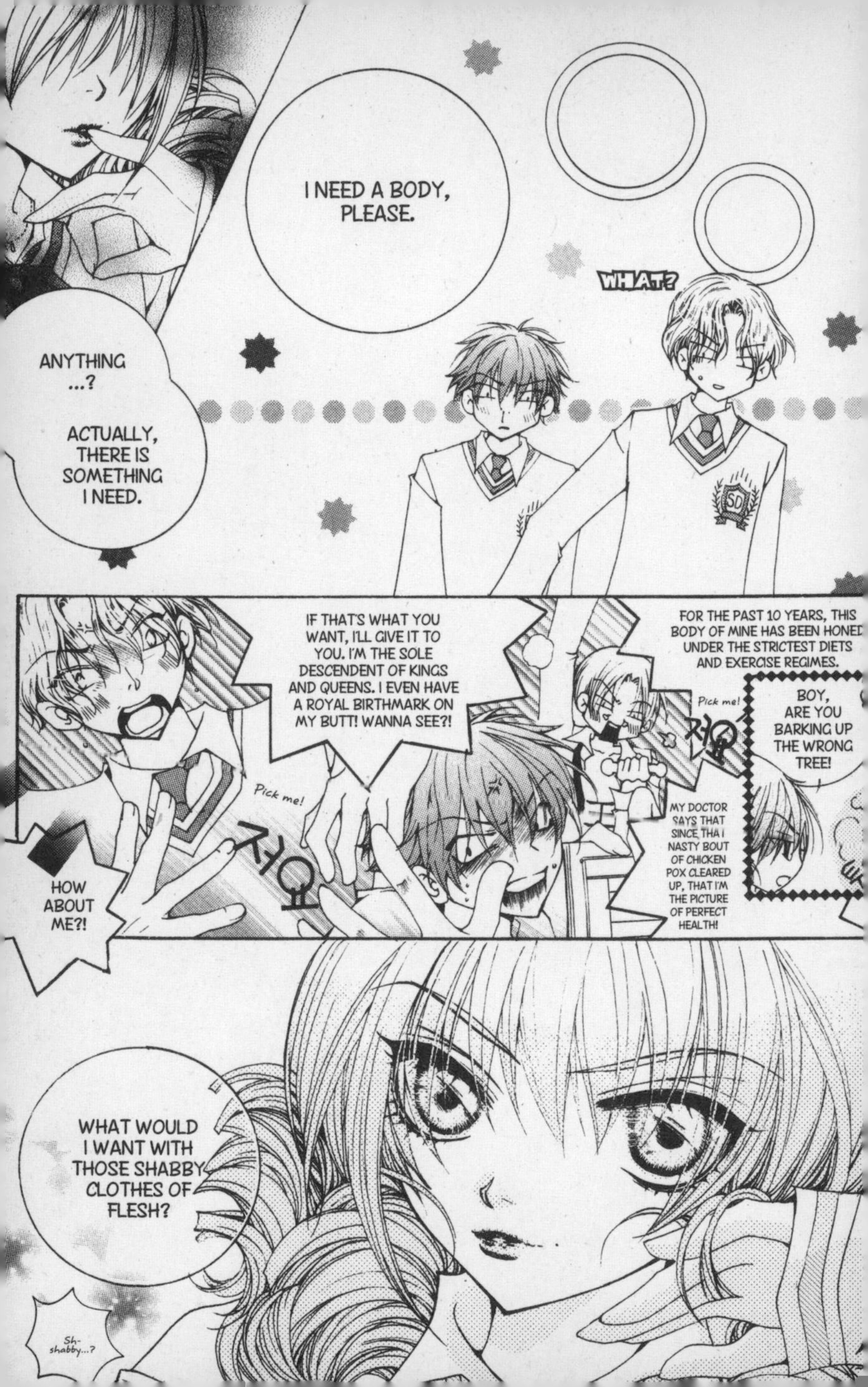
ANYTHING ...?
ACTUALLY, THERE IS SOMETHING I NEED.
I NEED A BODY, PLEASE.
WHAT?
HOW ABOUT ME?!
IF THAT'S WHAT YOU WANT, I'LL GIVE IT TO YOU. I'M THE SOLE DESCENDENT OF KINGS AND QUEENS. I EVEN HAVE A ROYAL BIRTHMARK ON MY BUTT! WANNA SEE?!
Pick me!
FOR THE PAST 10 YEARS, THIS BODY OF MINE HAS BEEN HONED UNDER THE STRICTEST DIETS AND EXERCISE REGIMES.
Pick me!
MY DOCTOR SAYS THAT SINCE THAT NASTY BOUT OF CHICKEN POX CLEARED UP, THAT I'M THE PICTURE OF PERFECT HEALTH!
BOY, ARE YOU BARKING UP THE WRONG TREE!
WHAT WOULD I WANT WITH THOSE SHABBY CLOTHES OF FLESH?
Sh-shabby...?

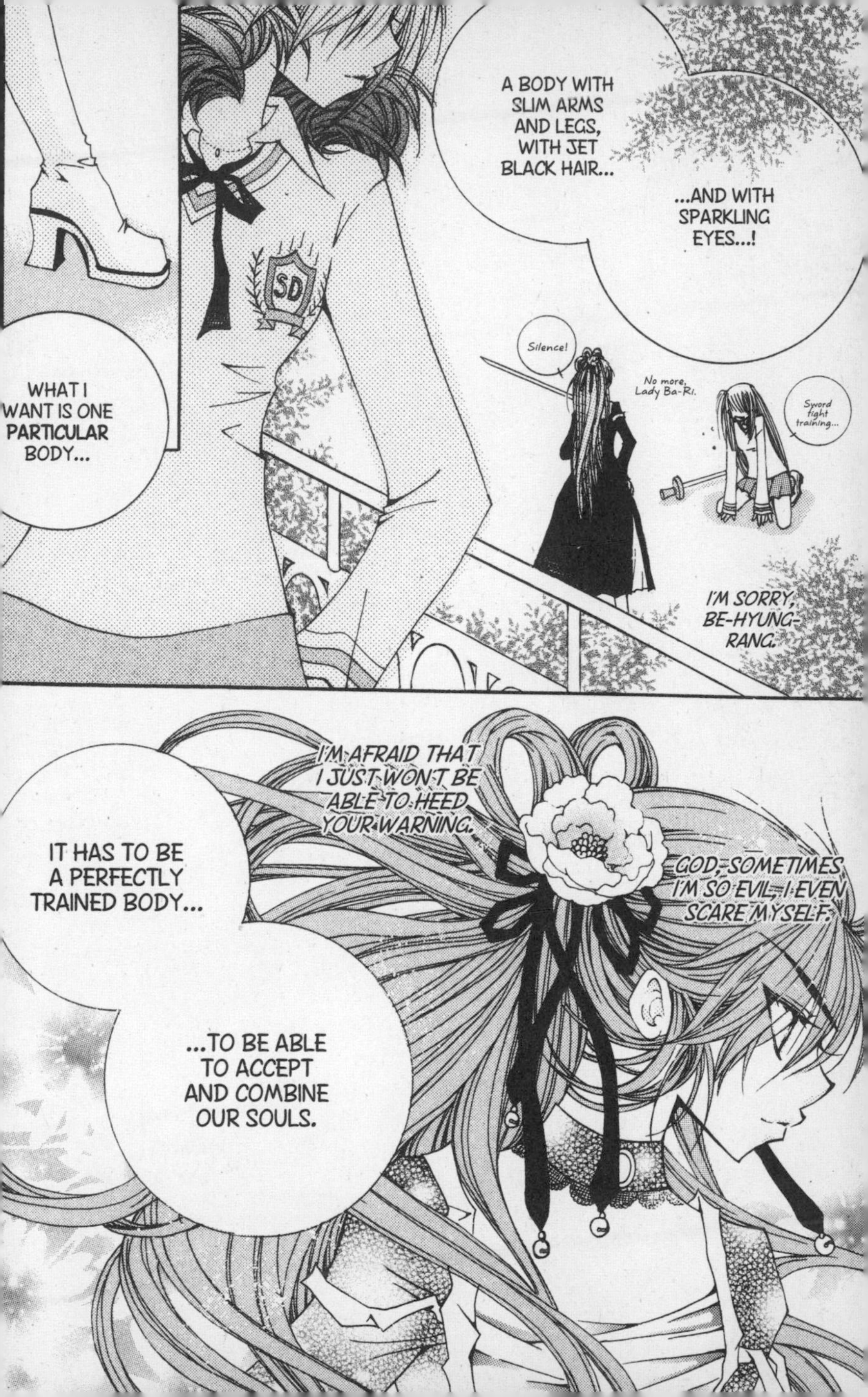

WHAT I WANT IS ONE **PARTICULAR** BODY...
A BODY WITH SLIM ARMS AND LEGS, WITH JET BLACK HAIR...
...AND WITH SPARKLING EYES...!
Silence!
No more, Lady Ba-Ri.
Sword fight training...
I'M SORRY, BE-HYUNG-RANG.
IT HAS TO BE A PERFECTLY TRAINED BODY...
...TO BE ABLE TO ACCEPT AND COMBINE OUR SOULS.
I'M AFRAID THAT I JUST WON'T BE ABLE TO HEED YOUR WARNING.
GOD, SOMETIMES I'M SO EVIL, I EVEN SCARE MYSELF.

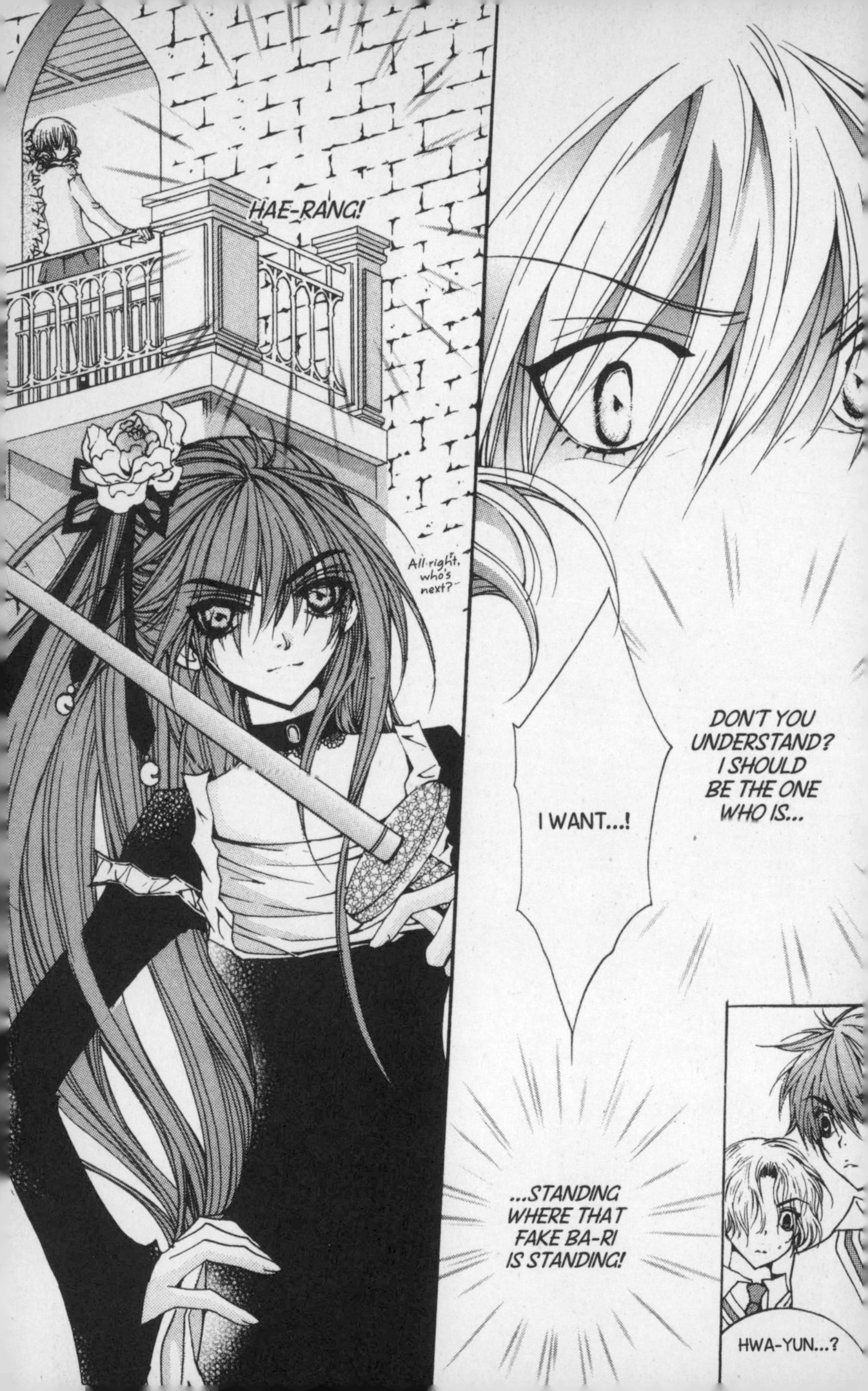
HAE-RANG!
All-right, who's next?
I WANT...!
DON'T YOU UNDERSTAND? I SHOULD BE THE ONE WHO IS...
...STANDING WHERE THAT FAKE BA-RI IS STANDING!
HWA-YUN...?

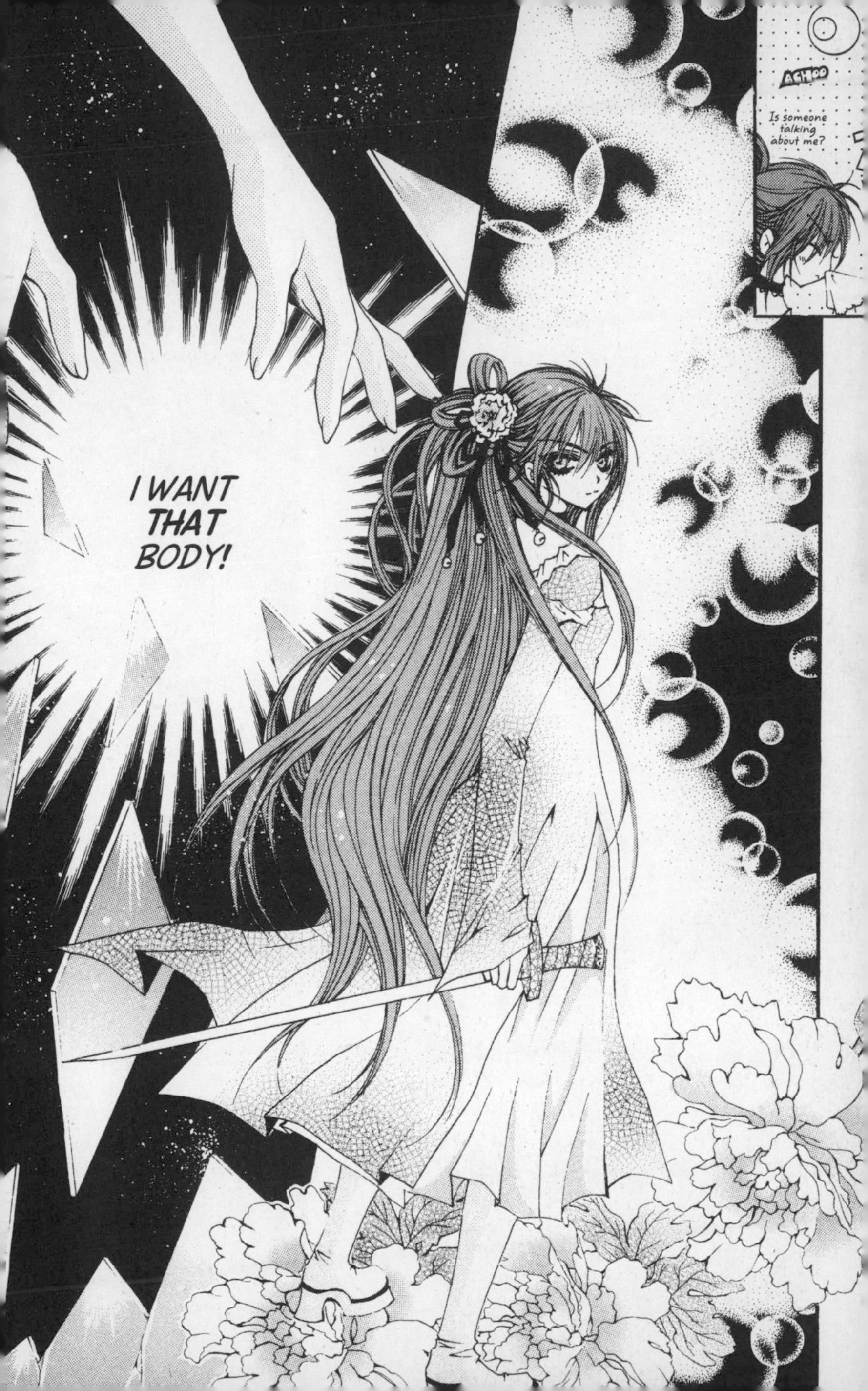
I WANT THAT BODY!
ACHOO
Is someone talking about me?

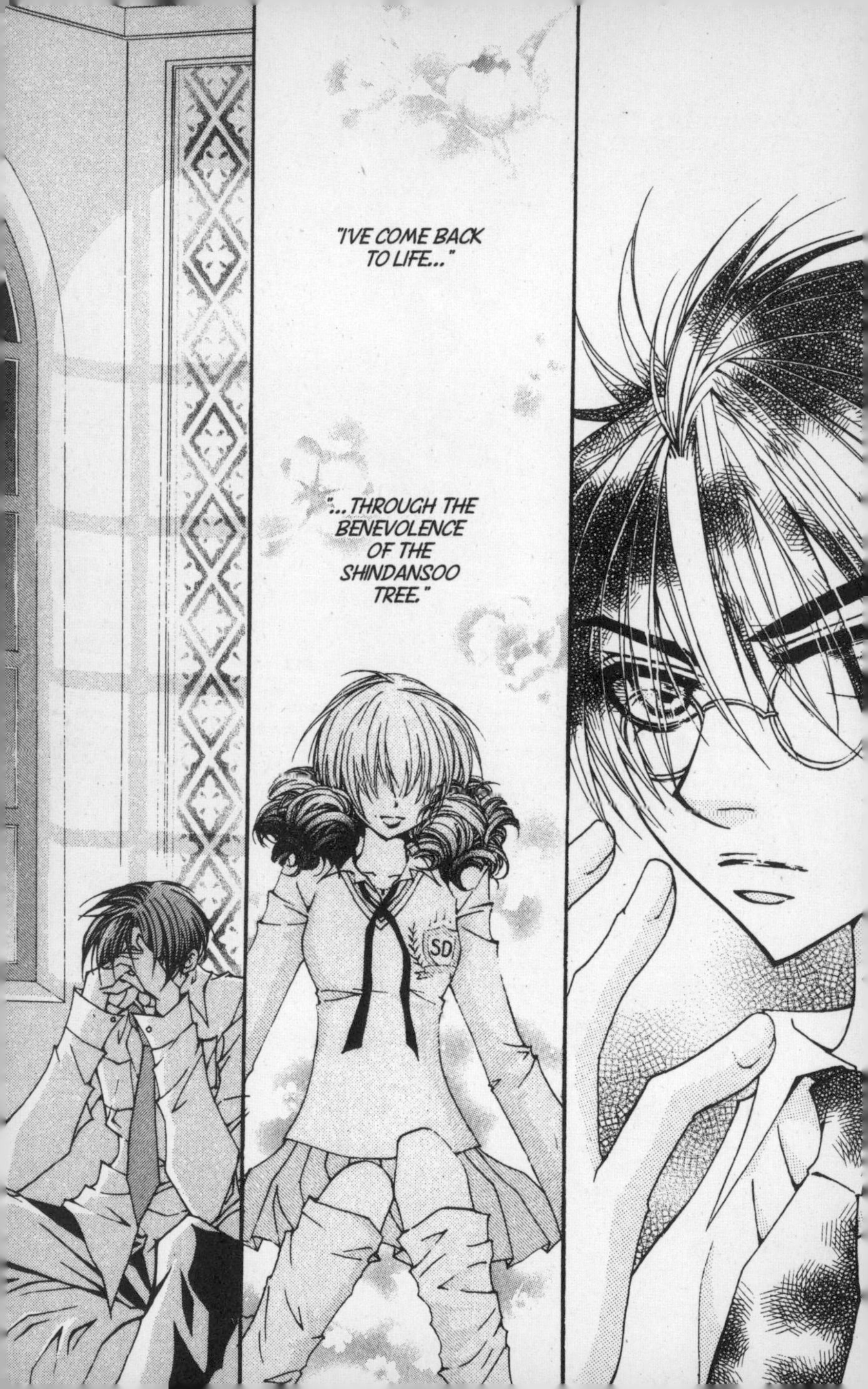
"I'VE COME BACK TO LIFE..."
"...THROUGH THE BENEVOLENCE OF THE SHINDANSOO TREE."
SD

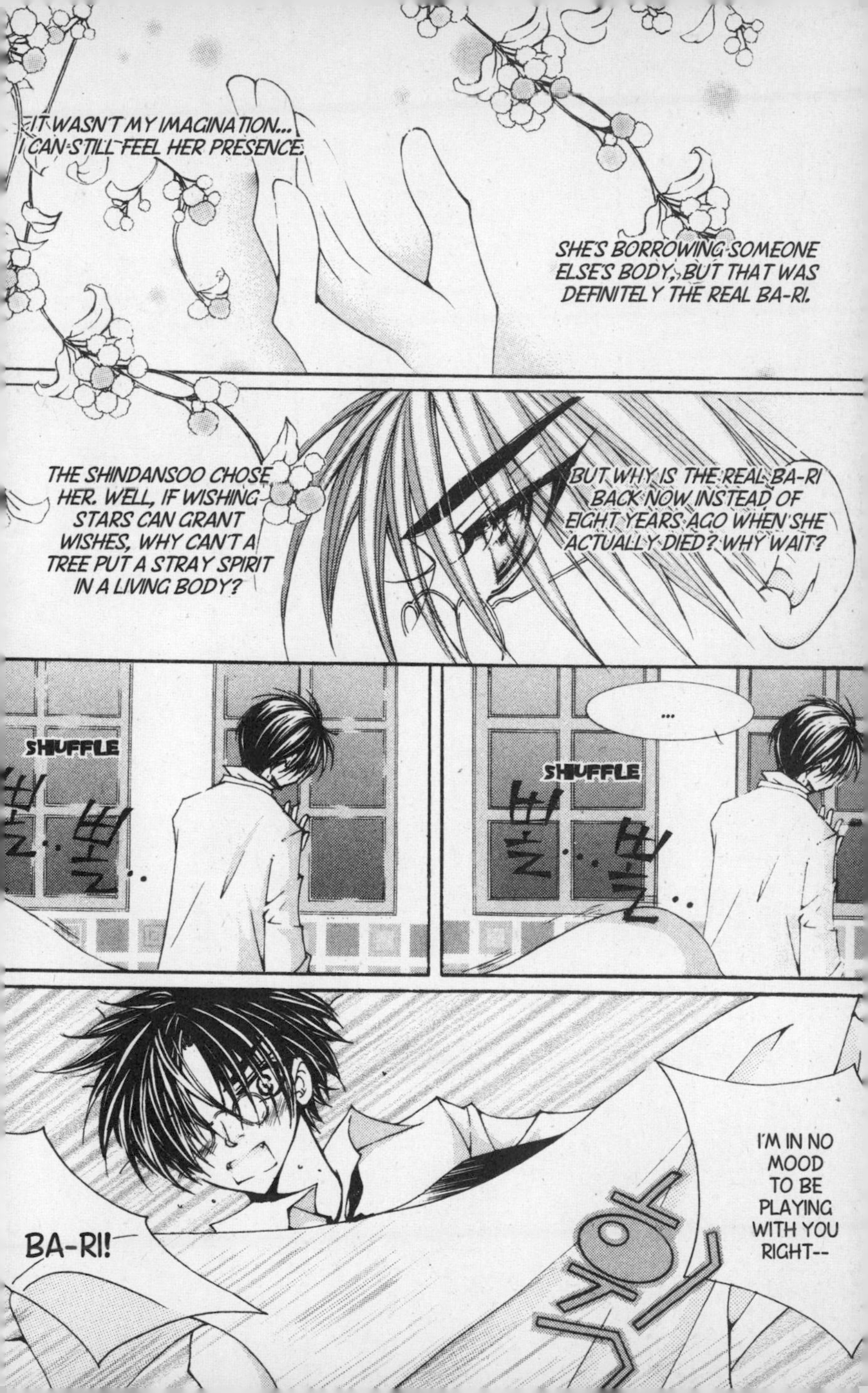
IT WASN'T MY IMAGINATION... I CAN STILL FEEL HER PRESENCE.
SHE'S BORROWING SOMEONE ELSE'S BODY, BUT THAT WAS DEFINITELY THE REAL BA-RI.
THE SHINDANSOO CHOSE HER. WELL, IF WISHING STARS CAN GRANT WISHES, WHY CAN'T A TREE PUT A STRAY SPIRIT IN A LIVING BODY?
BUT WHY IS THE REAL BA-RI BACK NOW INSTEAD OF EIGHT YEARS AGO WHEN SHE ACTUALLY DIED? WHY WAIT?
SHUFFLE
...
SHUFFLE
BA-RI!
I'M IN NO MOOD TO BE PLAYING WITH YOU RIGHT--

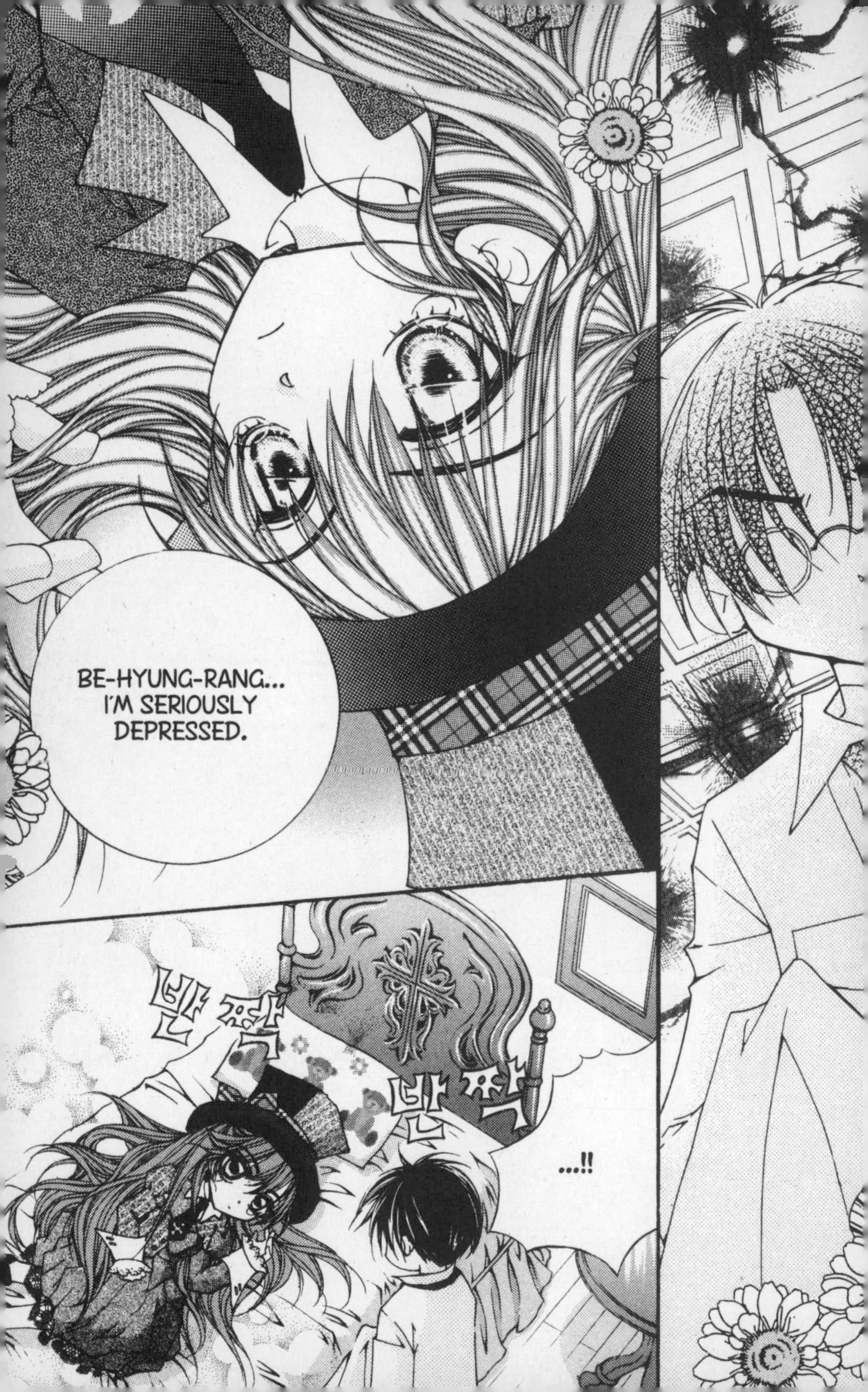
BE-HYUNG-RANG... I'M SERIOUSLY DEPRESSED.
...!!

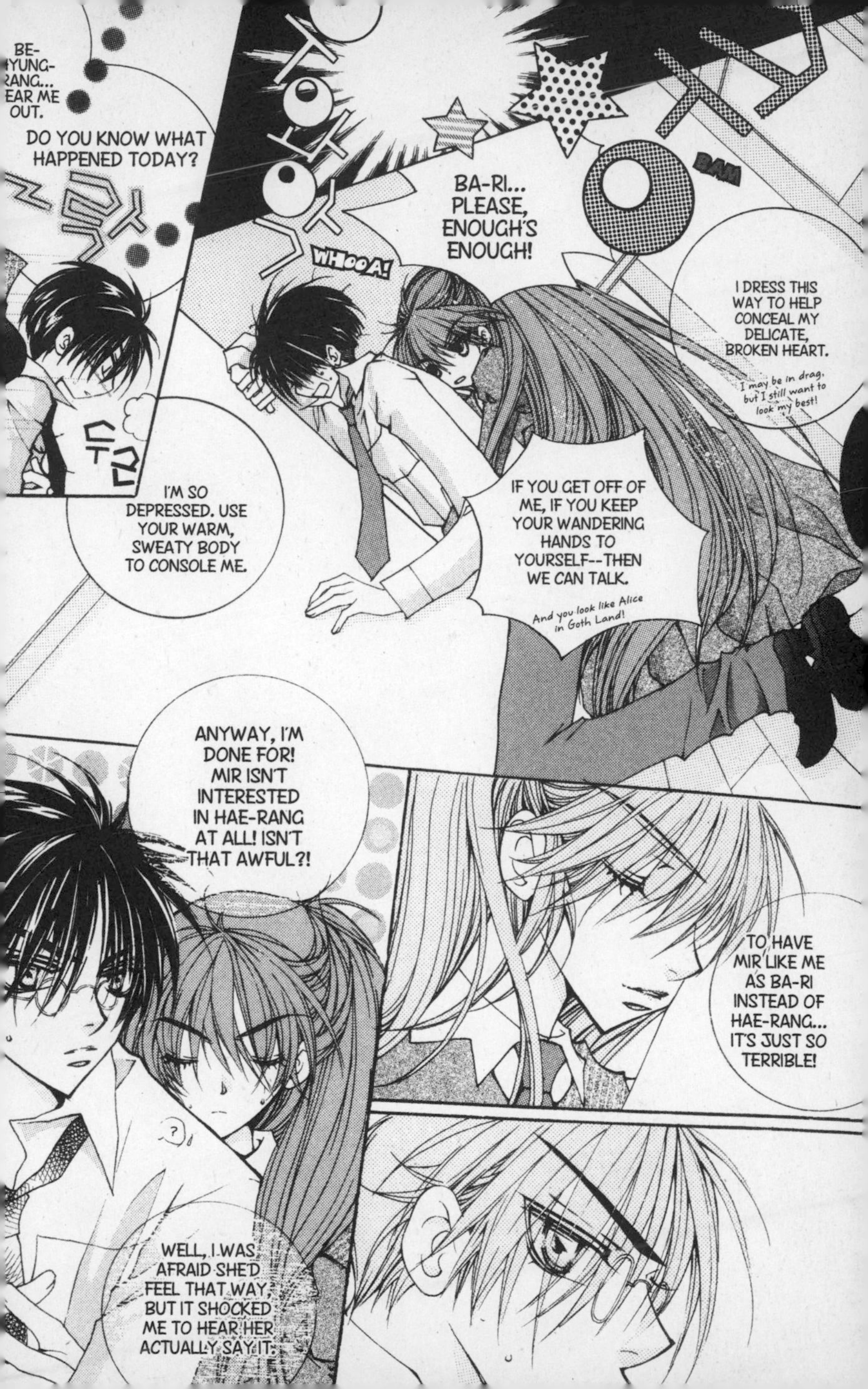
BE- YUNG- RANG... EAR ME OUT.
DO YOU KNOW WHAT HAPPENED TODAY?
I'M SO DEPRESSED. USE YOUR WARM, SWEATY BODY TO CONSOLE ME.
WHOOA!
BA-RI... PLEASE, ENOUGH'S ENOUGH!
BAM
I DRESS THIS WAY TO HELP CONCEAL MY DELICATE, BROKEN HEART.
I may be in drag, but I still want to look my best!
IF YOU GET OFF OF ME, IF YOU KEEP YOUR WANDERING HANDS TO YOURSELF--THEN WE CAN TALK.
And you look like Alice in Goth Land!
ANYWAY, I'M DONE FOR! MIR ISN'T INTERESTED IN HAE-RANG AT ALL! ISN'T THAT AWFUL?!
?
WELL, I WAS AFRAID SHE'D FEEL THAT WAY, BUT IT SHOCKED ME TO HEAR HER ACTUALLY SAY IT.
TO HAVE MIR LIKE ME AS BA-RI INSTEAD OF HAE-RANG... IT'S JUST SO TERRIBLE!

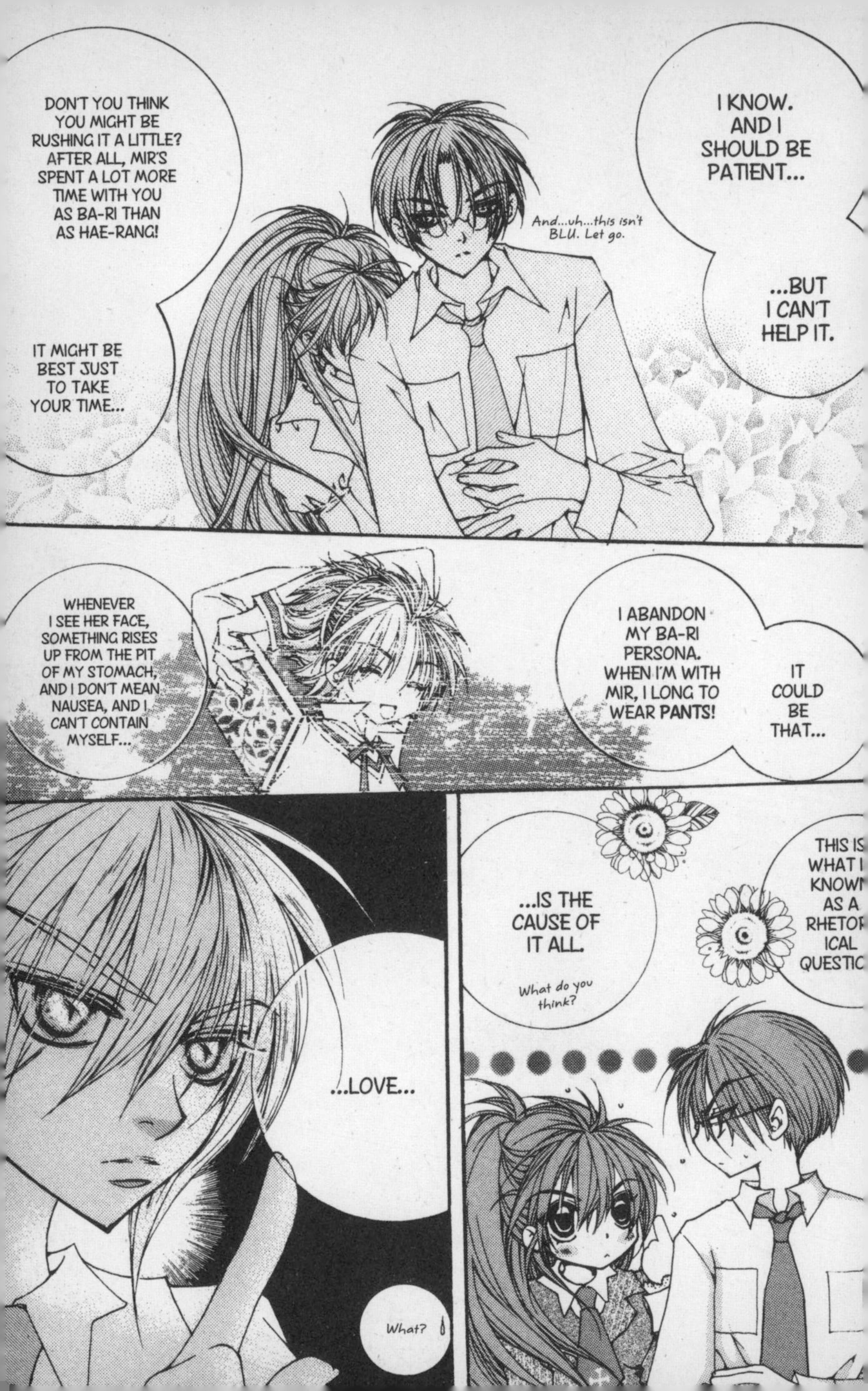

DON'T YOU THINK YOU MIGHT BE RUSHING IT A LITTLE? AFTER ALL, MIR'S SPENT A LOT MORE TIME WITH YOU AS BA-RI THAN AS HAE-RANG!
IT MIGHT BE BEST JUST TO TAKE YOUR TIME...
And...uh...this isn't BLU. Let go.
I KNOW. AND I SHOULD BE PATIENT...
...BUT I CAN'T HELP IT.
WHENEVER I SEE HER FACE, SOMETHING RISES UP FROM THE PIT OF MY STOMACH, AND I DON'T MEAN NAUSEA, AND I CAN'T CONTAIN MYSELF...
I ABANDON MY BA-RI PERSONA. WHEN I'M WITH MIR, I LONG TO WEAR PANTS!
IT COULD BE THAT...
...LOVE...
What?
...IS THE CAUSE OF IT ALL.
What do you think?
THIS IS WHAT I KNOWN AS A RHETOR ICAL QUESTIC

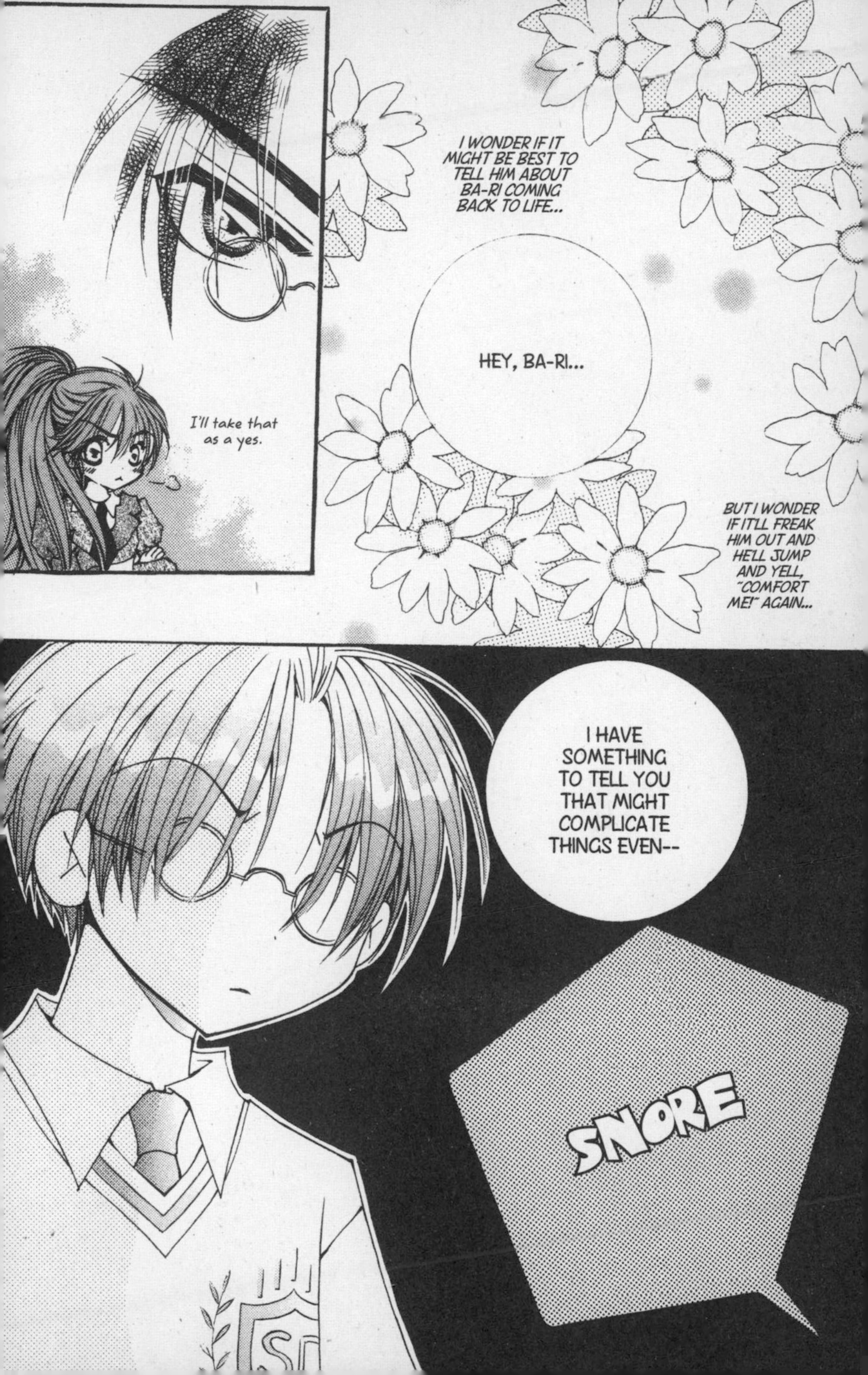
I'll take that as a yes.
I WONDER IF IT MIGHT BE BEST TO TELL HIM ABOUT BA-RI COMING BACK TO LIFE...
HEY, BA-RI...
BUT I WONDER IF IT'LL FREAK HIM OUT AND HE'LL JUMP AND YELL, "COMFORT ME!" AGAIN...
I HAVE SOMETHING TO TELL YOU THAT MIGHT COMPLICATE THINGS EVEN--
SNORE

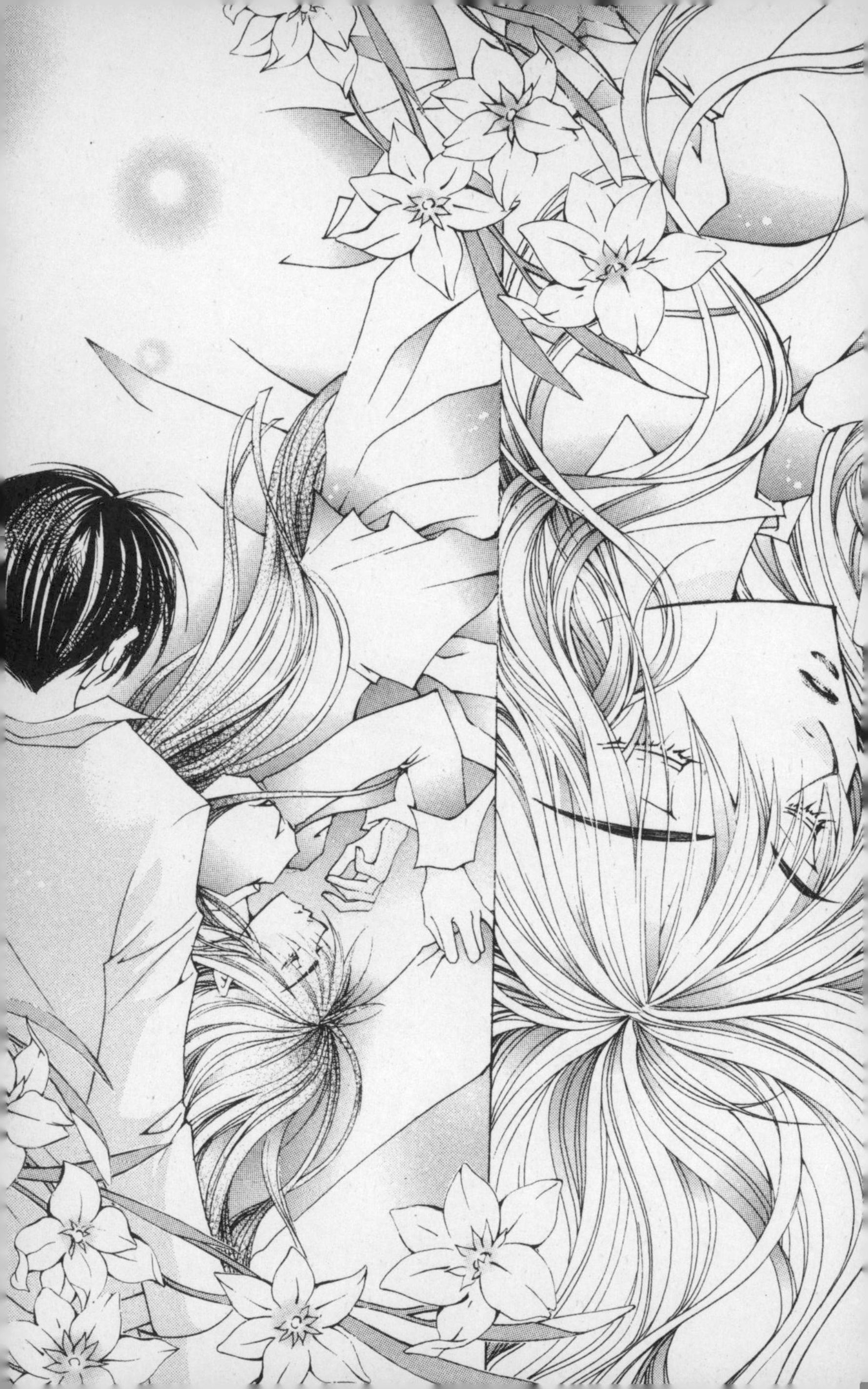

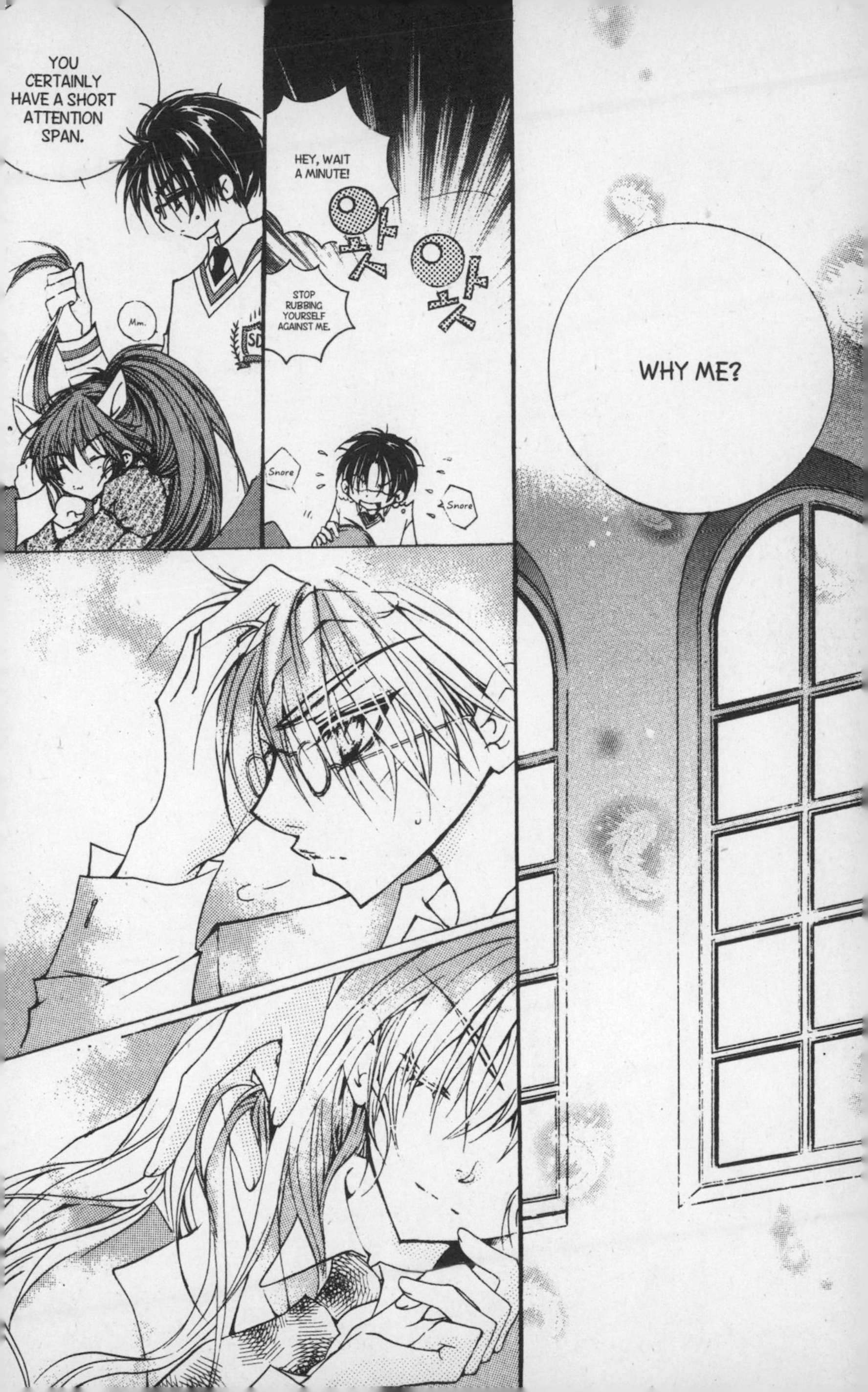
YOU CERTAINLY HAVE A SHORT ATTENTION SPAN.
Mm.
HEY, WAIT A MINUTE!
STOP RUBBING YOURSELF AGAINST ME.
Snore
Snore
WHY ME?

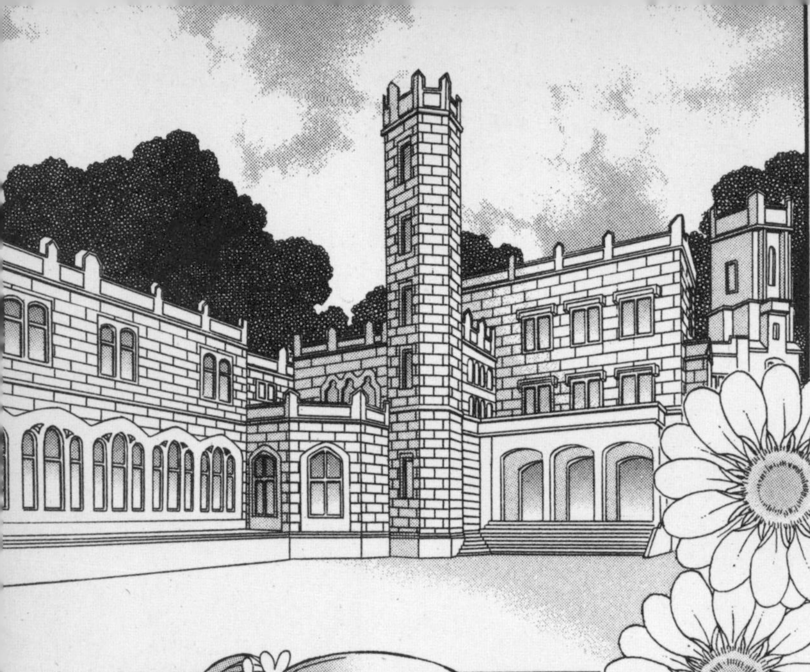
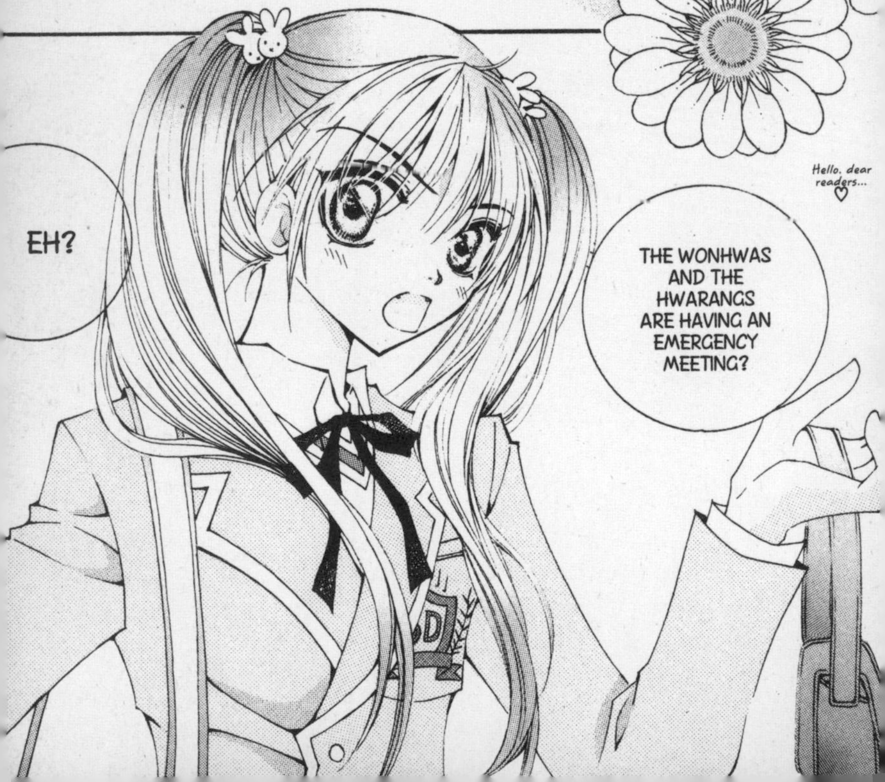
Hello, dear readers...♡
EH?
THE WONHWAS AND THE HWARANGS ARE HAVING AN EMERGENCY MEETING?

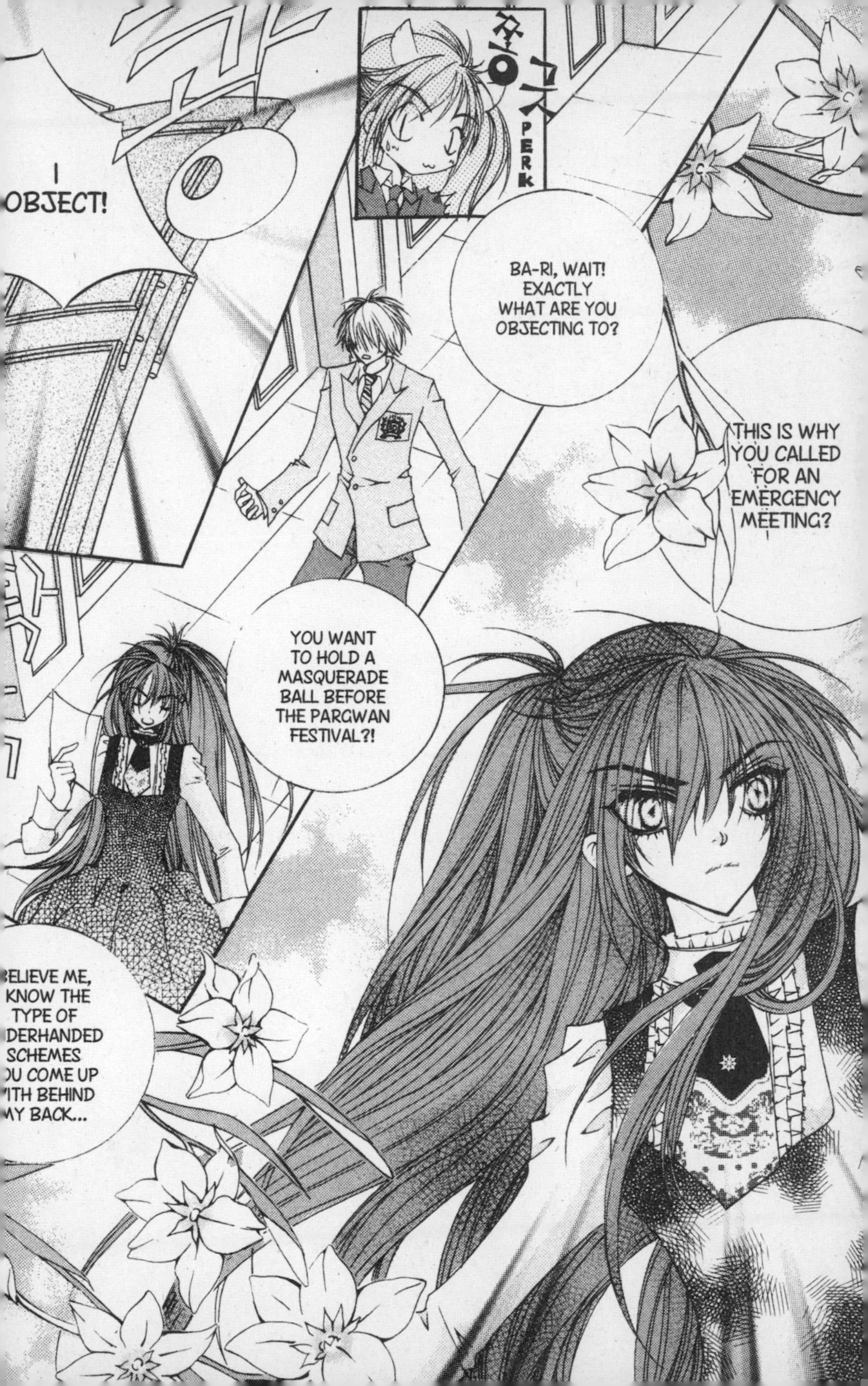
I OBJECT!
PERK
BA-RI, WAIT! EXACTLY WHAT ARE YOU OBJECTING TO?
THIS IS WHY YOU CALLED FOR AN EMERGENCY MEETING?
YOU WANT TO HOLD A MASQUERADE BALL BEFORE THE PARGWAN FESTIVAL?!
BELIEVE ME, KNOW THE TYPE OF DERHANDED SCHEMES OU COME UP ITH BEHIND MY BACK...

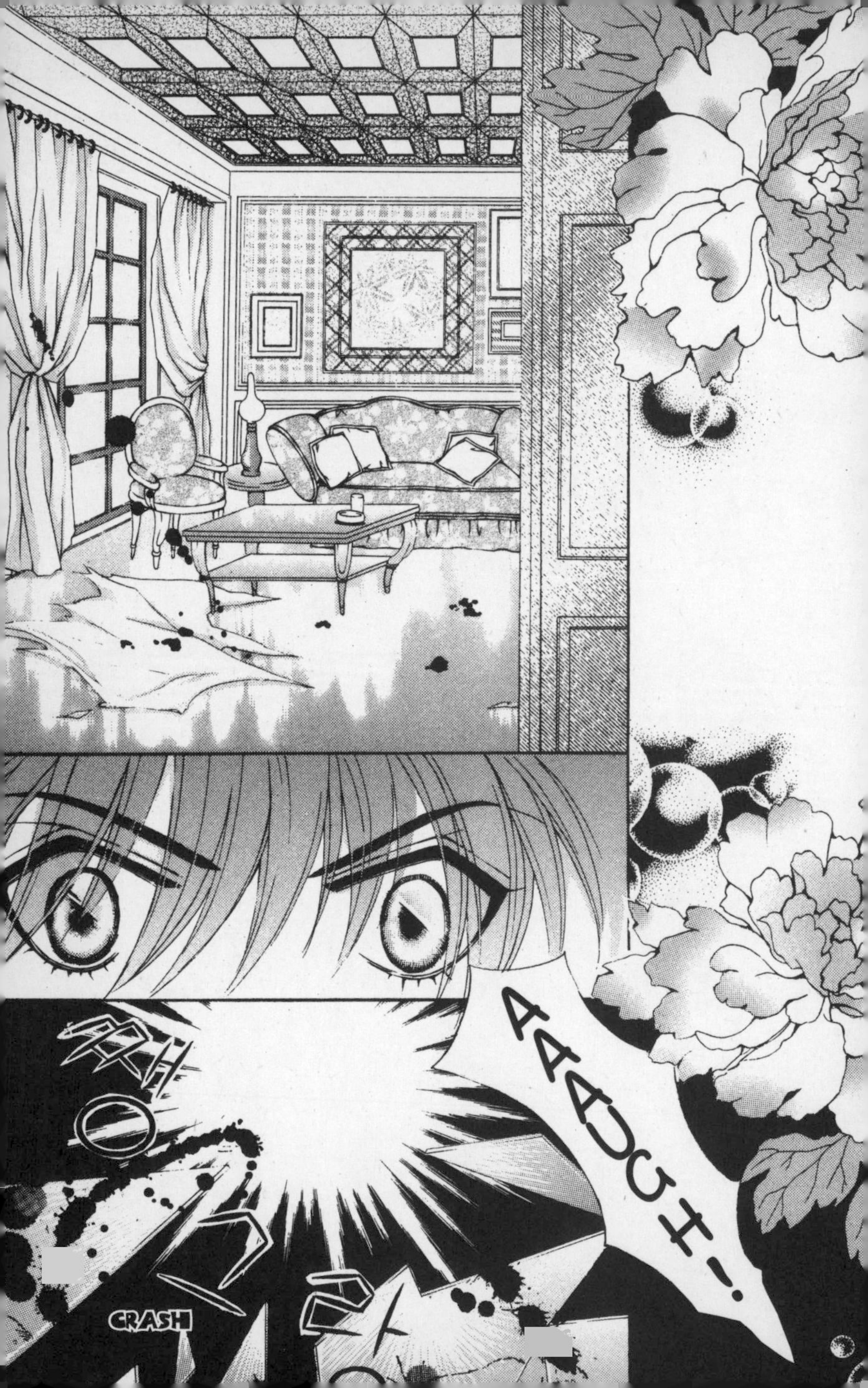
AAAUGH!!
CRASH

PART 7: HWA-YUN

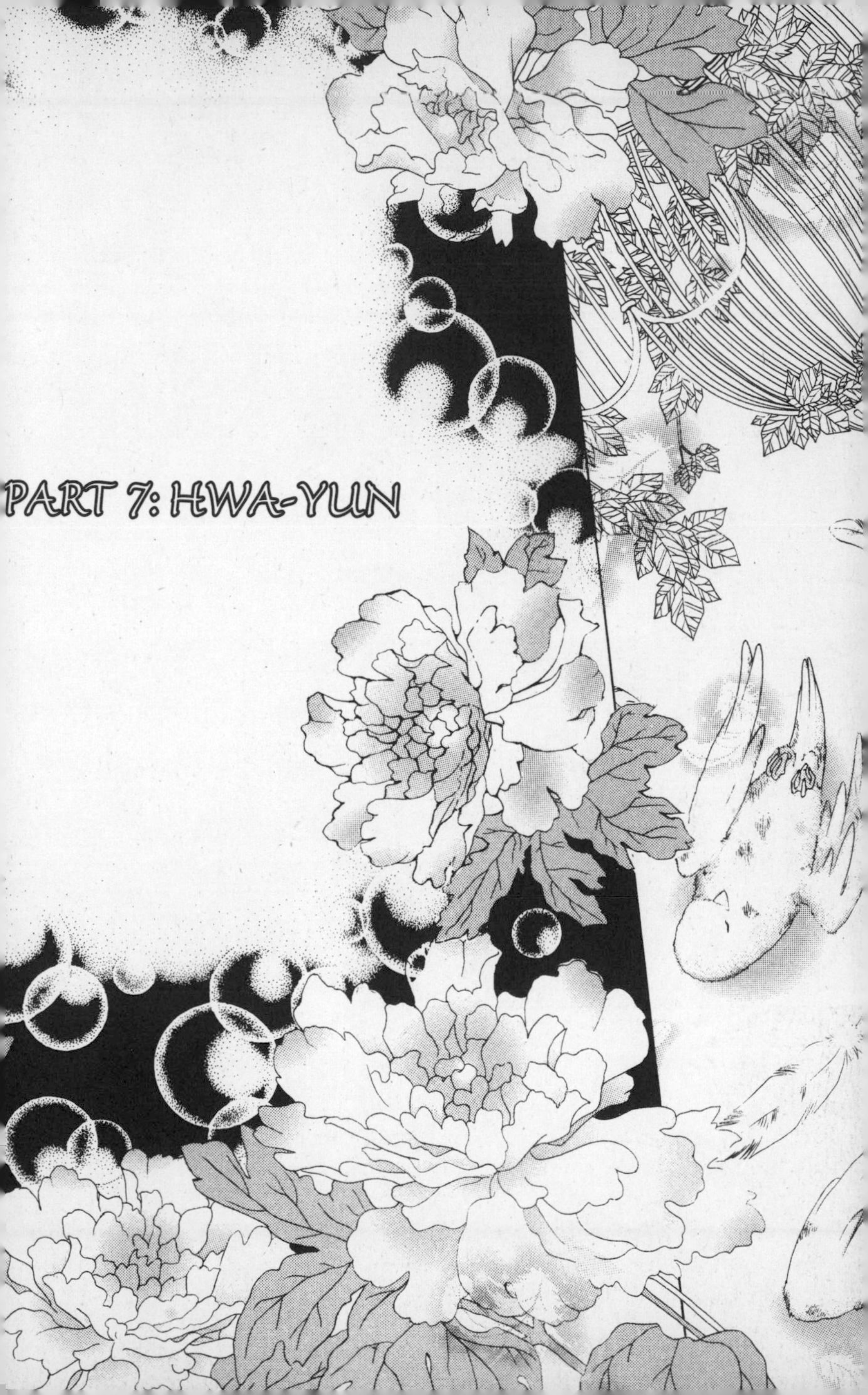

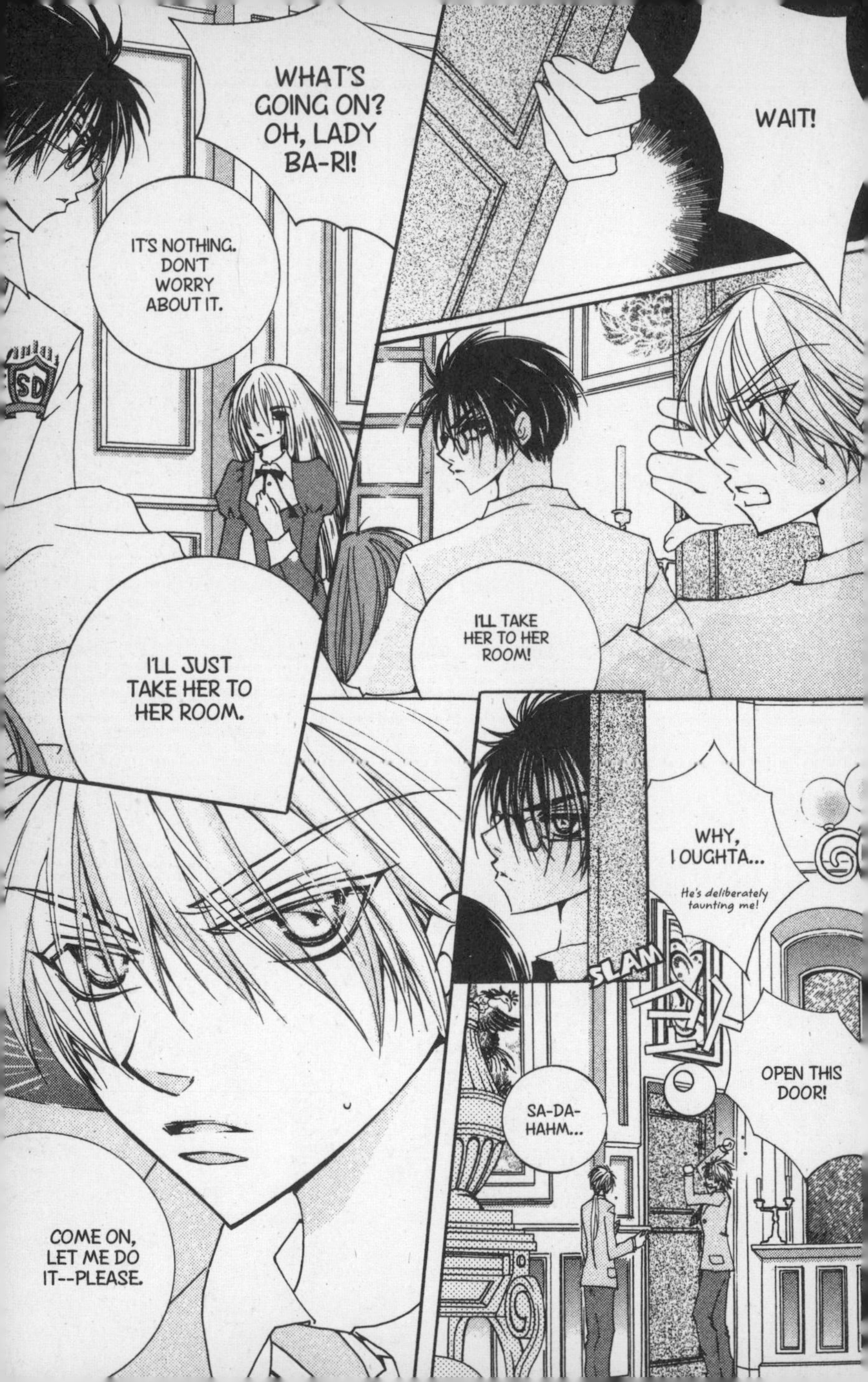
WHAT'S GOING ON? OH, LADY BA-RI!
IT'S NOTHING. DON'T WORRY ABOUT IT.
I'LL JUST TAKE HER TO HER ROOM.
WAIT!
I'LL TAKE HER TO HER ROOM!
COME ON, LET ME DO IT--PLEASE.
WHY, I OUGHTA...
He's deliberately taunting me!
SLAM
SA-DA-HAHM...
OPEN THIS DOOR!

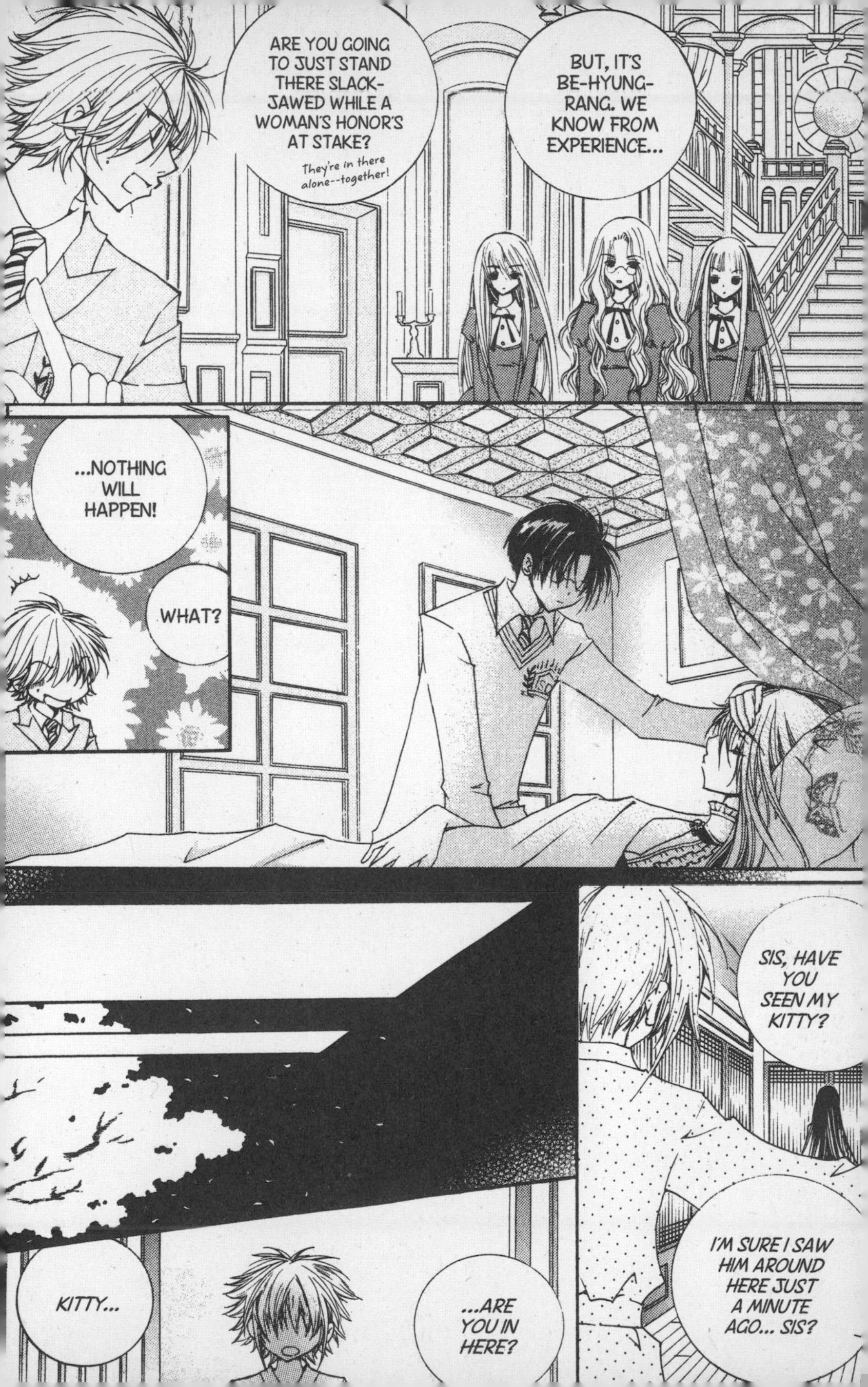
ARE YOU GOING TO JUST STAND THERE SLACK-JAWED WHILE A WOMAN'S HONOR'S AT STAKE?
They're in there alone--together!
BUT, IT'S BE-HYUNG-RANG. WE KNOW FROM EXPERIENCE...
...NOTHING WILL HAPPEN!
WHAT?
KITTY...
...ARE YOU IN HERE?
SIS, HAVE YOU SEEN MY KITTY?
I'M SURE I SAW HIM AROUND HERE JUST A MINUTE AGO... SIS?

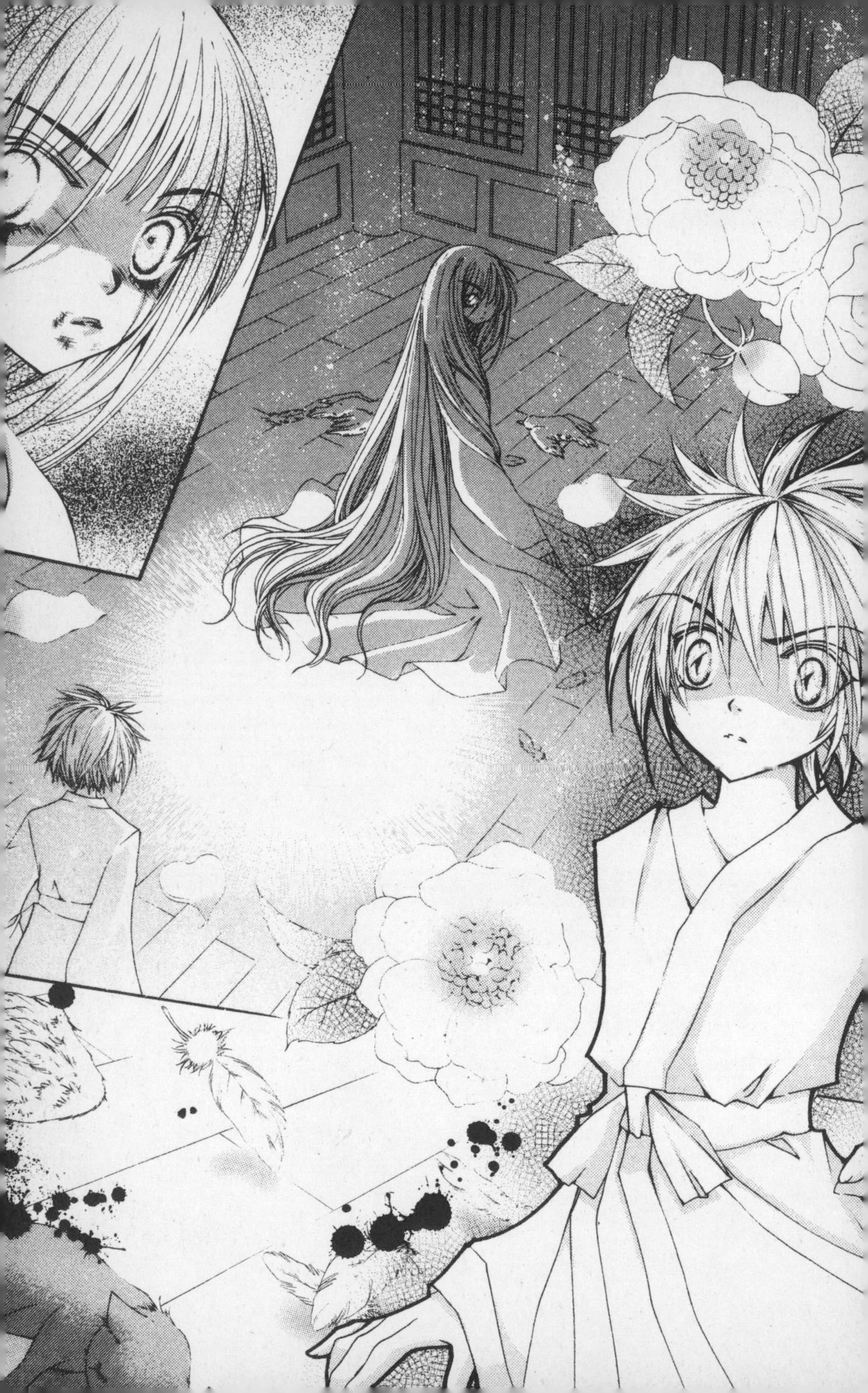

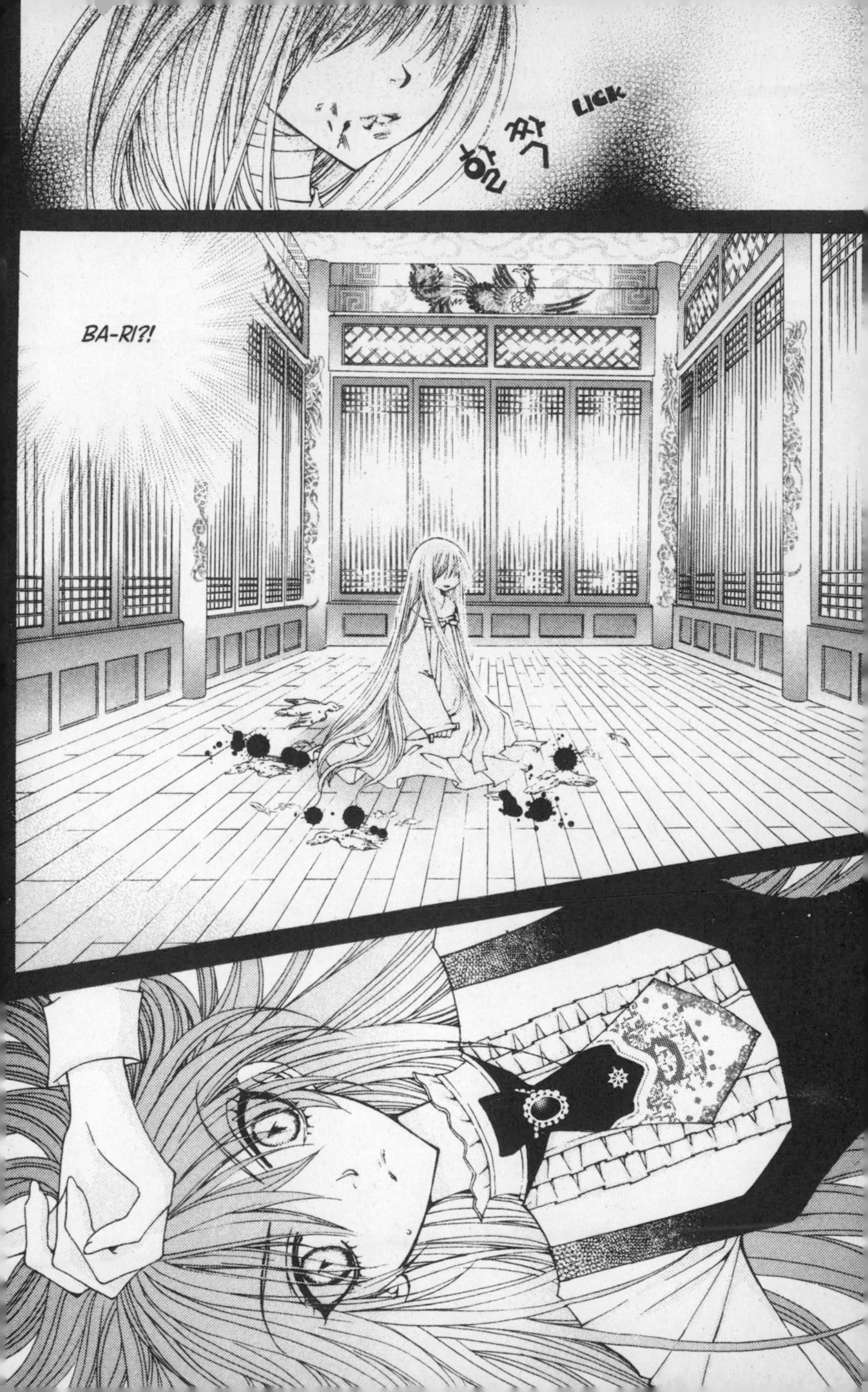
할짝
LICK
BA-RI?!

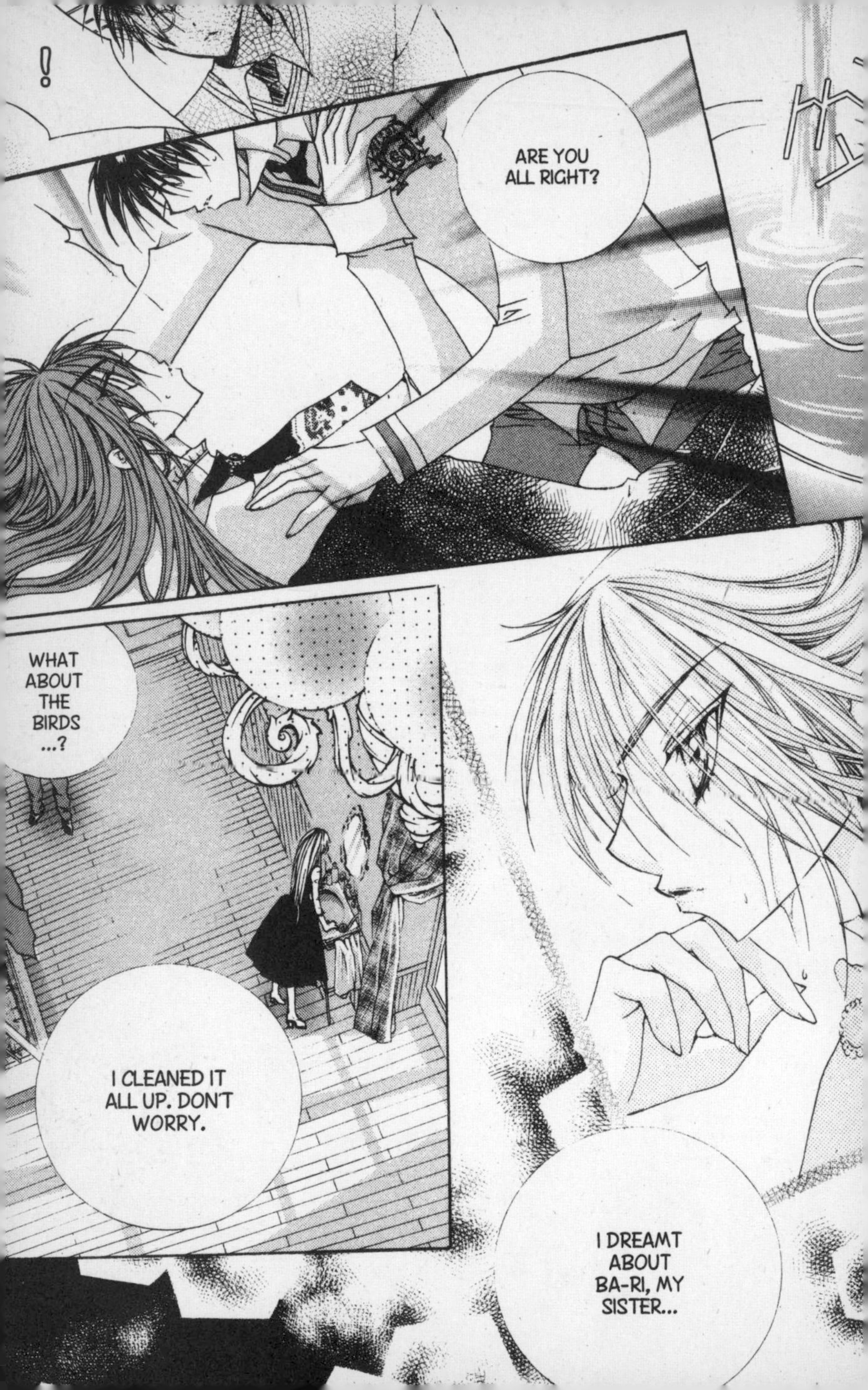
!
ARE YOU ALL RIGHT?
WHAT ABOUT THE BIRDS ...?
I CLEANED IT ALL UP. DON'T WORRY.
I DREAMT ABOUT BA-RI, MY SISTER...

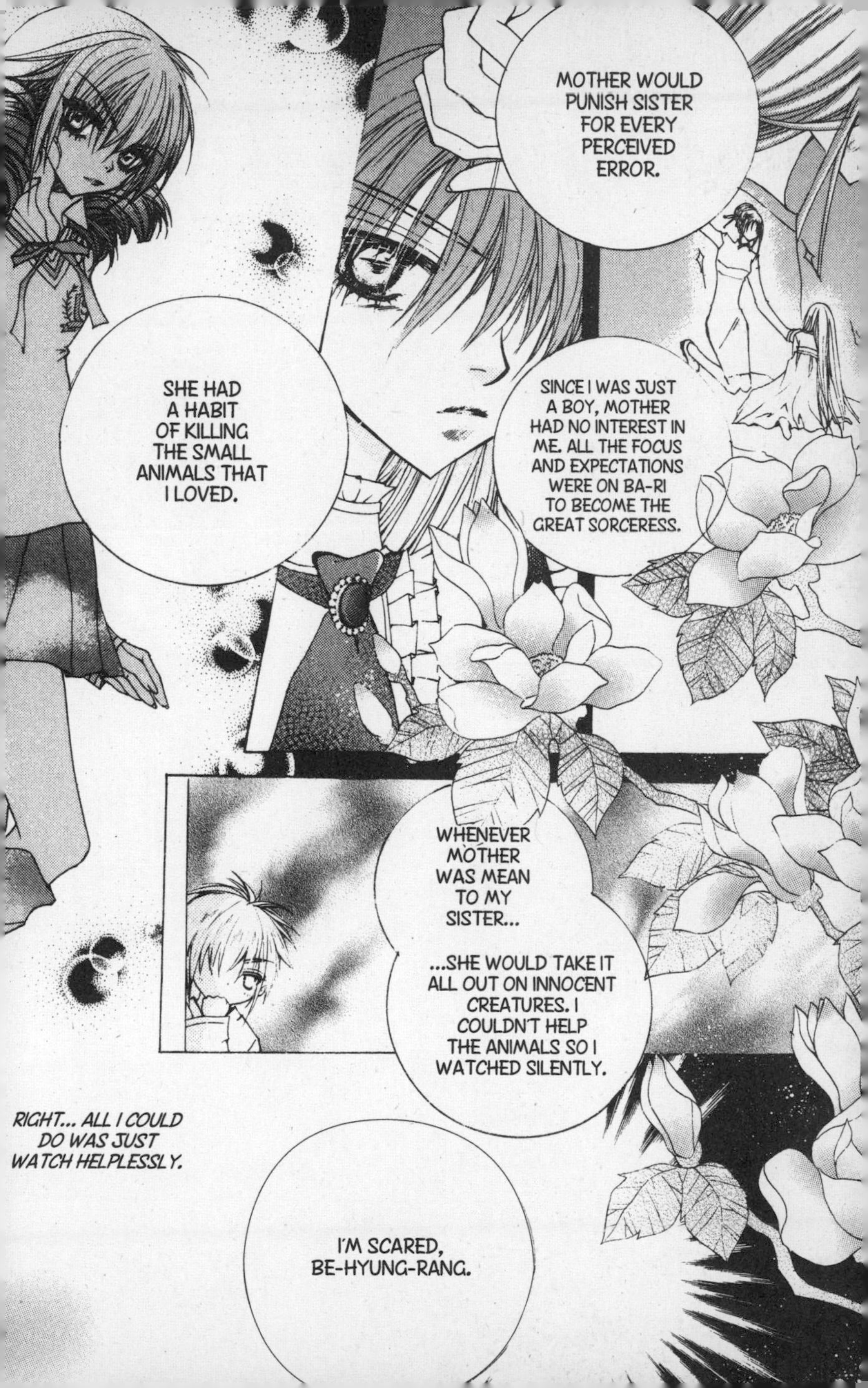
MOTHER WOULD PUNISH SISTER FOR EVERY PERCEIVED ERROR.
SHE HAD A HABIT OF KILLING THE SMALL ANIMALS THAT I LOVED.
SINCE I WAS JUST A BOY, MOTHER HAD NO INTEREST IN ME. ALL THE FOCUS AND EXPECTATIONS WERE ON BA-RI TO BECOME THE GREAT SORCERESS.
WHENEVER MOTHER WAS MEAN TO MY SISTER...
...SHE WOULD TAKE IT ALL OUT ON INNOCENT CREATURES. I COULDN'T HELP THE ANIMALS SO I WATCHED SILENTLY.
RIGHT... ALL I COULD DO WAS JUST WATCH HELPLESSLY.
I'M SCARED, BE-HYUNG-RANG.

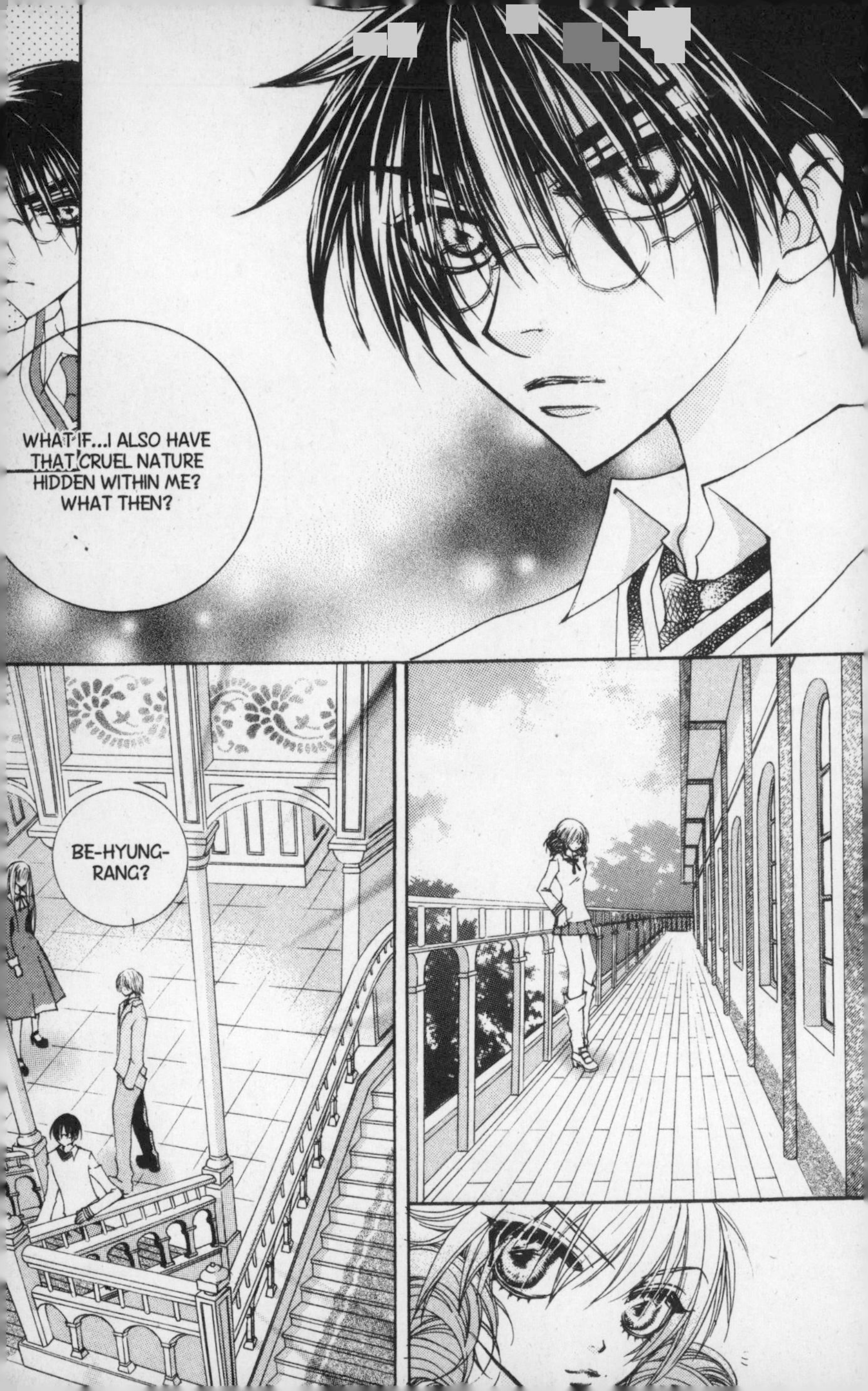
WHAT IF...I ALSO HAVE THAT CRUEL NATURE HIDDEN WITHIN ME? WHAT THEN?
BE-HYUNG-RANG?

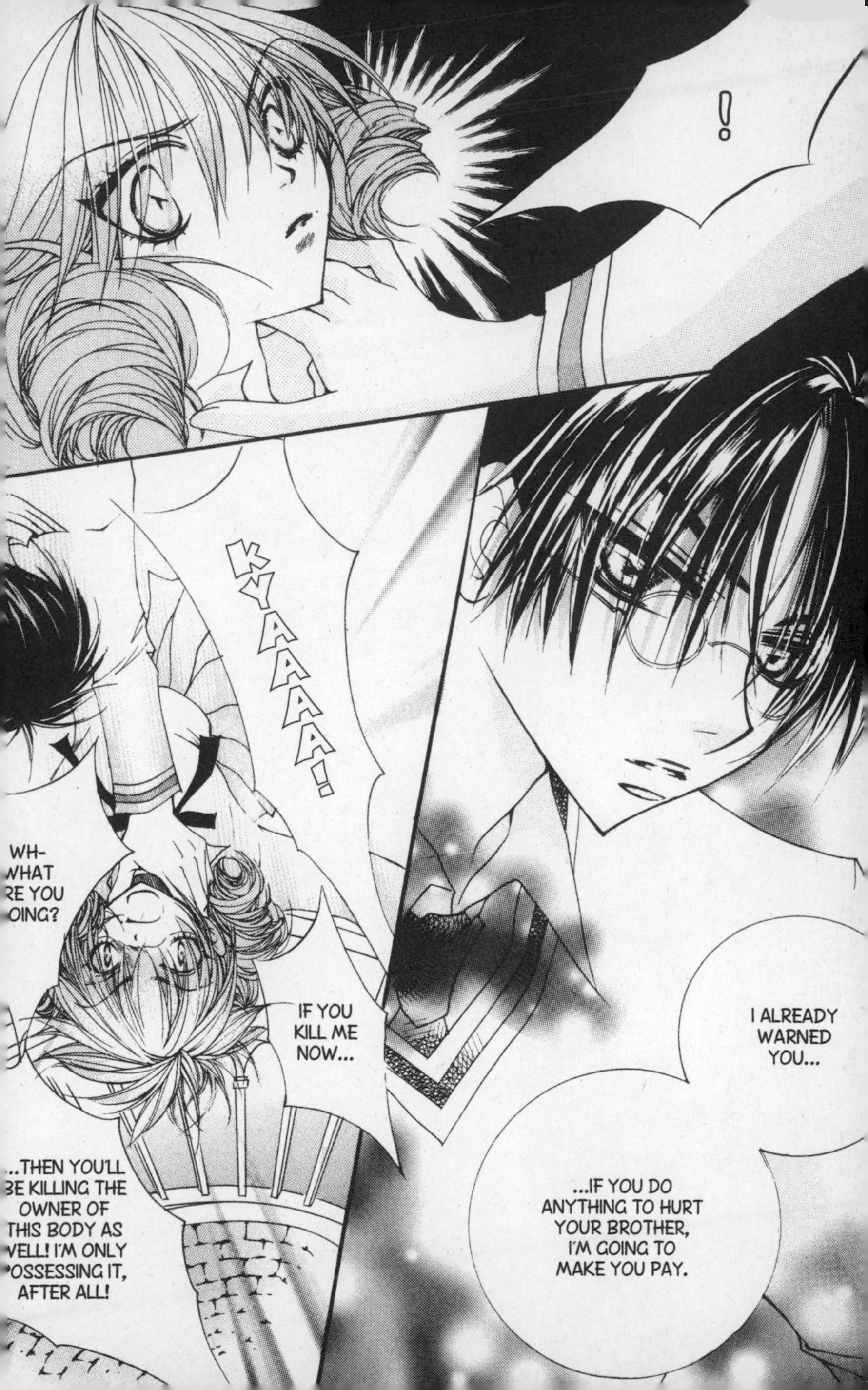
!
KYAAAAA!
WH- WHAT RE YOU OING?
IF YOU KILL ME NOW...
...THEN YOU'LL BE KILLING THE OWNER OF THIS BODY AS WELL! I'M ONLY POSSESSING IT, AFTER ALL!
I ALREADY WARNED YOU...
...IF YOU DO ANYTHING TO HURT YOUR BROTHER, I'M GOING TO MAKE YOU PAY.

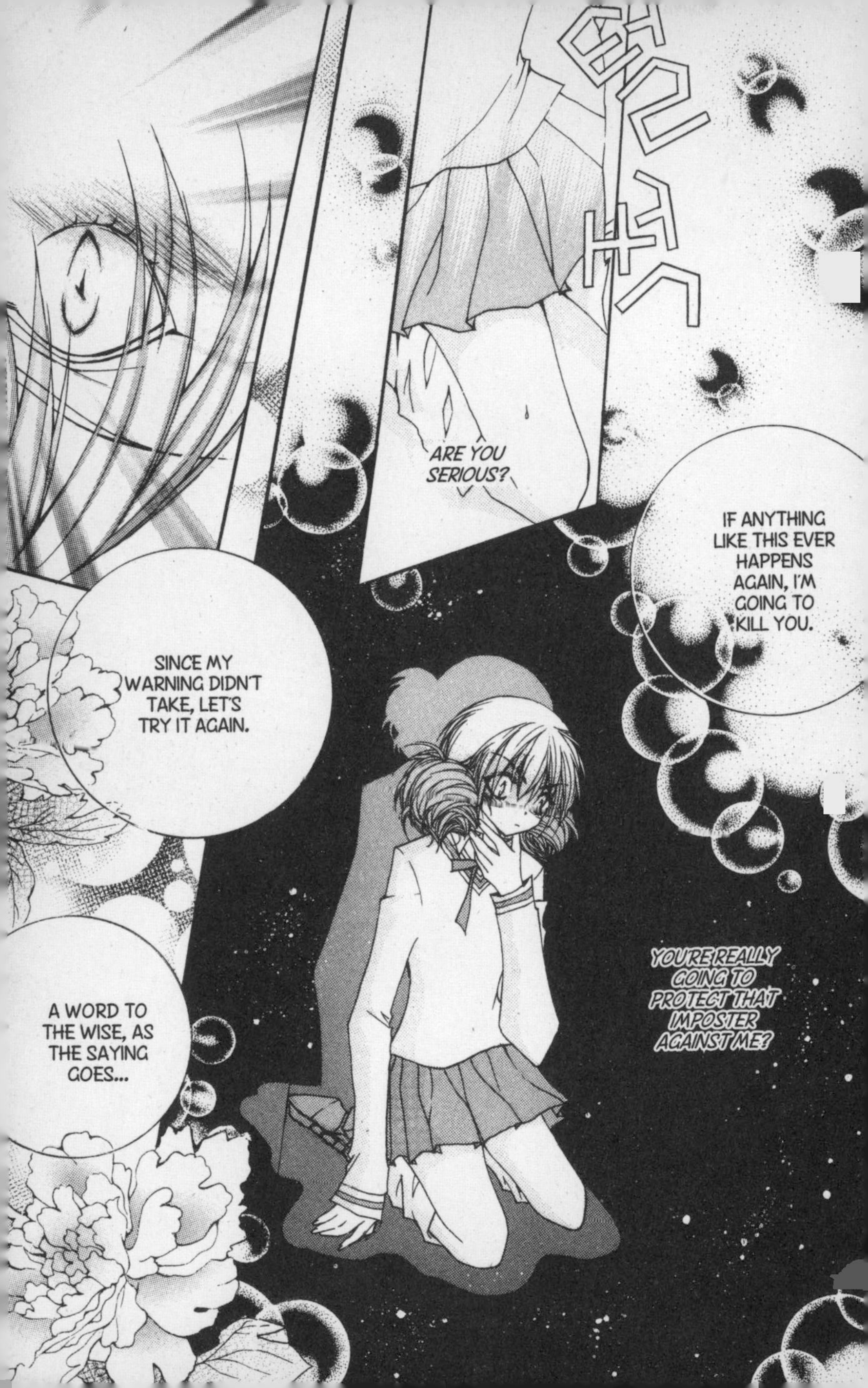

ARE YOU SERIOUS?
IF ANYTHING LIKE THIS EVER HAPPENS AGAIN, I'M GOING TO KILL YOU.
SINCE MY WARNING DIDN'T TAKE, LET'S TRY IT AGAIN.
A WORD TO THE WISE, AS THE SAYING GOES...
YOU'RE REALLY GOING TO PROTECT THAT IMPOSTER AGAINST ME?

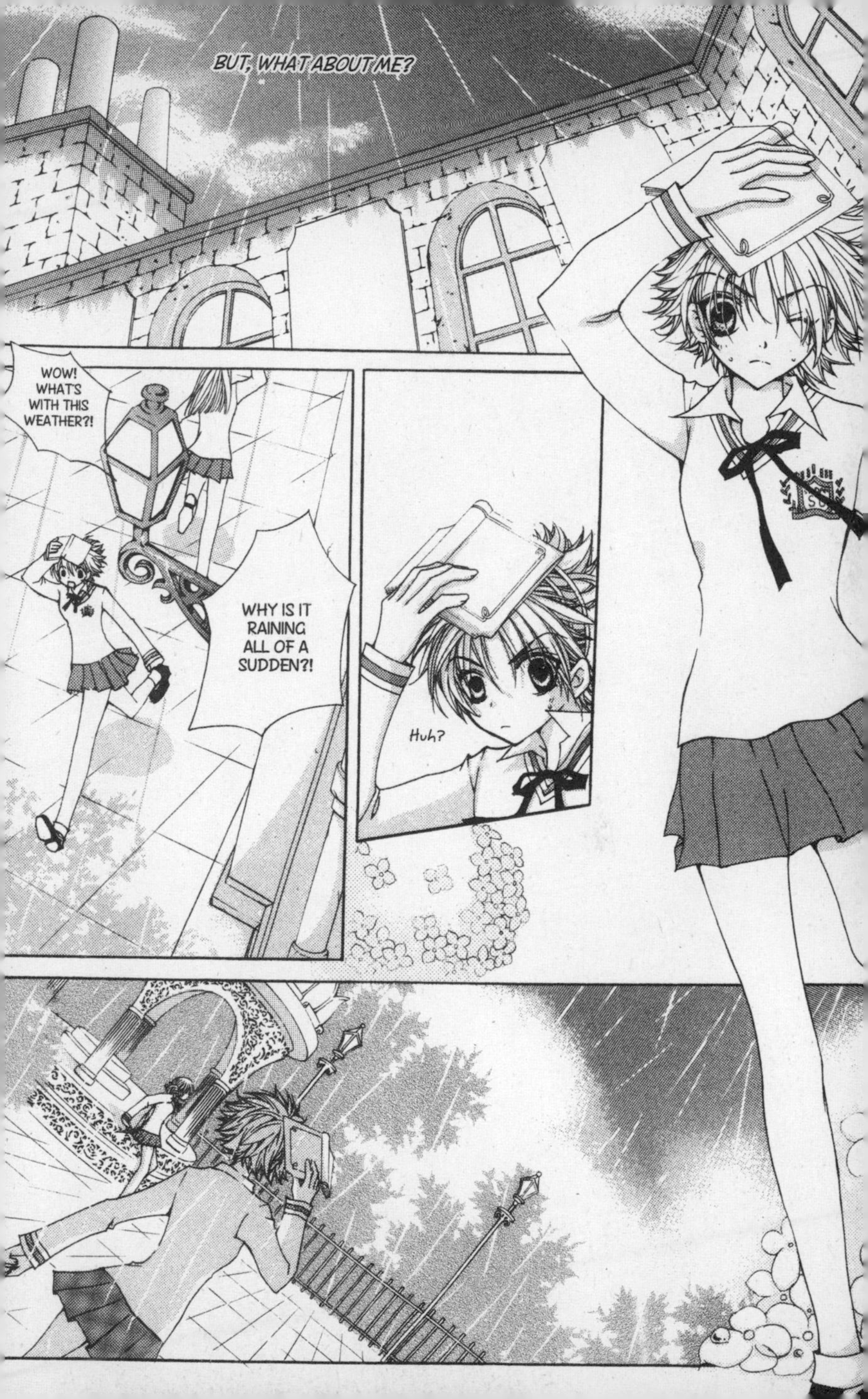
BUT, WHAT ABOUT ME?
WOW! WHAT'S WITH THIS WEATHER?!
WHY IS IT RAINING ALL OF A SUDDEN?!
Huh?

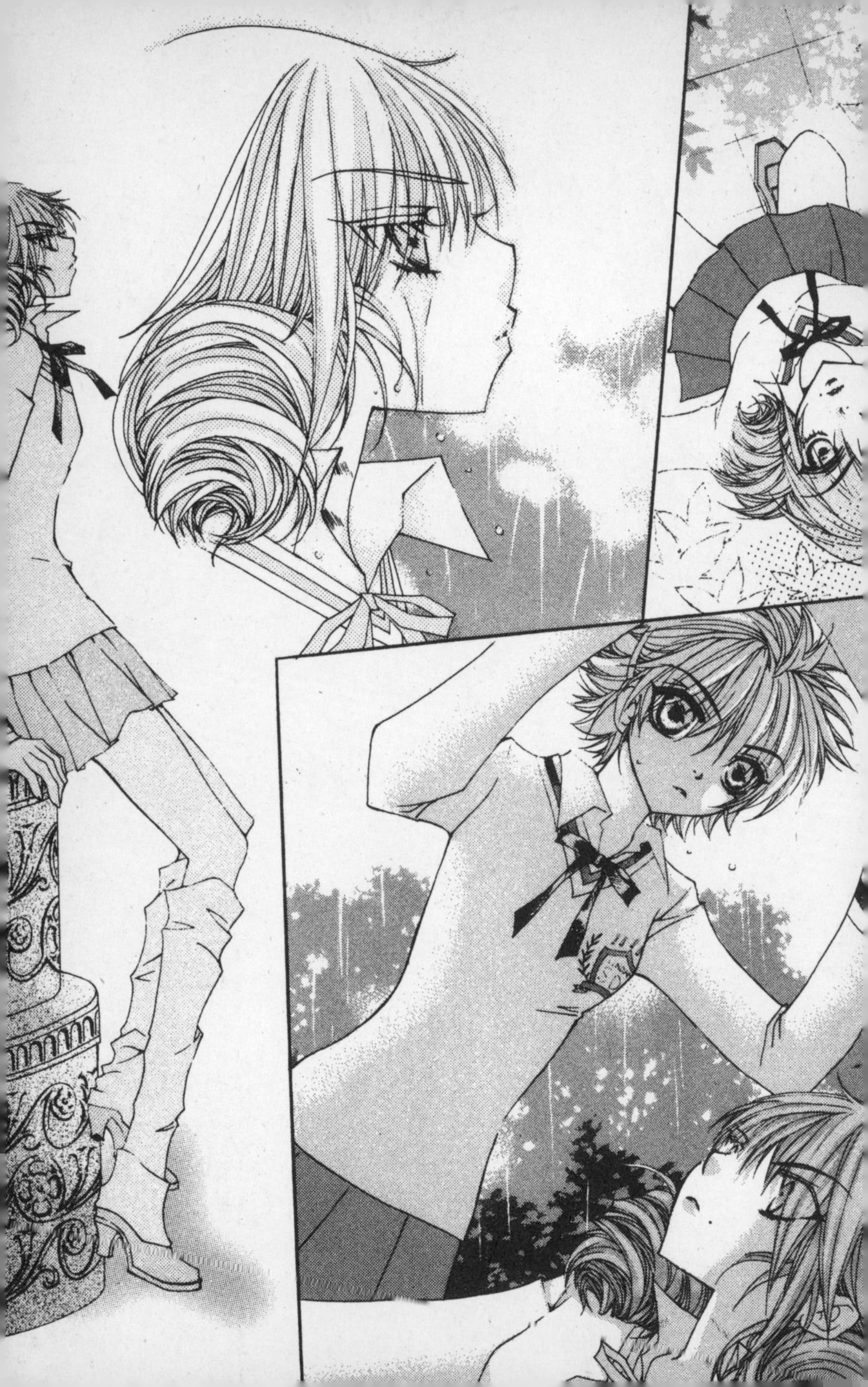

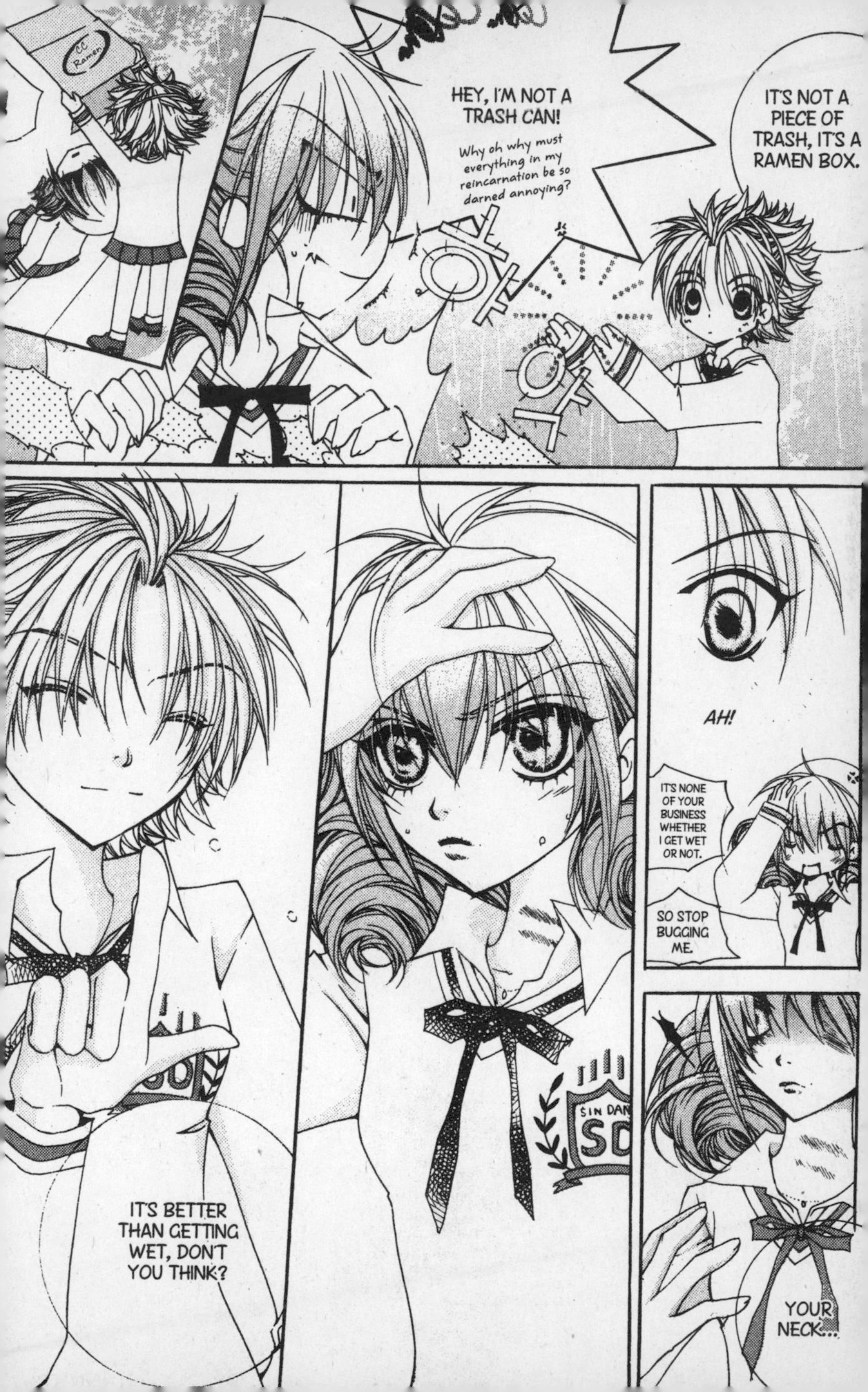
CC Ramen
HEY, I'M NOT A TRASH CAN!
Why oh why must everything in my reincarnation be so darned annoying?
IT'S NOT A PIECE OF TRASH, IT'S A RAMEN BOX.
IT'S BETTER THAN GETTING WET, DON'T YOU THINK?
SIN DAN SD
AH!
IT'S NONE OF YOUR BUSINESS WHETHER I GET WET OR NOT.
SO STOP BUGGING ME.
YOUR NECK...

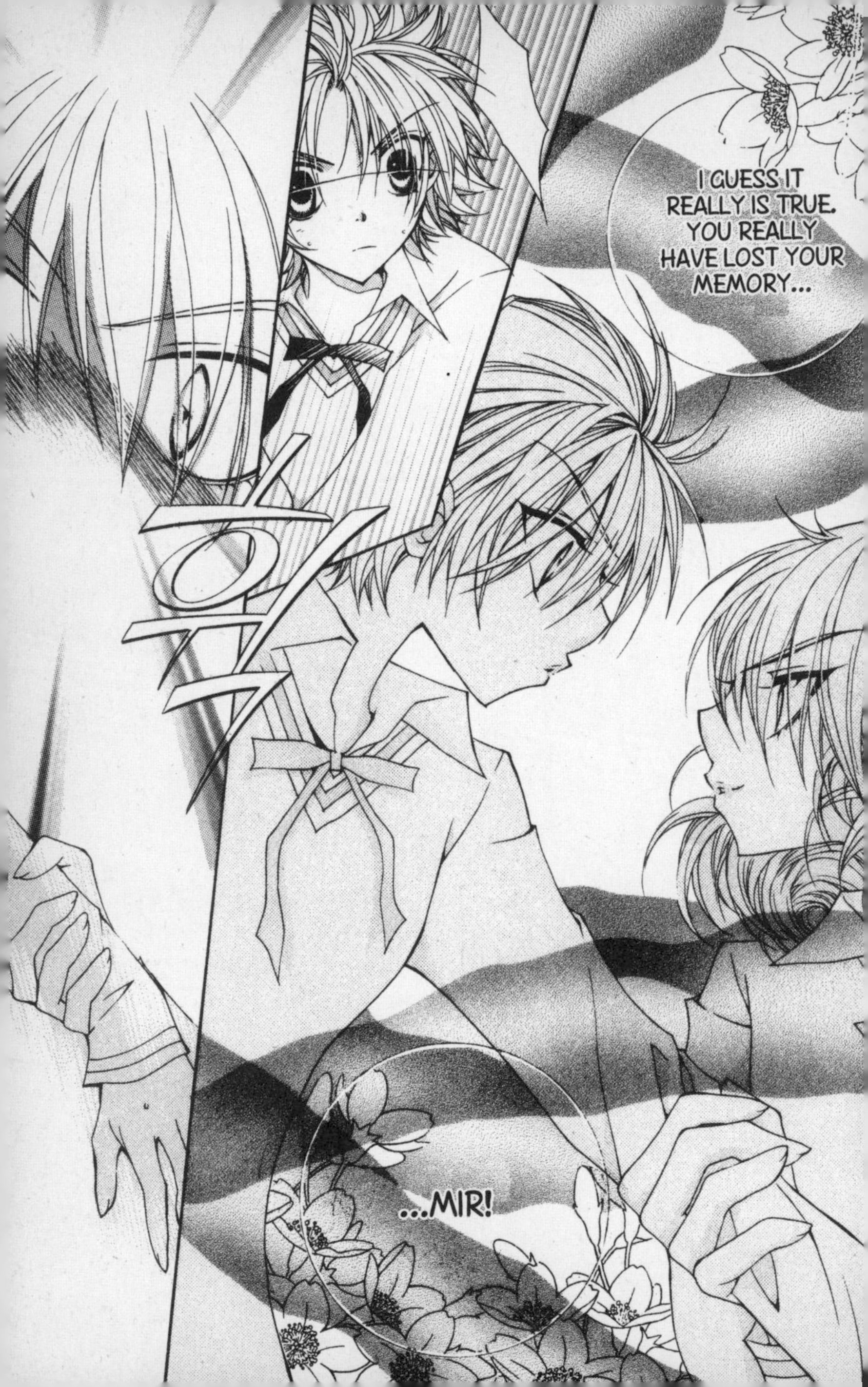
I GUESS IT REALLY IS TRUE. YOU REALLY HAVE LOST YOUR MEMORY...
...MIR!

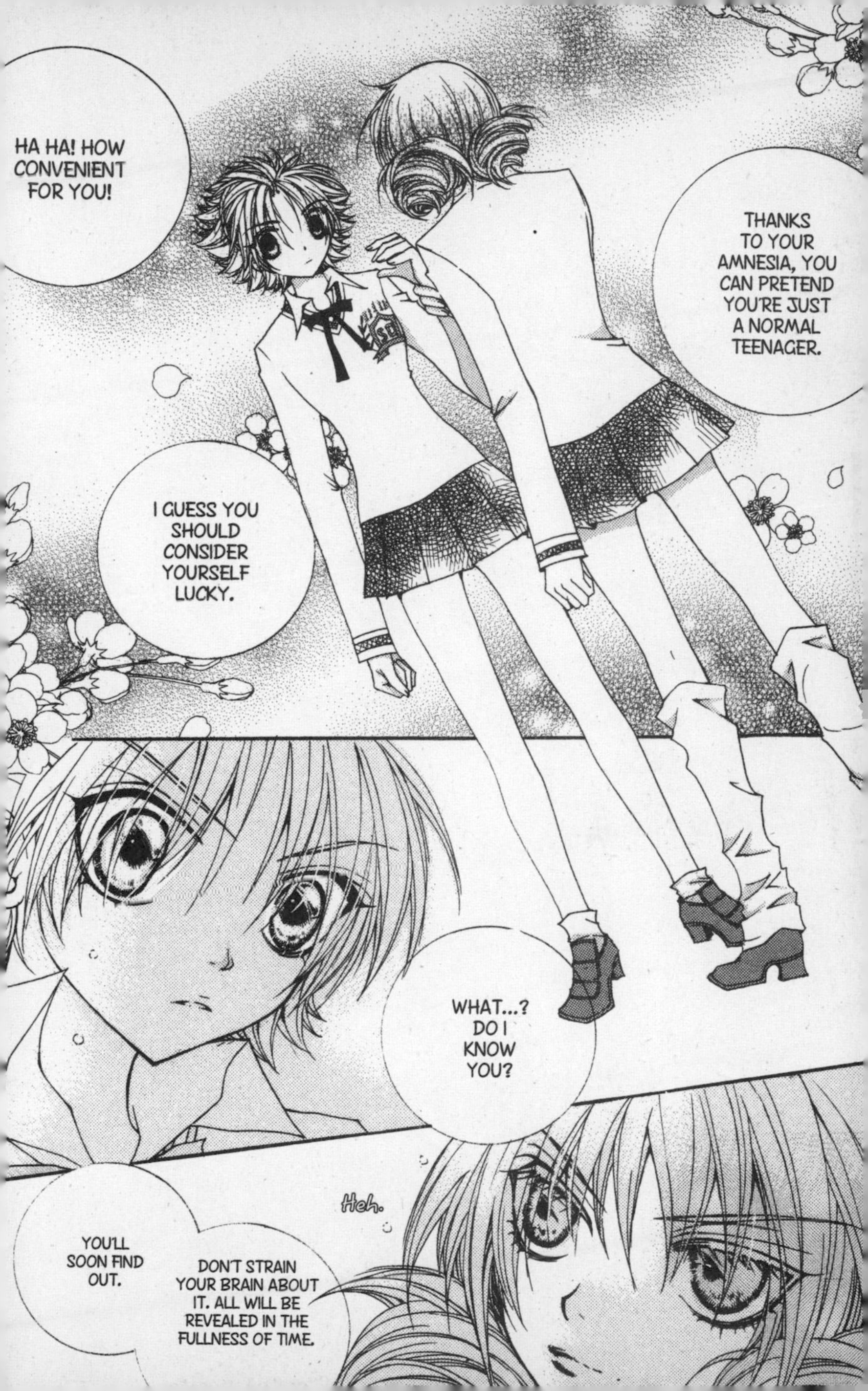
HA HA! HOW CONVENIENT FOR YOU!
THANKS TO YOUR AMNESIA, YOU CAN PRETEND YOU'RE JUST A NORMAL TEENAGER.
I GUESS YOU SHOULD CONSIDER YOURSELF LUCKY.
WHAT...? DO I KNOW YOU?
YOU'LL SOON FIND OUT.
Heh.
DON'T STRAIN YOUR BRAIN ABOUT IT. ALL WILL BE REVEALED IN THE FULLNESS OF TIME.

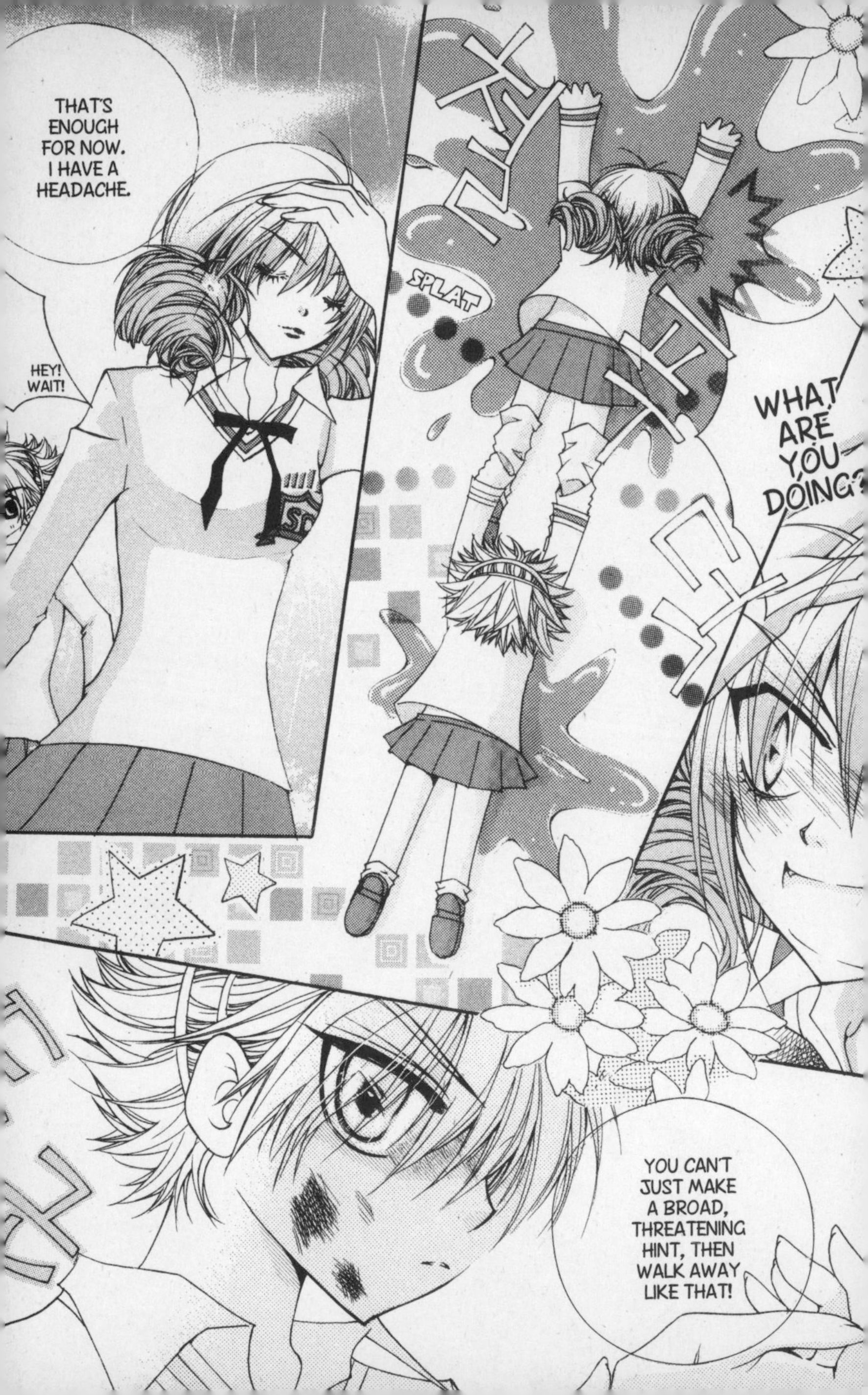
THAT'S ENOUGH FOR NOW. I HAVE A HEADACHE.
HEY! WAIT!
SPLAT
WHAT ARE YOU DOING?
YOU CAN'T JUST MAKE A BROAD, THREATENING HINT, THEN WALK AWAY LIKE THAT!

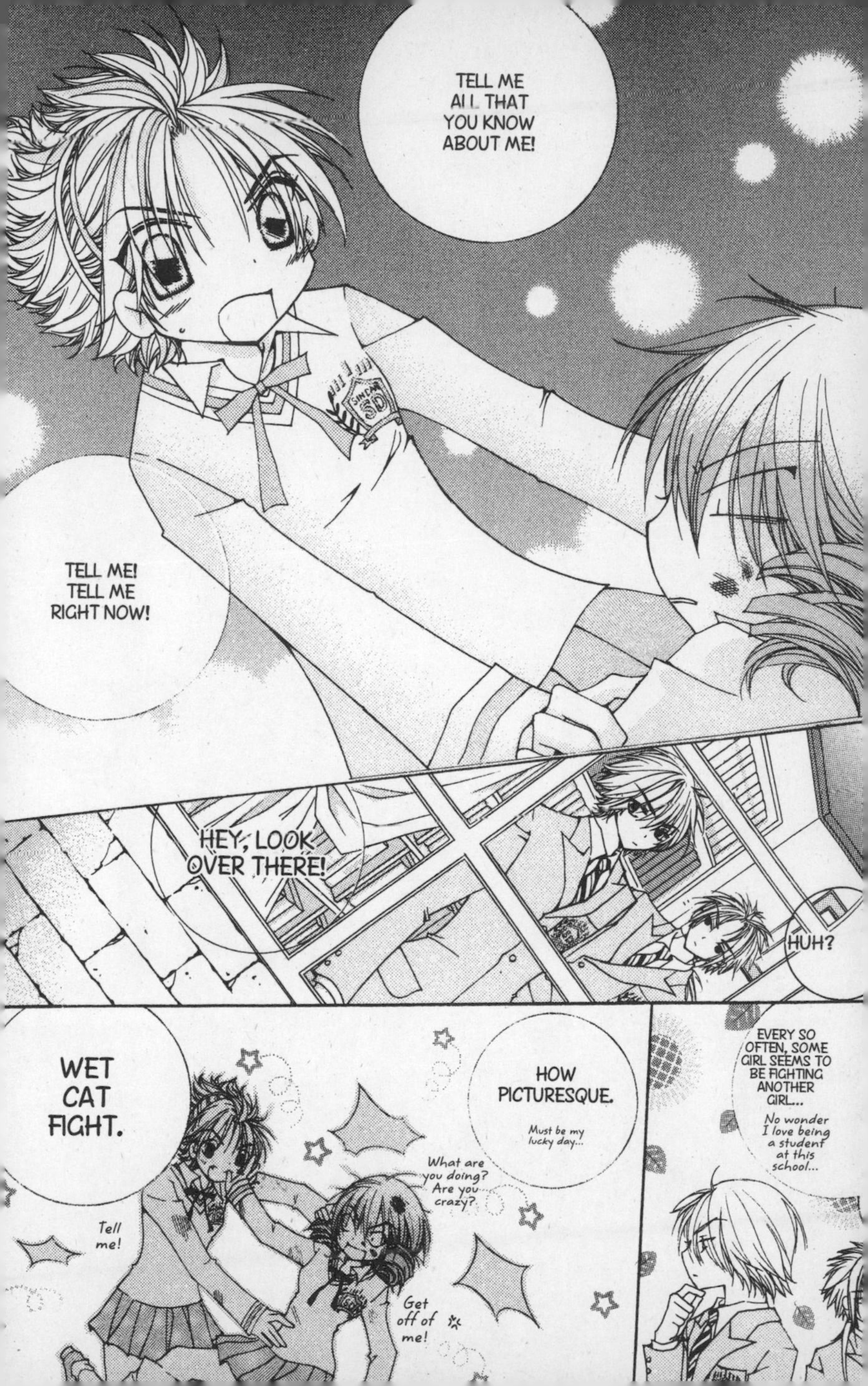
TELL ME ALL THAT YOU KNOW ABOUT ME!
TELL ME! TELL ME RIGHT NOW!
HEY, LOOK OVER THERE!
HUH?
WET CAT FIGHT.
Tell me!
What are you doing? Are you crazy?
Get off of me!
HOW PICTURESQUE.
Must be my lucky day...
EVERY SO OFTEN, SOME GIRL SEEMS TO BE FIGHTING ANOTHER GIRL...
No wonder I love being a student at this school...

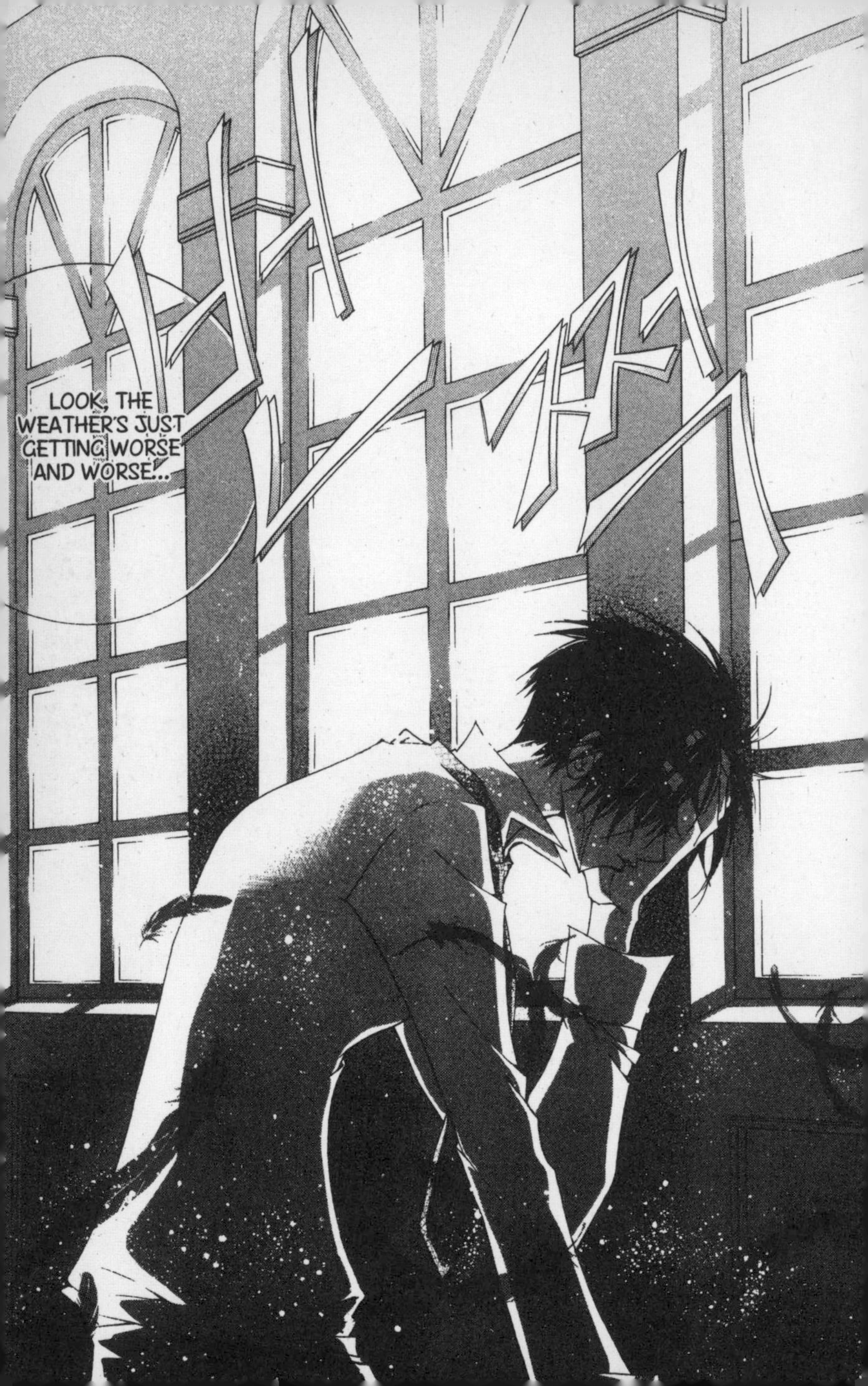
LOOK, THE WEATHER'S JUST GETTING WORSE AND WORSE...

FANTAMIR

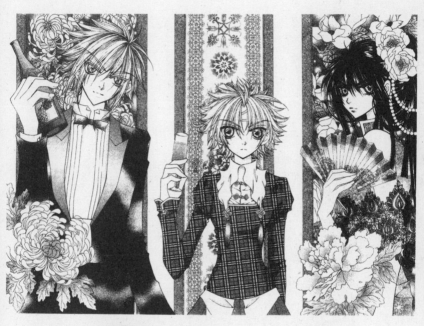

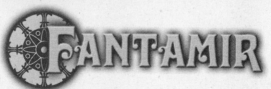

FANTAMIR

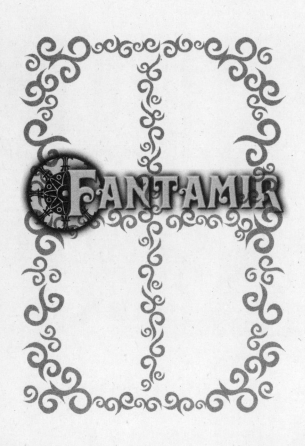

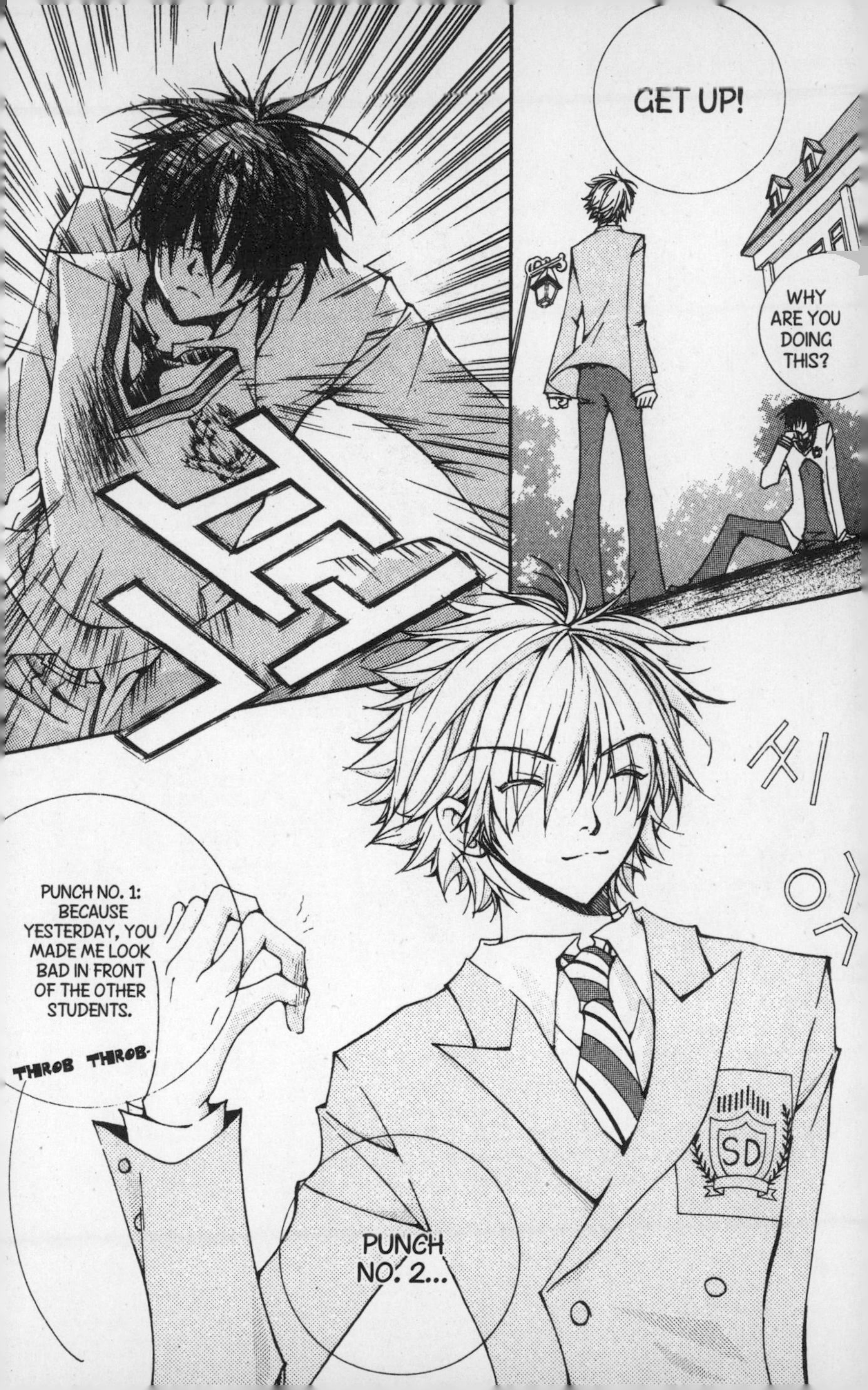
GET UP!
WHY ARE YOU DOING THIS?
PUNCH NO. 1: BECAUSE YESTERDAY, YOU MADE ME LOOK BAD IN FRONT OF THE OTHER STUDENTS.
THROB THROB
PUNCH NO. 2...

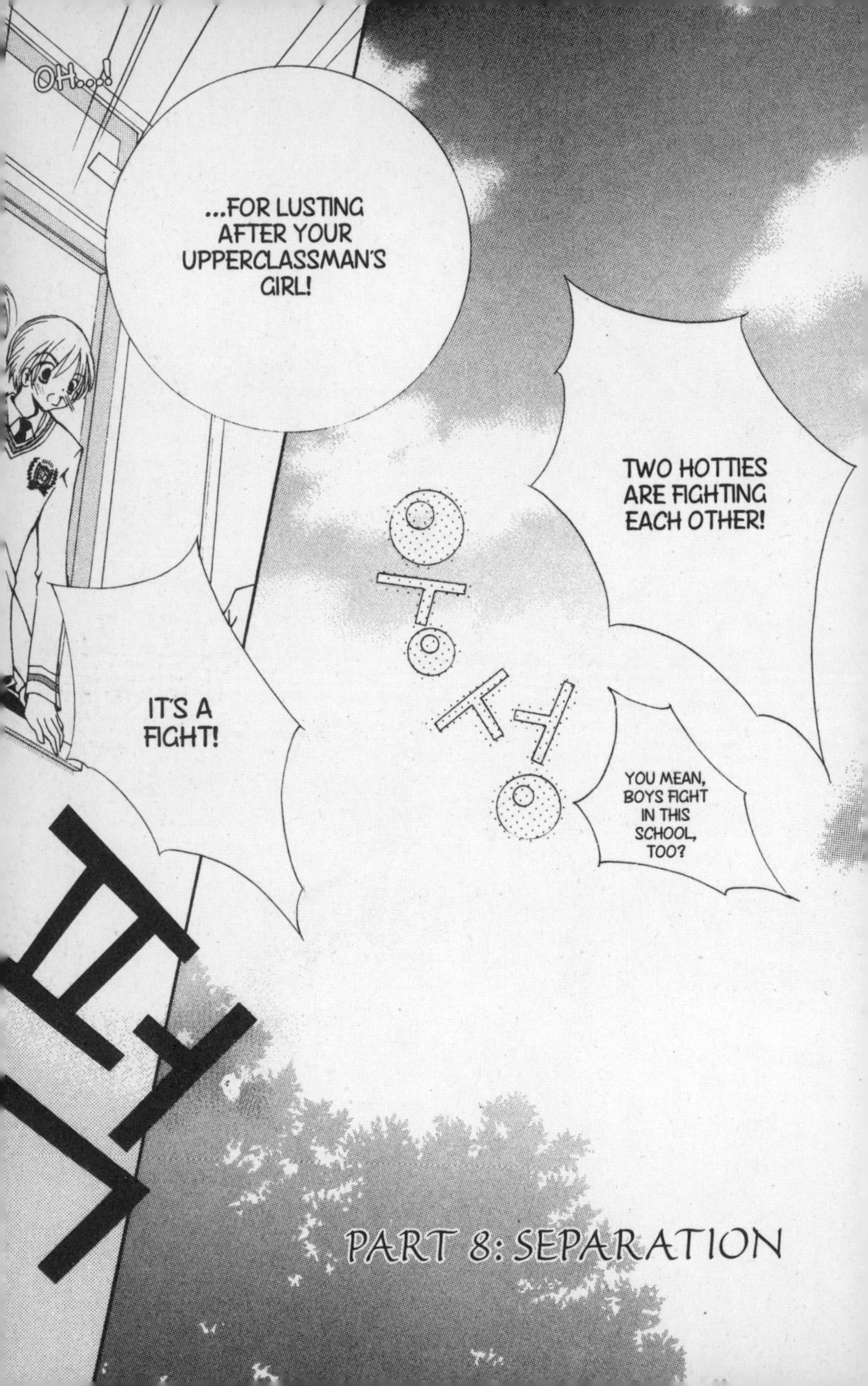
OH...!
...FOR LUSTING AFTER YOUR UPPERCLASSMAN'S GIRL!
IT'S A FIGHT!
TWO HOTTIES ARE FIGHTING EACH OTHER!
YOU MEAN, BOYS FIGHT IN THIS SCHOOL, TOO?
PART 8: SEPARATION

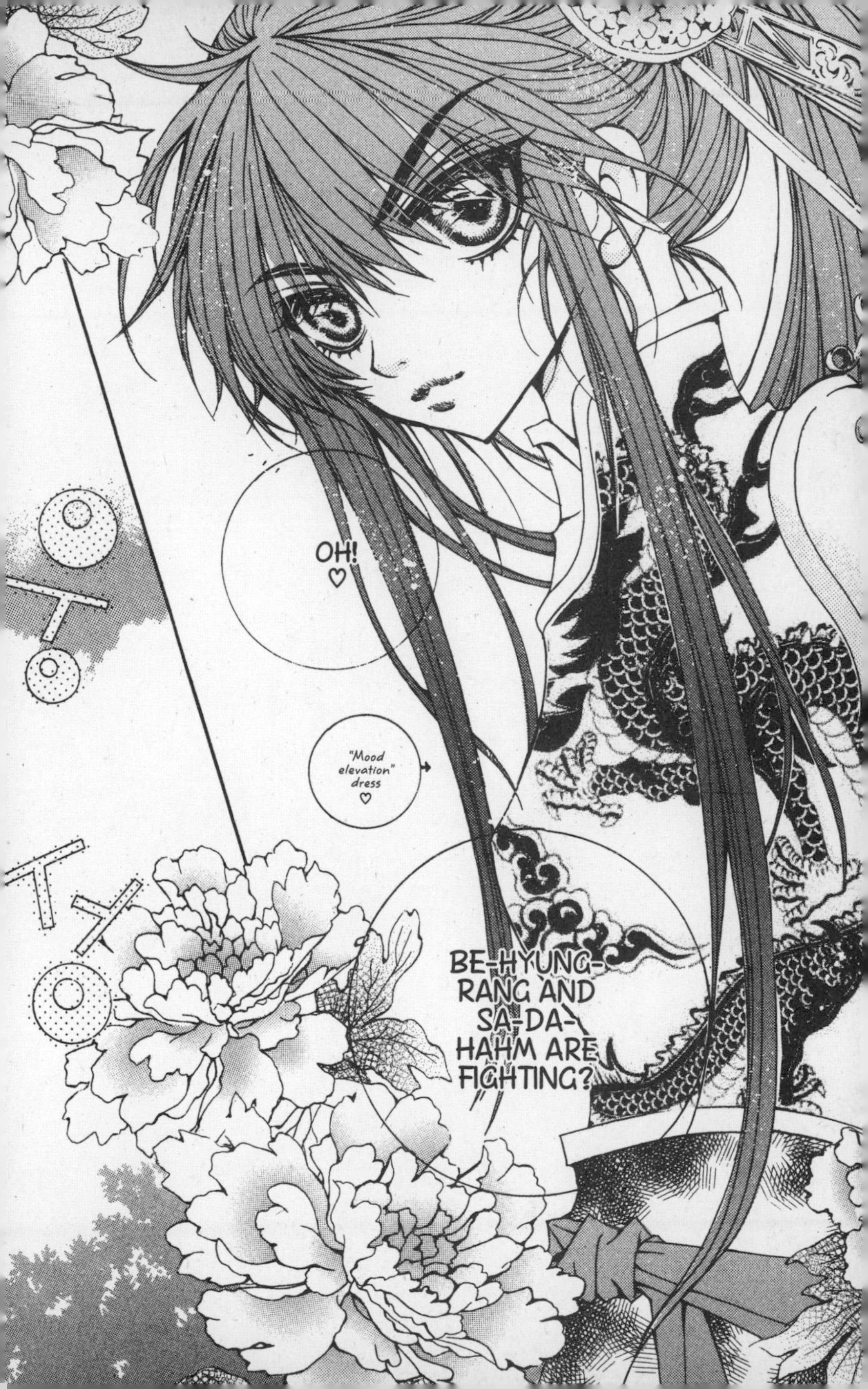
OH! ♡
"Mood elevation" dress ♡
BE-HYUNG-RANG AND SA-DA-HAHM ARE FIGHTING?

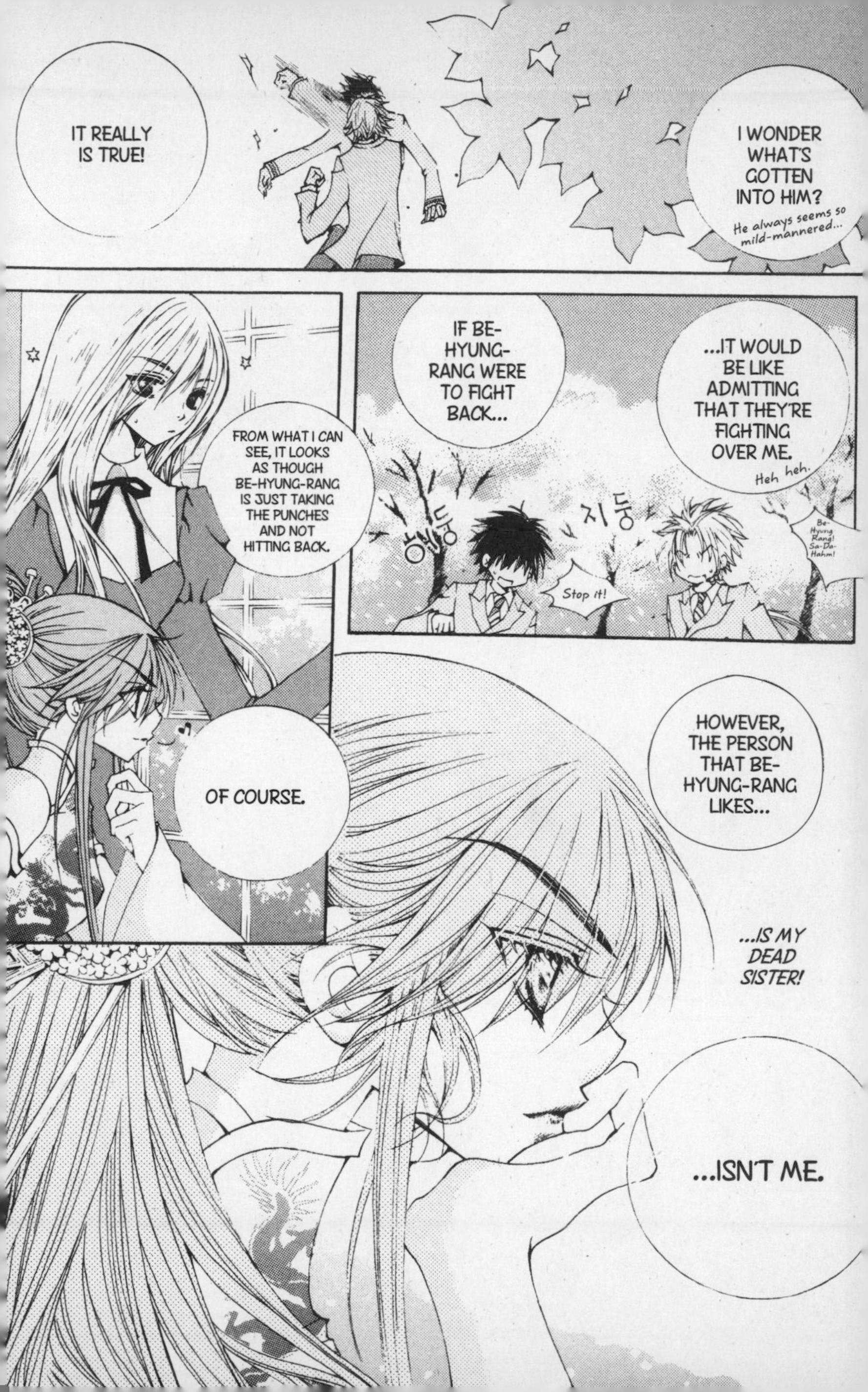
IT REALLY IS TRUE!
I WONDER WHAT'S GOTTEN INTO HIM?
He always seems so mild-mannered...
FROM WHAT I CAN SEE, IT LOOKS AS THOUGH BE-HYUNG-RANG IS JUST TAKING THE PUNCHES AND NOT HITTING BACK.
IF BE-HYUNG-RANG WERE TO FIGHT BACK...
...IT WOULD BE LIKE ADMITTING THAT THEY'RE FIGHTING OVER ME.
Heh heh.
지둥
Stop it!
Be-Hyung Rang! Sa-Da-Hahm!
OF COURSE.
HOWEVER, THE PERSON THAT BE-HYUNG-RANG LIKES...
...IS MY DEAD SISTER!
...ISN'T ME.

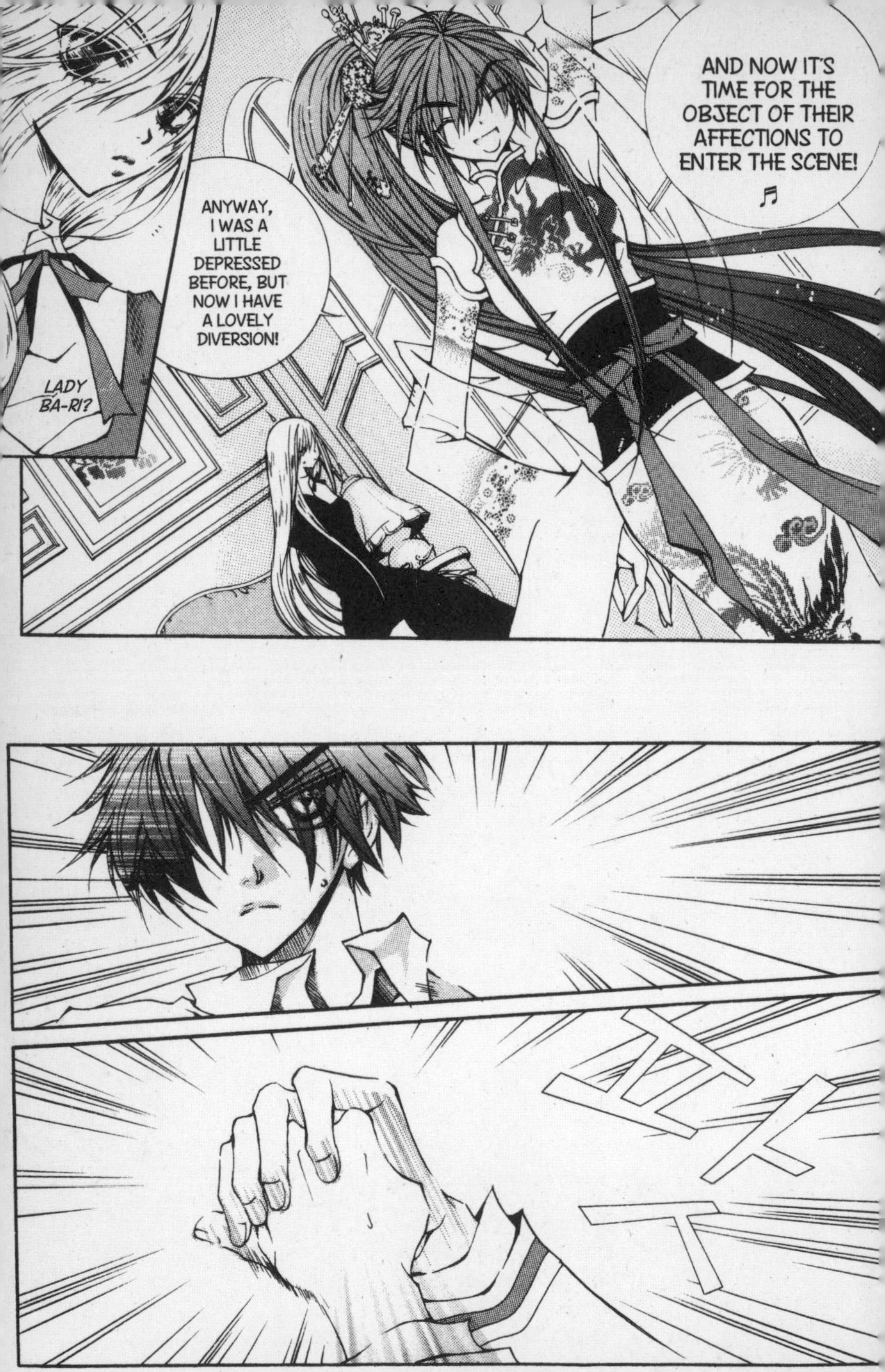
LADY BA-RI?
ANYWAY, I WAS A LITTLE DEPRESSED BEFORE, BUT NOW I HAVE A LOVELY DIVERSION!
AND NOW IT'S TIME FOR THE OBJECT OF THEIR AFFECTIONS TO ENTER THE SCENE! ♬

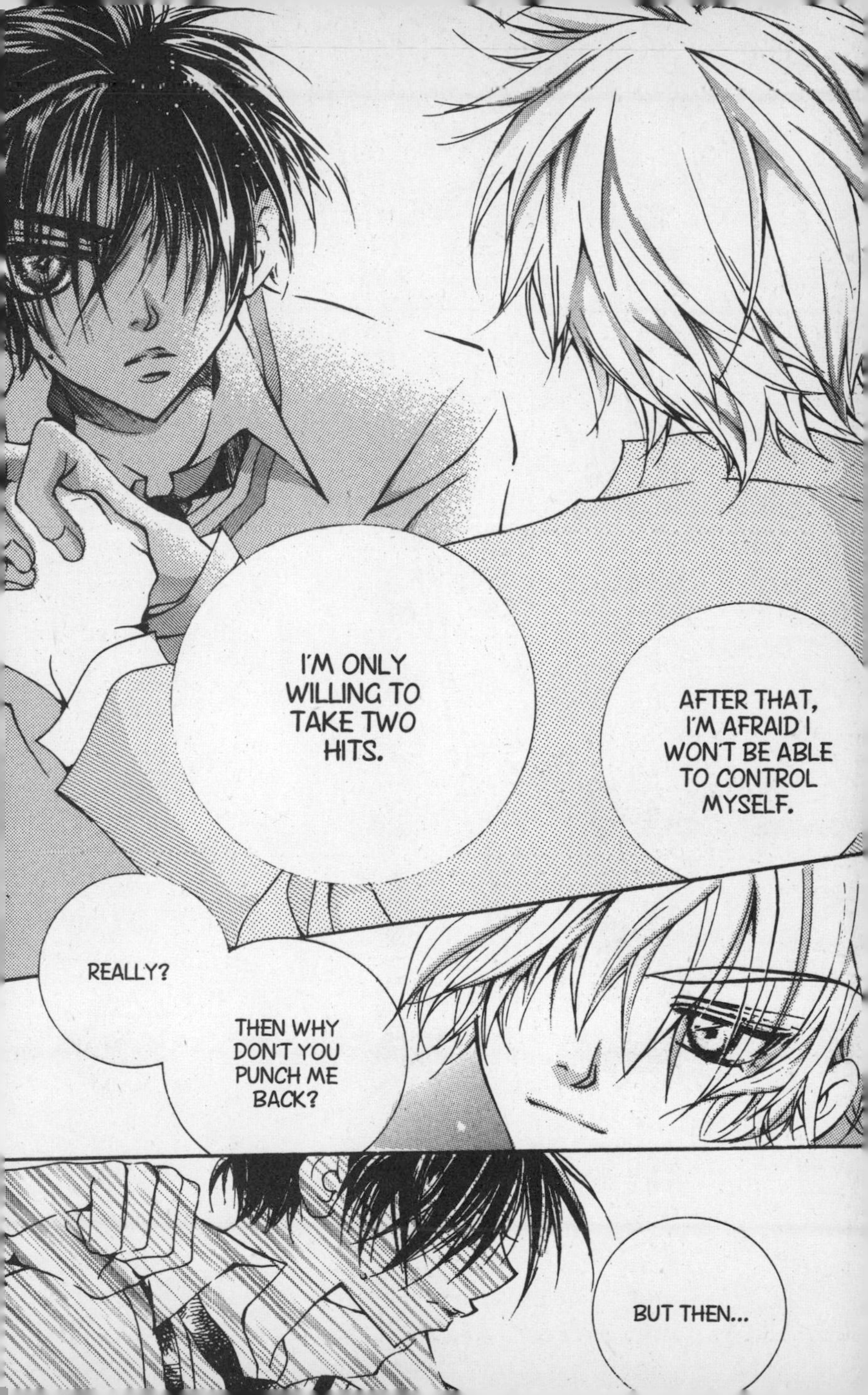
I'M ONLY WILLING TO TAKE TWO HITS.
AFTER THAT, I'M AFRAID I WON'T BE ABLE TO CONTROL MYSELF.
REALLY?
THEN WHY DON'T YOU PUNCH ME BACK?
BUT THEN...

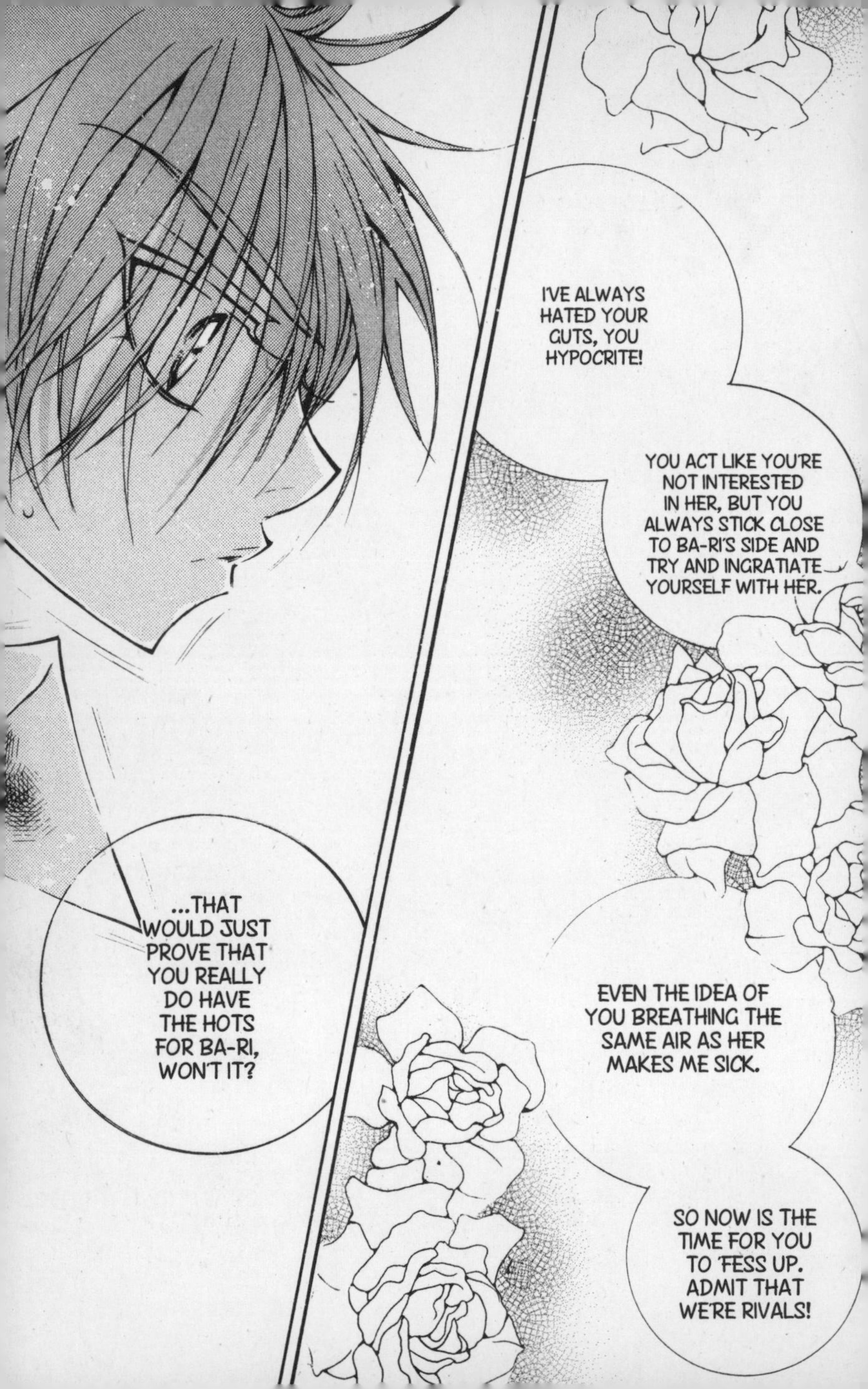
...THAT WOULD JUST PROVE THAT YOU REALLY DO HAVE THE HOTS FOR BA-RI, WON'T IT?
I'VE ALWAYS HATED YOUR GUTS, YOU HYPOCRITE!
YOU ACT LIKE YOU'RE NOT INTERESTED IN HER, BUT YOU ALWAYS STICK CLOSE TO BA-RI'S SIDE AND TRY AND INGRATIATE YOURSELF WITH HER.
EVEN THE IDEA OF YOU BREATHING THE SAME AIR AS HER MAKES ME SICK.
SO NOW IS THE TIME FOR YOU TO 'FESS UP. ADMIT THAT WE'RE RIVALS!

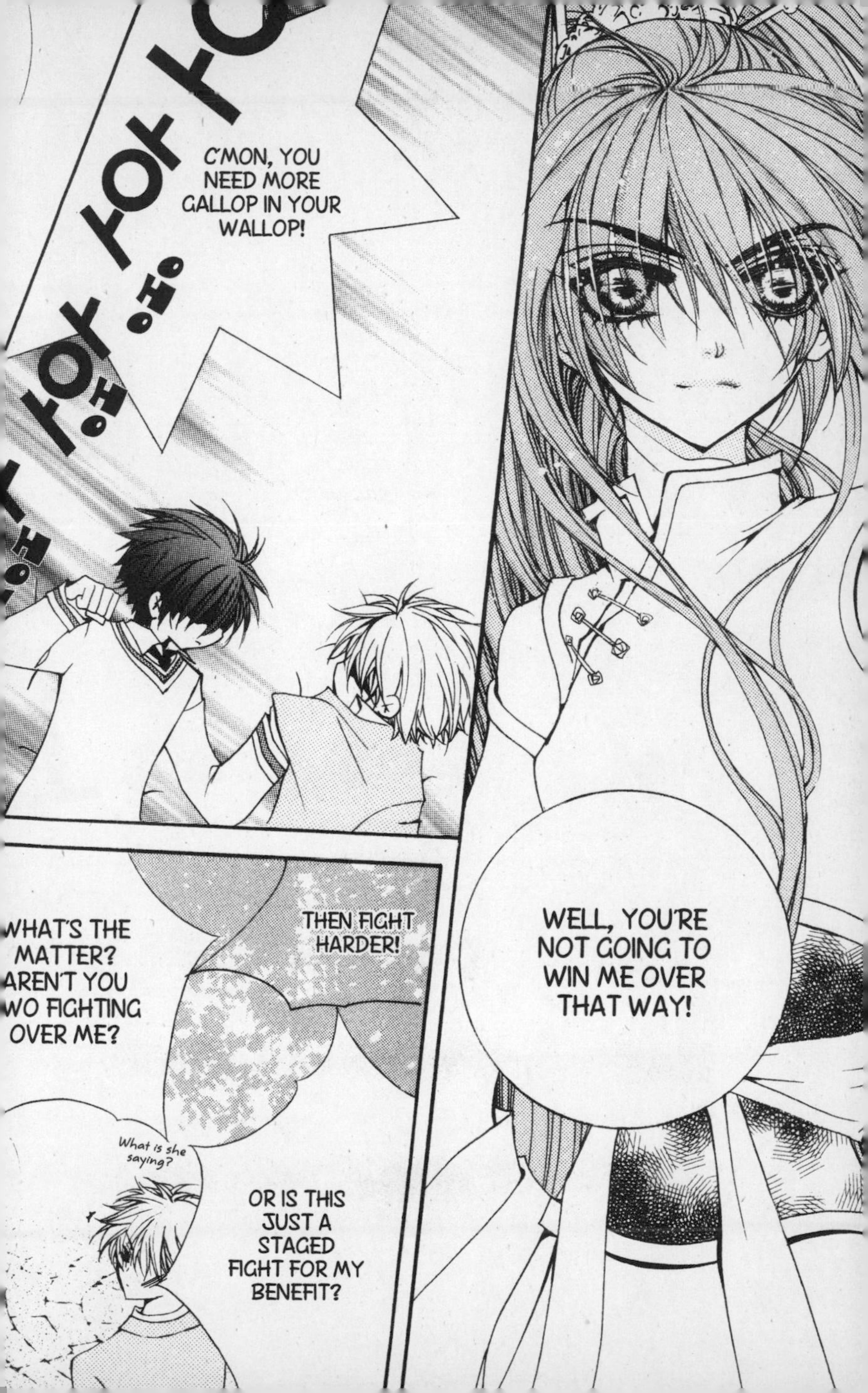
C'MON, YOU NEED MORE GALLOP IN YOUR WALLOP!
VHAT'S THE MATTER? AREN'T YOU WO FIGHTING OVER ME?
THEN FIGHT HARDER!
What is she saying?
OR IS THIS JUST A STAGED FIGHT FOR MY BENEFIT?
WELL, YOU'RE NOT GOING TO WIN ME OVER THAT WAY!

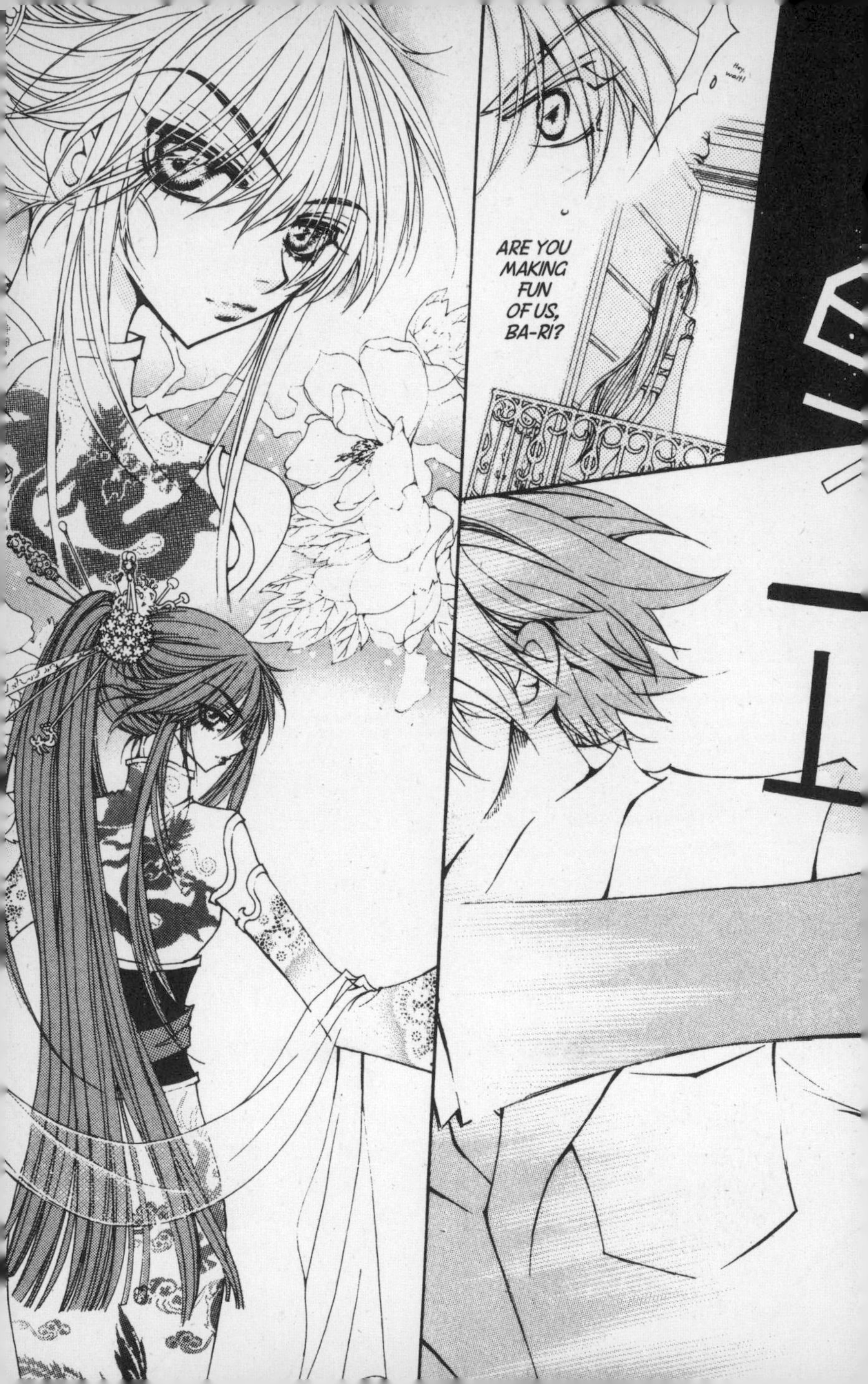
Hey, wait!
ARE YOU MAKING FUN OF US, BA-RI?

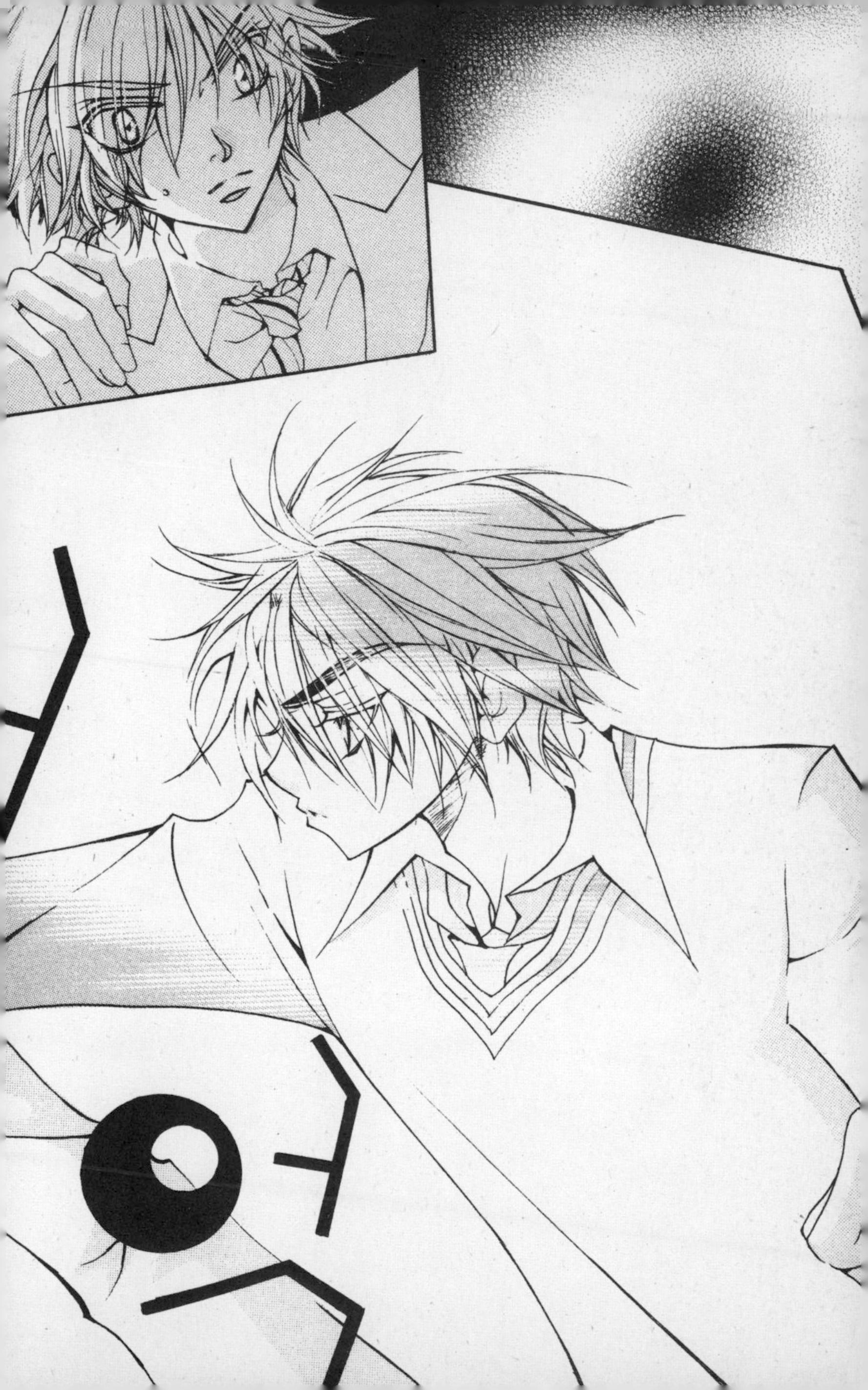

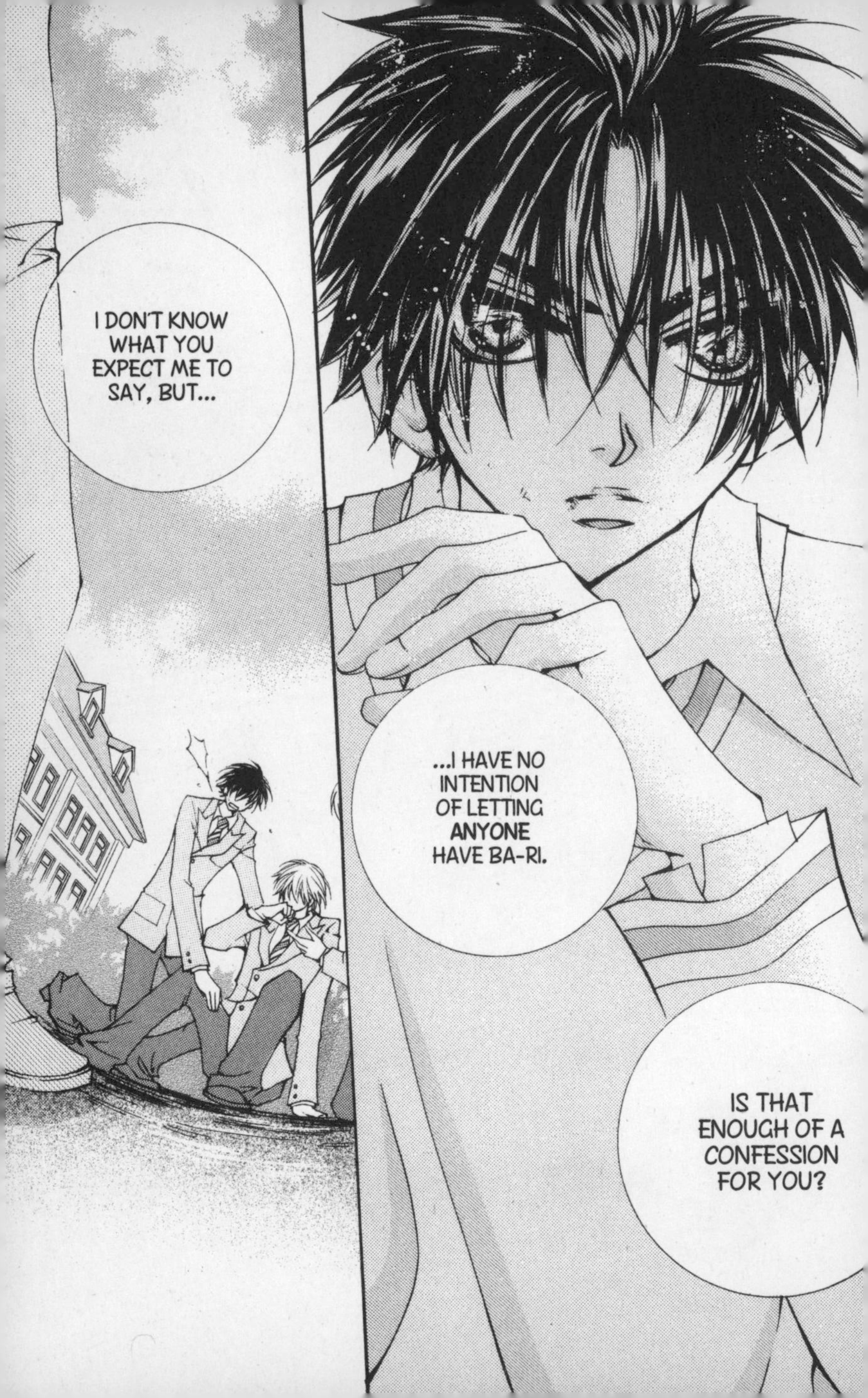
I DON'T KNOW WHAT YOU EXPECT ME TO SAY, BUT...
...I HAVE NO INTENTION OF LETTING ANYONE HAVE BA-RI.
IS THAT ENOUGH OF A CONFESSION FOR YOU?

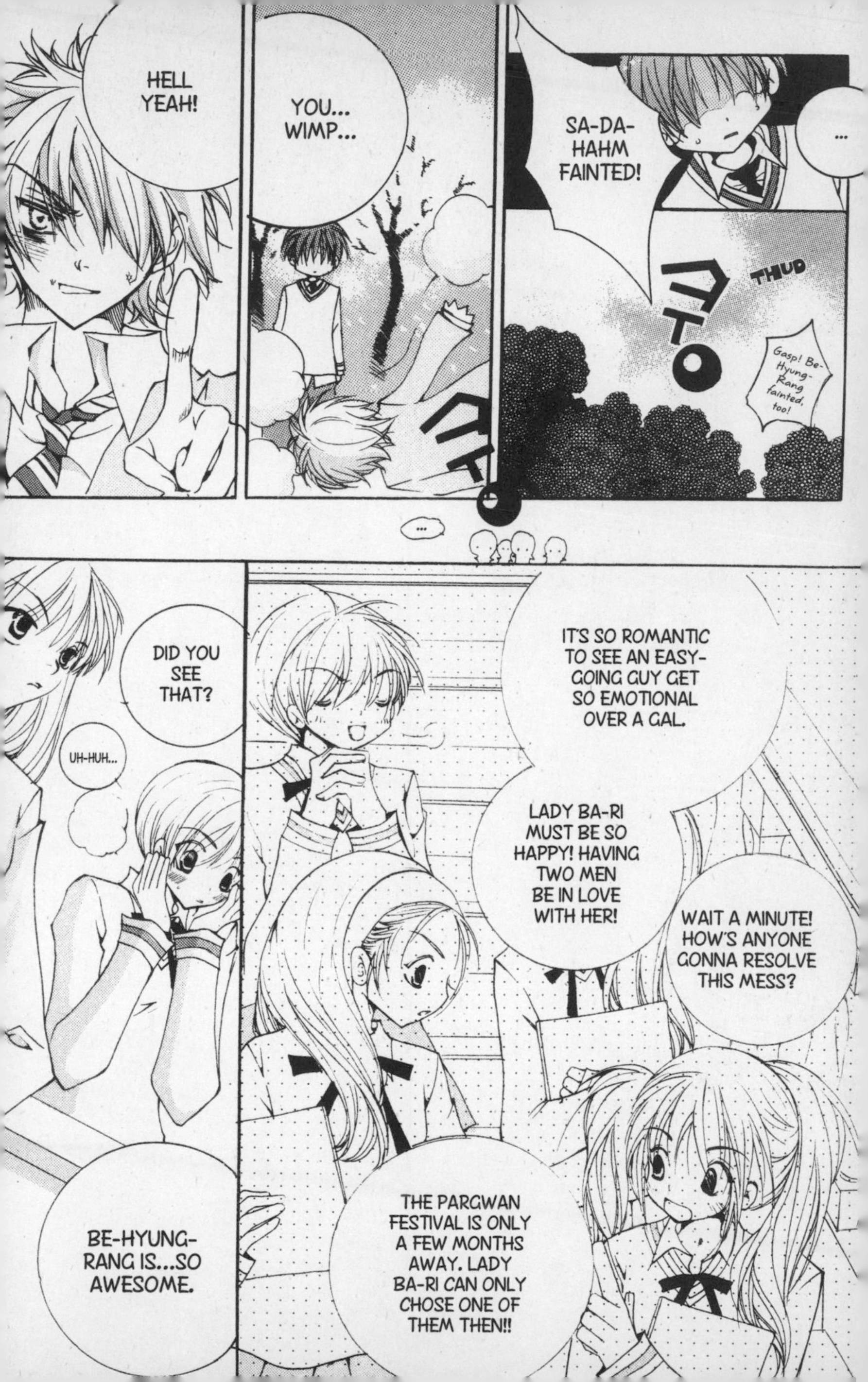
HELL YEAH!
YOU... WIMP...
SA-DA-HAHM FAINTED!
...
THUD
Gasp! Be-Hyung-Rang fainted, too!
...
DID YOU SEE THAT?
UH-HUH...
BE-HYUNG-RANG IS...SO AWESOME.
IT'S SO ROMANTIC TO SEE AN EASY-GOING GUY GET SO EMOTIONAL OVER A GAL.
LADY BA-RI MUST BE SO HAPPY! HAVING TWO MEN BE IN LOVE WITH HER!
WAIT A MINUTE! HOW'S ANYONE GONNA RESOLVE THIS MESS?
THE PARGWAN FESTIVAL IS ONLY A FEW MONTHS AWAY. LADY BA-RI CAN ONLY CHOSE ONE OF THEM THEN!!

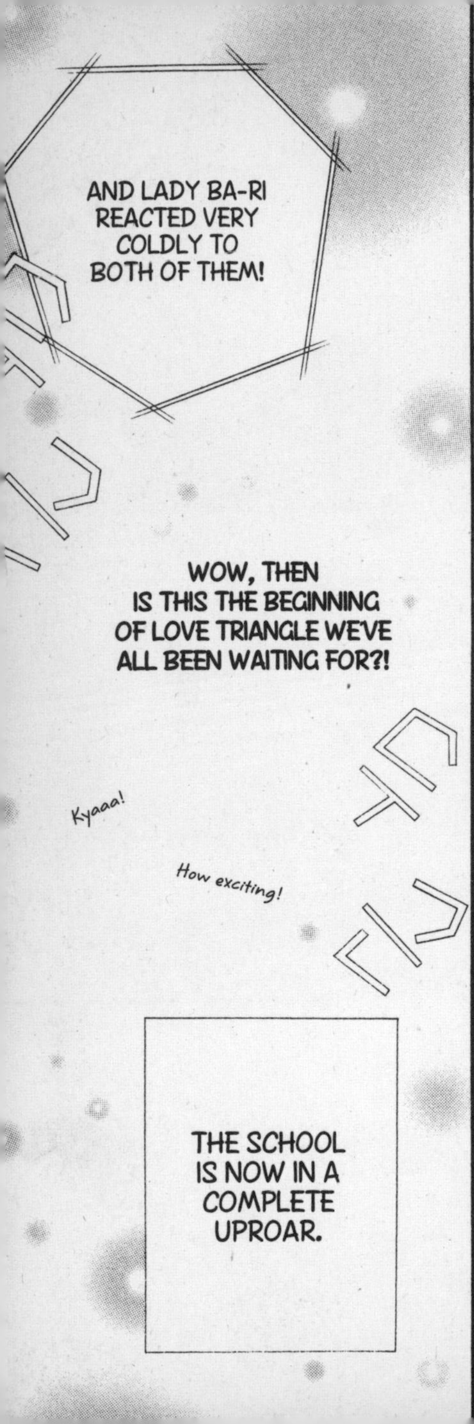
AND LADY BA-RI REACTED VERY COLDLY TO BOTH OF THEM!
WOW, THEN IS THIS THE BEGINNING OF LOVE TRIANGLE WE'VE ALL BEEN WAITING FOR?!
Kyaaa!
How exciting!
THE SCHOOL IS NOW IN A COMPLETE UPROAR.
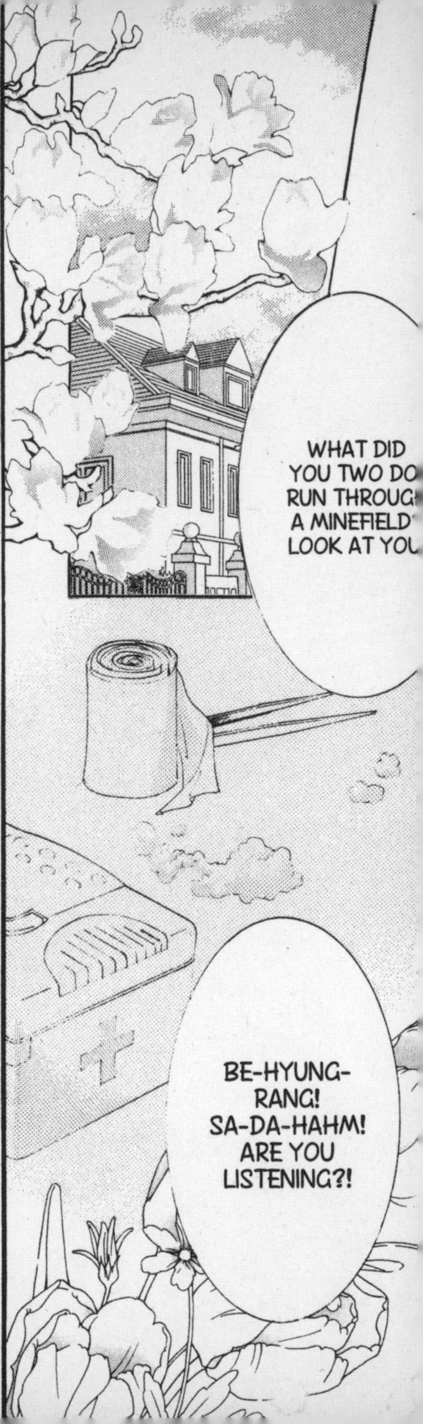
WHAT DID YOU TWO DO RUN THROUG A MINEFIELD LOOK AT YOU
BE-HYUNG-RANG! SA-DA-HAHM! ARE YOU LISTENING?!

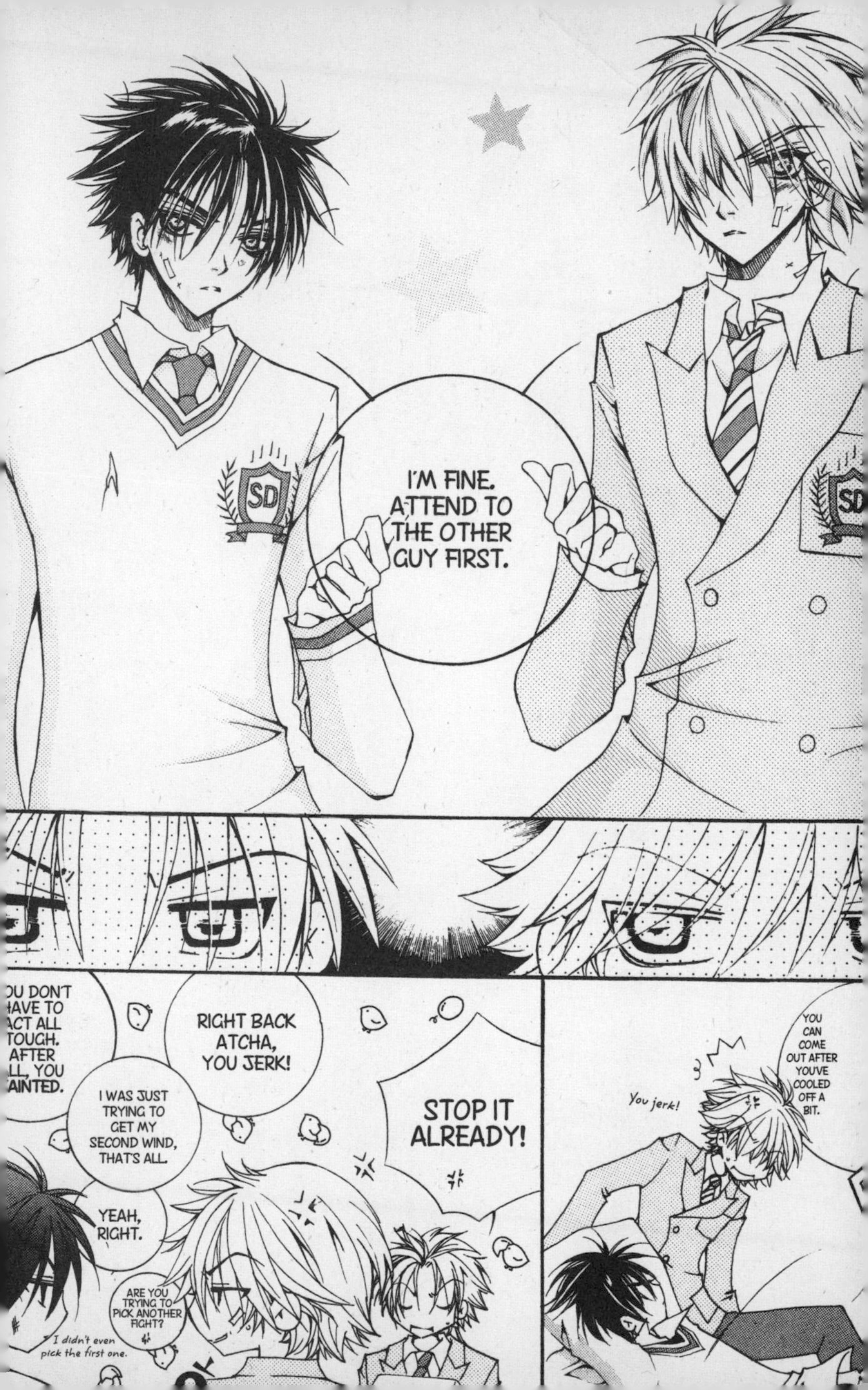
I'M FINE. ATTEND TO THE OTHER GUY FIRST.
OU DON'T HAVE TO ACT ALL TOUGH. AFTER LL, YOU AINTED.
RIGHT BACK ATCHA, YOU JERK!
I WAS JUST TRYING TO GET MY SECOND WIND, THAT'S ALL.
YEAH, RIGHT.
ARE YOU TRYING TO PICK ANOTHER FIGHT?
I didn't even pick the first one.
STOP IT ALREADY!
You jerk!
YOU CAN COME OUT AFTER YOU'VE COOLED OFF A BIT.

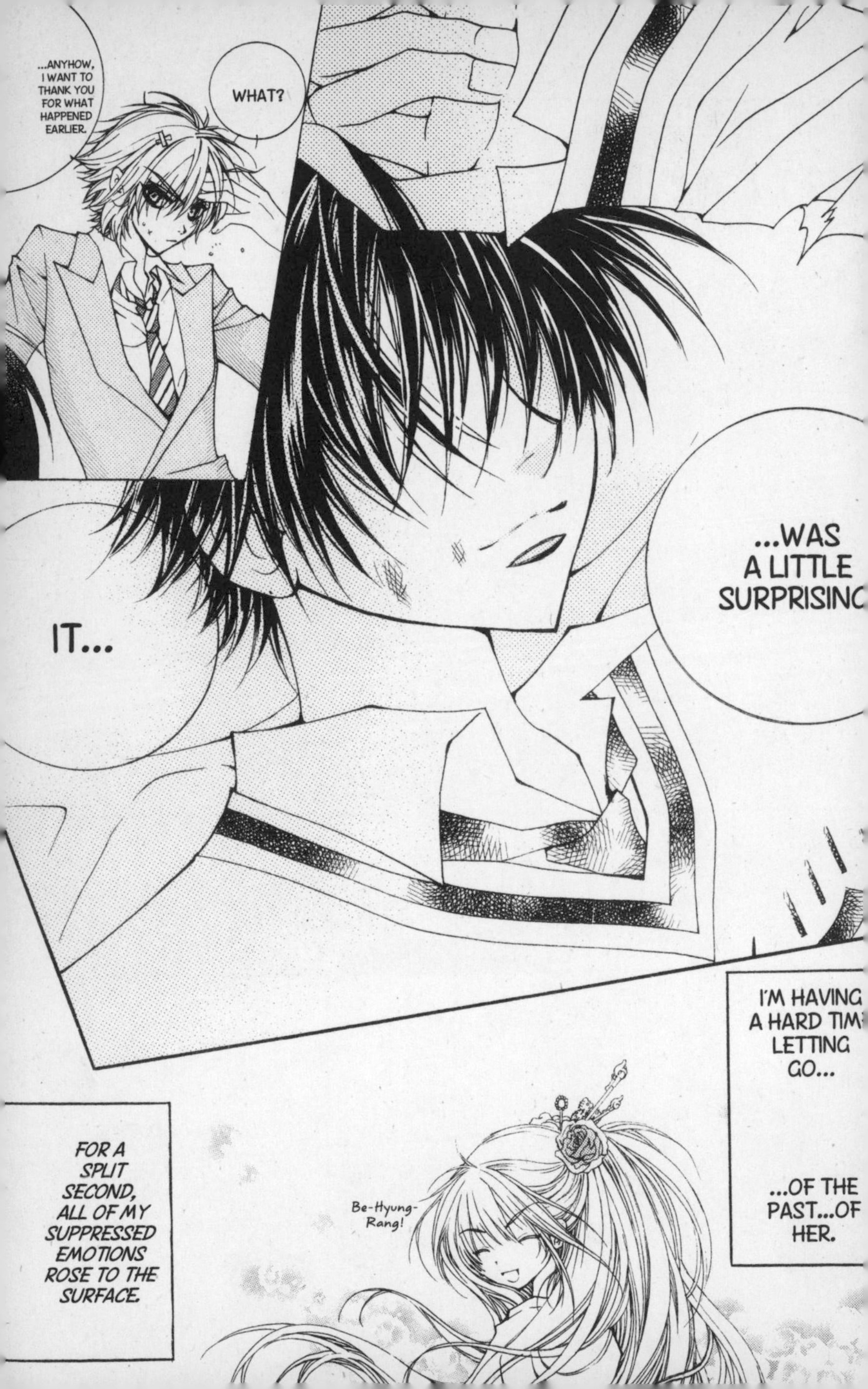
...ANYHOW, I WANT TO THANK YOU FOR WHAT HAPPENED EARLIER.
WHAT?
IT...
...WAS A LITTLE SURPRISING
I'M HAVING A HARD TIM LETTING GO...
...OF THE PAST...OF HER.
FOR A SPLIT SECOND, ALL OF MY SUPPRESSED EMOTIONS ROSE TO THE SURFACE.
Be-Hyung-Rang!

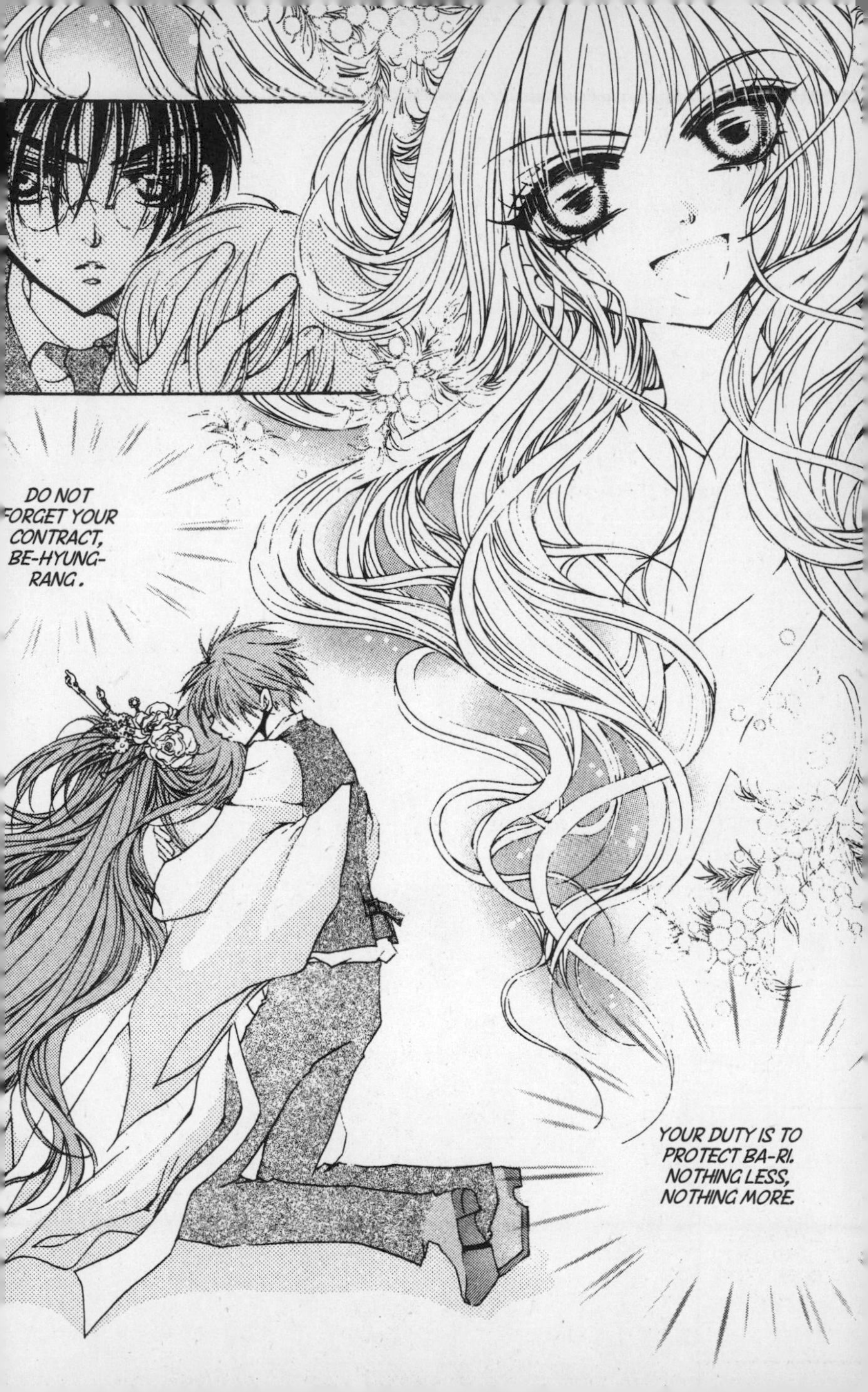
DO NOT FORGET YOUR CONTRACT, BE-HYUNG-RANG.
YOUR DUTY IS TO PROTECT BA-RI. NOTHING LESS, NOTHING MORE.

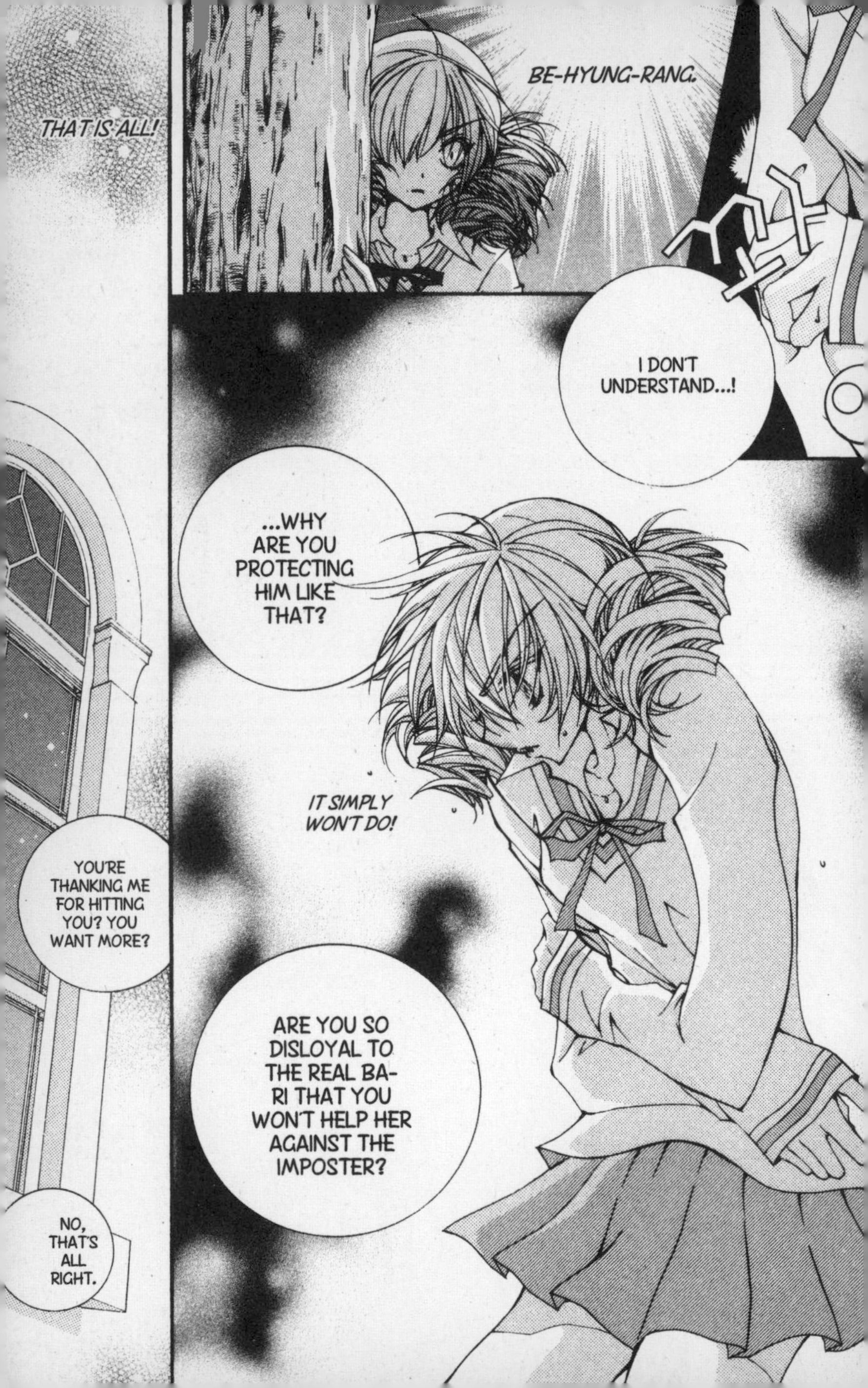
THAT IS ALL!
YOU'RE THANKING ME FOR HITTING YOU? YOU WANT MORE?
NO, THAT'S ALL RIGHT.
BE-HYUNG-RANG.
I DON'T UNDERSTAND...!
...WHY ARE YOU PROTECTING HIM LIKE THAT?
IT SIMPLY WON'T DO!
ARE YOU SO DISLOYAL TO THE REAL BA-RI THAT YOU WON'T HELP HER AGAINST THE IMPOSTER?

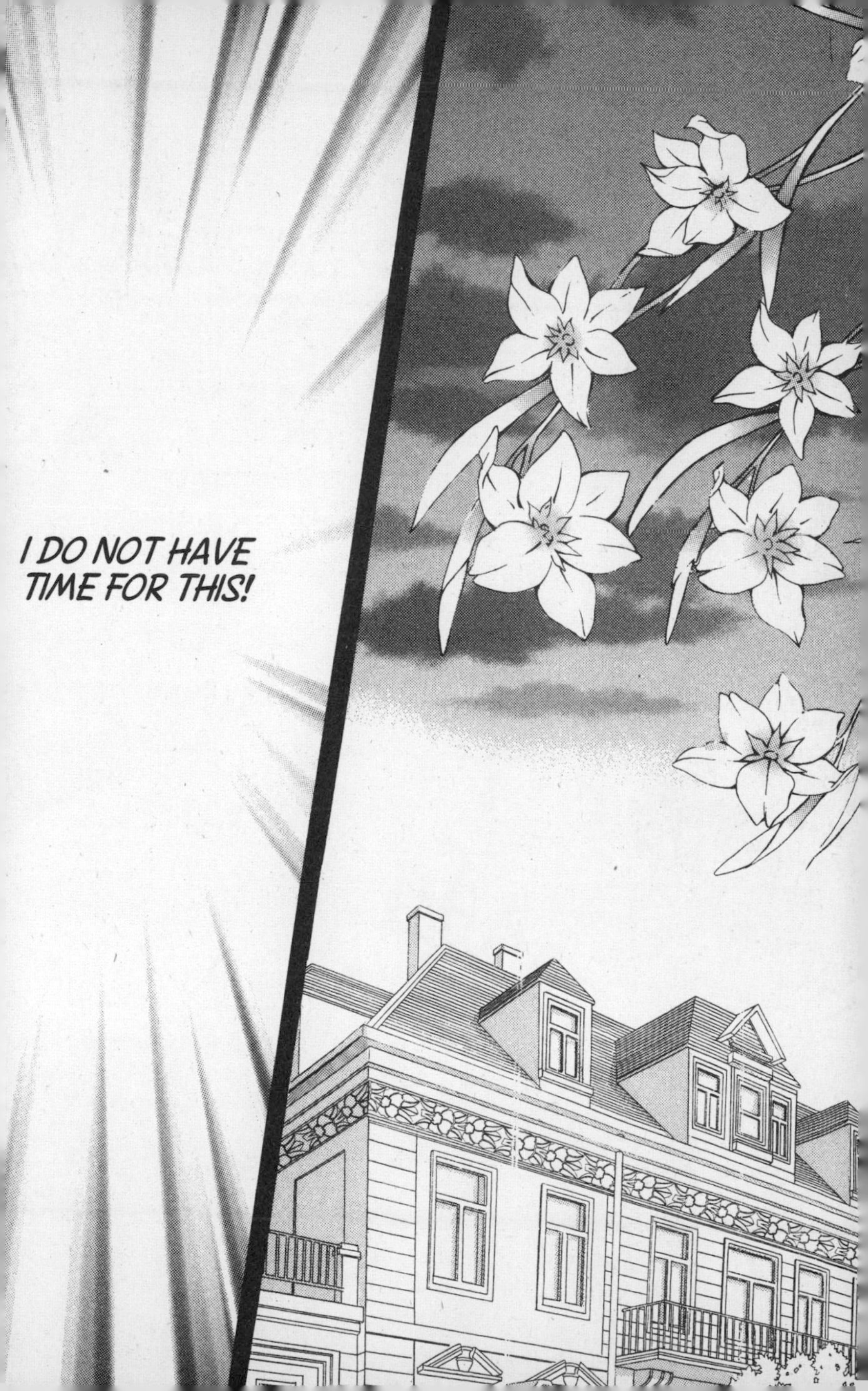
I DO NOT HAVE TIME FOR THIS!

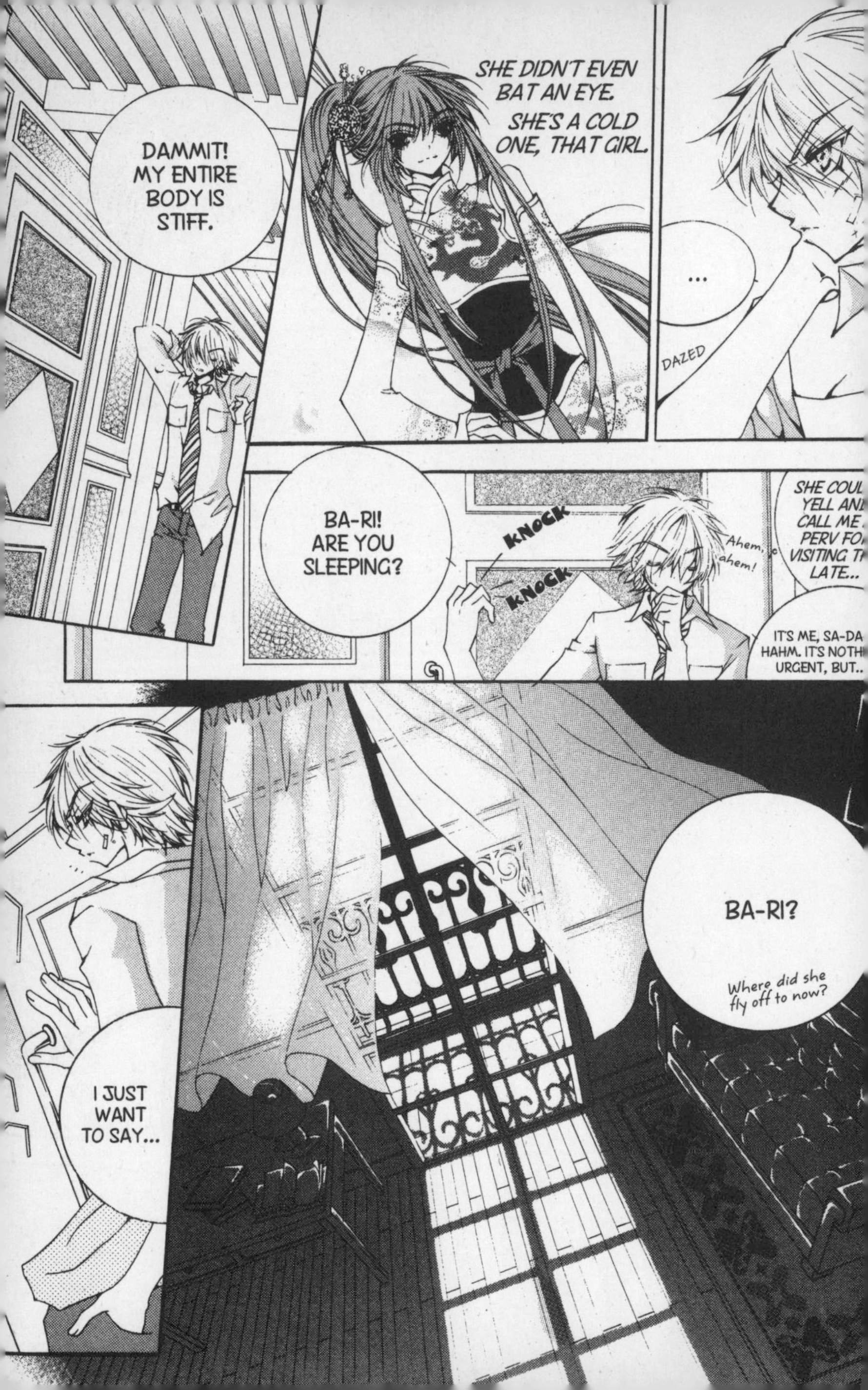
DAMMIT! MY ENTIRE BODY IS STIFF.
SHE DIDN'T EVEN BAT AN EYE.
SHE'S A COLD ONE, THAT GIRL.
...
DAZED
BA-RI! ARE YOU SLEEPING?
KNOCK
KNOCK
Ahem, ahem!
SHE COUL YELL AN CALL ME PERV FO VISITING T LATE...
IT'S ME, SA-DA HAHM. IT'S NOTH URGENT, BUT...
I JUST WANT TO SAY...
BA-RI?
Where did she fly off to now?

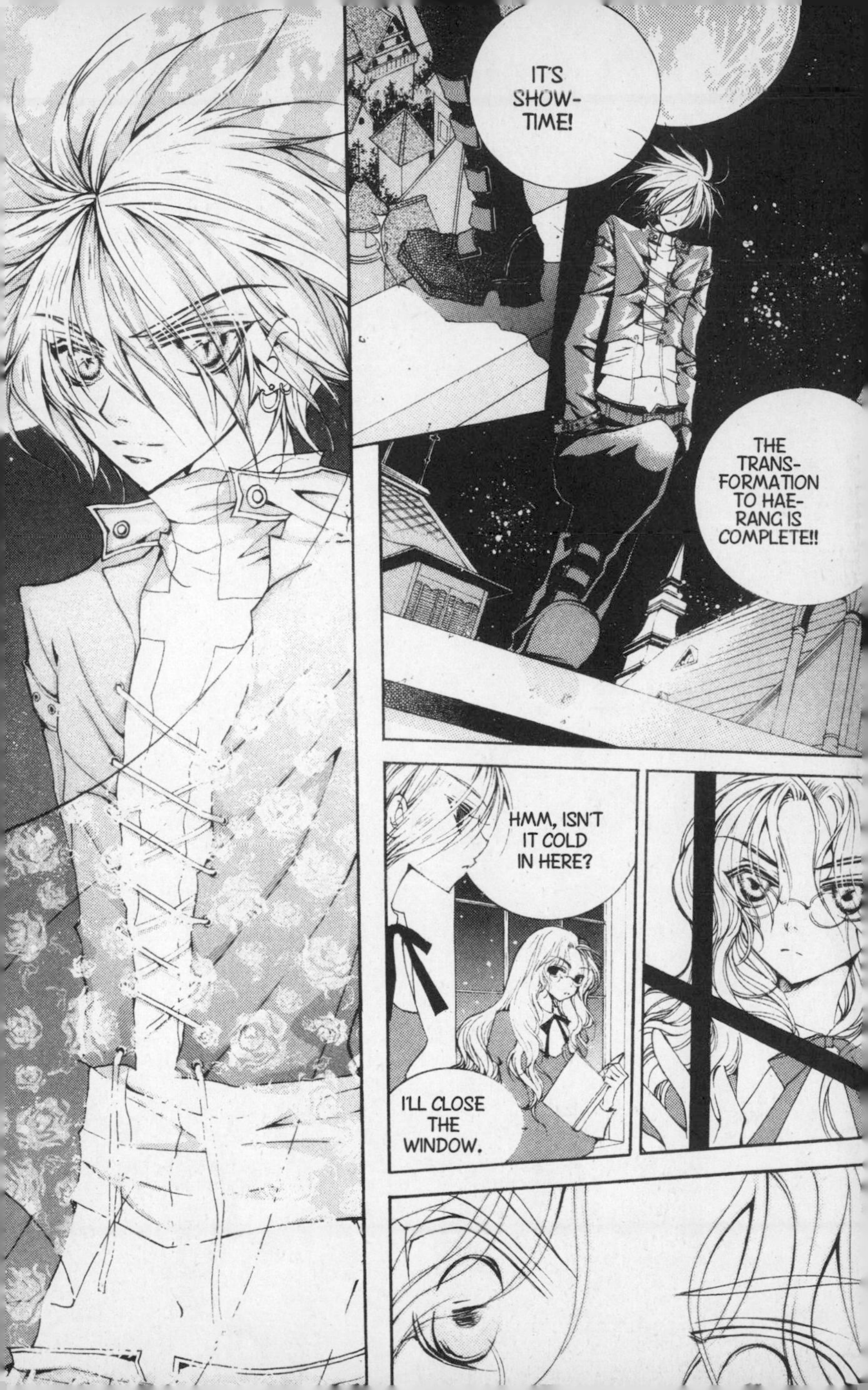
IT'S SHOW-TIME!
THE TRANS-FORMATION TO HAE-RANG IS COMPLETE!!
HMM, ISN'T IT COLD IN HERE?
I'LL CLOSE THE WINDOW.

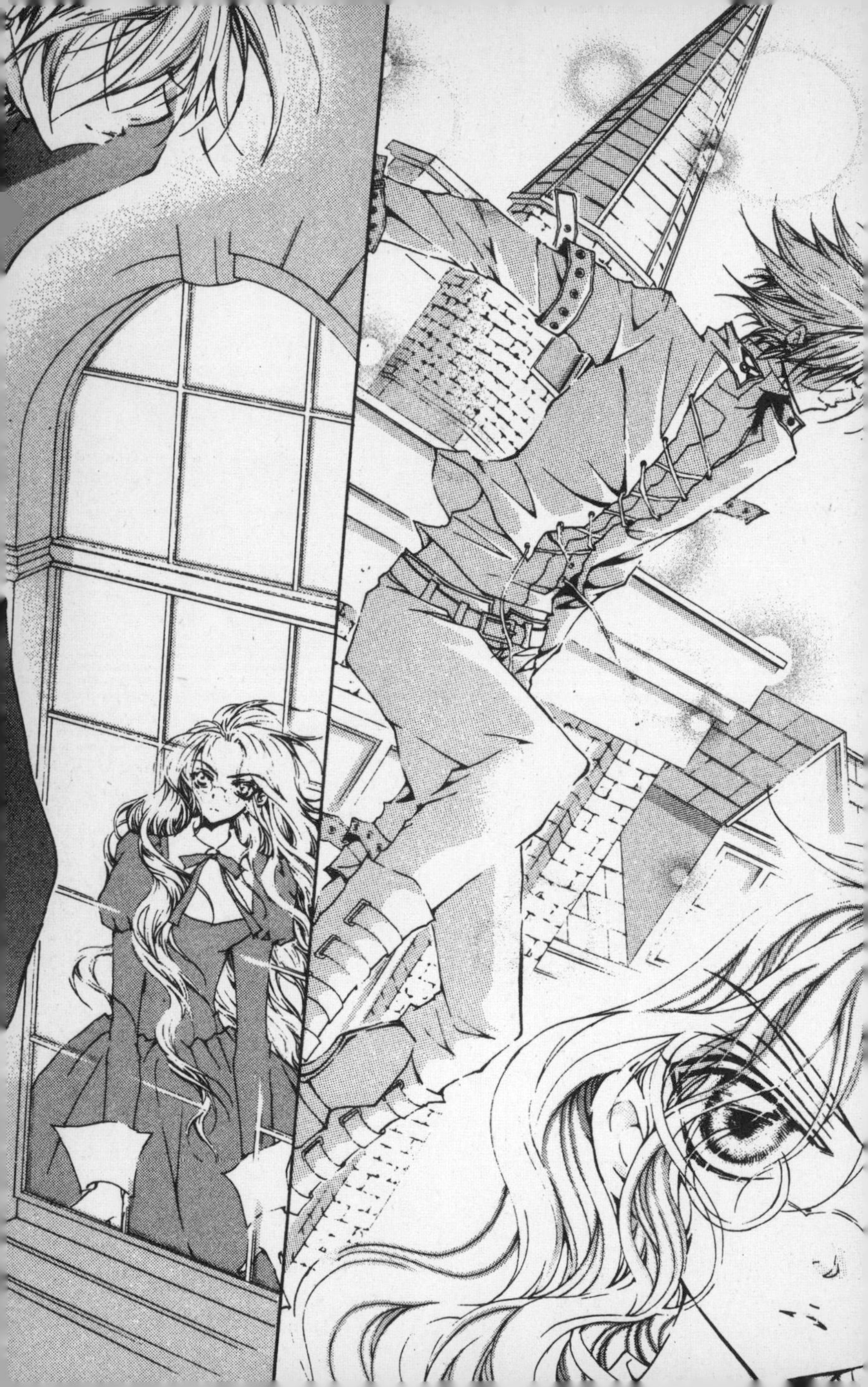

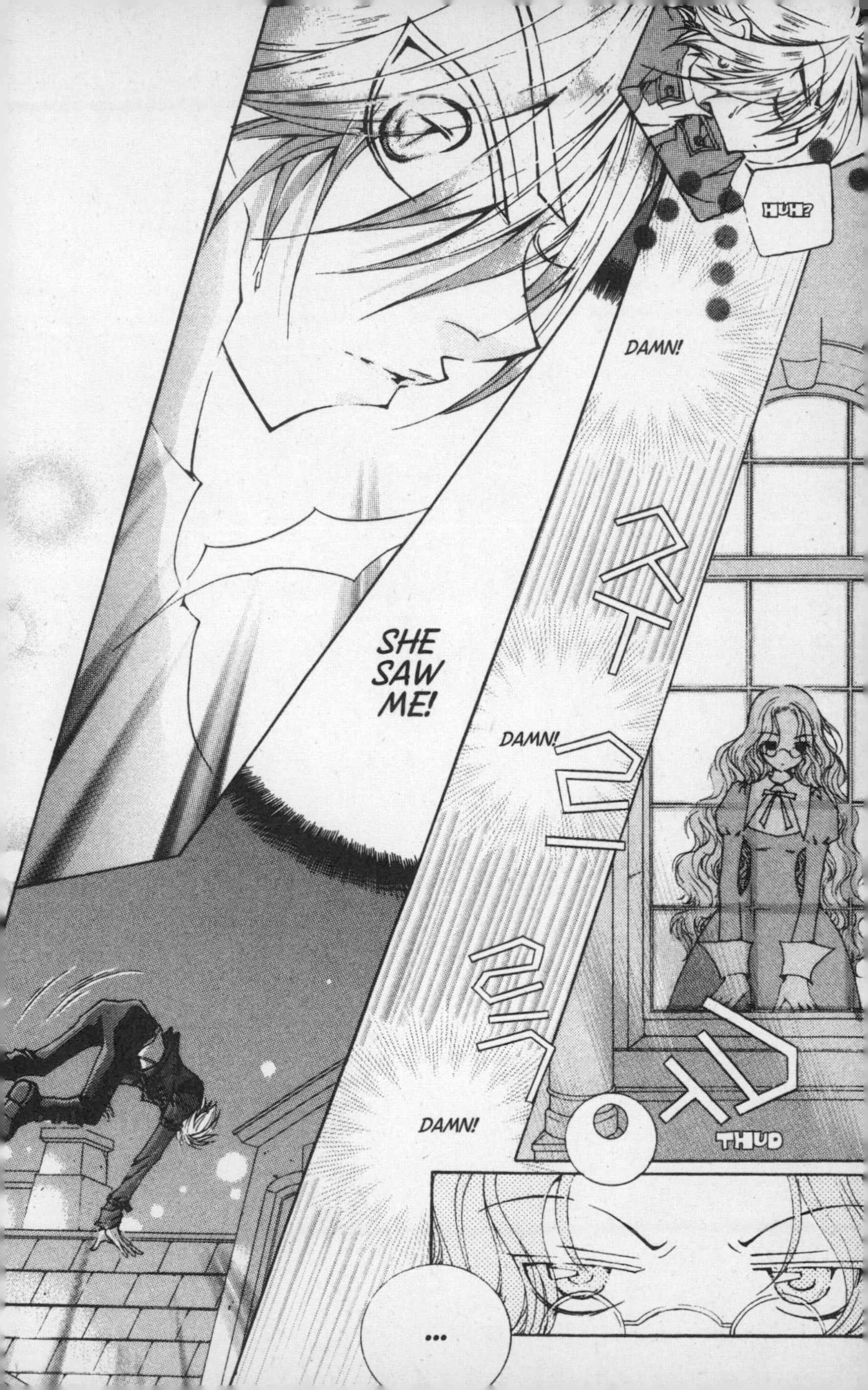
SHE SAW ME!
HUH?
DAMN!
DAMN!
DAMN!
THUD
...

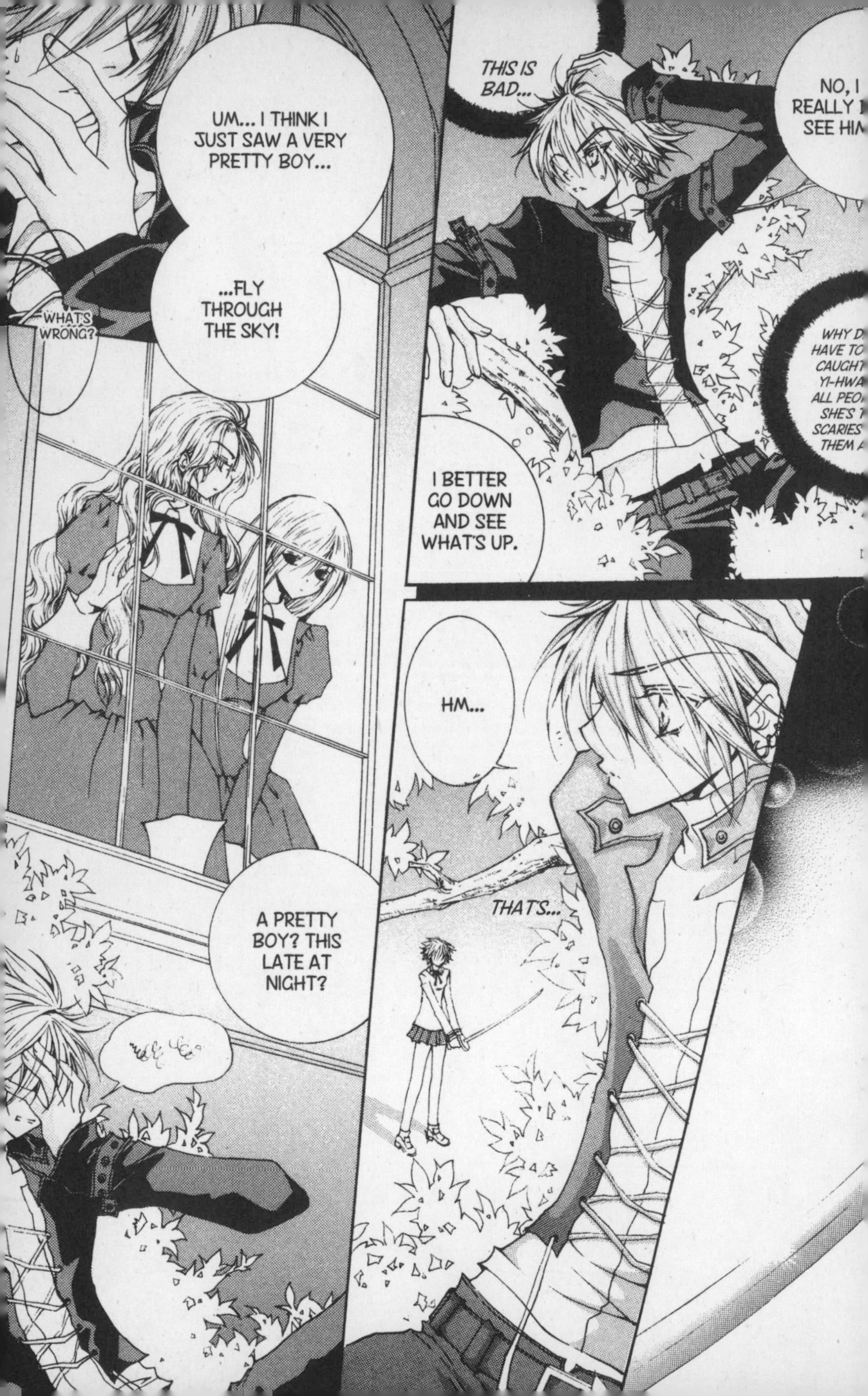
WHAT'S WRONG?
UM... I THINK I JUST SAW A VERY PRETTY BOY...
...FLY THROUGH THE SKY!
A PRETTY BOY? THIS LATE AT NIGHT?
THIS IS BAD...
NO, I REALLY
I BETTER GO DOWN AND SEE WHAT'S UP.
HM...
THAT'S...

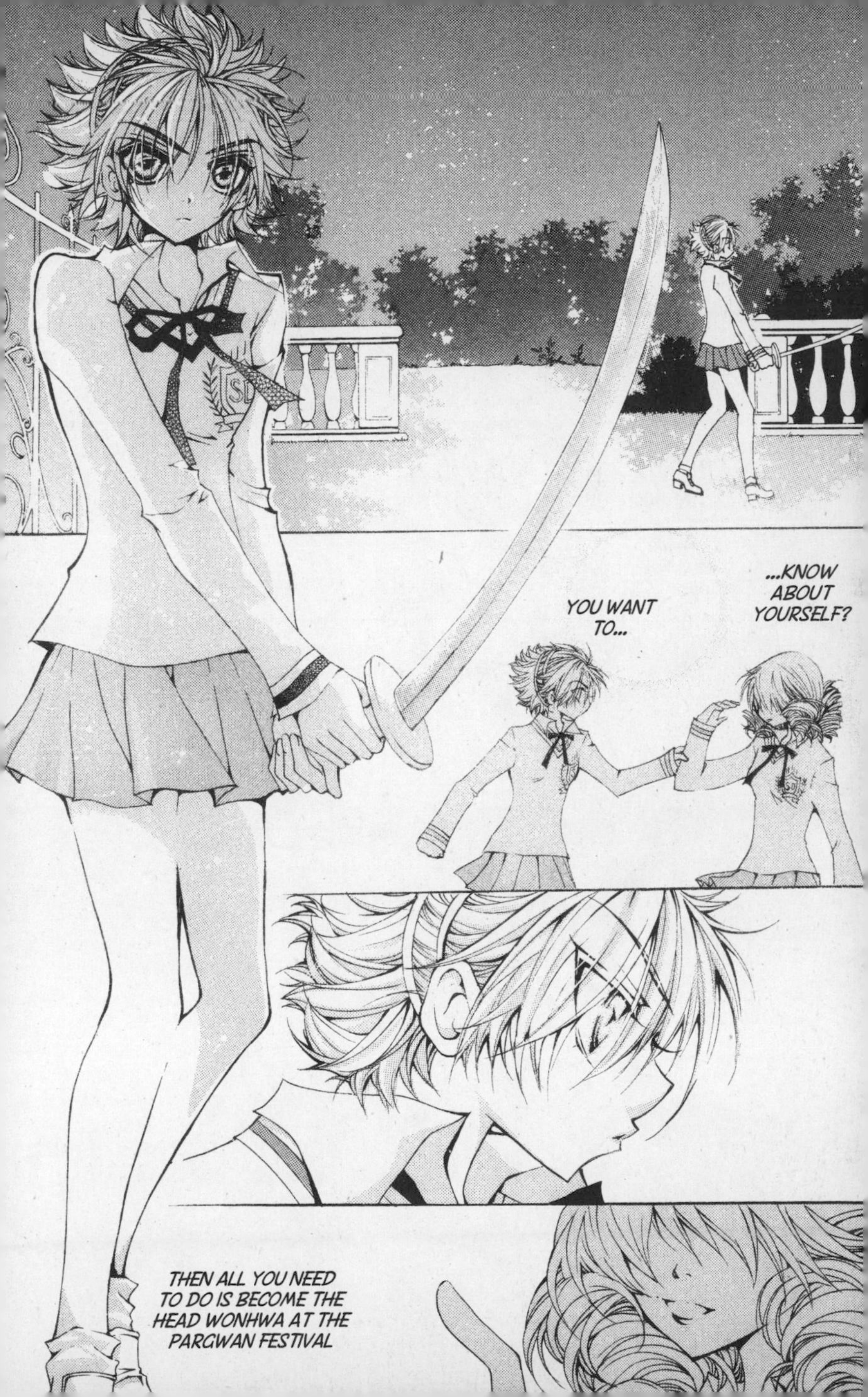
YOU WANT TO...
...KNOW ABOUT YOURSELF?
THEN ALL YOU NEED TO DO IS BECOME THE HEAD WONHWA AT THE PARGWAN FESTIVAL

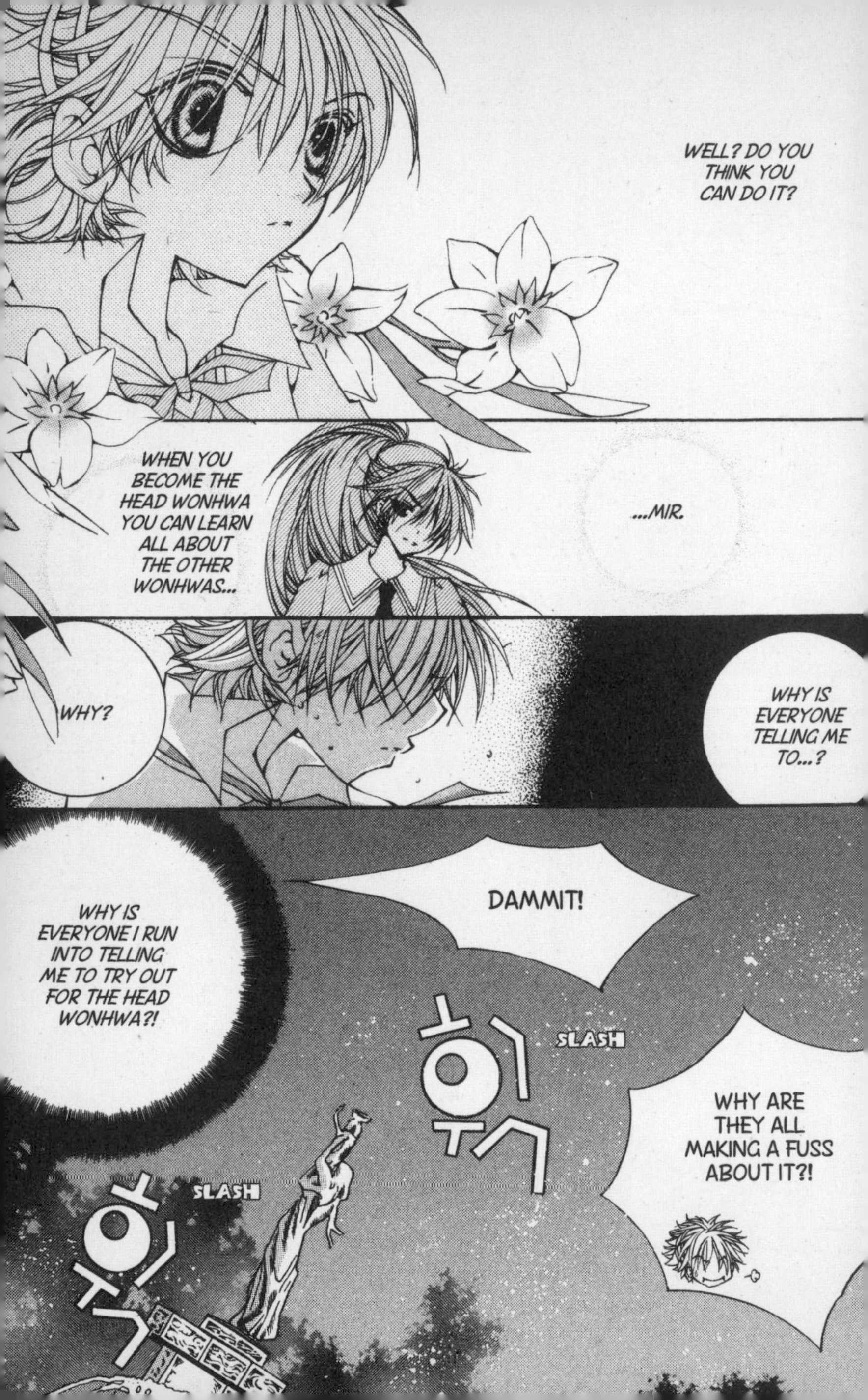
WELL? DO YOU THINK YOU CAN DO IT?
WHEN YOU BECOME THE HEAD WONHWA YOU CAN LEARN ALL ABOUT THE OTHER WONHWAS...
...MIR.
WHY?
WHY IS EVERYONE TELLING ME TO...?
WHY IS EVERYONE I RUN INTO TELLING ME TO TRY OUT FOR THE HEAD WONHWA?!
DAMMIT!
휙
SLASH
WHY ARE THEY ALL MAKING A FUSS ABOUT IT?!
휙
SLASH

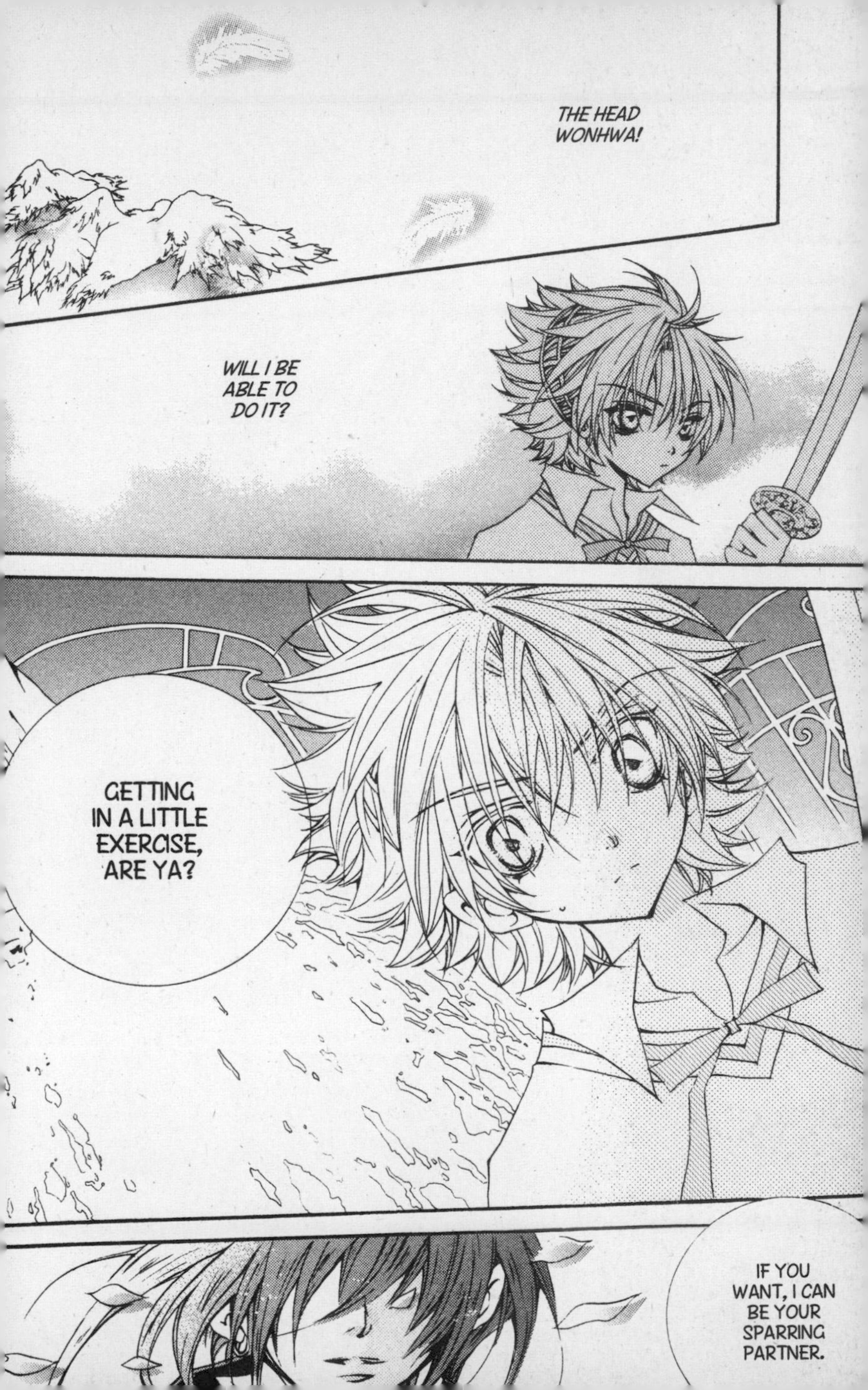
THE HEAD WONHWA!
WILL I BE ABLE TO DO IT?
GETTING IN A LITTLE EXERCISE, ARE YA?
IF YOU WANT, I CAN BE YOUR SPARRING PARTNER.

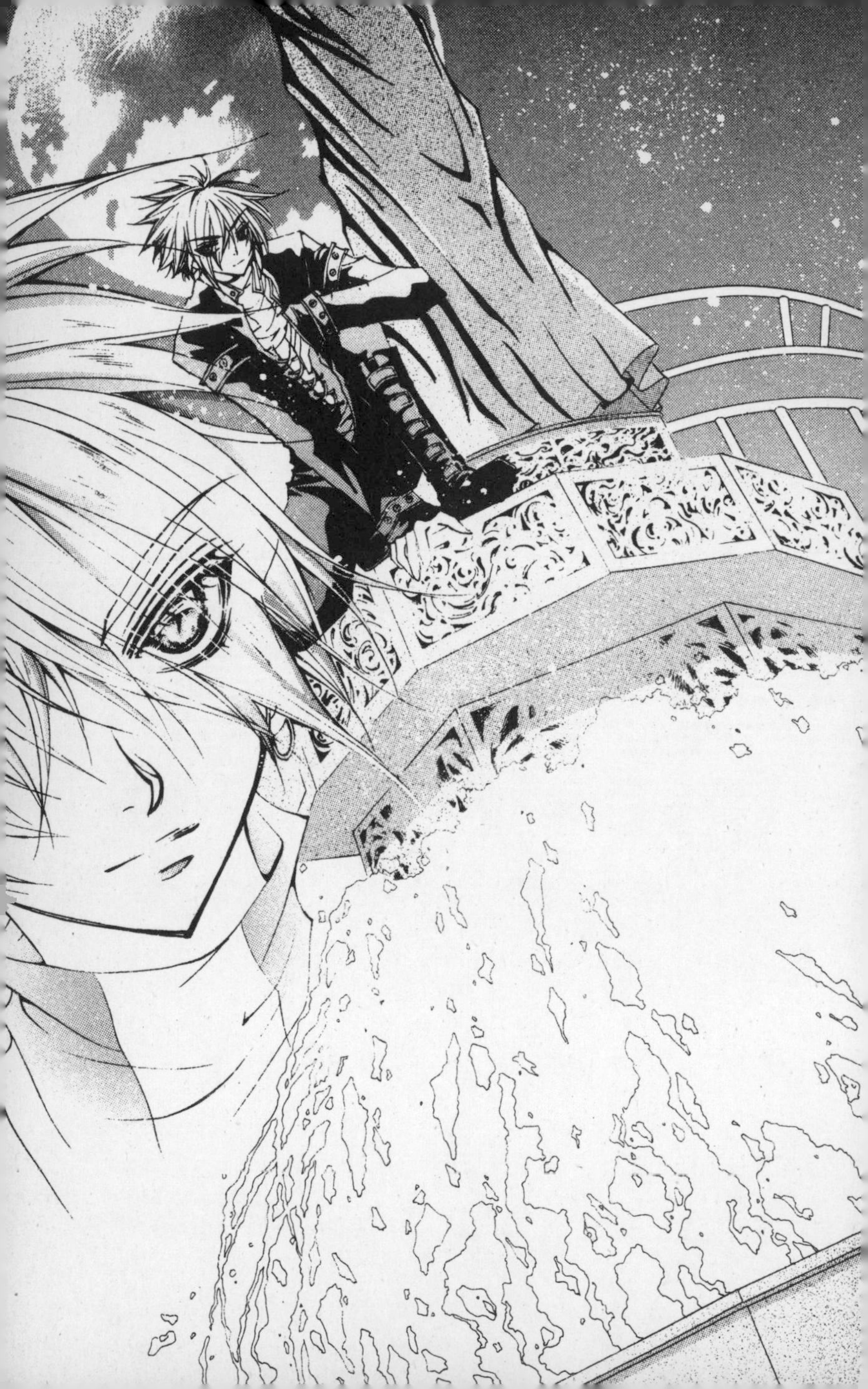

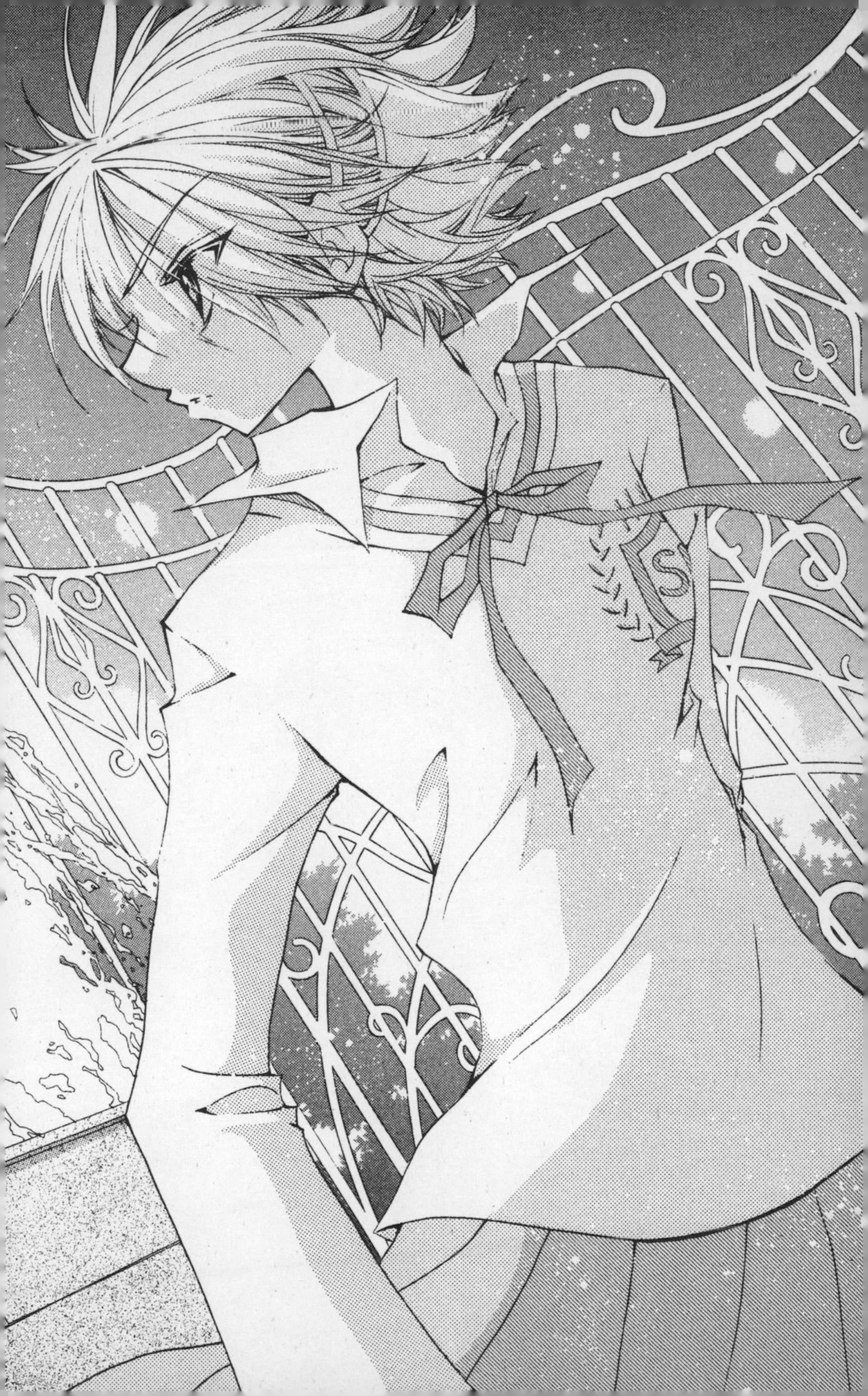

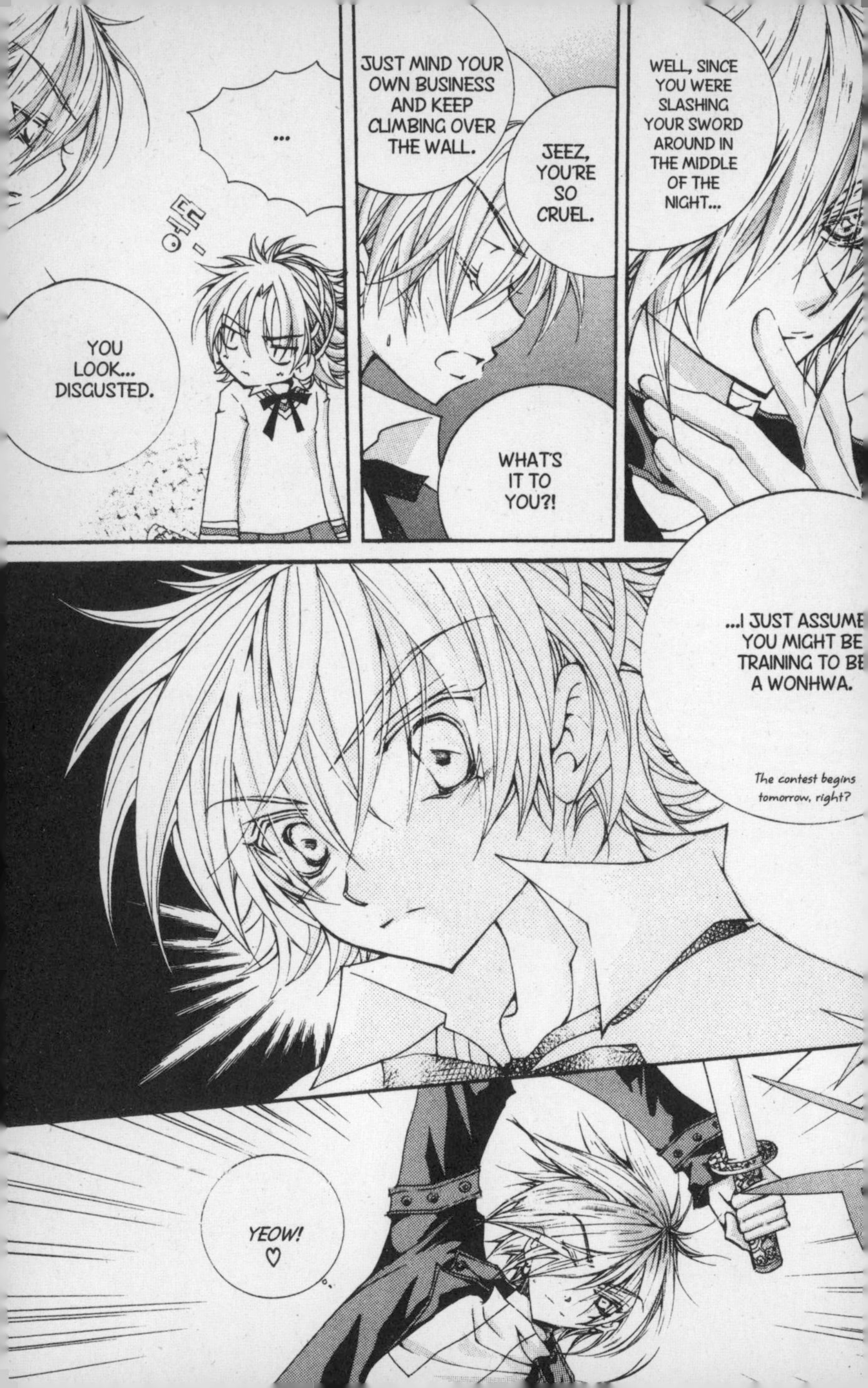
...
YOU LOOK... DISGUSTED.
JUST MIND YOUR OWN BUSINESS AND KEEP CLIMBING OVER THE WALL.
JEEZ, YOU'RE SO CRUEL.
WHAT'S IT TO YOU?!
WELL, SINCE YOU WERE SLASHING YOUR SWORD AROUND IN THE MIDDLE OF THE NIGHT...
...I JUST ASSUME YOU MIGHT BE TRAINING TO BE A WONHWA.
The contest begins tomorrow, right?
YEOW! ♡

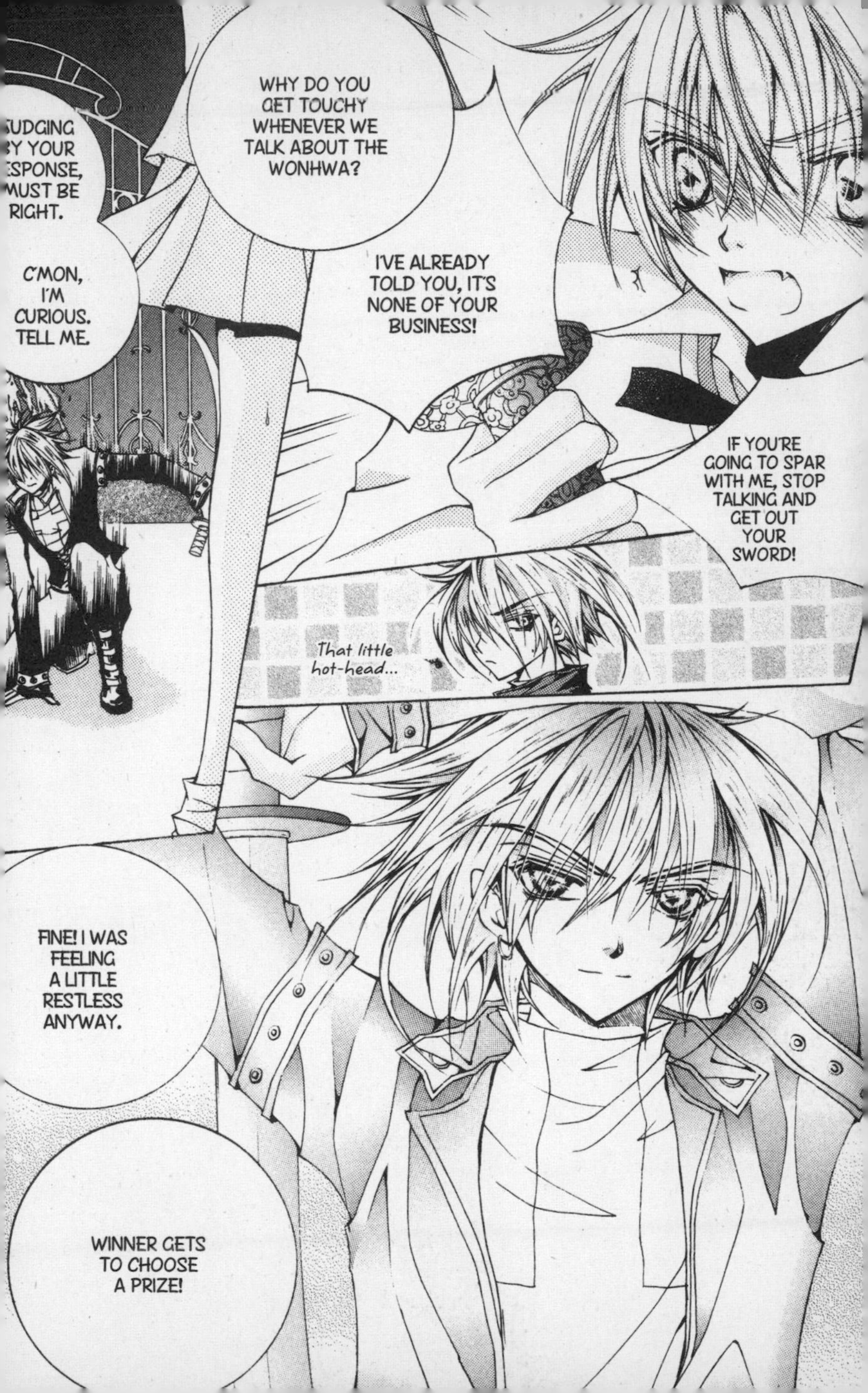

UDGING Y YOUR ESPONSE, MUST BE RIGHT.
C'MON, I'M CURIOUS. TELL ME.
WHY DO YOU GET TOUCHY WHENEVER WE TALK ABOUT THE WONHWA?
I'VE ALREADY TOLD YOU, IT'S NONE OF YOUR BUSINESS!
IF YOU'RE GOING TO SPAR WITH ME, STOP TALKING AND GET OUT YOUR SWORD!
That little hot-head...
FINE! I WAS FEELING A LITTLE RESTLESS ANYWAY.
WINNER GETS TO CHOOSE A PRIZE!

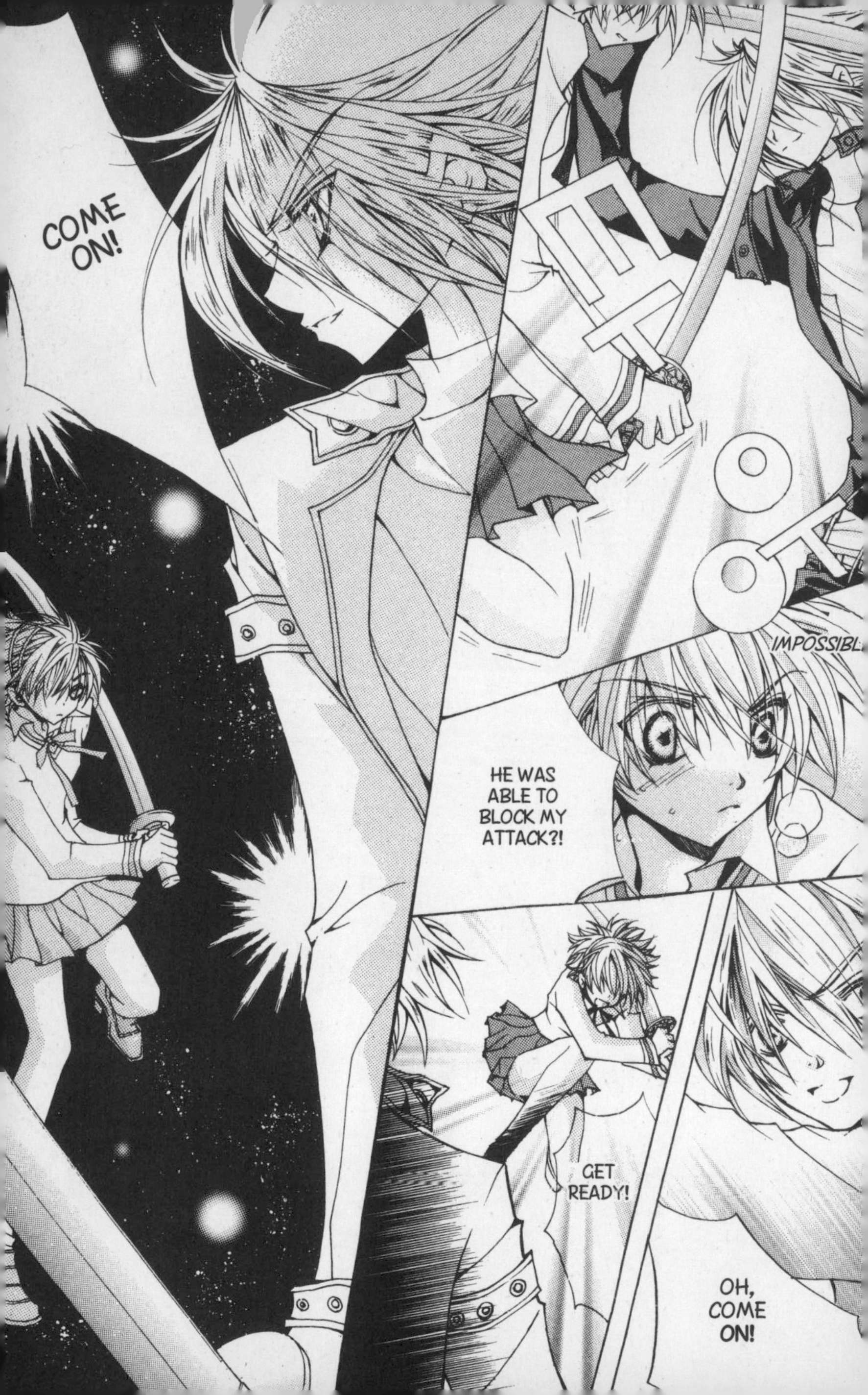
COME ON!
IMPOSSIBL
HE WAS ABLE TO BLOCK MY ATTACK?!
GET READY!
OH, COME ON!

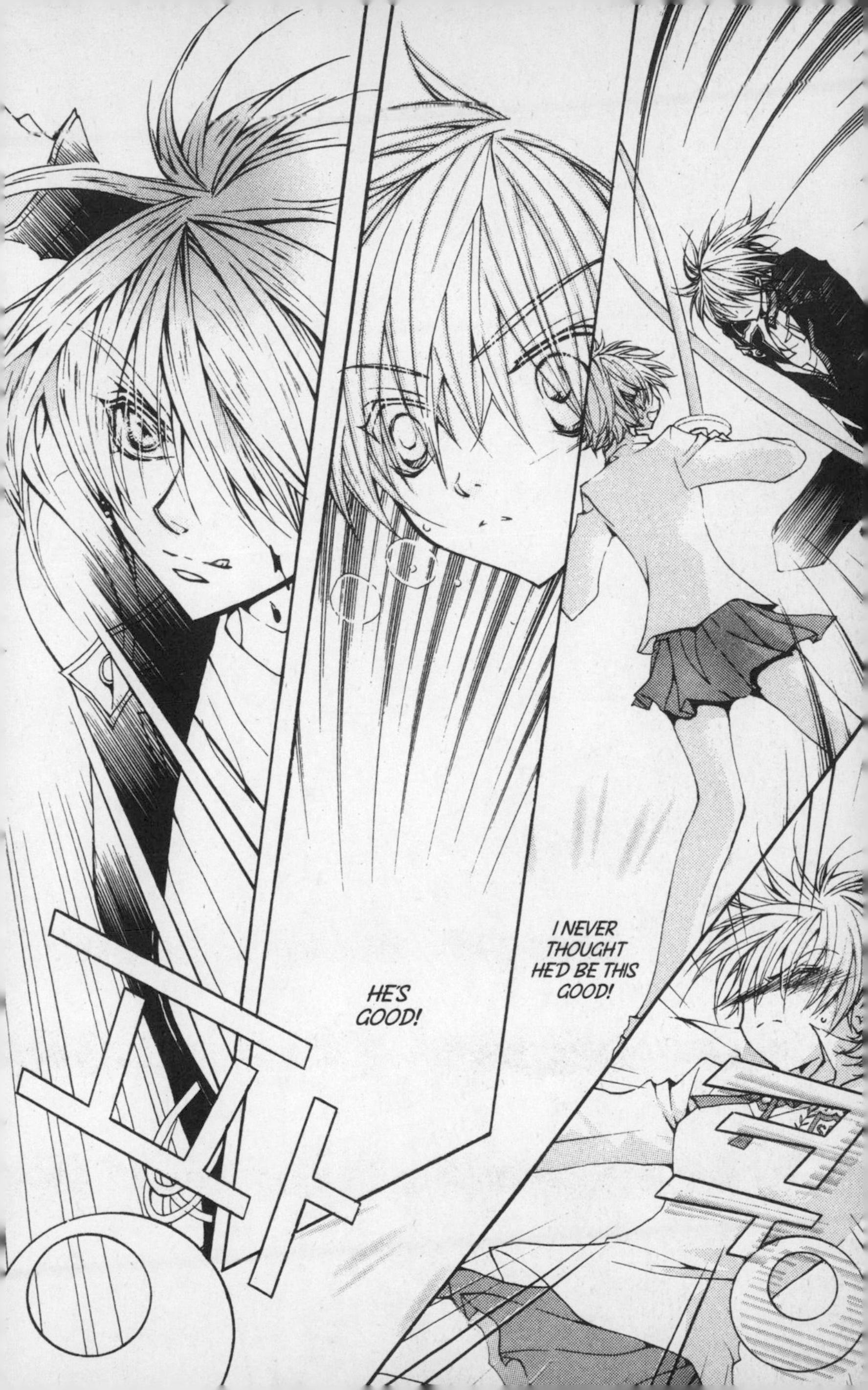
HE'S GOOD!
I NEVER THOUGHT HE'D BE THIS GOOD!

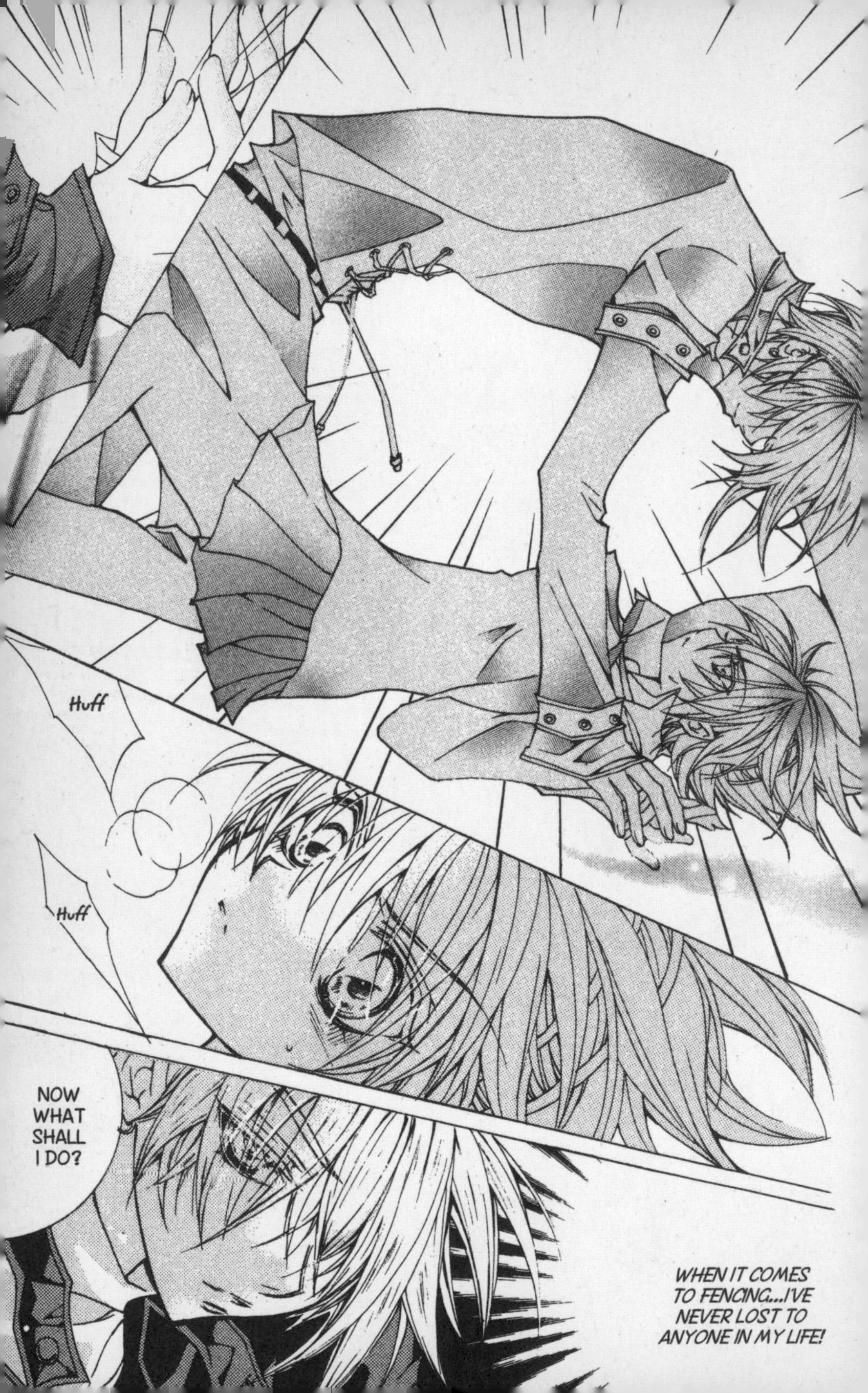
Huff
Huff
NOW WHAT SHALL I DO?
WHEN IT COMES TO FENCING...I'VE NEVER LOST TO ANYONE IN MY LIFE!

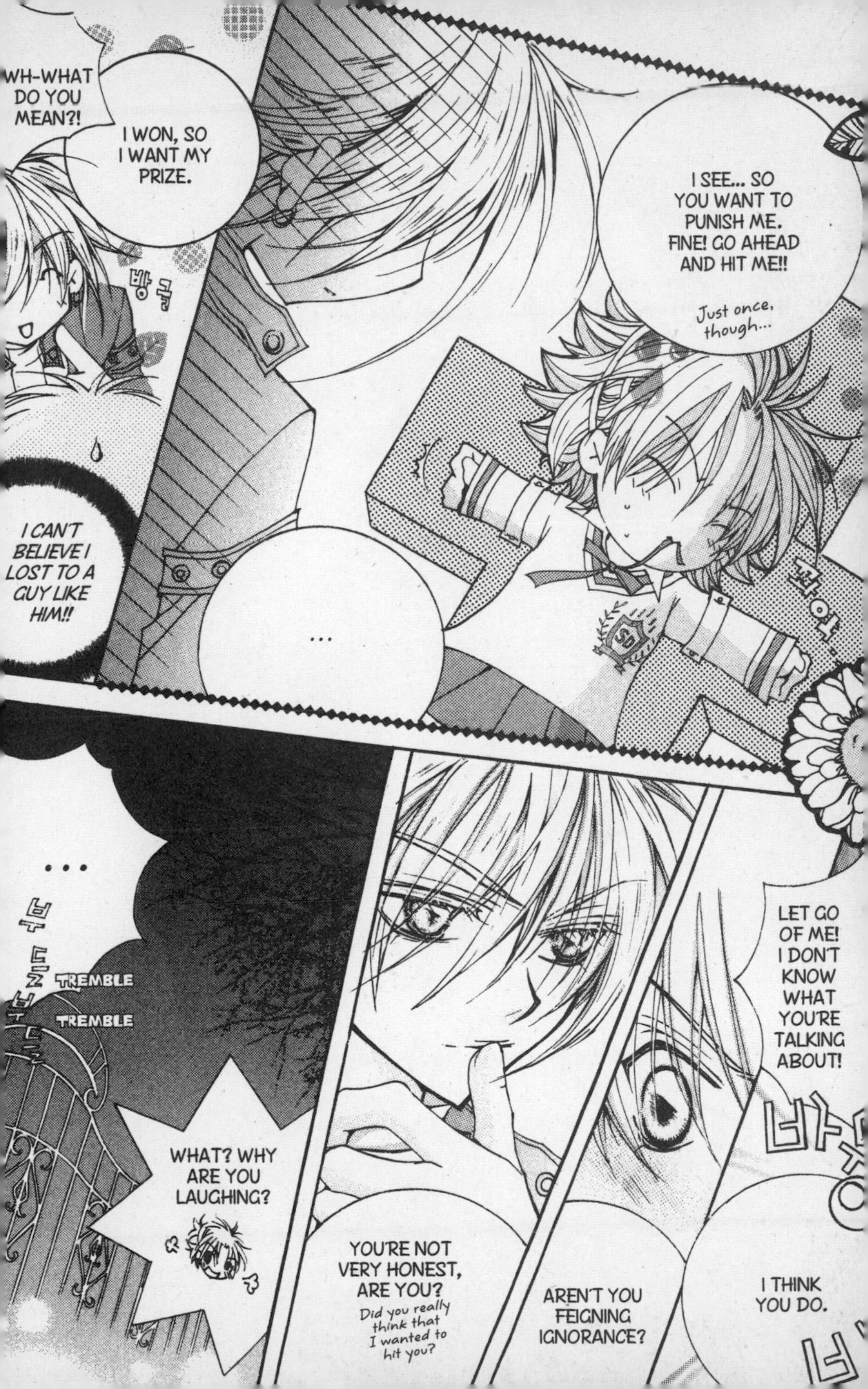
WH-WHAT DO YOU MEAN?!
I WON, SO I WANT MY PRIZE.
I CAN'T BELIEVE I LOST TO A GUY LIKE HIM!!
...
I SEE... SO YOU WANT TO PUNISH ME. FINE! GO AHEAD AND HIT ME!!
Just once, though...
...
TREMBLE
TREMBLE
WHAT? WHY ARE YOU LAUGHING?
YOU'RE NOT VERY HONEST, ARE YOU?
Did you really think that I wanted to hit you?
AREN'T YOU FEIGNING IGNORANCE?
LET GO OF ME! I DON'T KNOW WHAT YOU'RE TALKING ABOUT!
I THINK YOU DO.

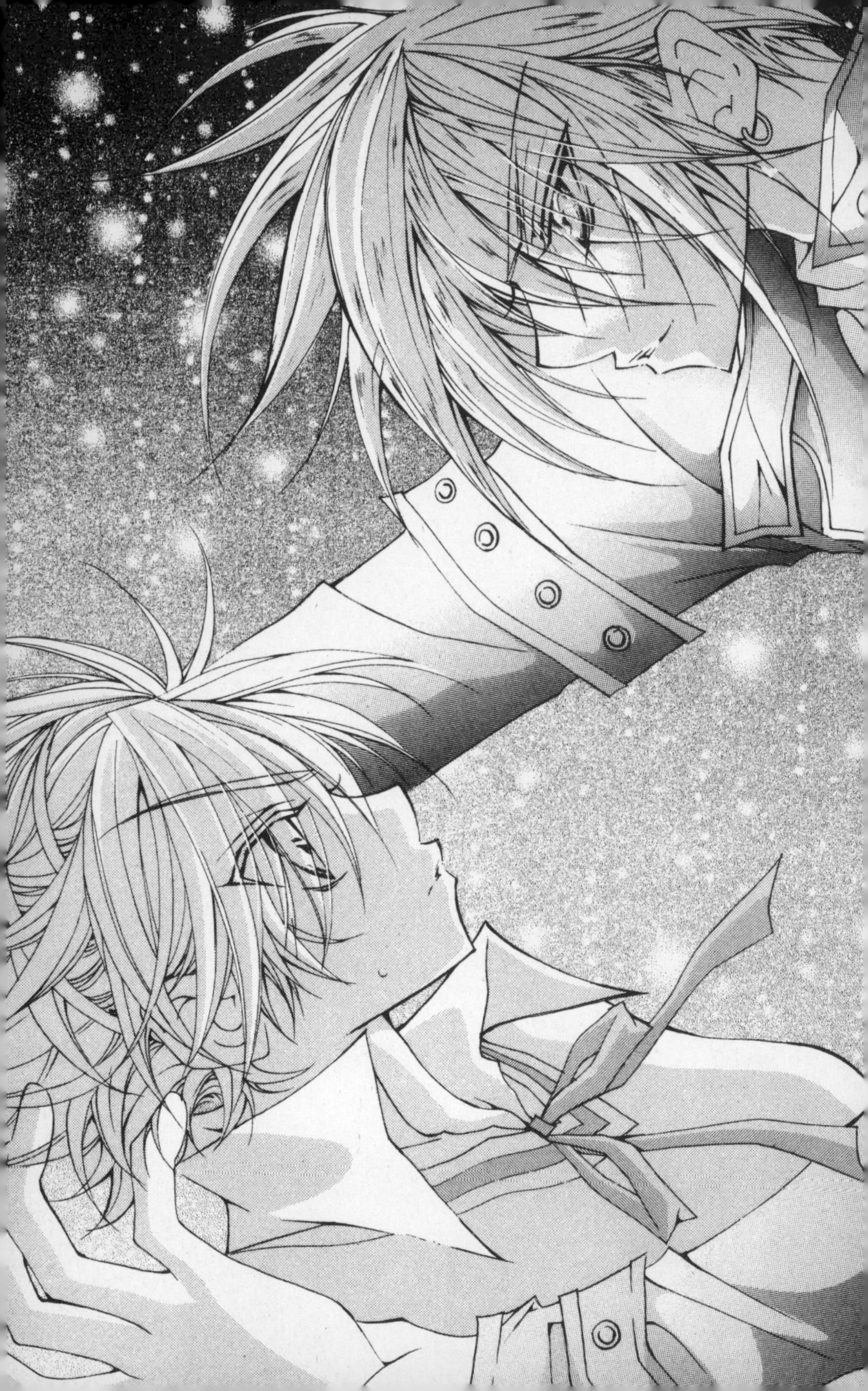

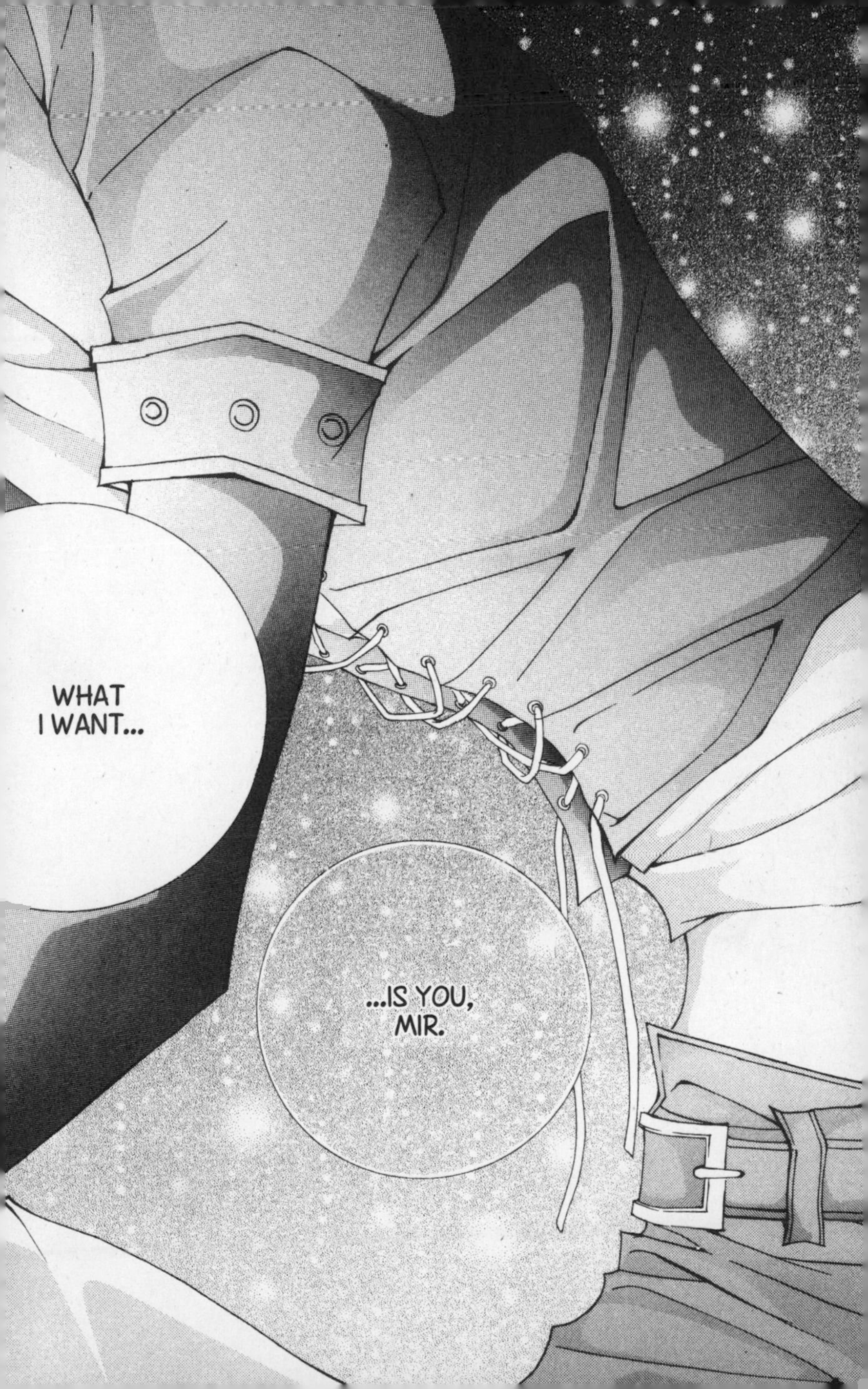
WHAT I WANT...
...IS YOU, MIR.

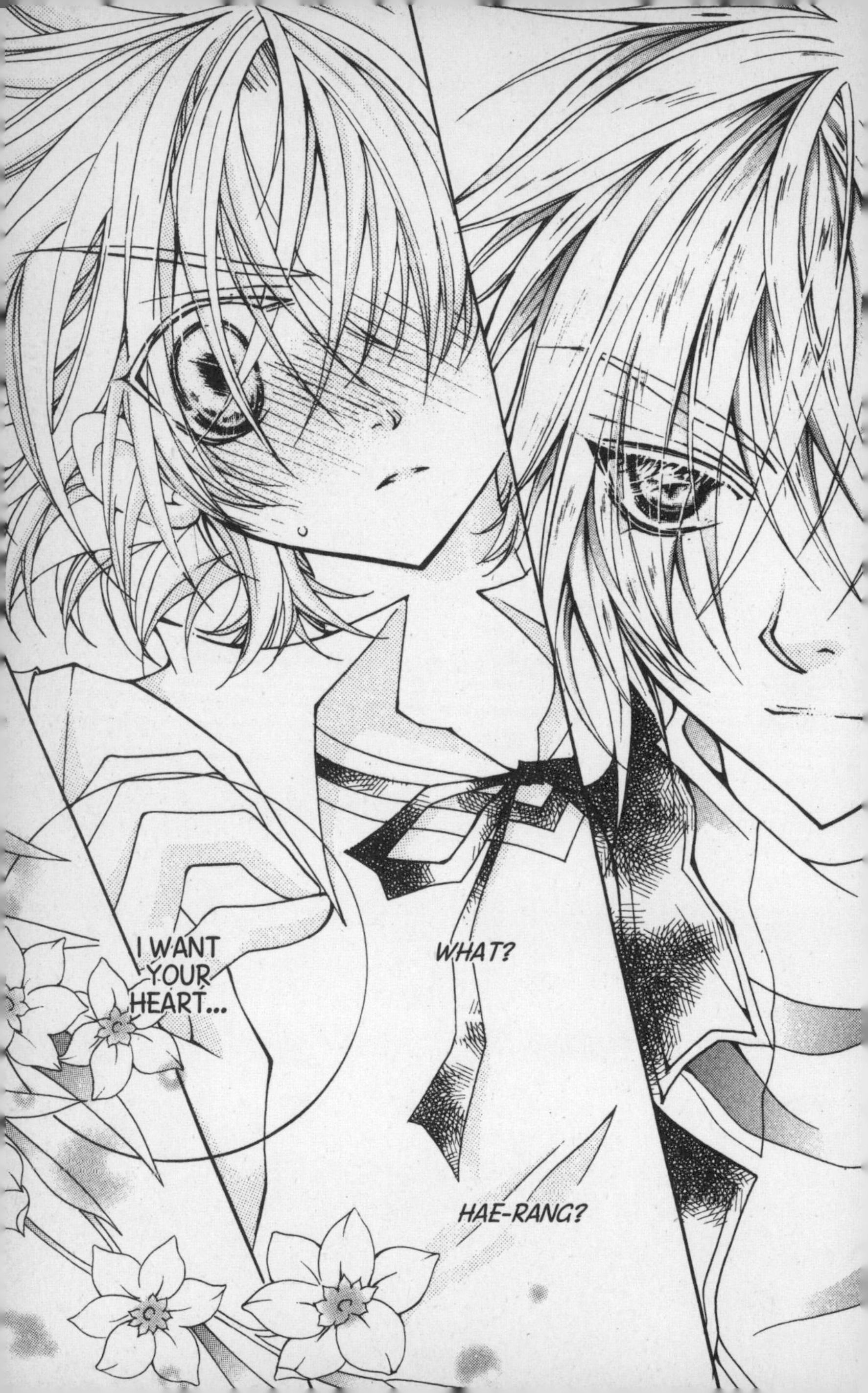
I WANT YOUR HEART...
WHAT?
HAE-RANG?

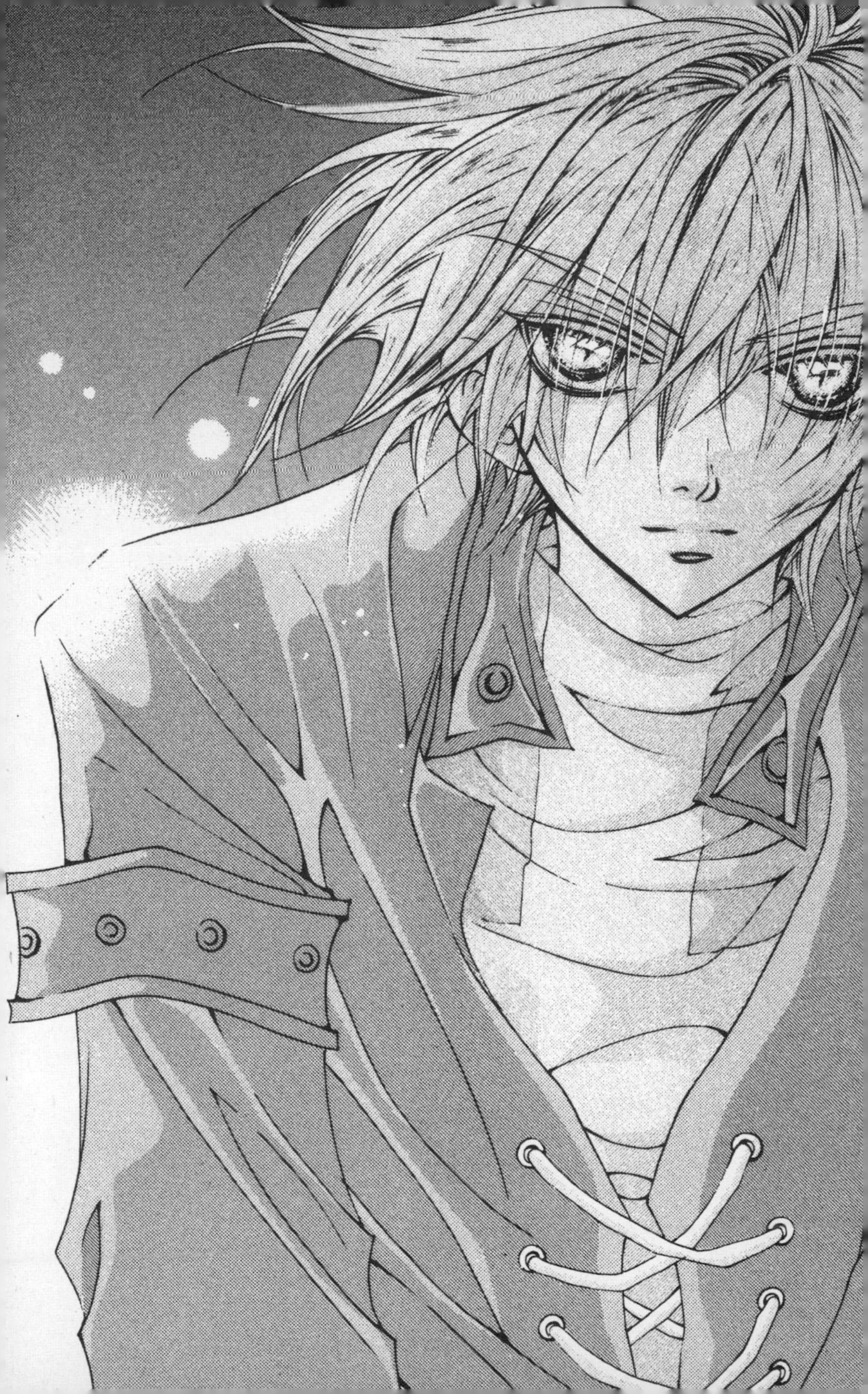

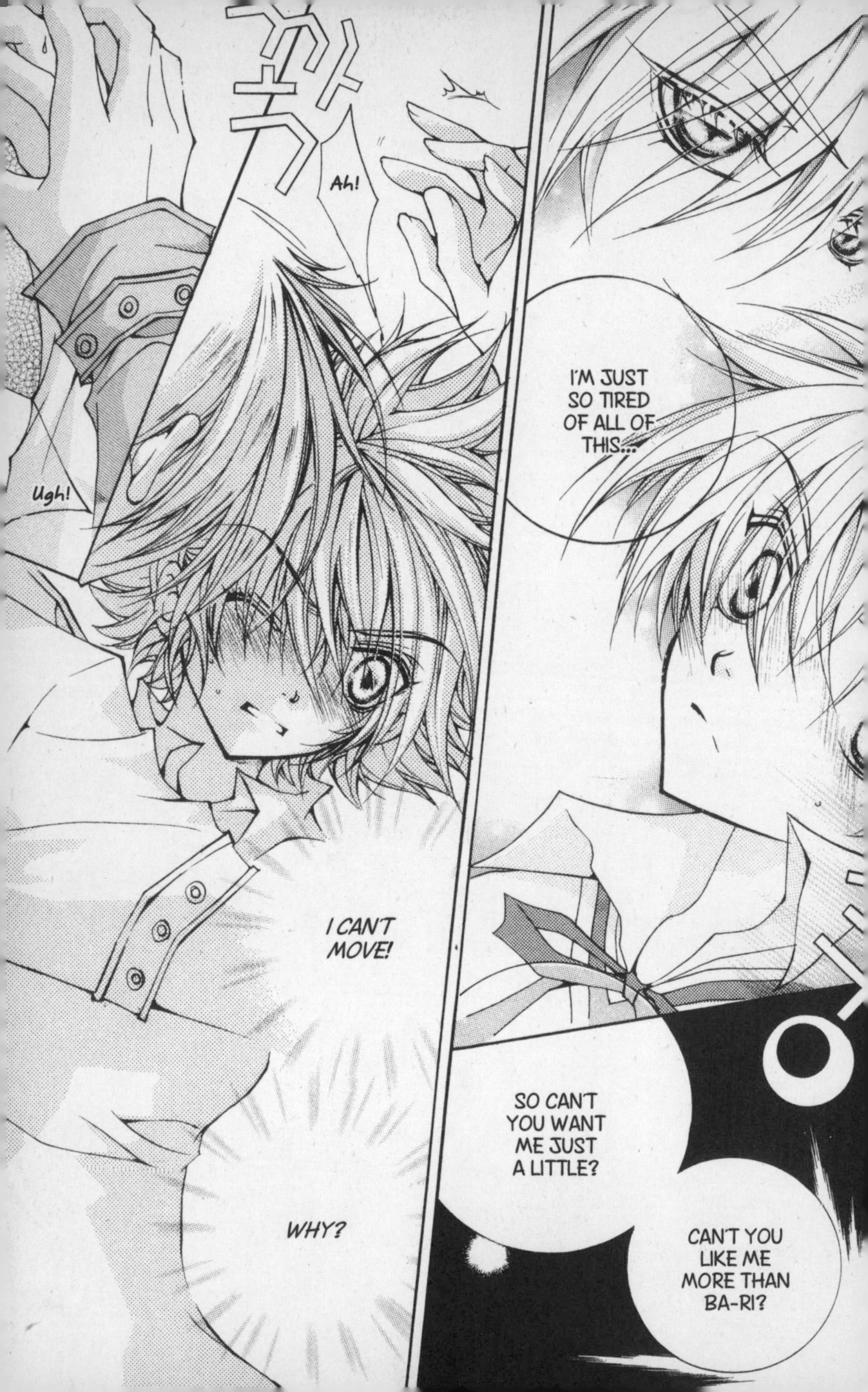
Ah!
Ugh!
I CAN'T MOVE!
WHY?
I'M JUST SO TIRED OF ALL OF THIS...
SO CAN'T YOU WANT ME JUST A LITTLE?
CAN'T YOU LIKE ME MORE THAN BA-RI?

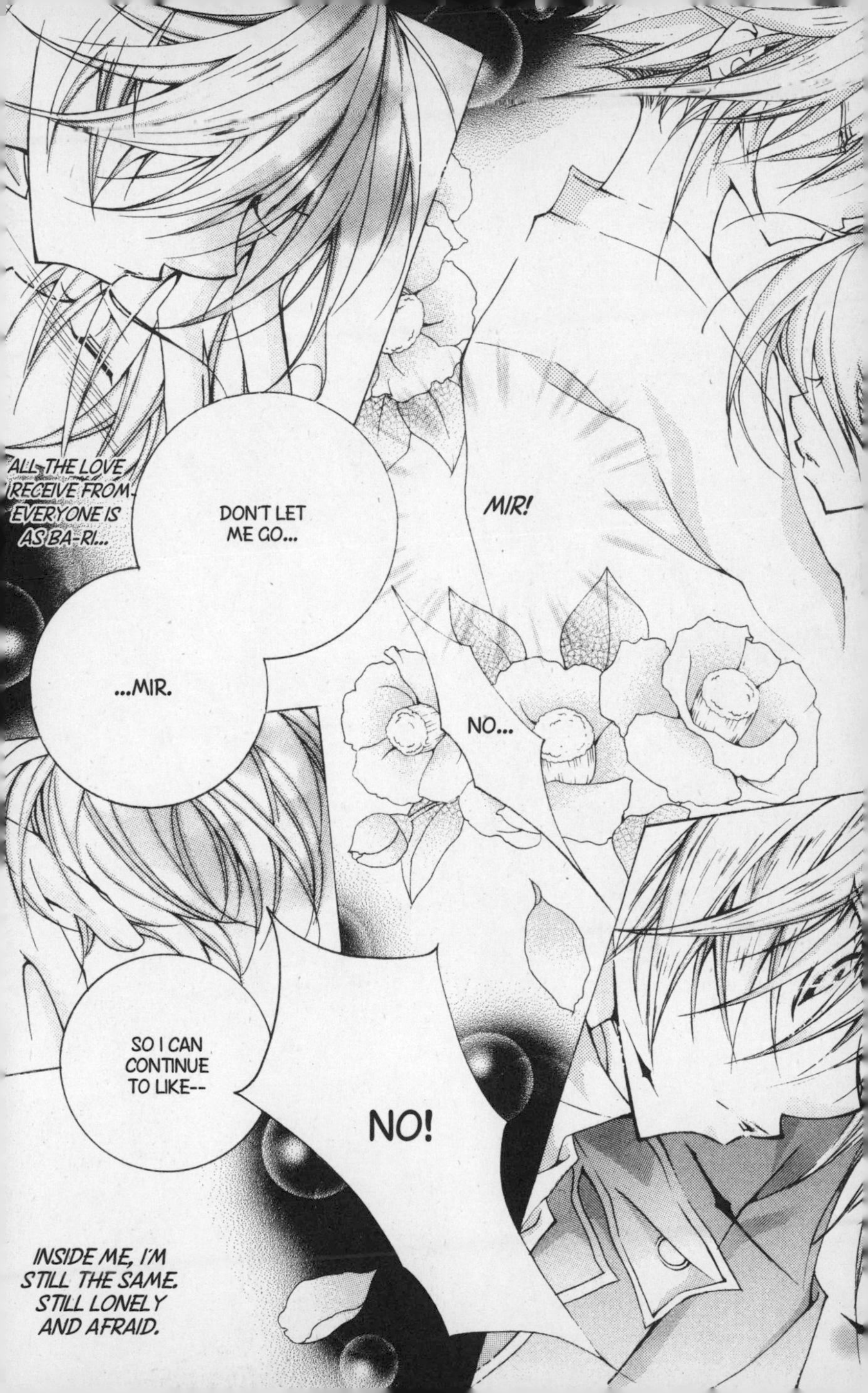
ALL THE LOVE RECEIVE FROM EVERYONE IS AS BA-RI...
DON'T LET ME GO...
MIR!
...MIR.
NO...
SO I CAN CONTINUE TO LIKE--
NO!
INSIDE ME, I'M STILL THE SAME. STILL LONELY AND AFRAID.

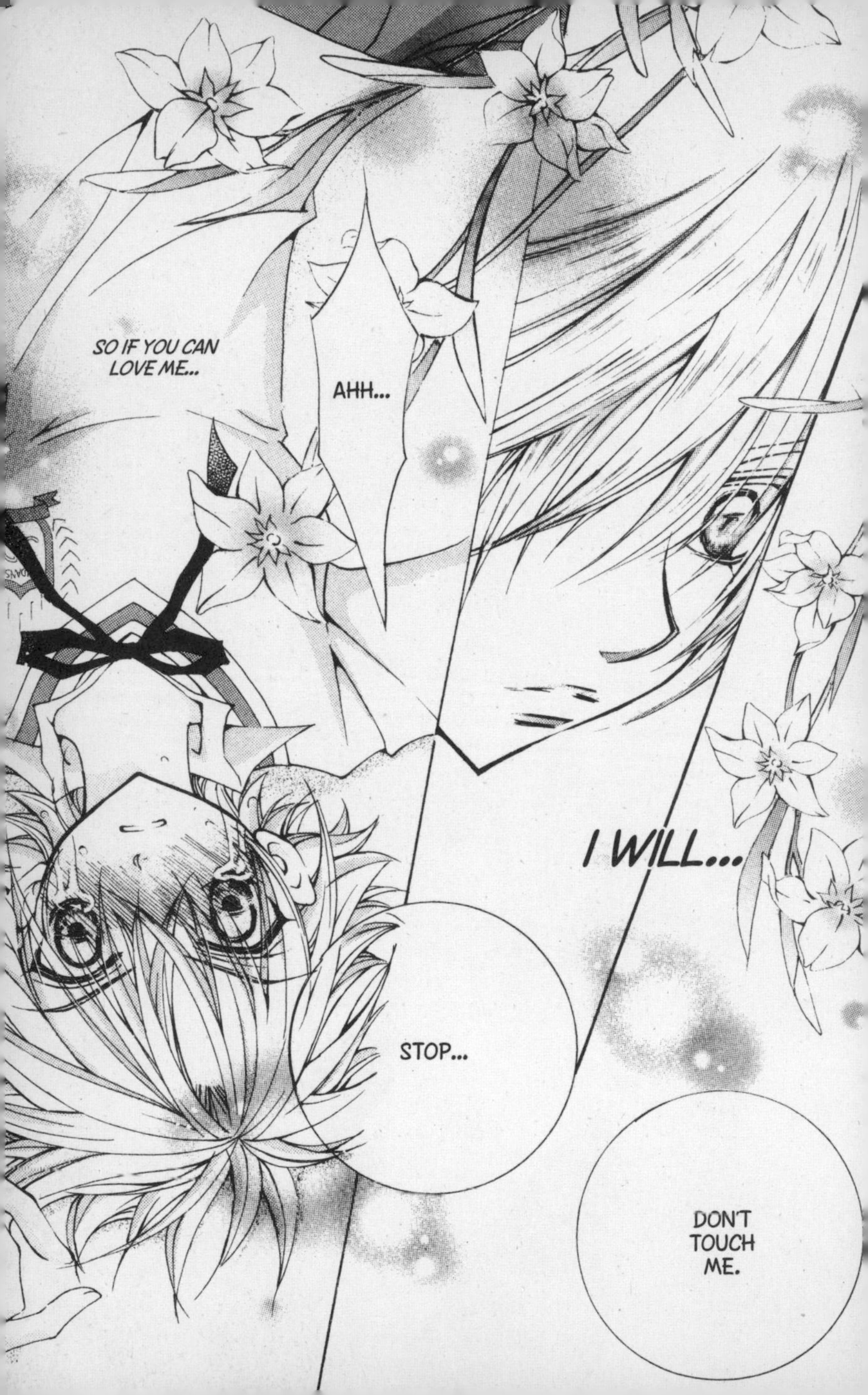
SO IF YOU CAN LOVE ME...
AHH...
I WILL...
STOP...
DON'T TOUCH ME.

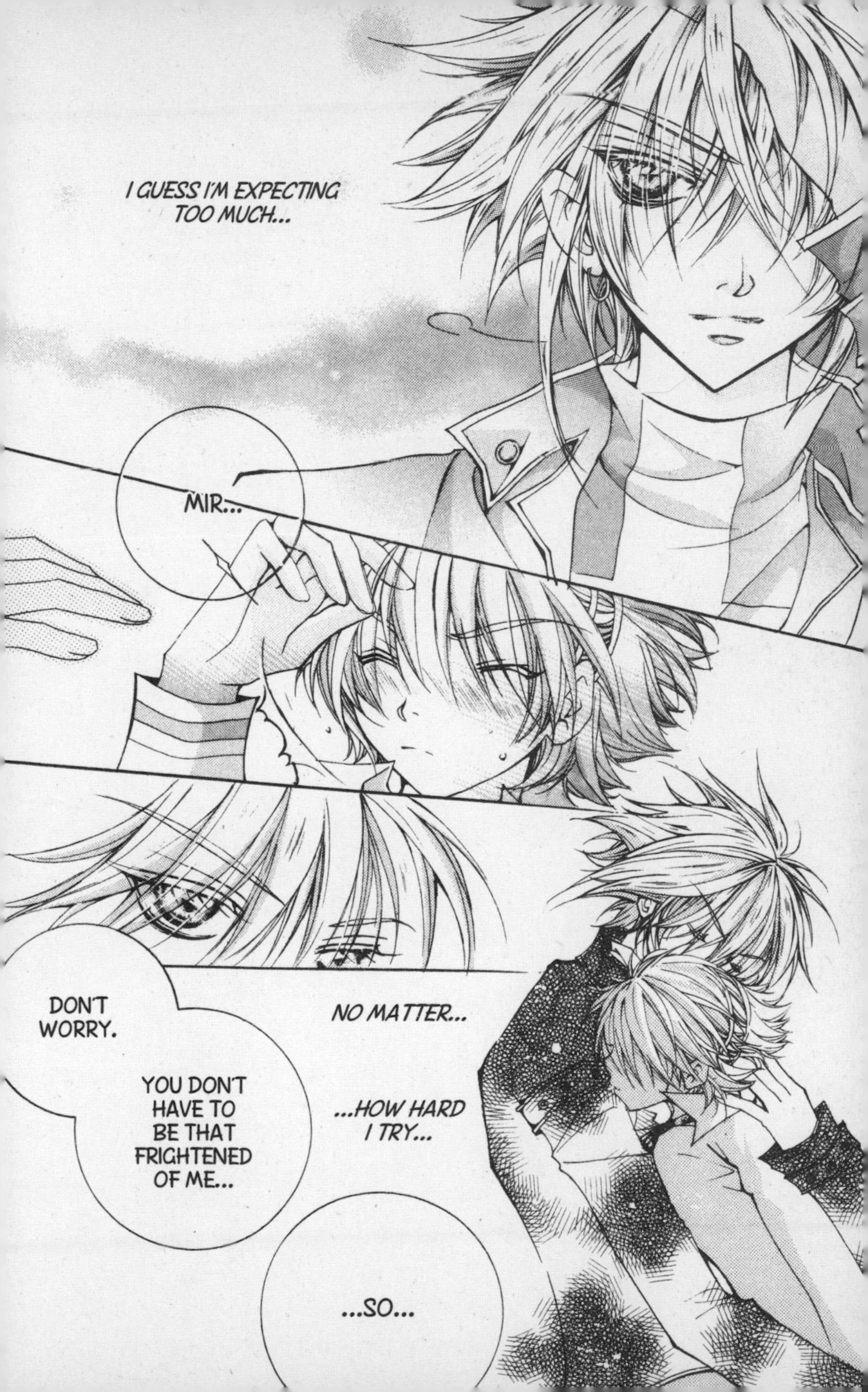

I GUESS I'M EXPECTING TOO MUCH...
MIR...
DON'T WORRY.
YOU DON'T HAVE TO BE THAT FRIGHTENED OF ME...
NO MATTER...
...HOW HARD I TRY...
...SO...

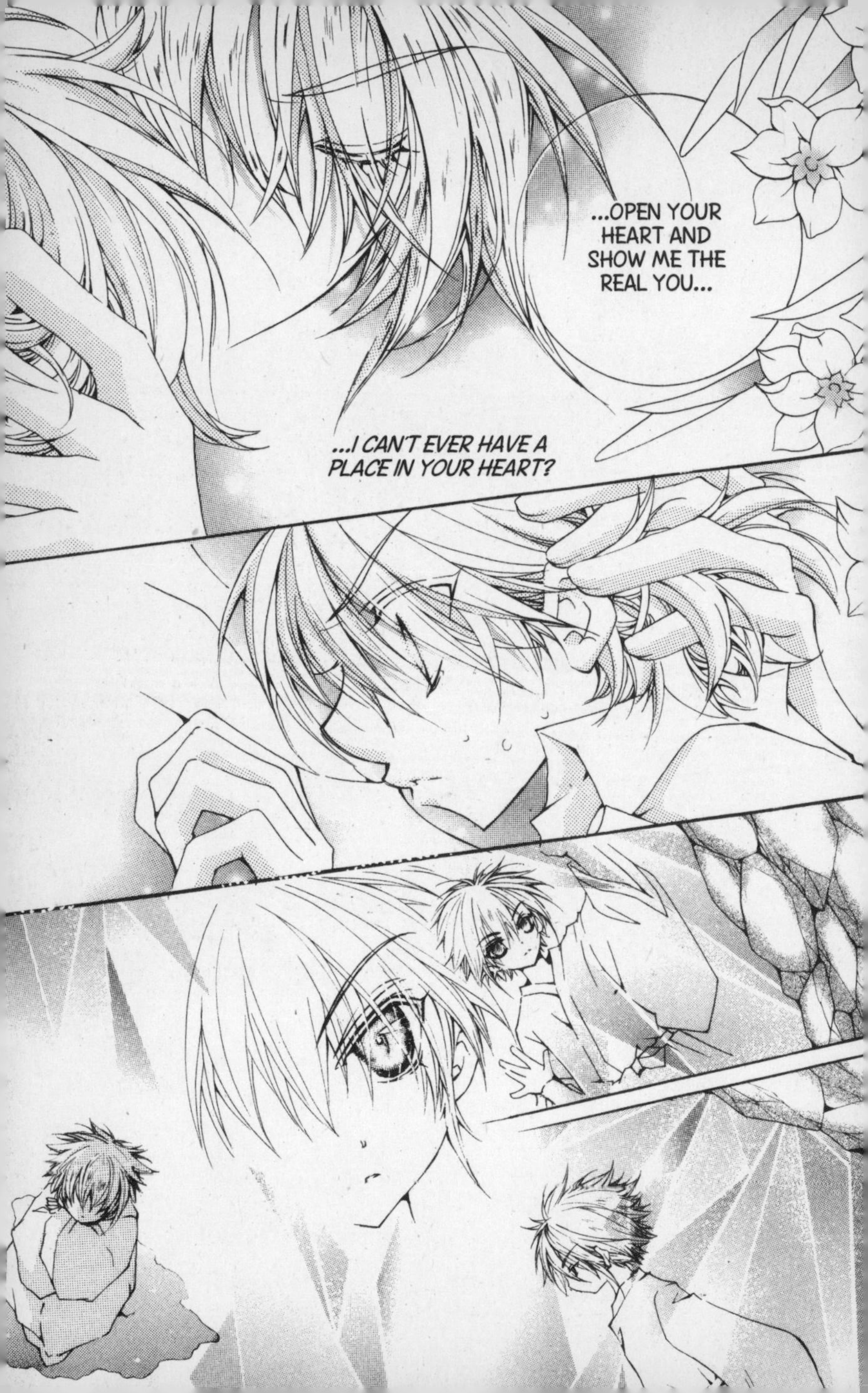
...OPEN YOUR HEART AND SHOW ME THE REAL YOU...
...I CAN'T EVER HAVE A PLACE IN YOUR HEART?

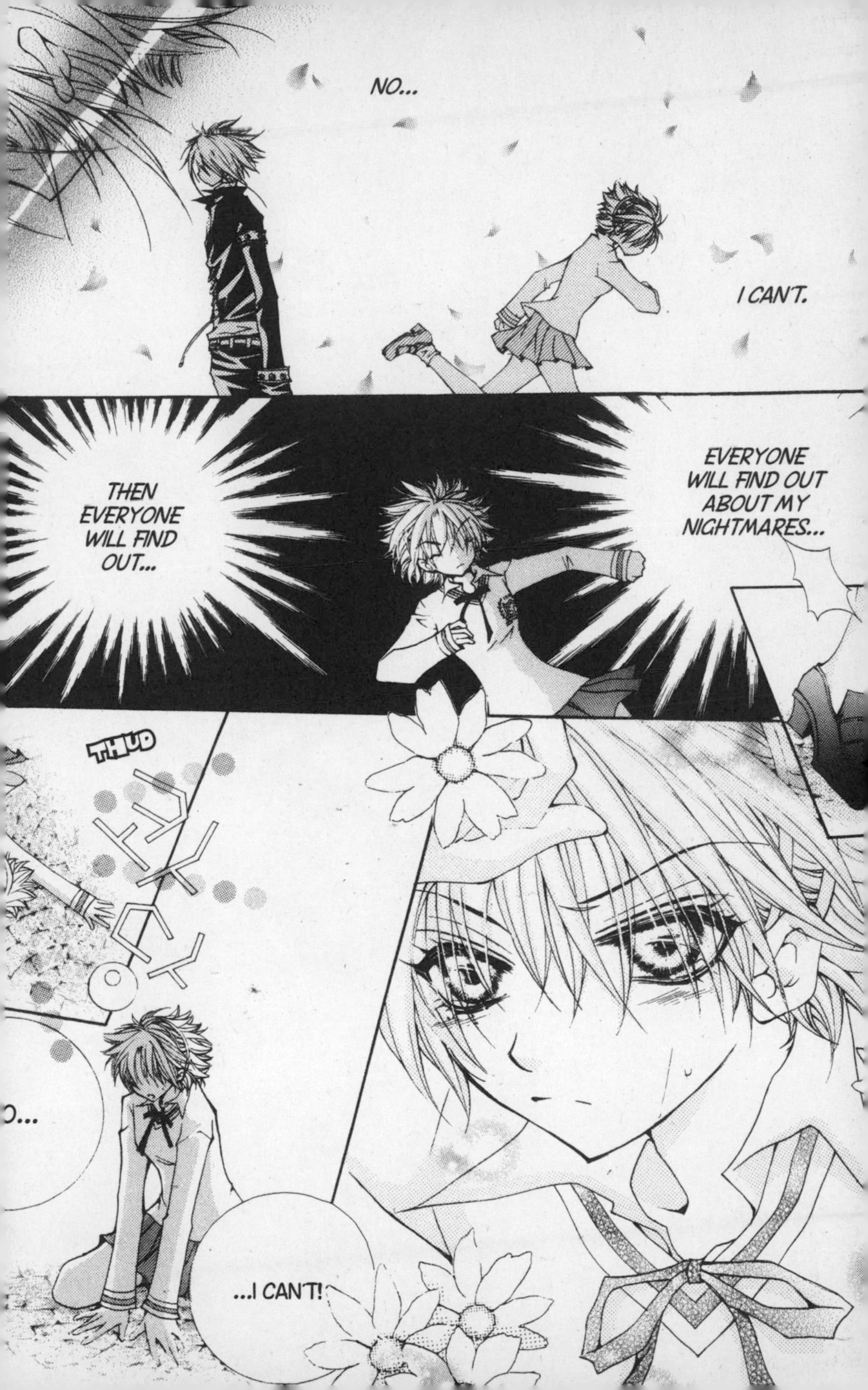
NO...
I CAN'T.
THEN EVERYONE WILL FIND OUT...
EVERYONE WILL FIND OUT ABOUT MY NIGHTMARES...
THUD
...I CAN'T!

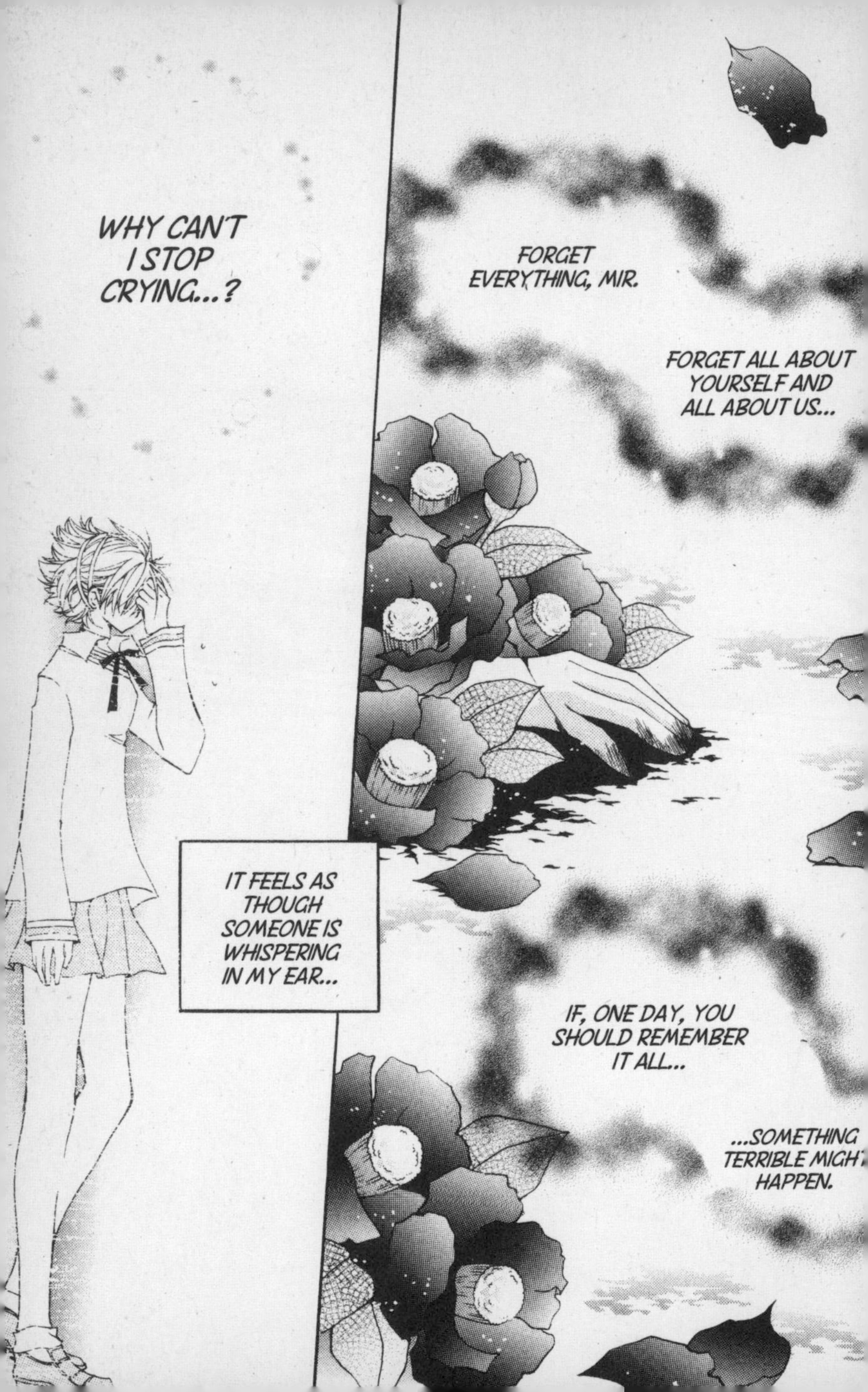
WHY CAN'T I STOP CRYING...?
IT FEELS AS THOUGH SOMEONE IS WHISPERING IN MY EAR...
FORGET EVERYTHING, MIR.
FORGET ALL ABOUT YOURSELF AND ALL ABOUT US...
IF, ONE DAY, YOU SHOULD REMEMBER IT ALL...
...SOMETHING TERRIBLE MIGHT HAPPEN.

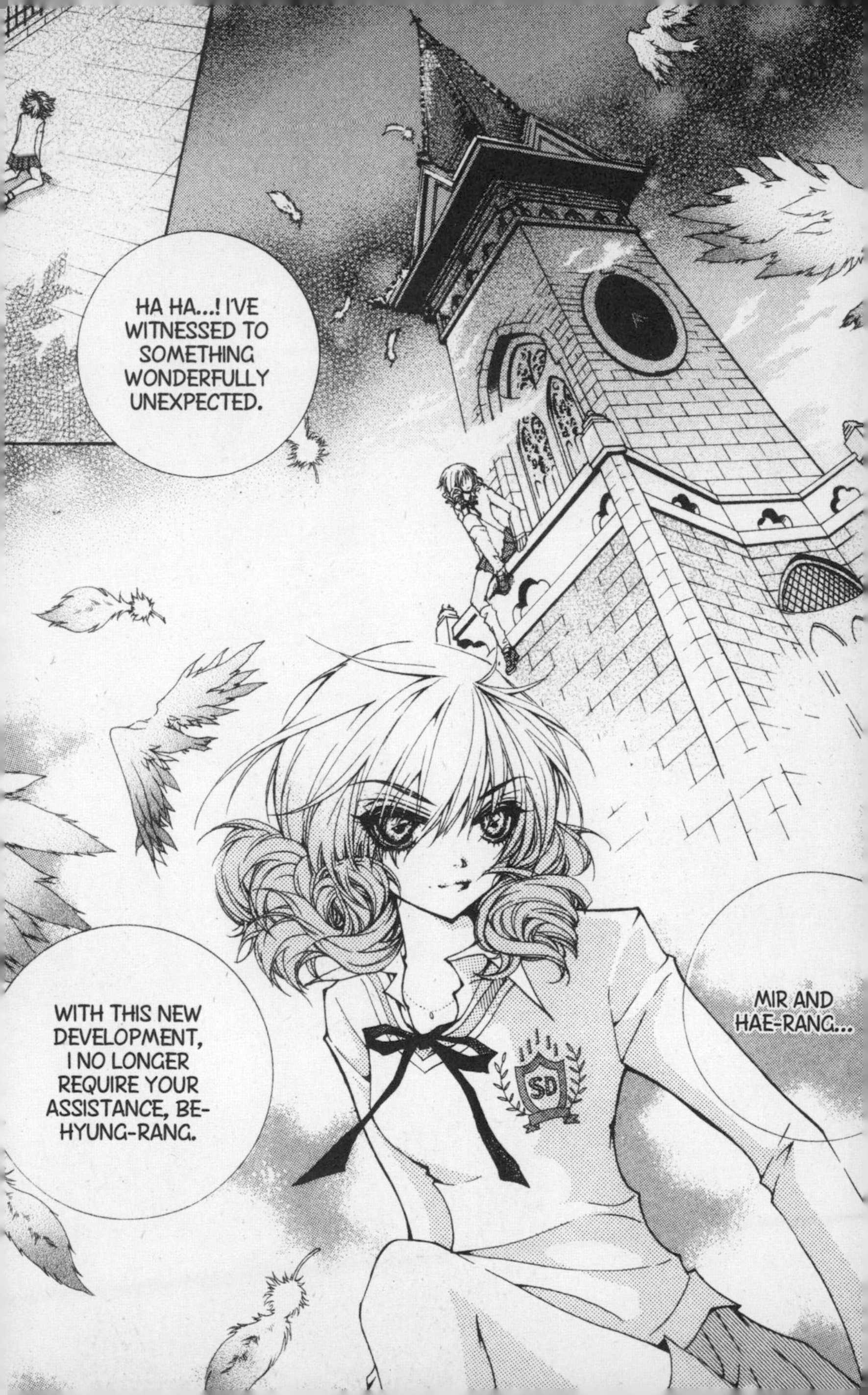
HA HA...! I'VE WITNESSED TO SOMETHING WONDERFULLY UNEXPECTED.
WITH THIS NEW DEVELOPMENT, I NO LONGER REQUIRE YOUR ASSISTANCE, BE-HYUNG-RANG.
MIR AND HAE-RANG...
SD

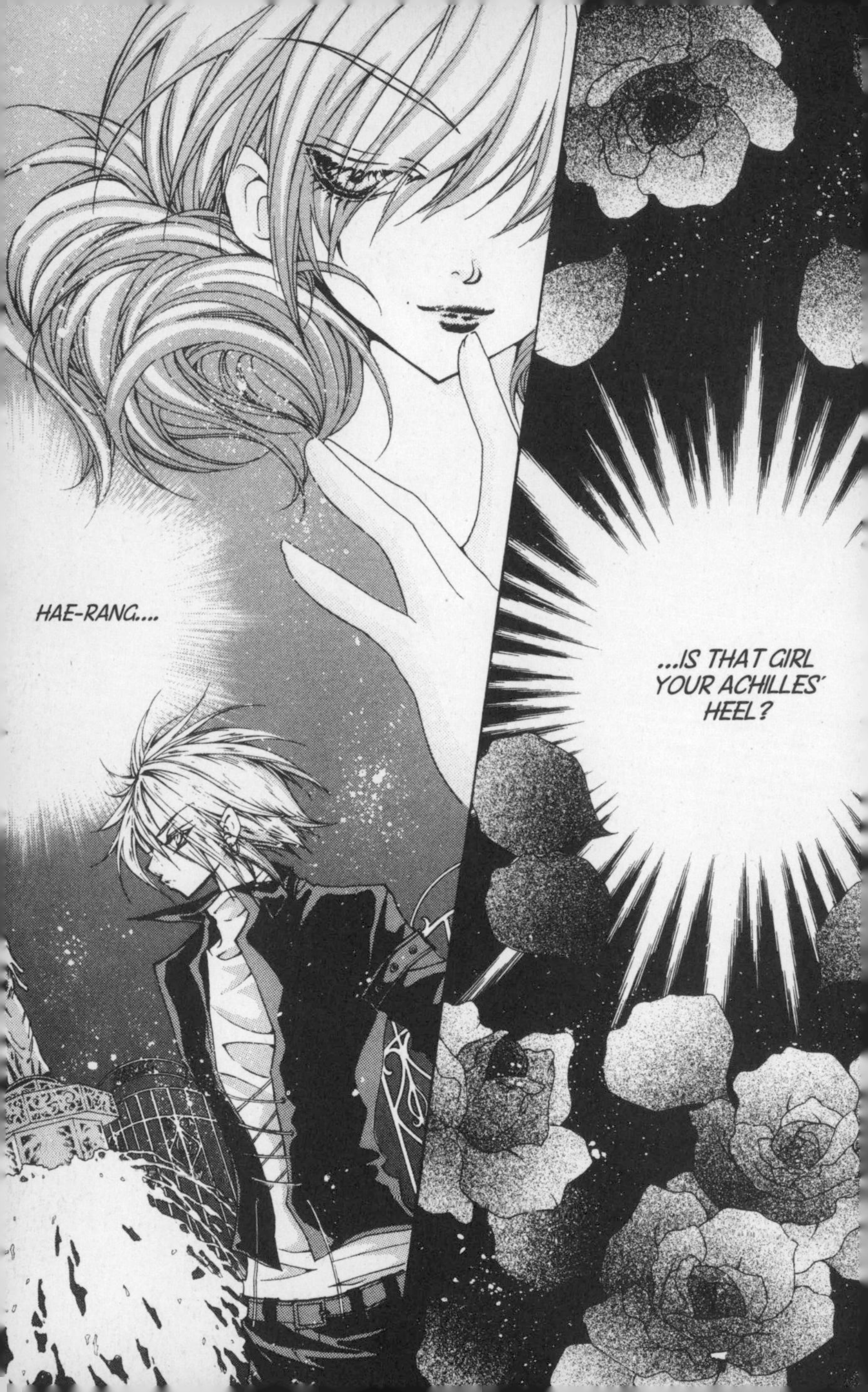
HAE-RANG....
...IS THAT GIRL YOUR ACHILLES' HEEL?

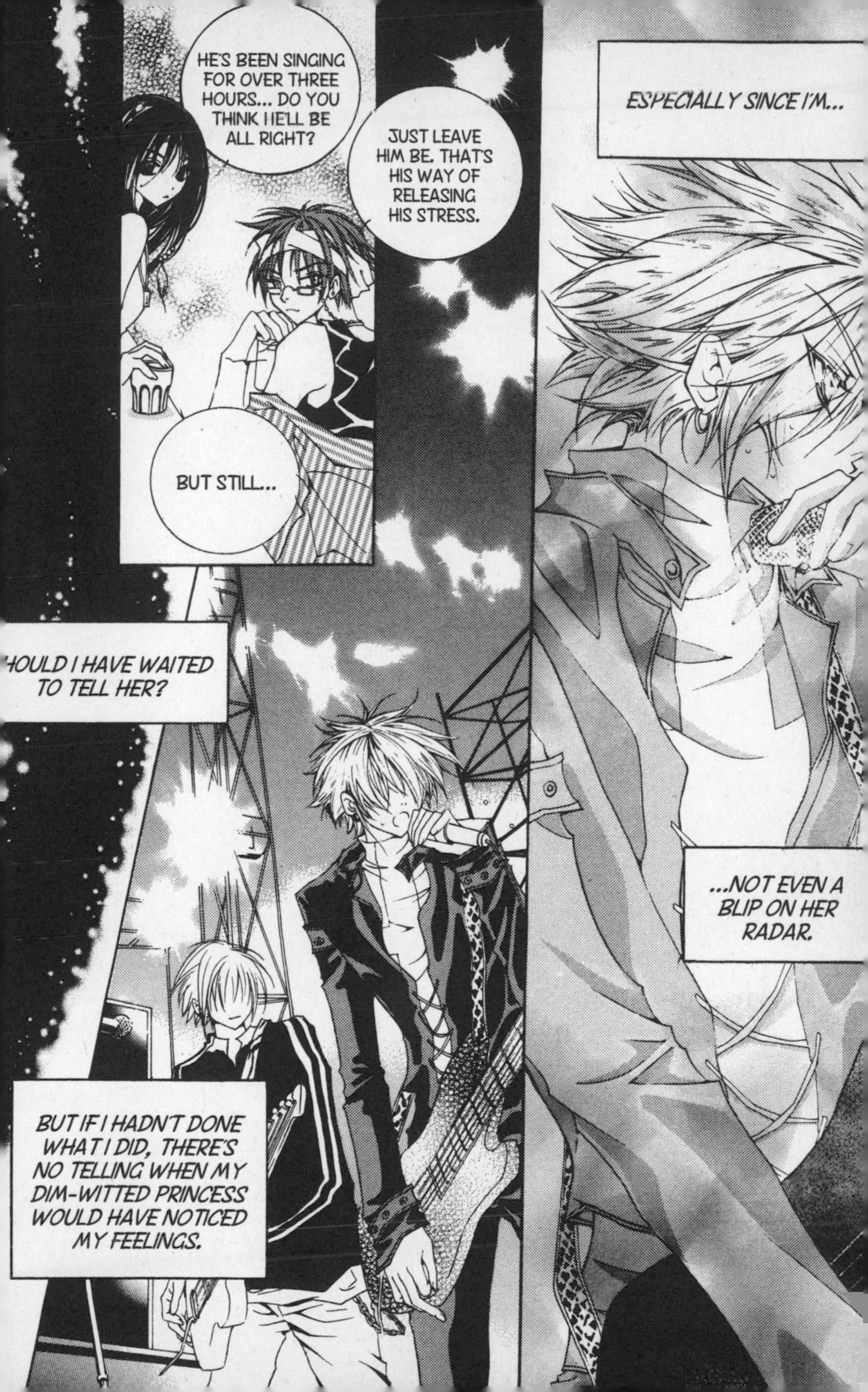

HE'S BEEN SINGING FOR OVER THREE HOURS... DO YOU THINK HE'LL BE ALL RIGHT?
JUST LEAVE HIM BE. THAT'S HIS WAY OF RELEASING HIS STRESS.
BUT STILL...
HOULD I HAVE WAITED TO TELL HER?
BUT IF I HADN'T DONE WHAT I DID, THERE'S NO TELLING WHEN MY DIM-WITTED PRINCESS WOULD HAVE NOTICED MY FEELINGS.
ESPECIALLY SINCE I'M...
...NOT EVEN A BLIP ON HER RADAR.

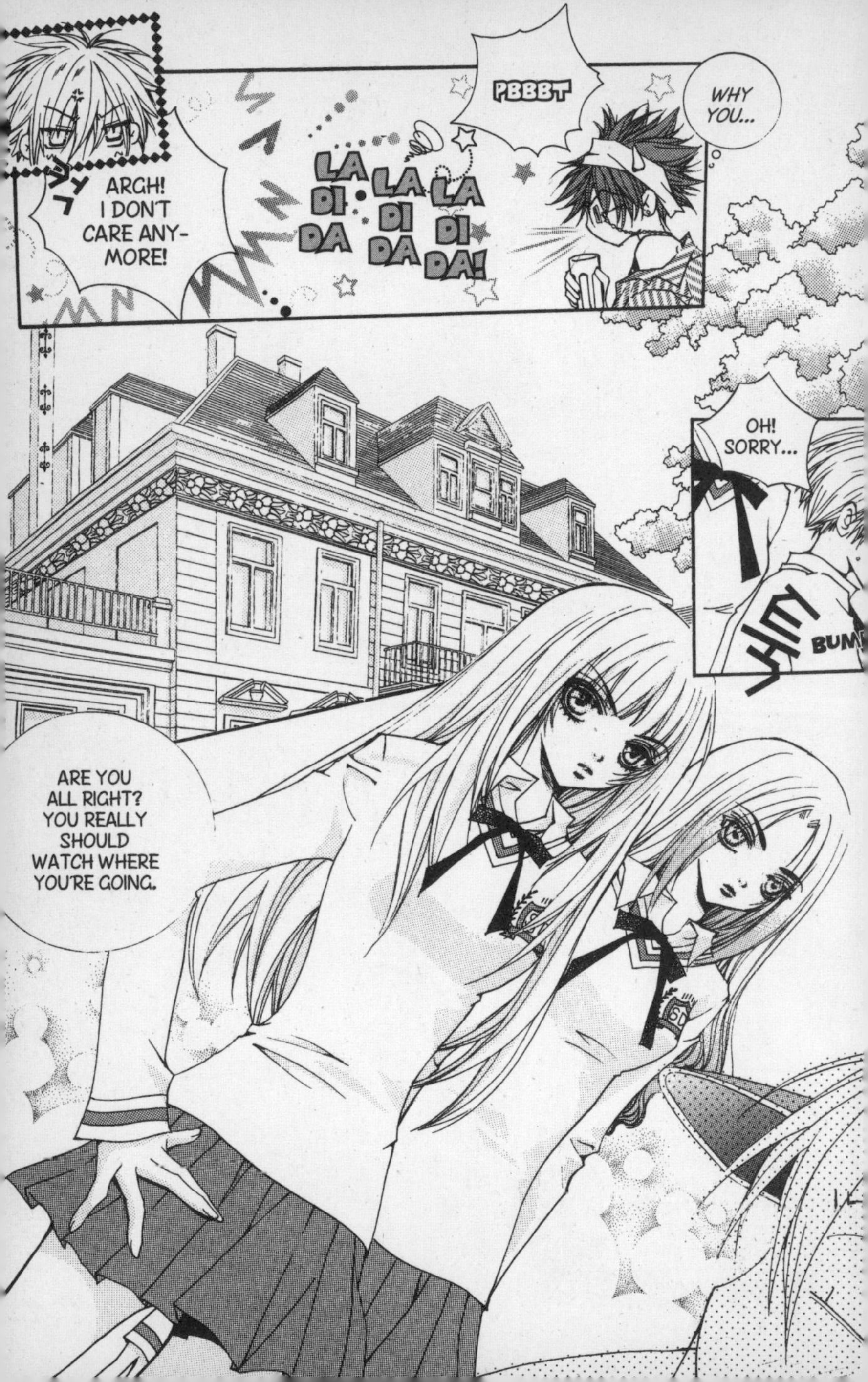
ARGH! I DON'T CARE ANY-MORE!
LA DI DA LA DI DA LA DI DA!
PBBBT
WHY YOU...
ARE YOU ALL RIGHT? YOU REALLY SHOULD WATCH WHERE YOU'RE GOING.
OH! SORRY...
HEY
BUM

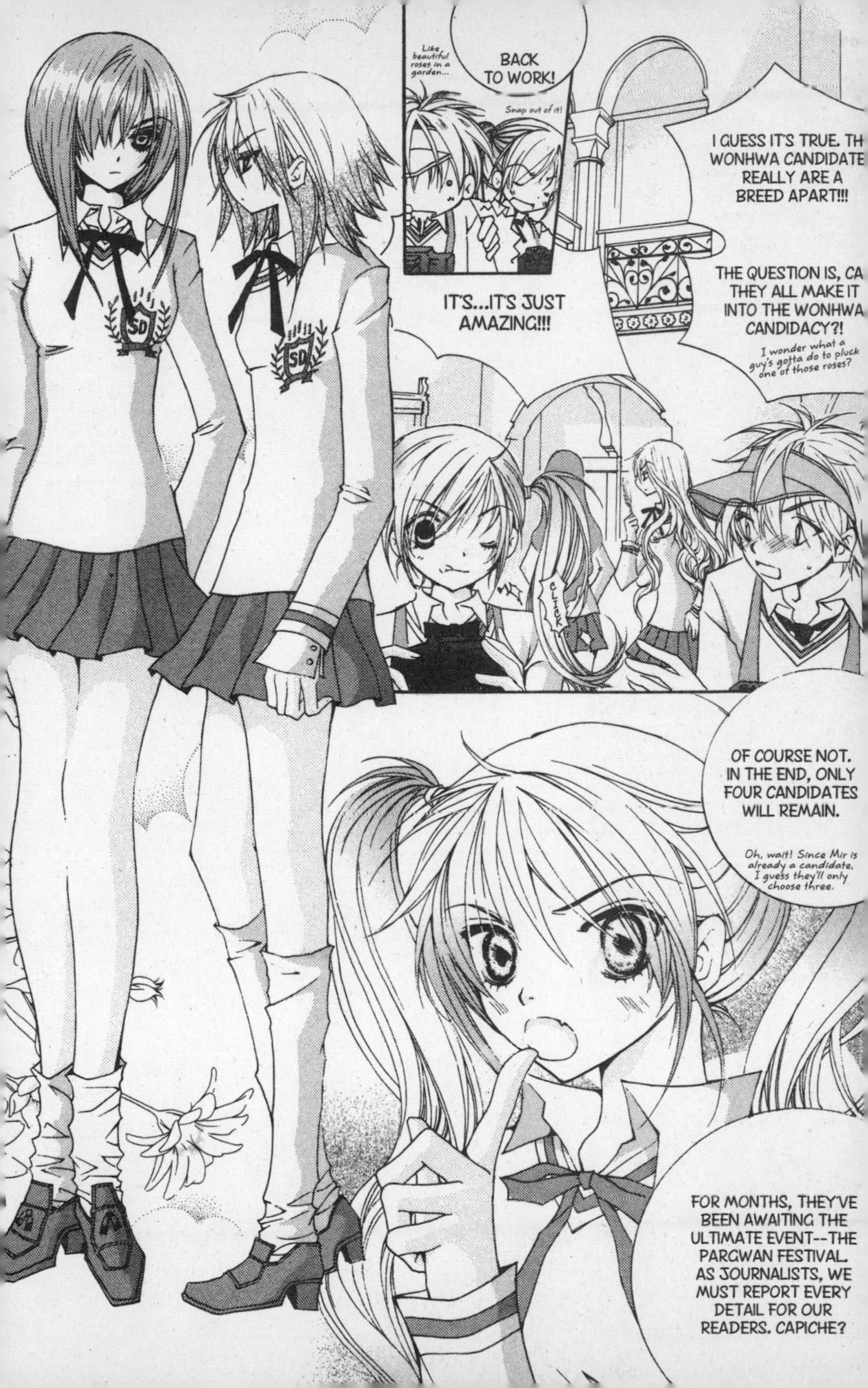

Like beautiful roses in a garden...
BACK TO WORK!
Snap out of it!
IT'S...IT'S JUST AMAZING!!!
I GUESS IT'S TRUE. TH WONHWA CANDIDATE REALLY ARE A BREED APART!!!
THE QUESTION IS, CA THEY ALL MAKE IT INTO THE WONHWA CANDIDACY?!
I wonder what a guy's gotta do to pluck one of those roses?
CLICK
OF COURSE NOT. IN THE END, ONLY FOUR CANDIDATES WILL REMAIN.
Oh, wait! Since Mir is already a candidate, I guess they'll only choose three.
FOR MONTHS, THEY'VE BEEN AWAITING THE ULTIMATE EVENT--THE PARGWAN FESTIVAL. AS JOURNALISTS, WE MUST REPORT EVERY DETAIL FOR OUR READERS. CAPICHE?

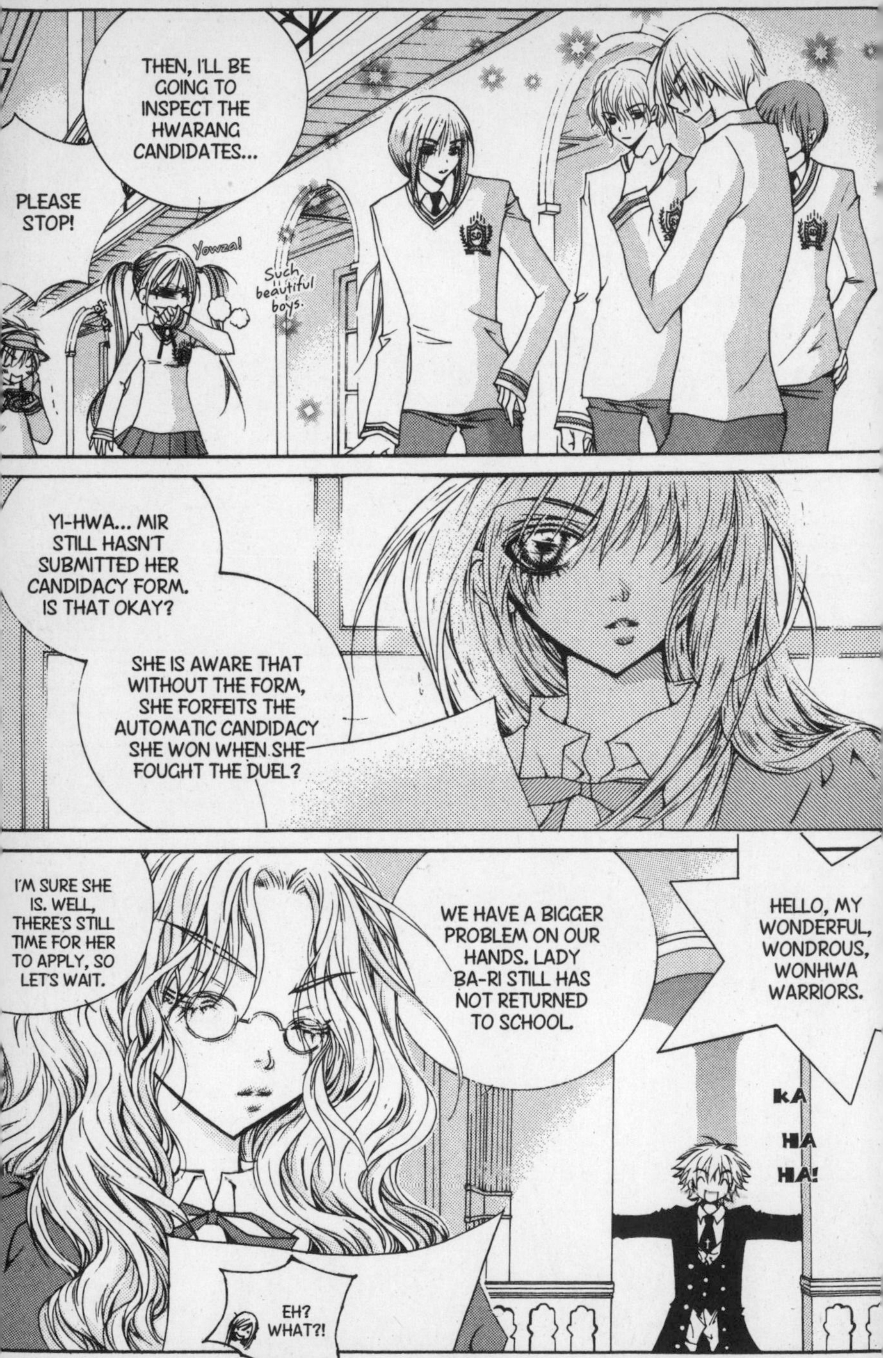
THEN, I'LL BE GOING TO INSPECT THE HWARANG CANDIDATES...
PLEASE STOP!
Yowza!
Such beautiful boys.
YI-HWA... MIR STILL HASN'T SUBMITTED HER CANDIDACY FORM. IS THAT OKAY?
SHE IS AWARE THAT WITHOUT THE FORM, SHE FORFEITS THE AUTOMATIC CANDIDACY SHE WON WHEN SHE FOUGHT THE DUEL?
I'M SURE SHE IS. WELL, THERE'S STILL TIME FOR HER TO APPLY, SO LET'S WAIT.
WE HAVE A BIGGER PROBLEM ON OUR HANDS. LADY BA-RI STILL HAS NOT RETURNED TO SCHOOL.
EH? WHAT?!
HELLO, MY WONDERFUL, WONDROUS, WONHWA WARRIORS.
KA
HA
HA!

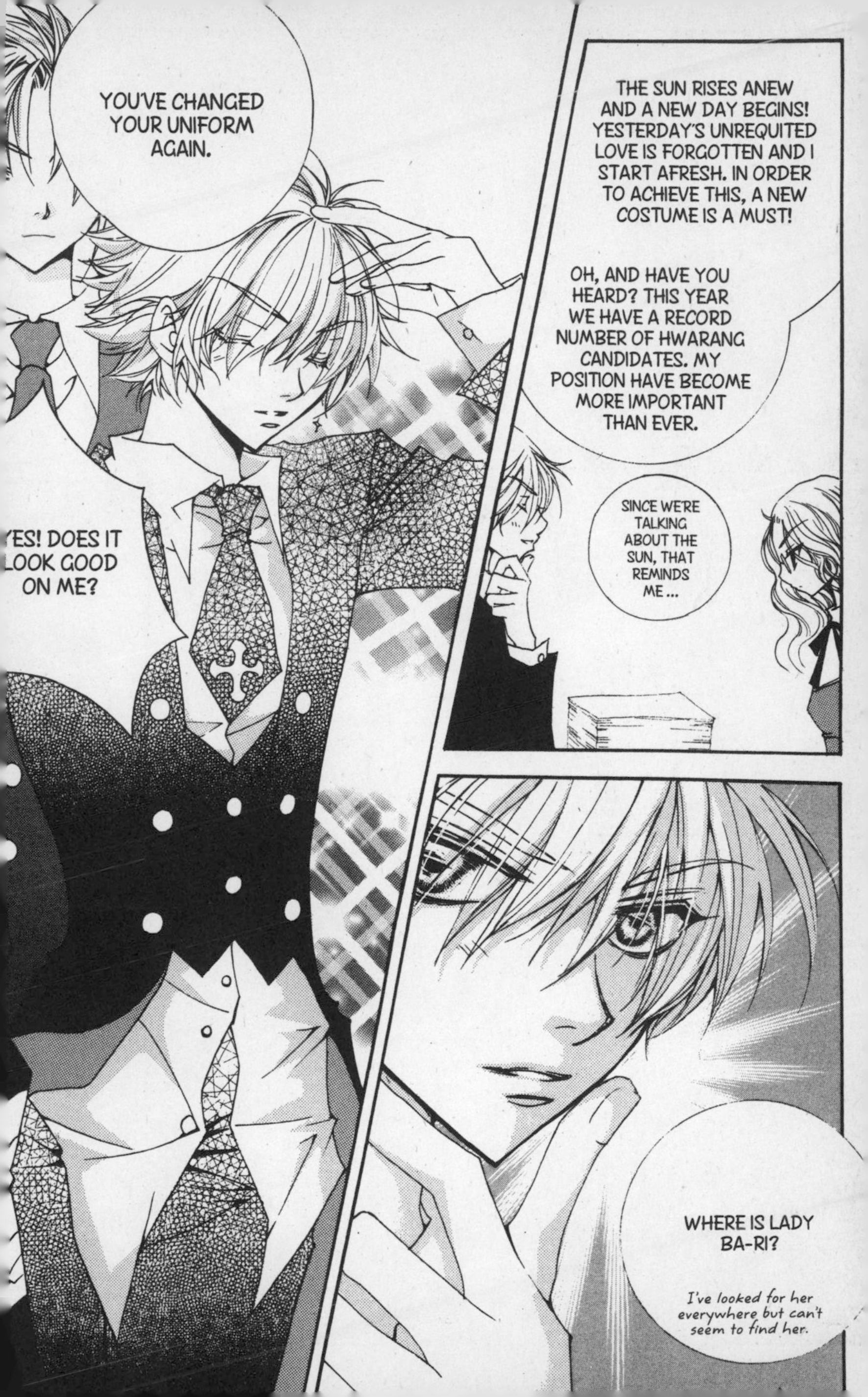

YOU'VE CHANGED YOUR UNIFORM AGAIN.
YES! DOES IT LOOK GOOD ON ME?
THE SUN RISES ANEW AND A NEW DAY BEGINS! YESTERDAY'S UNREQUITED LOVE IS FORGOTTEN AND I START AFRESH. IN ORDER TO ACHIEVE THIS, A NEW COSTUME IS A MUST!
OH, AND HAVE YOU HEARD? THIS YEAR WE HAVE A RECORD NUMBER OF HWARANG CANDIDATES. MY POSITION HAVE BECOME MORE IMPORTANT THAN EVER.
SINCE WE'RE TALKING ABOUT THE SUN, THAT REMINDS ME...
WHERE IS LADY BA-RI?
I've looked for her everywhere but can't seem to find her.

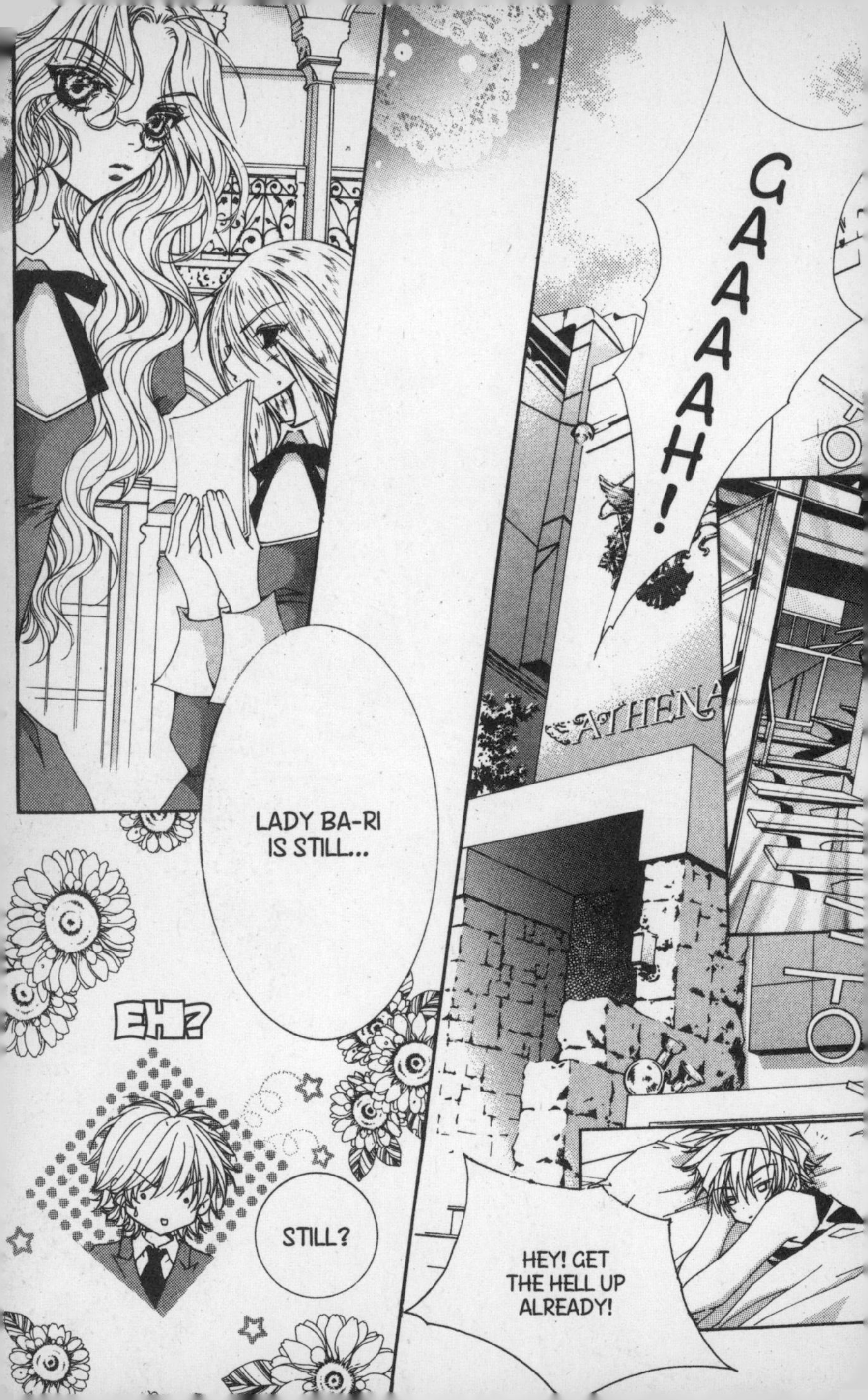
LADY BA-RI IS STILL...
EH?
STILL?
GAAAAH!
ATHENA
HEY! GET THE HELL UP ALREADY!

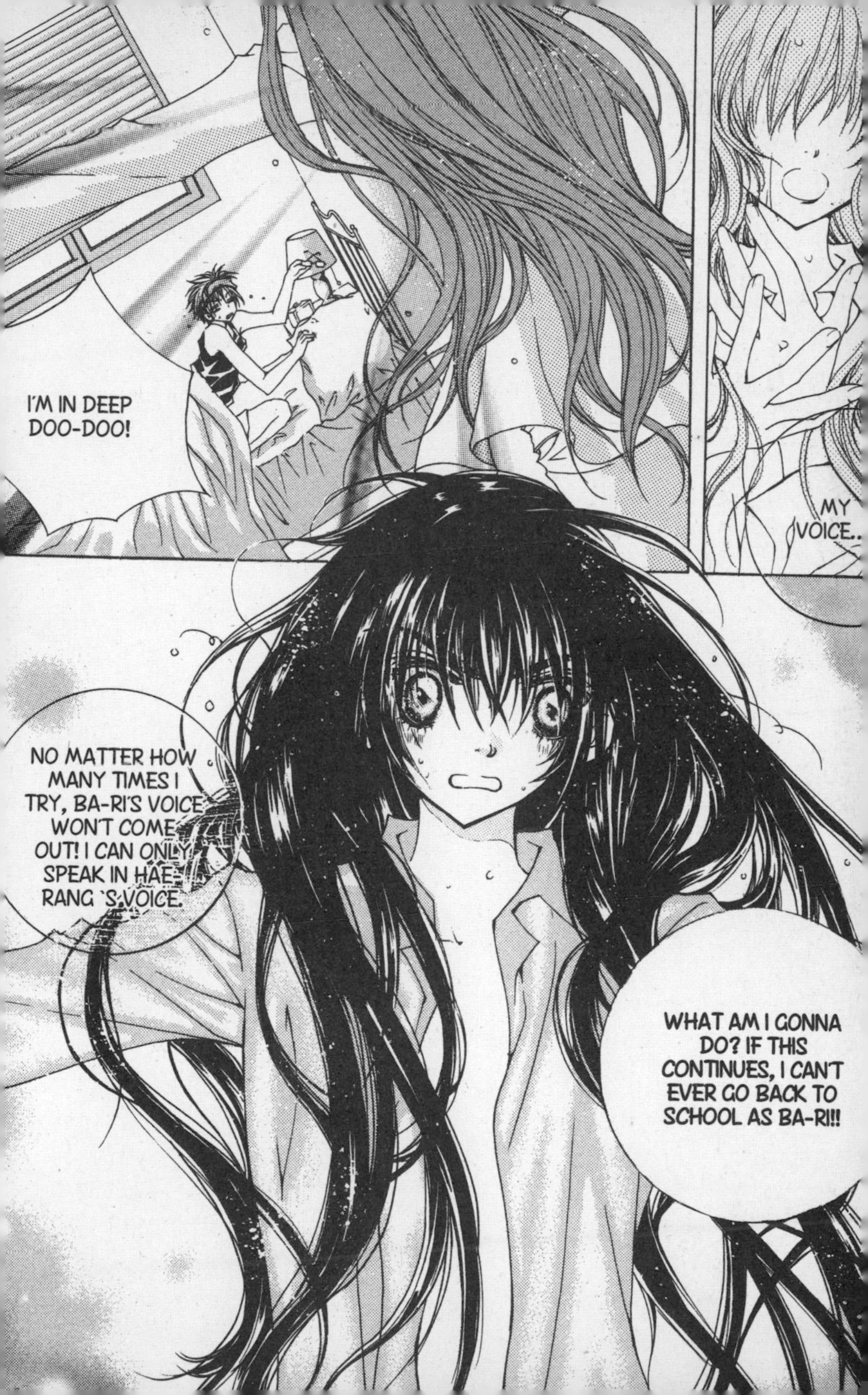
I'M IN DEEP DOO-DOO!
MY VOICE..
NO MATTER HOW MANY TIMES I TRY, BA-RI'S VOICE WON'T COME OUT! I CAN ONLY SPEAK IN HAE-RANG 'S VOICE.
WHAT AM I GONNA DO? IF THIS CONTINUES, I CAN'T EVER GO BACK TO SCHOOL AS BA-RI!!

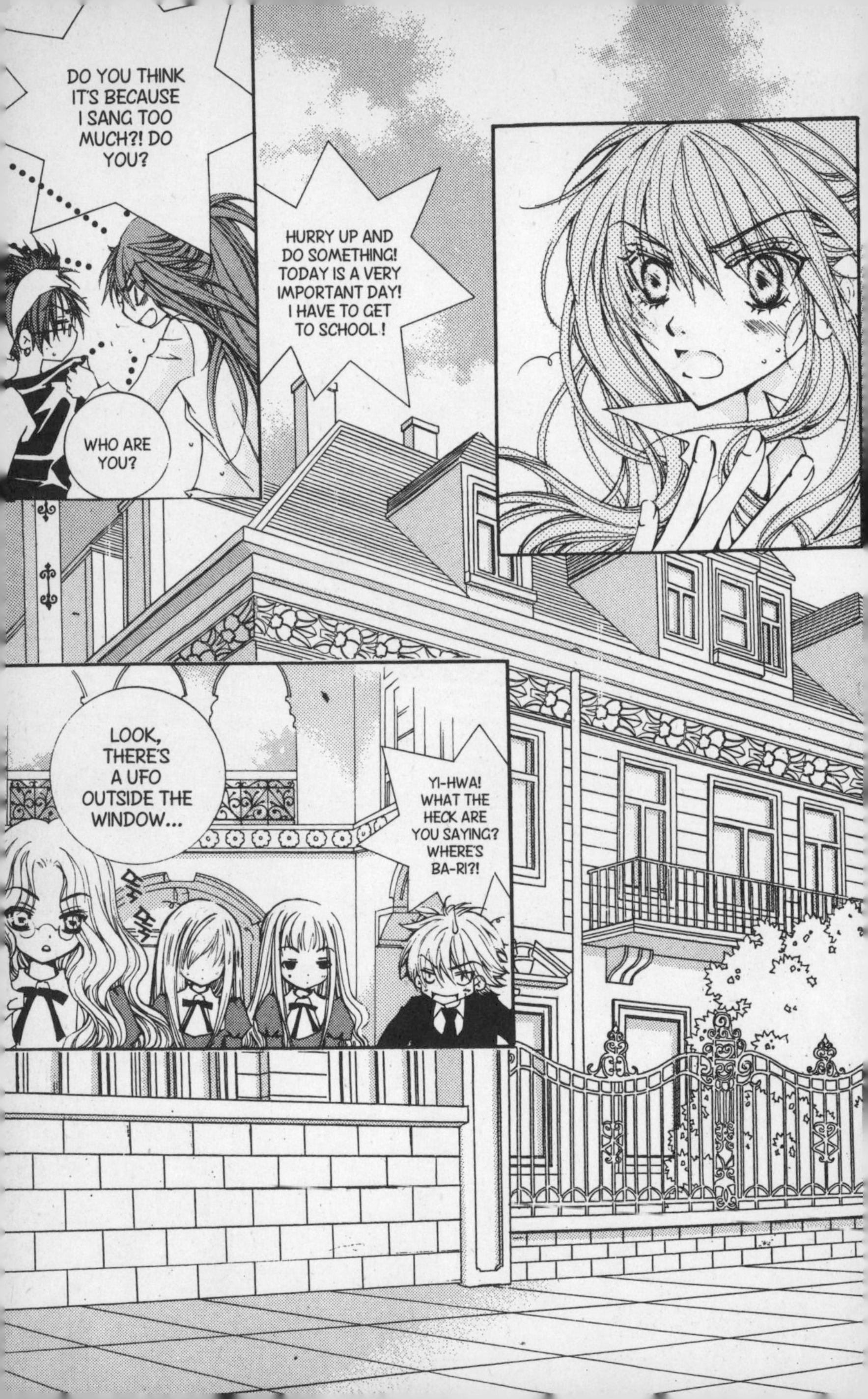
DO YOU THINK IT'S BECAUSE I SANG TOO MUCH?! DO YOU?
WHO ARE YOU?
HURRY UP AND DO SOMETHING! TODAY IS A VERY IMPORTANT DAY! I HAVE TO GET TO SCHOOL!
LOOK, THERE'S A UFO OUTSIDE THE WINDOW...
YI-HWA! WHAT THE HECK ARE YOU SAYING? WHERE'S BA-RI?!

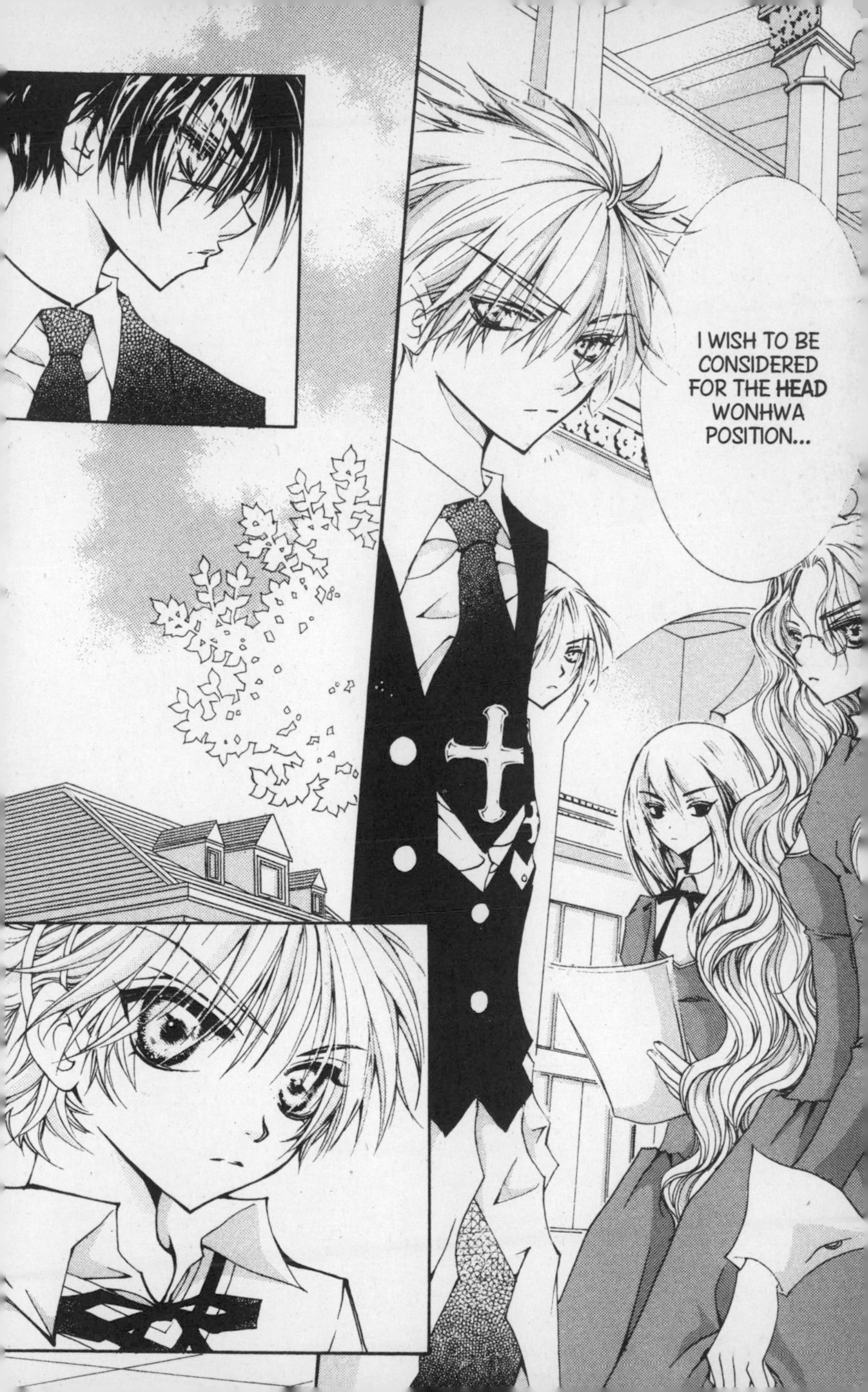
I WISH TO BE CONSIDERED FOR THE HEAD WONHWA POSITION...

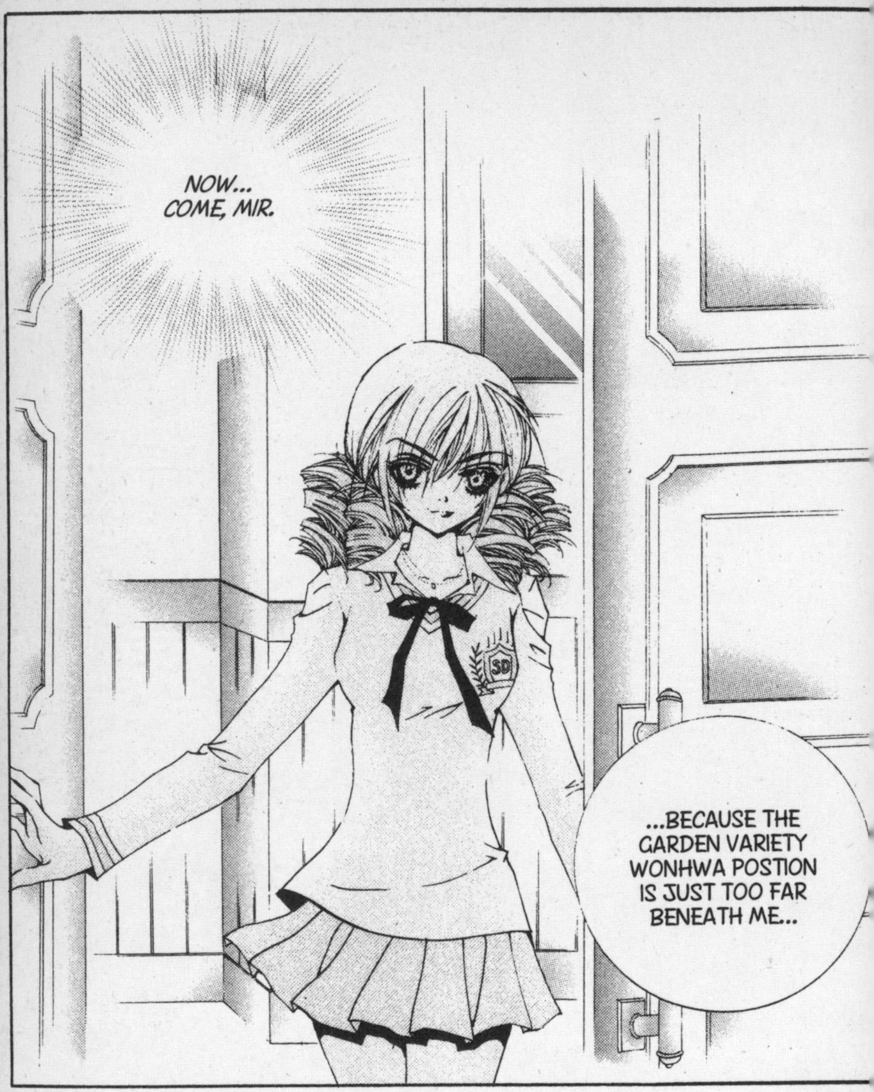
NOW...
COME, MIR.
...BECAUSE THE GARDEN VARIETY WONHWA POSTION IS JUST TOO FAR BENEATH ME...

I WILL MAKE THIS YOUR FINAL RESTING PLACE!

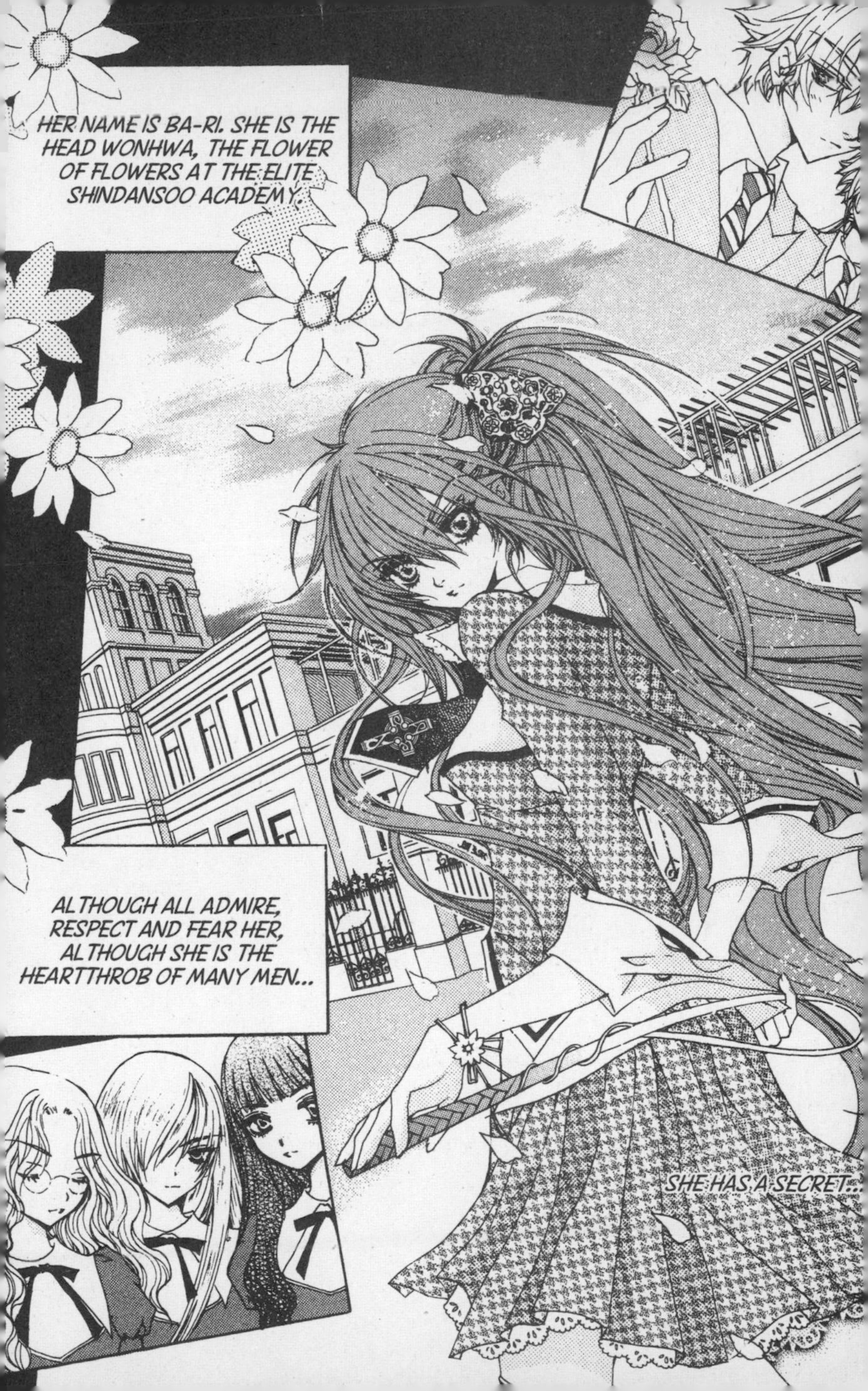
HER NAME IS BA-RI. SHE IS THE HEAD WONHWA, THE FLOWER OF FLOWERS AT THE ELITE SHINDANSOO ACADEMY.
ALTHOUGH ALL ADMIRE, RESPECT AND FEAR HER, ALTHOUGH SHE IS THE HEARTTHROB OF MANY MEN...
SHE HAS A SECRET...

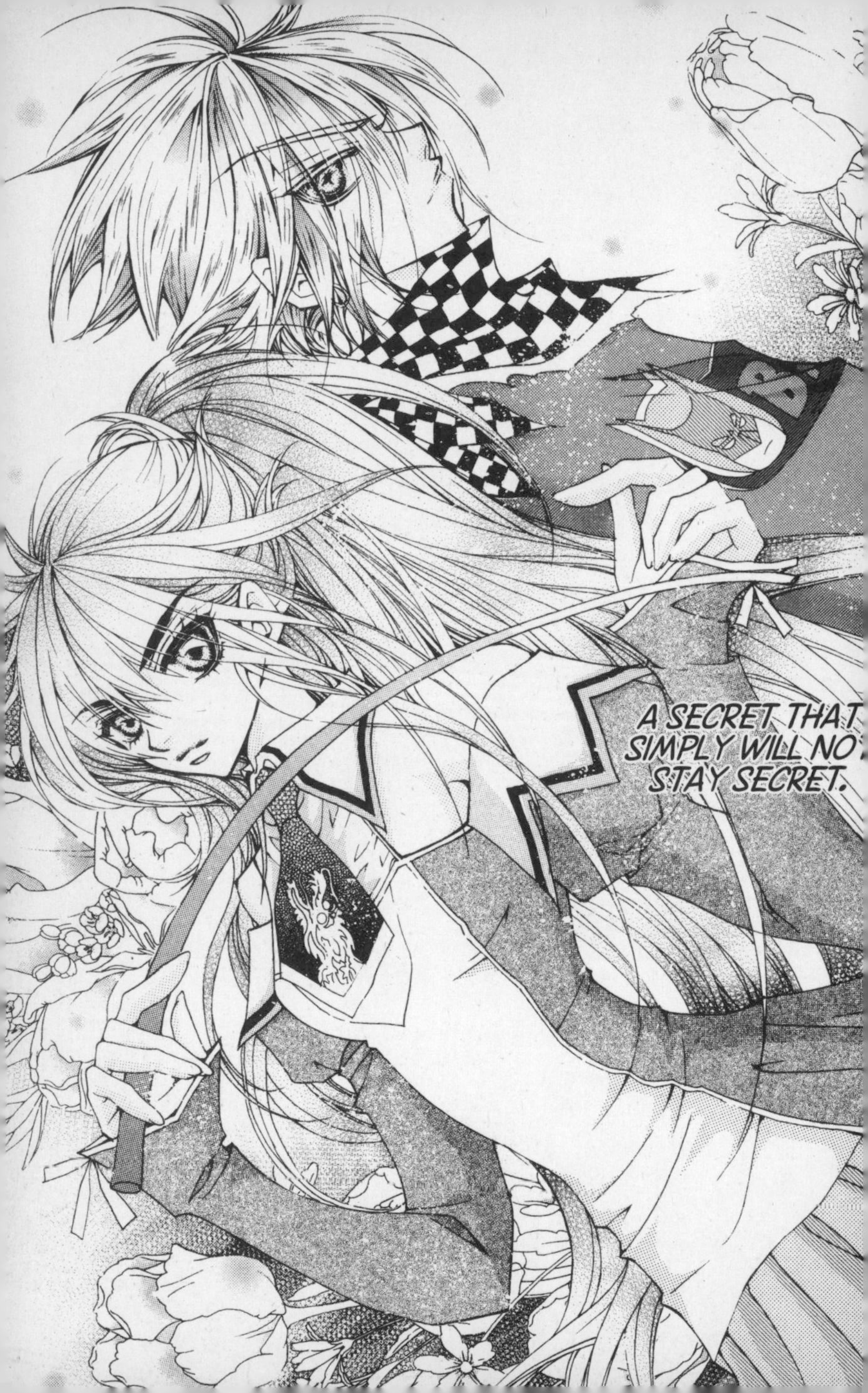
A SECRET THAT
SIMPLY WILL NO
STAY SECRET.

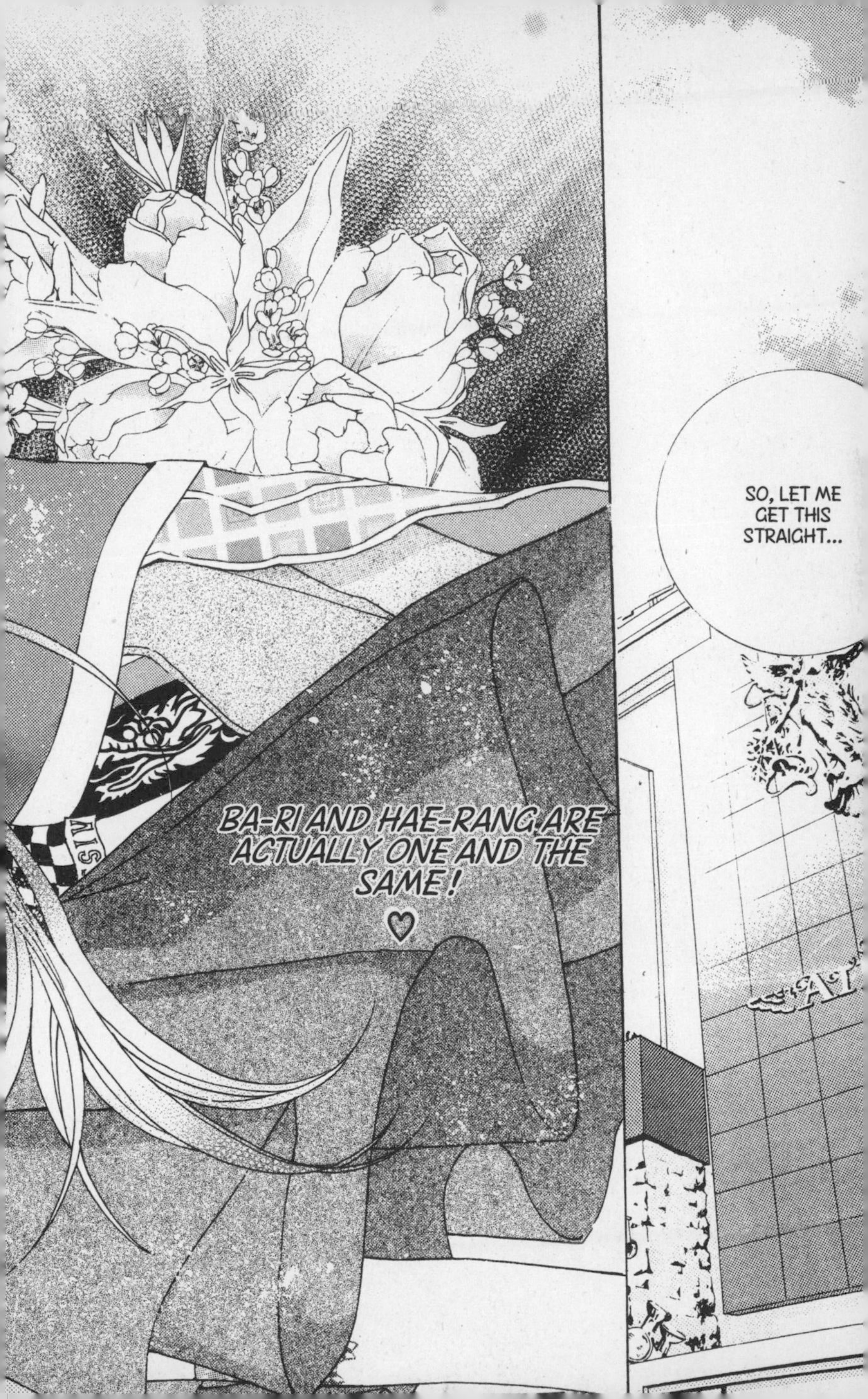
BA-RI AND HAE-RANG ARE ACTUALLY ONE AND THE SAME! ♡
SO, LET ME GET THIS STRAIGHT...

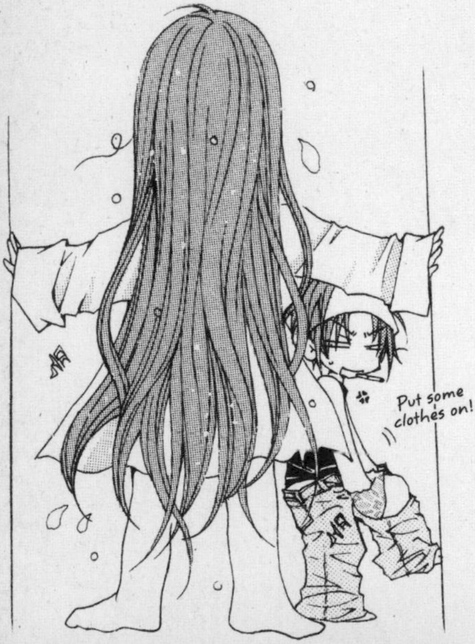
Put some clothes on!

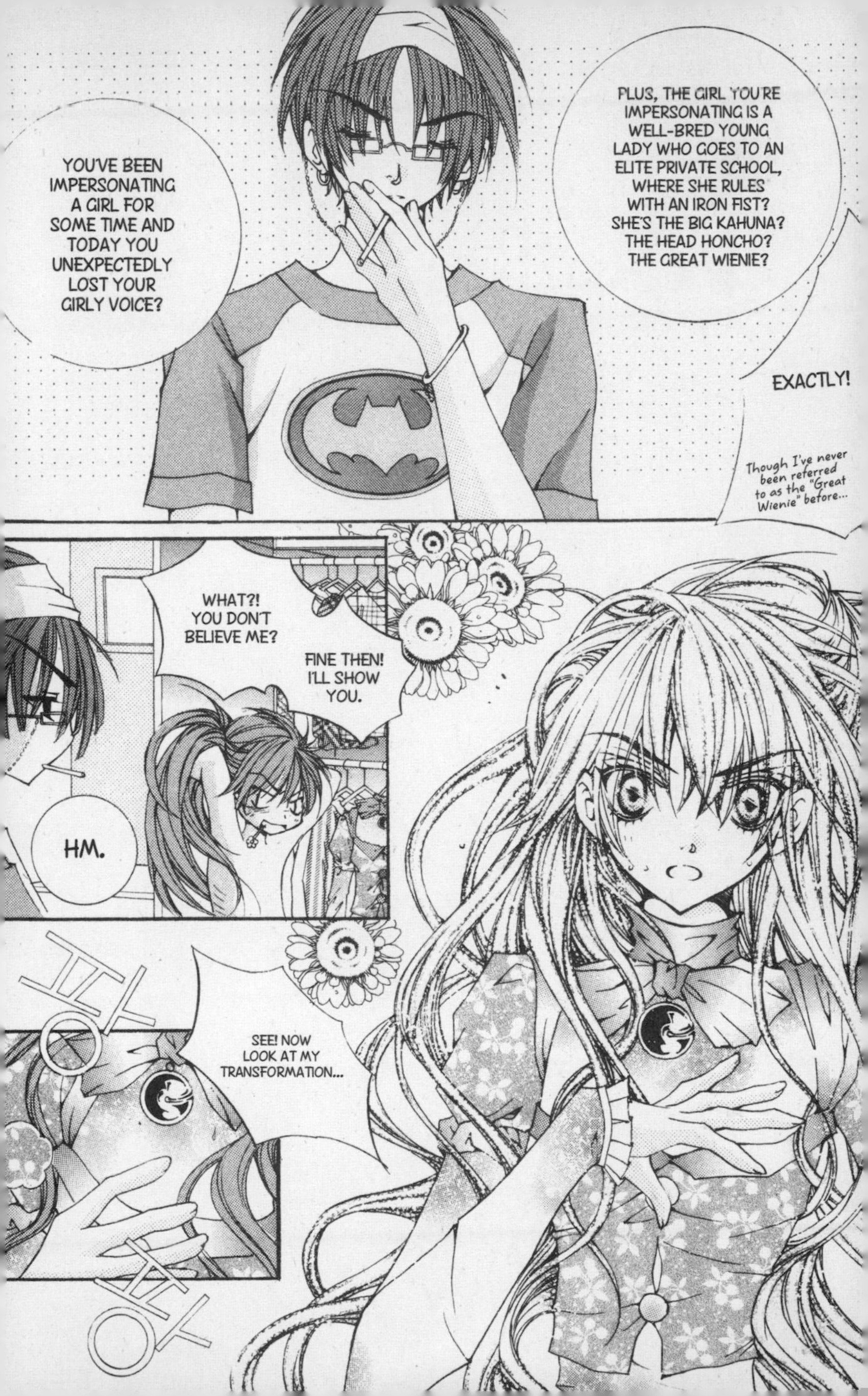
YOU'VE BEEN IMPERSONATING A GIRL FOR SOME TIME AND TODAY YOU UNEXPECTEDLY LOST YOUR GIRLY VOICE?
PLUS, THE GIRL YOU'RE IMPERSONATING IS A WELL-BRED YOUNG LADY WHO GOES TO AN ELITE PRIVATE SCHOOL, WHERE SHE RULES WITH AN IRON FIST? SHE'S THE BIG KAHUNA? THE HEAD HONCHO? THE GREAT WIENIE?
EXACTLY!
Though I've never been referred to as the "Great Wienie" before...
HM.
WHAT?! YOU DON'T BELIEVE ME?
FINE THEN! I'LL SHOW YOU.
SEE! NOW LOOK AT MY TRANSFORMATION...

NO! THIS ISN'T IT!

I LOOK LIKE HER BUT SOMETHING IS SLIGHTLY OFF. WAIT, I GOT IT! BA-RI IS A MORE HAUGHTY AND ELEGANT YOUNG LADY, AND I'M NOT...

...WHY ISN'T THIS WORKING? THIS HAS NEVER HAPPENED TO ME BEFORE.

...FOR SOME REASON, I CAN'T FOCUS ON BEING BA-RI. BUT WHY?!

MORE IMPORTANTLY...

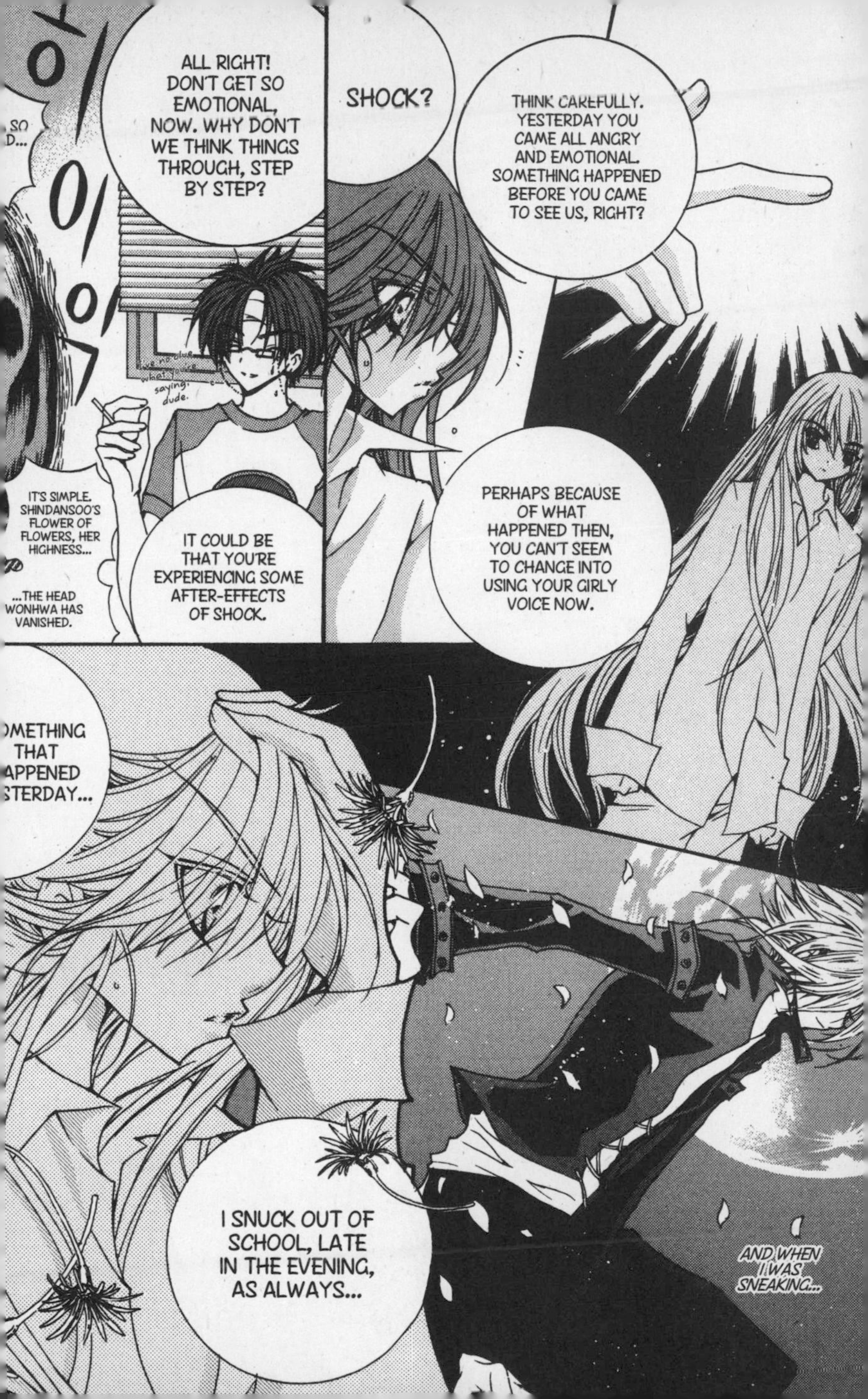
SO
D...
ALL RIGHT! DON'T GET SO EMOTIONAL, NOW. WHY DON'T WE THINK THINGS THROUGH, STEP BY STEP?
I've no clue what you're saying, dude.
IT'S SIMPLE. SHINDANSOO'S FLOWER OF FLOWERS, HER HIGHNESS...
...THE HEAD WONHWA HAS VANISHED.
IT COULD BE THAT YOU'RE EXPERIENCING SOME AFTER-EFFECTS OF SHOCK.
SHOCK?
THINK CAREFULLY. YESTERDAY YOU CAME ALL ANGRY AND EMOTIONAL. SOMETHING HAPPENED BEFORE YOU CAME TO SEE US, RIGHT?
PERHAPS BECAUSE OF WHAT HAPPENED THEN, YOU CAN'T SEEM TO CHANGE INTO USING YOUR GIRLY VOICE NOW.
OMETHING THAT APPENED STERDAY...
I SNUCK OUT OF SCHOOL, LATE IN THE EVENING, AS ALWAYS...
AND WHEN I WAS SNEAKING...

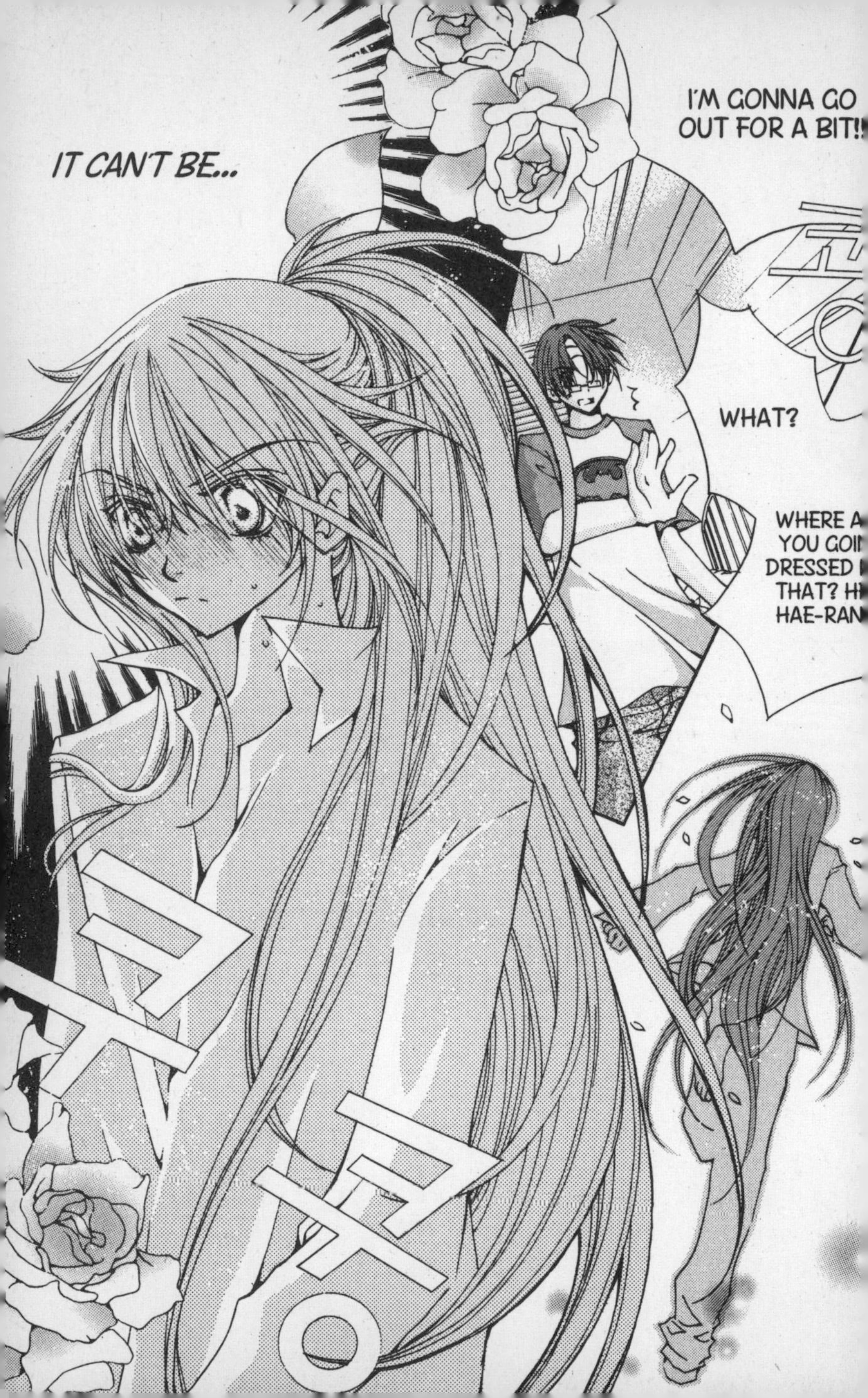
I'M GONNA GO OUT FOR A BIT!!
IT CAN'T BE...
WHAT?
WHERE A YOU GOI DRESSED THAT? H HAE-RAN

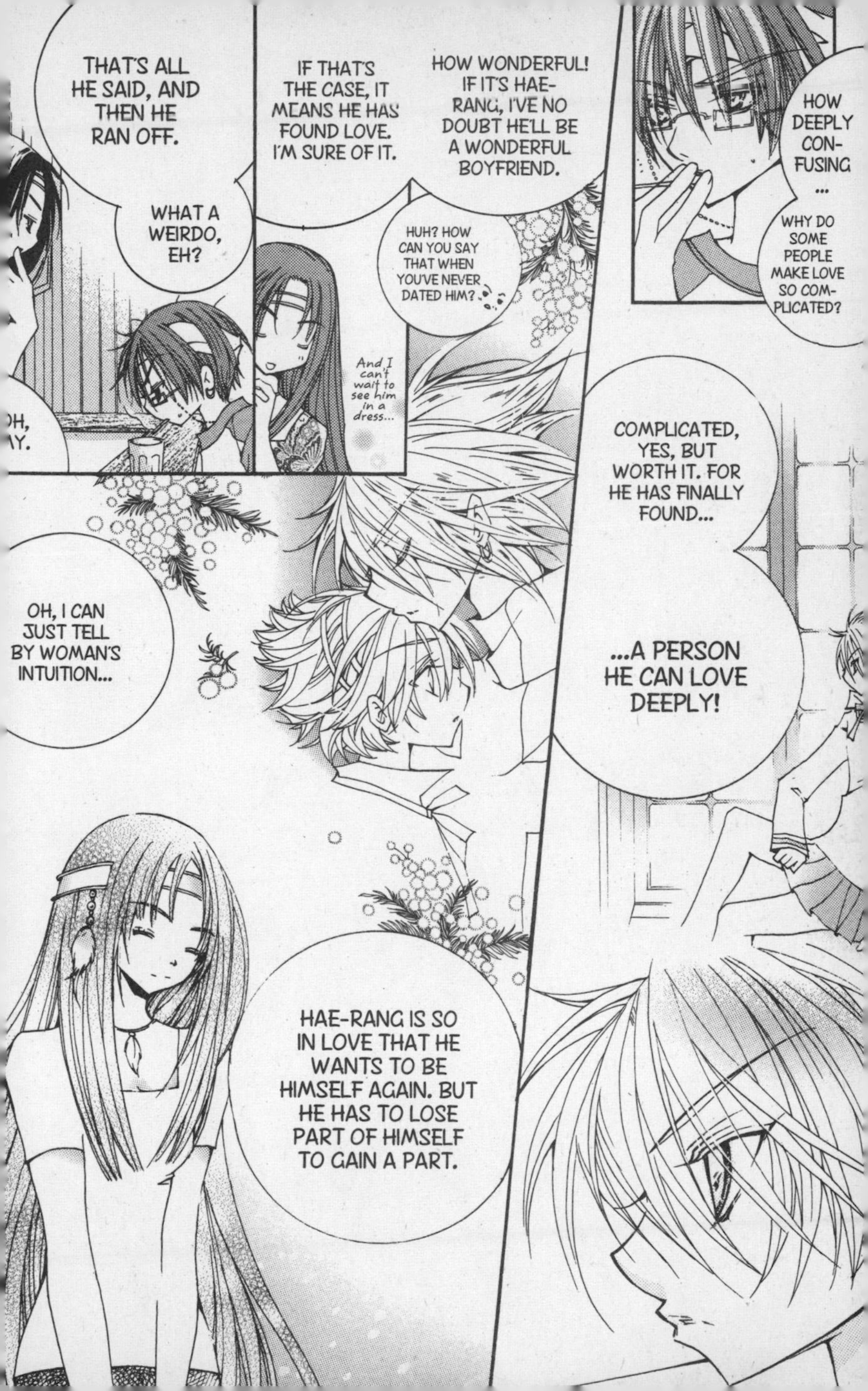
THAT'S ALL HE SAID, AND THEN HE RAN OFF.
WHAT A WEIRDO, EH?
IF THAT'S THE CASE, IT MEANS HE HAS FOUND LOVE. I'M SURE OF IT.
HOW WONDERFUL! IF IT'S HAE-RANG, I'VE NO DOUBT HE'LL BE A WONDERFUL BOYFRIEND.
HUH? HOW CAN YOU SAY THAT WHEN YOU'VE NEVER DATED HIM?
And I can't wait to see him in a dress...
HOW DEEPLY CON-FUSING...
WHY DO SOME PEOPLE MAKE LOVE SO COM-PLICATED?
OH, I CAN JUST TELL BY WOMAN'S INTUITION...
HAE-RANG IS SO IN LOVE THAT HE WANTS TO BE HIMSELF AGAIN. BUT HE HAS TO LOSE PART OF HIMSELF TO GAIN A PART.
COMPLICATED, YES, BUT WORTH IT. FOR HE HAS FINALLY FOUND...
...A PERSON HE CAN LOVE DEEPLY!

HOW DARE YOU?!

NOW I REMEMBER.

HWA-YUN... IS YOUR NAME?

OF COURSE. YOU AND ALL THE GIRLS HERE HAVE THE SAME OPPORTUNITY.

HOWEVER, HWA-YU YOU WILL NEVER REACH YOUR GOAL (SITTING IN THE HEA WONHWA'S SEAT.

FOR THE SAKE OF TH WONHWA NAME, I WIL STOP YOU.

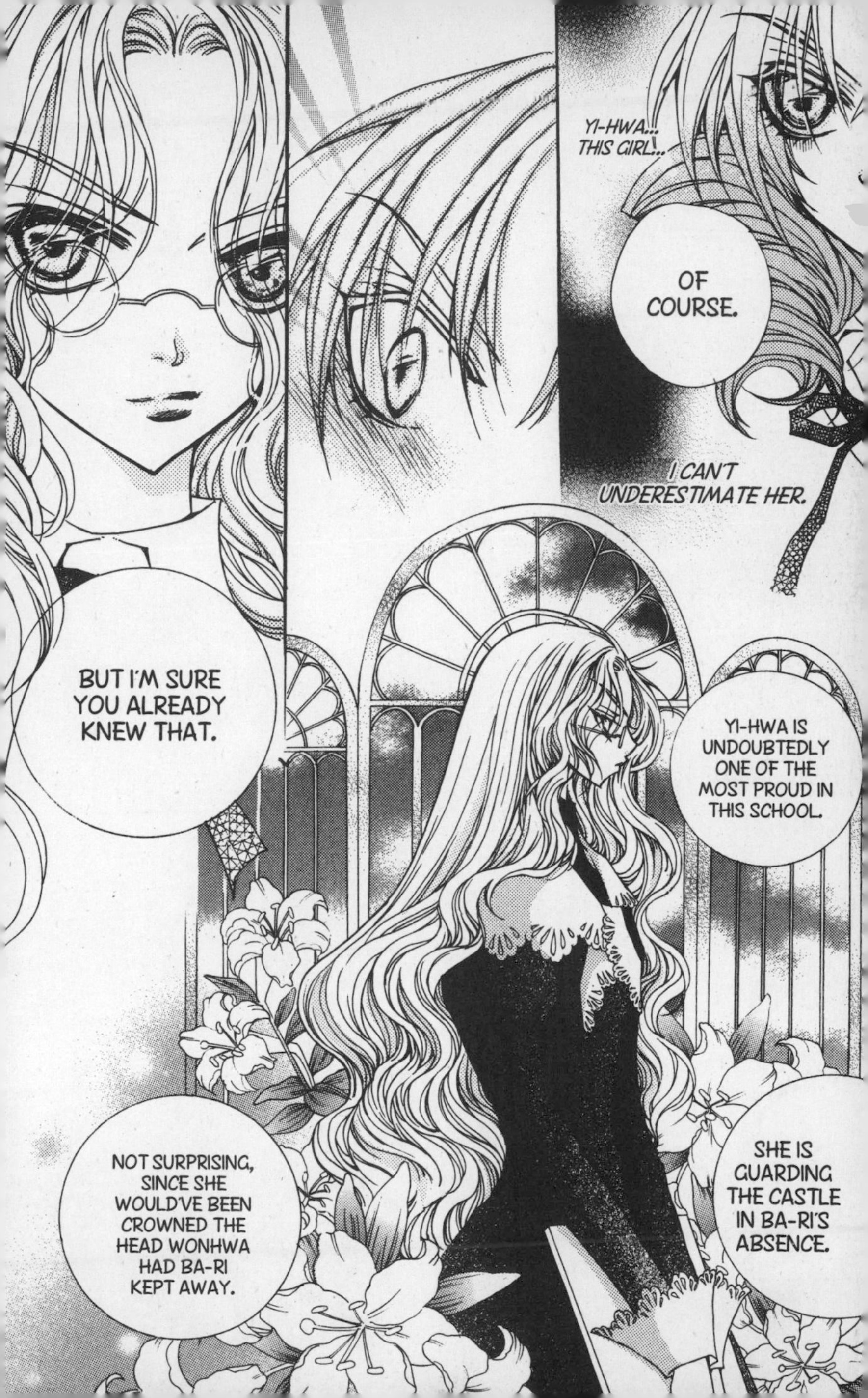
BUT I'M SURE YOU ALREADY KNEW THAT.
YI-HWA... THIS GIRL...
OF COURSE.
I CAN'T UNDERESTIMATE HER.
YI-HWA IS UNDOUBTEDLY ONE OF THE MOST PROUD IN THIS SCHOOL.
NOT SURPRISING, SINCE SHE WOULD'VE BEEN CROWNED THE HEAD WONHWA HAD BA-RI KEPT AWAY.
SHE IS GUARDING THE CASTLE IN BA-RI'S ABSENCE.

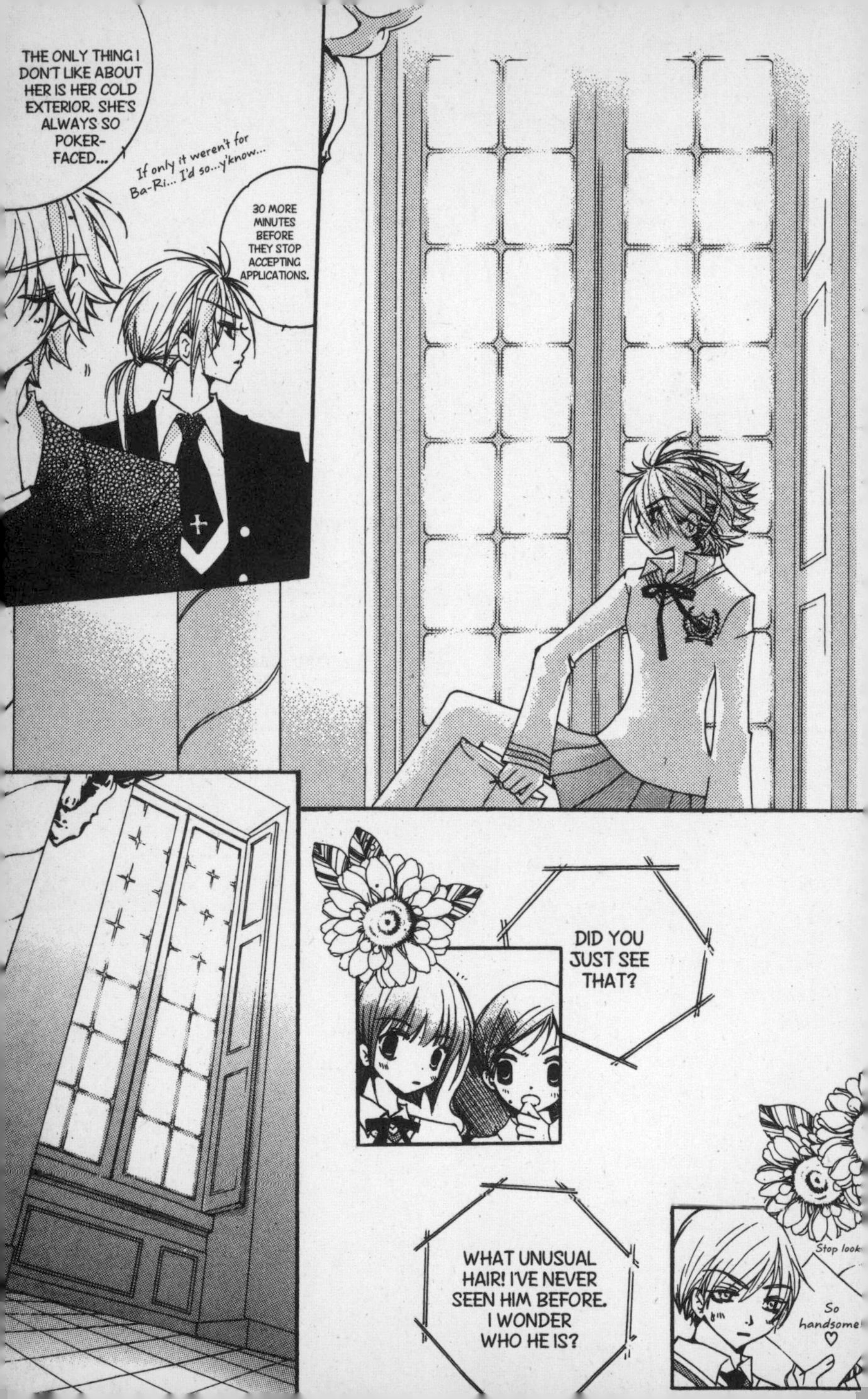
THE ONLY THING I DON'T LIKE ABOUT HER IS HER COLD EXTERIOR. SHE'S ALWAYS SO POKER-FACED...
If only it weren't for Ba-Ri... I'd so...y'know...
30 MORE MINUTES BEFORE THEY STOP ACCEPTING APPLICATIONS.
DID YOU JUST SEE THAT?
WHAT UNUSUAL HAIR! I'VE NEVER SEEN HIM BEFORE. I WONDER WHO HE IS?
Stop look
So handsome ♡

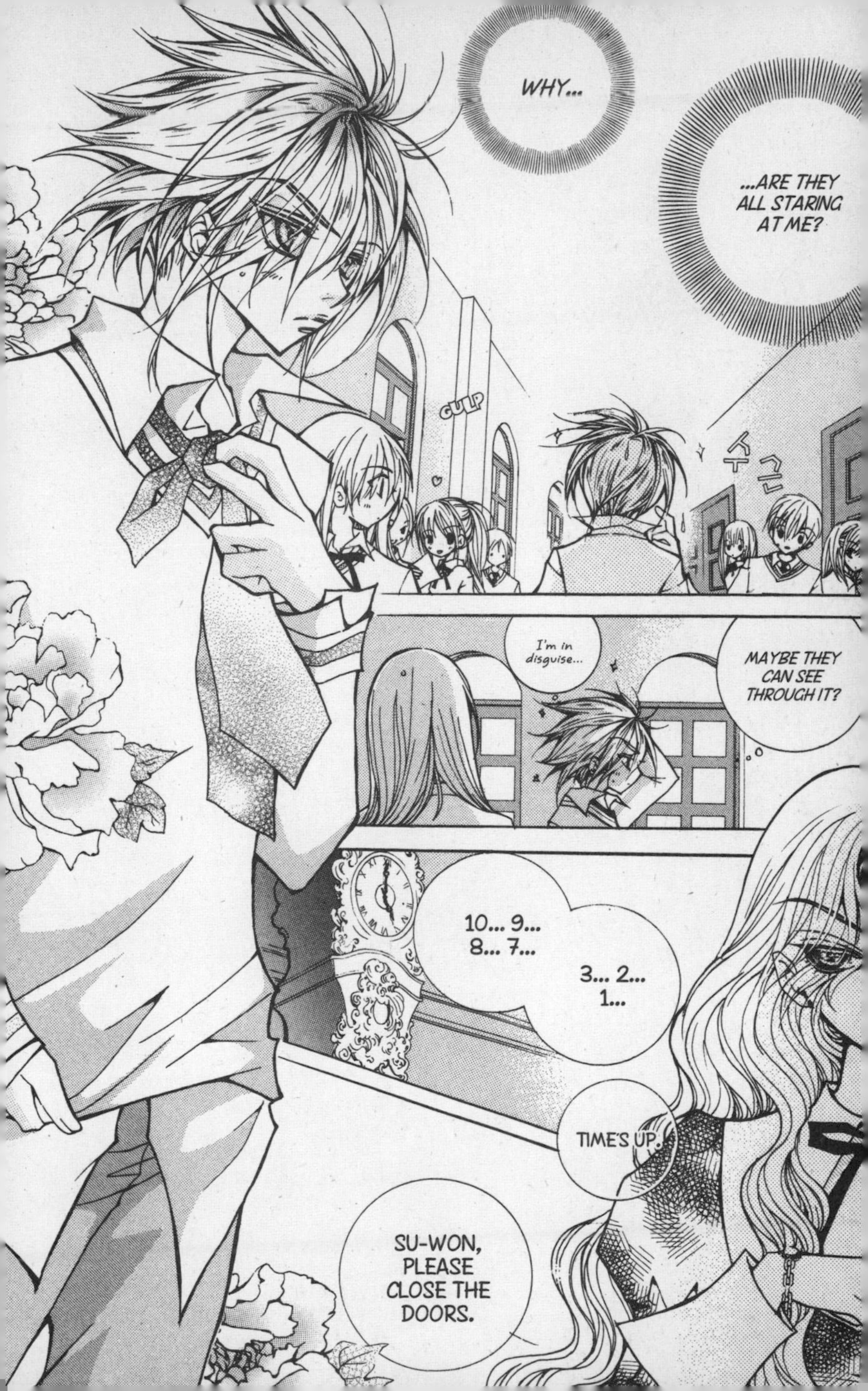
WHY...
...ARE THEY ALL STARING AT ME?
GULP
I'm in disguise...
MAYBE THEY CAN SEE THROUGH IT?
10... 9... 8... 7...
3... 2... 1...
TIME'S UP.
SU-WON, PLEASE CLOSE THE DOORS.

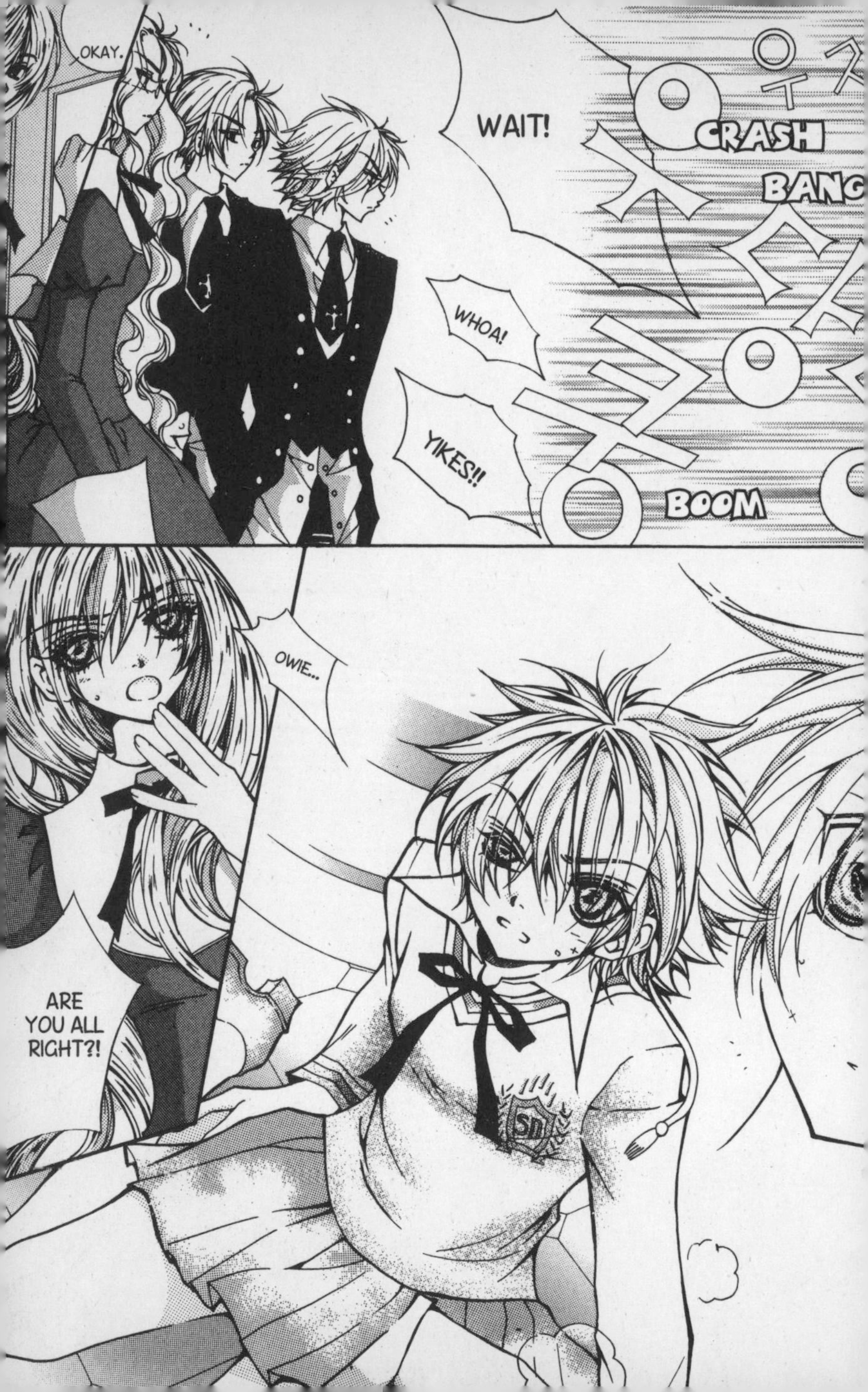

OKAY.
...
WAIT!
CRASH
BANG
WHOA!
YIKES!!
BOOM
OWIE..
ARE YOU ALL RIGHT?!

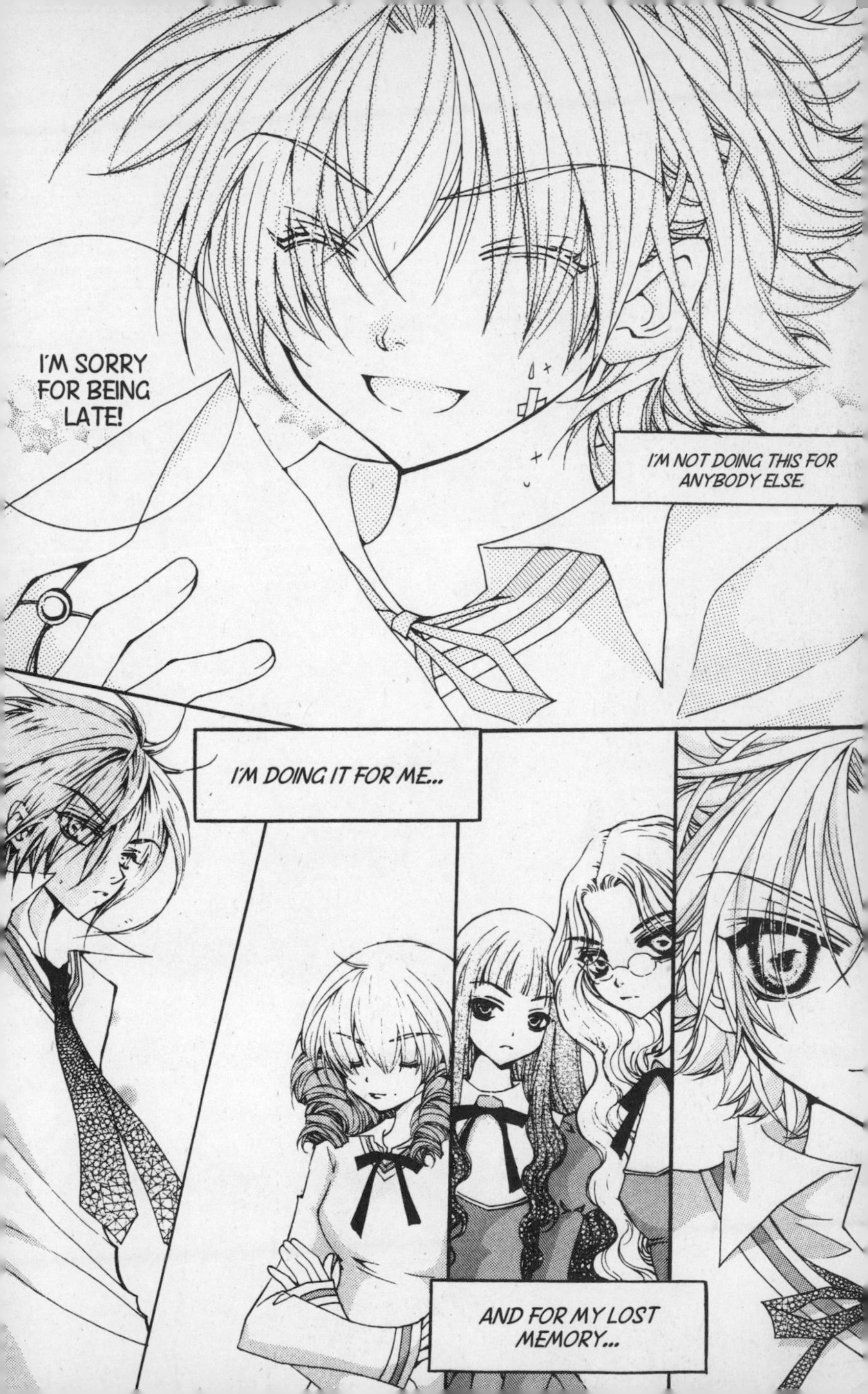
I'M SORRY FOR BEING LATE!
I'M NOT DOING THIS FOR ANYBODY ELSE.
I'M DOING IT FOR ME...
AND FOR MY LOST MEMORY...

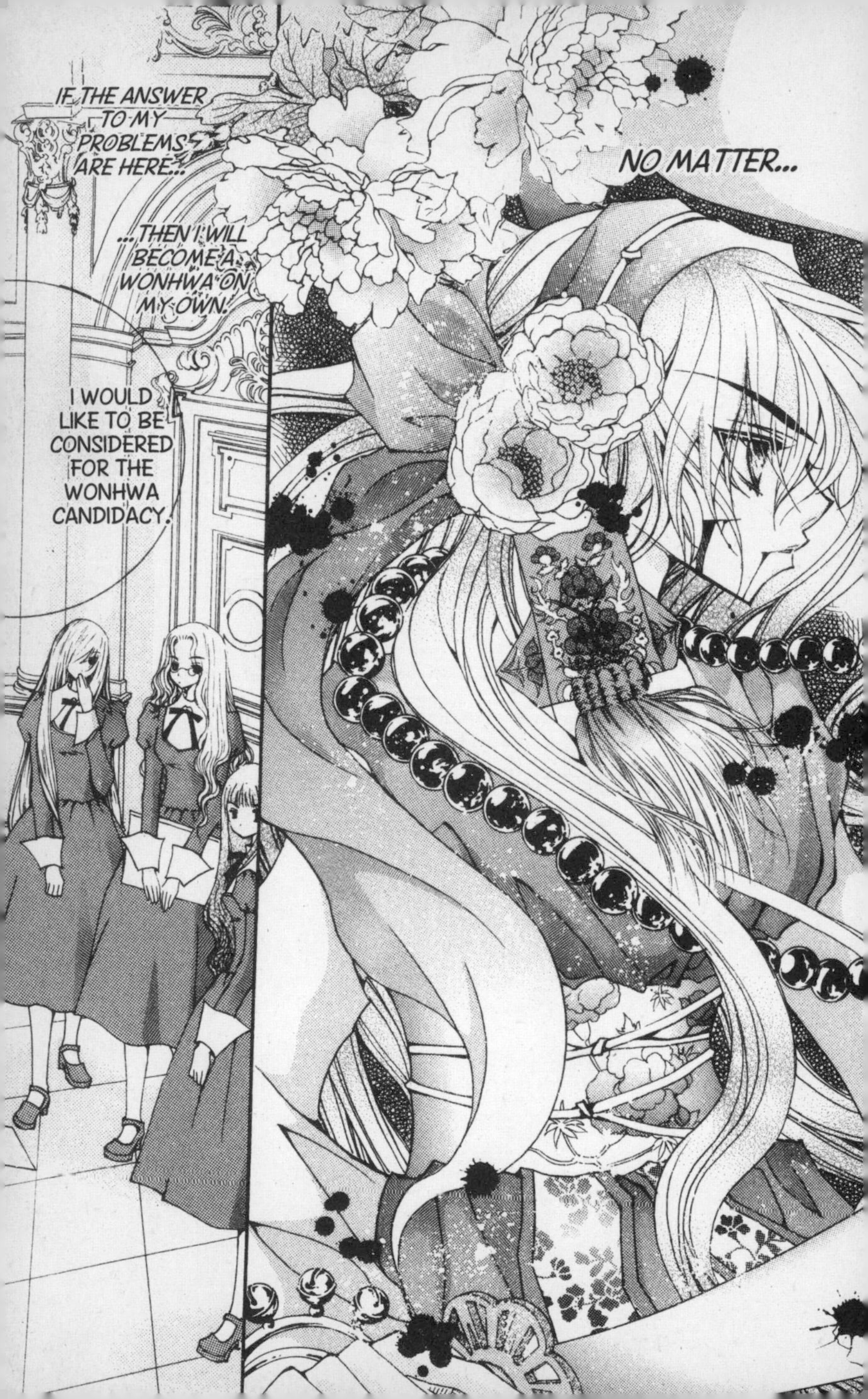
IF THE ANSWER TO MY PROBLEMS ARE HERE...
...THEN I WILL BECOME A WONHWA ON MY OWN.
I WOULD LIKE TO BE CONSIDERED FOR THE WONHWA CANDIDACY.
NO MATTER...

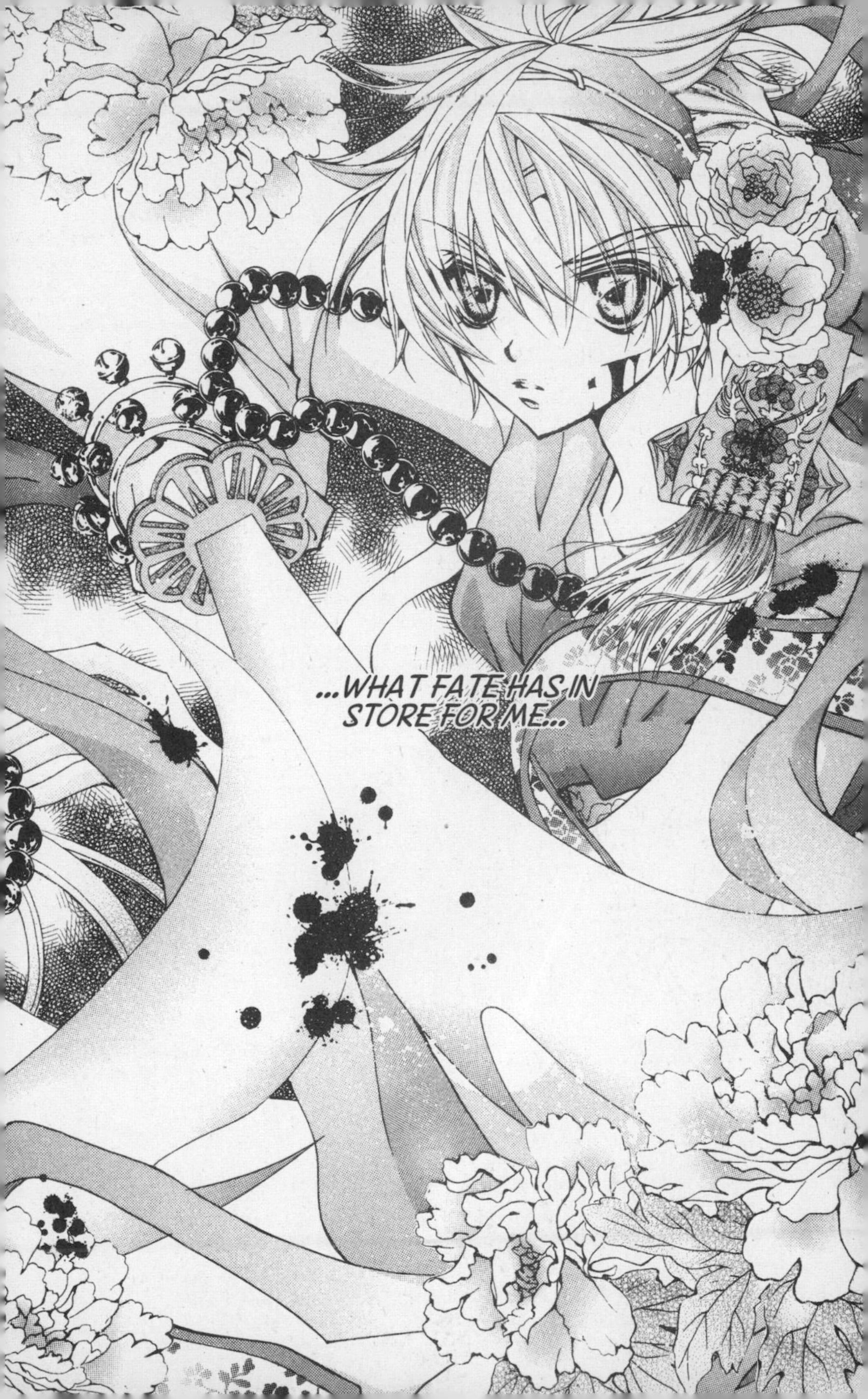
...WHAT FATE HAS IN
STORE FOR ME...

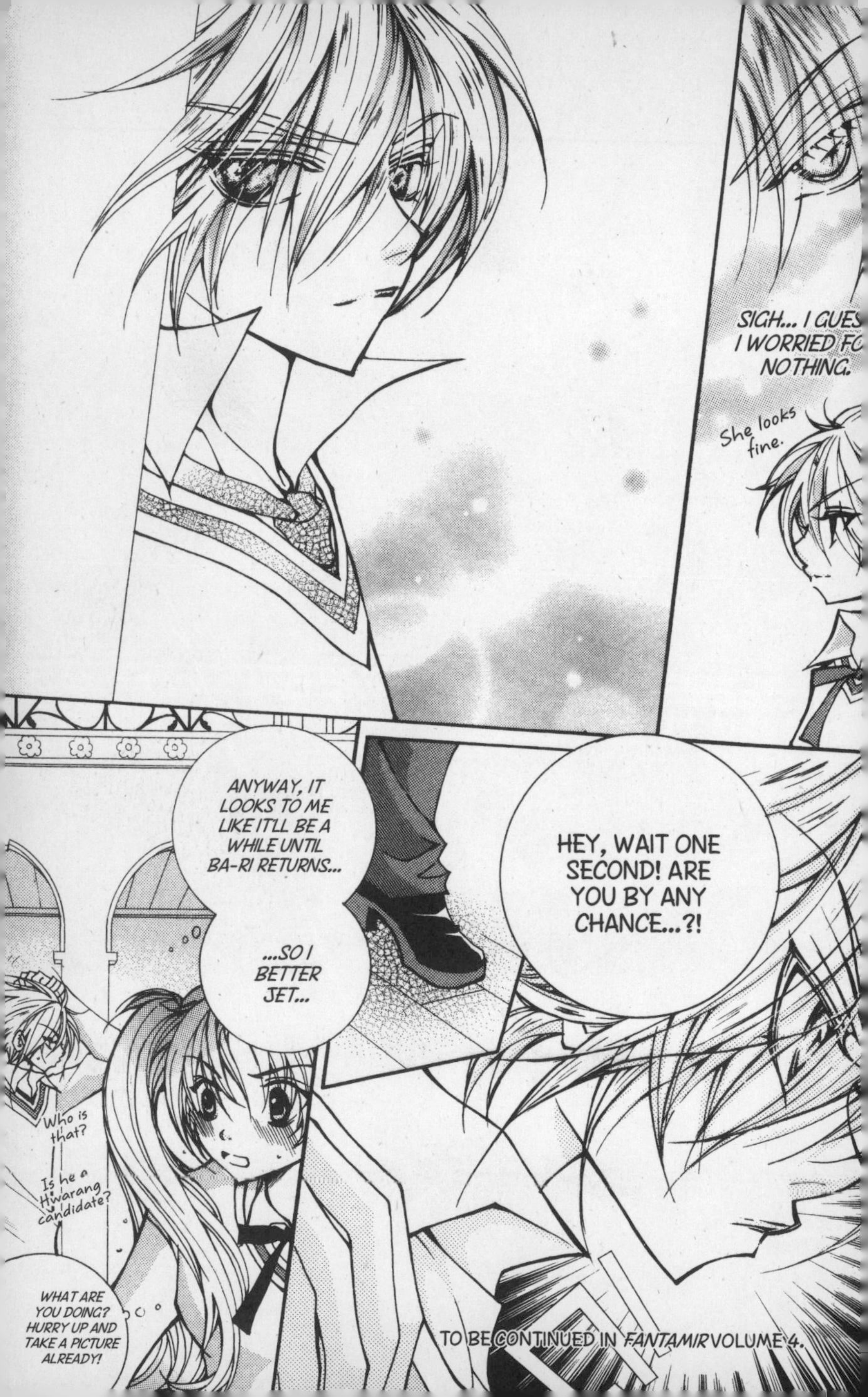
SIGH... I GUES
I WORRIED FO
NOTHING.
She looks fine.
Who is that?
Is he a Hwarang candidate?
WHAT ARE YOU DOING? HURRY UP AND TAKE A PICTURE ALREADY!
ANYWAY, IT LOOKS TO ME LIKE IT'LL BE A WHILE UNTIL BA-RI RETURNS...
...SO I BETTER JET...
HEY, WAIT ONE SECOND! ARE YOU BY ANY CHANCE...?!
TO BE CONTINUED IN FANTAMIR VOLUME 4.

FANTAMIR

WONHWA VS. HWARANG

WONHWA:

BY THE 6TH CENTURY, SHILLA HAD BEGUN TO STABILIZE AND BEGAN A SERIES OF REFORMS TO CONCRETIZE ITS NEWFOUND STATUS AS A COUNTRY. THE GOVERNMENT RECOGNIZED THE NEED FOR A SYSTEM IN WHICH NEW, YOUNG TALENTS COULD BE FOUND AND TRAINED, WITH THE GOAL OF ULTIMATELY BECOMING LEADERS OF THE COUNTRY ONE DAY. THUS, SHILLA'S 24TH KING, JIN-HEUNG (534-576 AD) ADOPTED THE SYSTEM OF WONHWA KNOWN AS WONHWA-JEDO. THERE IS SOME DISPUTE AS TO WHETHER THIS WAS AN EXCLUSIVE ORGANIZATION OF MALES LIKE THE HWARANG, BUT AS ITS LEADERS WERE TWO WOMEN, MOST SEE IT LIKELY THAT FEMALE PARTICIPATION WAS NOT FORBIDDEN IN WONHWA. THE TWO WOMEN SELECTED TO LEAD THE WONHWA WERE NAM-MO AND JOON-JUNG, AND THE KING HANDPICKED THEM, FOR THEY EXCELLED IN KNOWLEDGE, MARITAL ARTS, BEAUTY AND GRACE. THE TWO WOMEN CO-EXISTED PEACEFULLY, SHARING THEIR POWER AND AUTHORITY OVER THEIR GROWING NUMBER OF FOLLOWERS, UNTIL JOON-JUNG GREW JEALOUS OF NAM-MO'S INCREASING POPULARITY OVER HER OWN. JOON-JUNG SECRETLY INVITED NAM-MO OVER TO HER HOUSE ONE NIGHT, AND WHEN NAM-MO STARTED OUT TO RETURN TO HER HOME, JOON-JUNG PUSHED HER OFF A CLIFF. KING JIN-HEUNG WAS GREATLY ANGERED AND EXECUTED JOON-JUNG, DISSOLVED THE WONHWA-JEDO AND REPLACED IT WITH THE HWARANG-JEDO.

AFTER THE DEMISE OF ANCIENT CHOSON, THE KOREAN PENINSULA WAS DIVIDED INTO THREE WARRING STATES: SHILLA, KOGURYO, AND BAEKJAE...

HWARANG:

KING JIN-HEUNG'S EVERLASTING LEGACY LIES IN HIS IMPLEMENTING THE HWARANG-JEDO IN 576. AFTER THE NAM-MO/JOON-JUNG FIASCO, THE KING DECIDED THAT THE NEW SYSTEM AND INSTITUTION WOULD BE OPEN ONLY TO MALES. UNLIKE THE WONHWA, HWARANG WAS A COLLECTIVE OF CAREFULLY SELECTED YOUNG MEN. TO BE NOMINATED AS A CANDIDATE, A YOUNG MAN HAD TO BE OF NOBLE BLOOD, WITH HIS FAMILY IN GOOD SOCIAL STANDING, AND DISPLAY MENTAL AND PHYSICAL PROWESS. TO BE INDUCTED AS A HWARANG, HE HAD TO BE RECOMMENDED BY ONE OF THE HWARANG INSTRUCTORS AND POSSESS PHYSICAL BEAUTY.

A HWARANG'S DEFINING QUALITY WAS CONSIDERED TO BE PATRIOTISM, AS HE WAS EXPECTED TO GIVE HIS LIFE FOR THE BETTERMENT OF HIS COUNTRY. NOT SURPRISINGLY, HWARANGS CONCENTRATED HEAVILY ON MARTIAL ARTS (NOW CALLED TAEKWONDO/HWARANGDO) AND MANY YOUNG HWARANGS INDEED GREW UP TO BE FAMOUS GENERALS WHOSE FEATS ARE LEGENDARY IN KOREAN HISTORY. AND ALTHOUGH HWARANGS WERE EXPECTED TO BECOME GREAT WARRIORS, THEY WERE ALSO TRAINED TO BE EXCELLENT POETS, SINGERS AND DANCERS.

THE HWARANG-JEDO LASTED ALMOST A THOUSAND YEARS, DURING WHICH BOTH KORYO (DESCENDENTS OF KOGURYO, WHO WOULD LATER ULTIMATELY UNIFY THE PENINSULA AS KOREA) AND JAPAN BORROWED AND ADOPTED THEIR OWN GOOKSUN AND BUSHIDO SYSTEM, RESPECTIVELY.

IN THE NEXT VOLUME OF

FANTAMIR

HAE-RANG'S FINALLY AT THE SHINDANSOO
ACADEMY WEARING PANTS INSTEAD OF A DRESS,
BUT HAS SOMEONE NOTICED HIS "REAL" IDENTITY
BEFORE HE'S EVEN HAD A CHANCE TO CHECK OUT
THE BOYS' RESTROOM? AND WILL THE COLD AND
PRECISE YI-HWA ACCEPT MIR'S 0.9 SECONDS LATE
WONHWA ENTRY? STAY TUNED FOR MORE SWORD-
CLASHING, GENDER-SWITCHING, TREE-OBSESSING
FUN IN THE NEXT VOLUME OF FANTAMIR.

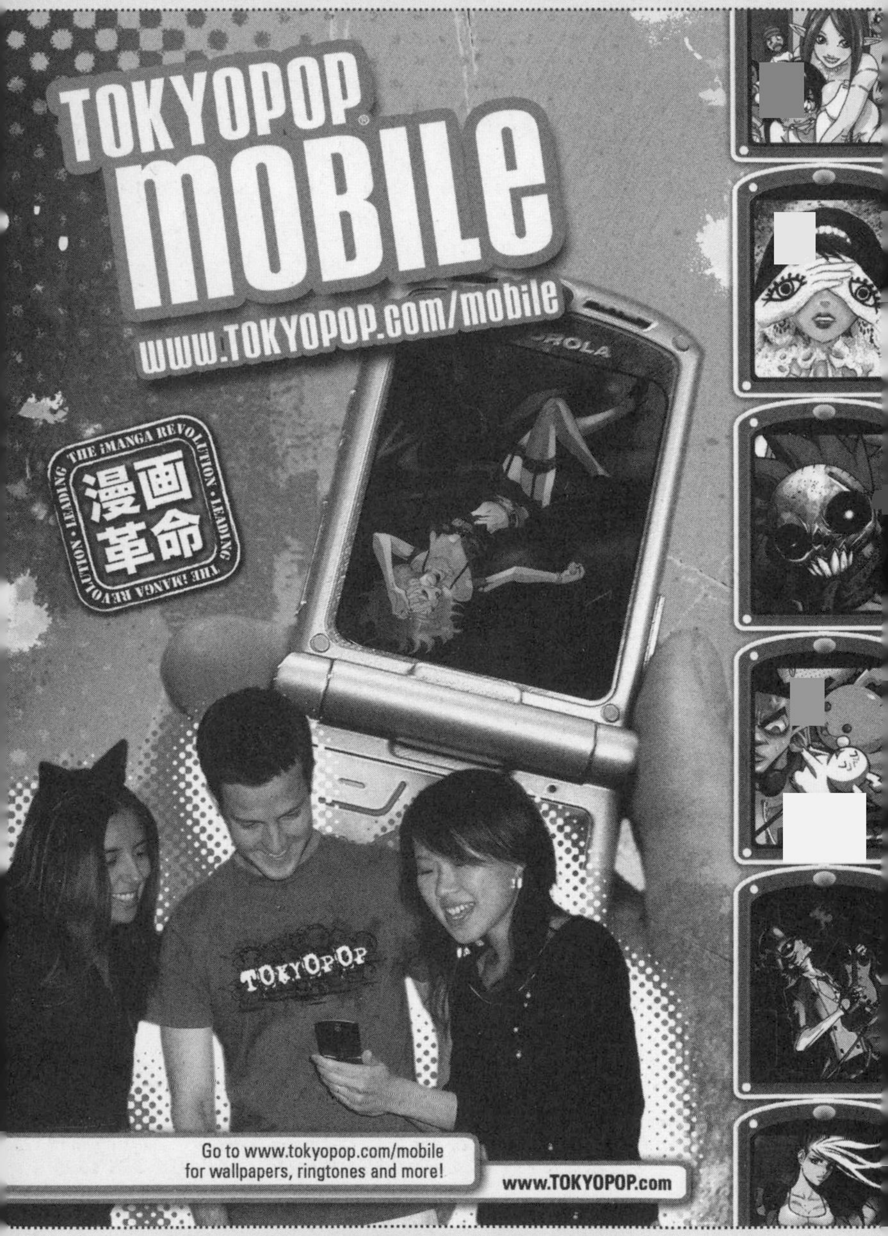
TOKYOPOP®
MOBILE
www.TOKYOPOP.com/mobile
THE iMANGA REVOLUTION · LEADING · THE iMANGA REVOLUTION · LEADING
漫画革命
TOKYOPOP
Go to www.tokyopop.com/mobile
for wallpapers, ringtones and more!
www.TOKYOPOP.com

Hotel AFRICA™

Anything can happen at the Hotel Africa

In the middle of nowhere, in the most desolate part of Utah, stands Hotel Africa—a hotel as unique as its guests. Join Elvis, the hotel's lifelong resident, as he revisits some of the most charming, crazy, heartwarming, and strange stories of life at the hotel. Between the family that runs the place and the strange characters who stay, one thing is certain: life at the Hotel Africa is anything but normal.

Also available from Hee Jung Park, Fever

Once you go to Fever, you will never be the same...

INCLUDES ORIGINAL COLOR ART!

© Hee-Jung Park